RACIALIZATION

before **7 – DAY LOAN**

LIVERPOOL  UNIVERSITY
.C.
634

D1332171

LIVERPOOL JMU LIBRARY

3   1111   01183   4304

LIVERPOOL JOHN MOORES UNIVERSITY
Aldham Robarts L.R.C.
TEL. 0151 231 3701/3634

RACIALIZATION
Studies in Theory and Practice

Edited by
KARIM MURJI
and
JOHN SOLOMOS

OXFORD
UNIVERSITY PRESS

OXFORD

UNIVERSITY PRESS

Great Clarendon Street, Oxford OX2 6DP

Oxford University Press is a department of the University of Oxford.
It furthers the University's objective of excellence in research, scholarship,
and education by publishing worldwide in

Oxford New York

Auckland Cape Town Dar es Salaam Hong Kong Karachi
Kuala Lumpur Madrid Melbourne Mexico City Nairobi
New Delhi Shanghai Taipei Toronto

With offices in

Argentina Austria Brazil Chile Czech Republic France Greece
Guatemala Hungary Italy Japan Souyth Korea Poland Portugal
Singapore Switzerland Thailand Turkey Ukraine Vietnam

Oxford is a registered trade mark of Oxford University Press
in the UK and in certain other countries

Published in the United States
by Oxford University Press Inc., New York

© the several contributors 2005

The moral rights of the author have been asserted
Database right Oxford University Press (maker)

First published 2005

All rights reserved. No part of this publication may be reproduced,
stored in a retrieval system, or transmitted, in any form or by any means,
without the prior permission in writing of Oxford University Press,
or as expressly permitted by law, or under terms agreed with the appropriate
reprographics rights organization. Enquiries concerning reproduction
outside the scope of the above should be sent to the Rights Department,
Oxford University Press, at the address above

You must not circulate this book in any other binding or cover
and you must impose this same condition on any acquirer

British Library Cataloguing in Publication Data
Data available
ISBN 0–19–925702–7 (hbk.)
ISBN 0–19–925703–5 (pbk.)

1 3 5 7 9 10 8 6 4 2

Typeset by Newgen Imaging Systems (P) Ltd., Chennai, India
Printed in Great Britain
on acid-free paper by
Biddles Ltd., King's Lynn

PREFACE

During the past two decades, the idea of *racialization* has become a commonplace term in scholarly debate in the social sciences and humanities. Inspired by the work of Robert Miles among others, researchers have used the term both in a descriptive and a conceptual sense. This expansion in the use of this term, and its increasing importance in the analysis of racial phenomena has, however, not been accompanied by a sustained analysis of its conceptual underpinnings or its usage in empirical social research. Indeed, it is perhaps this very lack of clarity about the concept that has led to its ever-increasing use by scholars and researchers working across a wide range of paradigms and fields of scholarship. This in itself may not be a problem, but we felt that there is a need for some critical reflection on what has become in many ways a core conceptual tool in race and ethnic studies. It is with this in mind that we invited a number of scholars actively researching in this field to provide us with their perspective on the possible uses of *racialization* as a concept and to reflect on how they have engaged with it in their own scholarly investigations. The outcome of this invitation is this collection of original chapters that reflect, we hope, a broad spectrum of opinion on this concept.

We are aware that a book of this kind raises a number of questions as well as providing some signposts about how to navigate contemporary debates in this ever-changing field of scholarship and research. We have tried to tackle some of these questions in the introductory chapter, and in the process we have also highlighted some of the recurrent themes and debates that run through the volume as a whole. We hope, however, that in reading the divergent perspectives collected together in this volume, you will agree that current debates about the processes that go under the generic label of racialization have the potential to open up avenues for further theoretical and empirical research.

In putting an edited volume such as this together, we have inevitably accumulated a number of debts to friends and colleagues. number of them are represented in the book itself, but in addition hank Claire Alexander, Les Back, Chetan Bhatt, Alice Bloch, la Bojadjijev, Max Farrar, Rosemarie Mallett, Robert Miles, Neal, Steve Pile, Liza Schuster, and Satnam Virdee. John

Solomos would also like to thank West Bromwich Albion for getting promotion to the Premier League in April 2004, and cheering him up as this volume neared completion. As this volume neared completion, Karim Murji was cheered up by an even more life changing event, namely the birth of his son, Rafi, in March 2004. We would also like to say thank you to Dominic Byatt and other staff at Oxford University Press for their support for this project.

KARIM MURJI
Open University

JOHN SOLOMOS
City University, London

May 2004

CONTENTS

ABBREVIATIONS

BNP   British National Party
DP   Democratic Party
HGDP Human Genome Diversity Project
HGP   Human Genome Project
OBE   Order of the British Empire

NOTES ON CONTRIBUTORS

Michael Banton was Professor of Sociology at the University of Bristol, 1965–92. He was the former chairman of the United Nations Committee on the Elimination of Racial Discrimination and a past president of the Royal Anthropological Institute of Great Britain and Ireland. His most recent book is *The International Politics of Race* (2002).

Avtar Brah teaches at Birkbeck College, University of London. Her research and publications cover areas such as gender and feminist theory, 'race' and ethnicity, intergenerational change, and globalization. Books include *Cartographies of Diaspora: Contesting Identities* (1996) and *Hybridity and its Discontents: Politics, Science, and Culture* (edited, with Annie Coombes, 2000).

Philomena Essed is Senior Researcher at the Amsterdam Institute for Metropolitan and International Development Studies, University of Amsterdam and Visiting Professor in Women's Studies and African American Studies at the University of California, Irvine. She is author of the monographs *Everyday Racism: Reports from Women in Two Cultures* (1990), *Understanding Everyday Racism: An Interdisciplinary Theory* (1991), *Diversity: Gender, Color, and Culture* (1996), and co-editor of *Race Critical Theories: Text and Context* (2002), *Refugees and the Transformation of Societies: Agency, Policy, Ethics and Politics* (2004), and *A Companion to Gender Studies* (2004).

David Theo Goldberg is the Director of the system-wide University of California Humanities Research Institute and Professor of African American Studies and Criminology, Law, and Society, and a Fellow of the Critical Theory Institute, University of California, Irvine. He was formerly Director and Professor of the School of Justice Studies, a law and social science programme, at Arizona State University. He is the author of *Racist Culture: Philosophy and the Politics of Meaning* (1993), *Racial Subjects: Writing on Race in America* (1997), *The Racial State* (2002), and *Ethical Theory and Social Issues* (1990/1995). He has edited or co-edited *Anatomy of Racism* (1990), *Multiculturalism: A Critical Reader* (1995), *Between Law and Culture* (2001), *Race Critical Theories* (2002), *A Companion on Racial and*

Ethnic Studies (2002), and *Relocating Postcolonialism* (2002). He is the founding co-editor of *Social Identities: Journal for the Study of Race, Nation and Culture.*

Ghassan Hage is Associate Professor of Social Anthropology at the University of Sydney. His work in the areas of multiculturalism, nationalism, and racism are published in many international journals. He is currently working on an ethnography of Lebanese transnational families. His books include *White Nation: Fantasies of White Supremacy in a Multicultural Society* (2000), *Arab-Australians: Citizenship and Belonging* (2001), and most recently *Against Paranoid Nationalism: Searching for Hope in a Shrinking Society* (2003).

Michael Keith is the Director of the Centre for Urban and Community Research at Goldsmiths College, University of London (www.goldsmiths.ac.uk/cucr). His research has focused on the nature of contemporary urbanism, with particular reference to issues of racism and multiculture. He is the author of *After the Cosmopolitan: Multicultural Cities and the Future of Racism* (2005).

Tony Kushner is Professor of Jewish/non-Jewish relations in the Department of History and Parkes Institute, University of Southampton. He has written widely on Jewish history, anti-Semitism, racism, immigration, and refugees and has recently completed two studies, *We Europeans? Mass-Observation, 'Race' and British Identity in the Twentieth Century* (2005) and, with Donald Bloxham, *The Holocaust: A Counter History* (2004). He is co-editor of the journal *Patterns of Prejudice.*

Eugene McLaughlin is Professor of Criminology in the Department of Sociology, City University, London. He has published extensively in the fields of criminological studies, race and policing, and race, news media, and public policy.

Karim Murji is a Senior Lecturer in Sociology at the Open University. He has published mainly in criminology and in ethnic and racial studies, including three authored or co-authored books on drugs. He is a member of the editorial board of *Sociology.*

Anoop Nayak is a Lecturer in the School of Geography, Politics, and Sociology, University of Newcastle upon Tyne. His research areas include race and ethnic studies, masculinities and social change, and theorizing the body. His most recent book is *Race, Place and Globalization: Youth Cultures in a Changing World* (2003).

Ann Phoenix is Professor of Social and Developmental Psychology at the Open University. Her research interests centre on social identities and the ways in which psychological experiences and social processes are inextricably interlinked. Her research includes work on gendered, racialized, social class, and national identities as well as on motherhood and the identities associated with young people's consumption. Her books include *Young Mothers?* (1991), *Black, White, or Mixed Race? Race and Racism in the Lives of Young People of Mixed Parentage* (1993/2002, with Barbara Tizard), and *Young Masculinities: Understanding Boys in Contemporary Society* (2002, with Stephen Frosh and Rob Pattman).

Ali Rattansi is Visiting Professor of Sociology, City University, London. His books include *Marx and the Division of Labour* (1982), *Postmodernism and Society* (1990, with Roy Boyne), *'Race', Culture and Difference* (1992, with James Donald) and *Racism, Modernity, and Identity* (1994, with Sallie Westwood). He is a member of the editorial board of *Economy and Society*.

John Solomos is Professor of Sociology at City University, London. He has researched and written widely on race and ethnic relations. His recent books are *Race and Racism in Britain* (3rd edn., 2003) and *The Changing Face of Football: Racism, Identity, and Multiculture in the English Game* (2001, with Les Back and Tim Crabbe). He has also co-edited *Researching Race and Racism* (2004, with Martin Bulmer) and *A Companion to Racial and Ethnic Studies* (2002, with David Theo Goldberg). He is Associate Editor of the journal *Ethnic and Racial Studies*.

Brett St Louis is a sociologist teaching ethnic studies at the University of California, San Diego. He has published a number of articles on race in relation to intellectual work and sport and is currently completing a manuscript on C. L. R. James's social and political thought.

Vron Ware is author of *Beyond the Pale: White Women, Racism, and History* (1992) and co-author, with Les Back, of *Out of Whiteness: Color, Politics, and Culture* (2002). She is from London but currently based at Yale University, teaching sociology and women's and gender studies.

Introduction: Racialization in Theory and Practice

KARIM MURJI AND JOHN SOLOMOS

What is in a word? When that word is *racialization*, the short answer is a great deal and, perhaps, too much. Racialization has become a widely used term in discussions of racial and ethnic relations—indeed, it could be argued that it has become a core concept in the analysis of racial phenomena, particularly to signal the processes by which ideas about race are constructed, come to be regarded as meaningful, and are acted upon. Racialization is commonplace as a descriptor and as a concept in most or all social science disciplines and across the humanities. The idea of racialization has been applied in various ways and its scope extends to a huge variety of issues, concerns, and topics that extend well beyond ethnic and racial studies, and even beyond sociology and other disciplines in which the study of race has been prominent. Immigration, the media, political discourses, crime and policing, housing and residential patterns, and poverty are among the leading topics or issues analysed in terms of racialization in the United Kingdom since the 1970s. The years since have witnessed the expansion and extension of the application of racialization so that cultures, bodies, institutions, images, representations, technologies, landscape, the environment, and art history have all been analysed through racialization. It is now almost routine to hear about the racialization of whiteness, of the Irish, Italians, Slavs, Chinese, and many other ethnonational or ethnoracial groups. Racialization is applied to whole institutions such as the police, educational or legal systems, or entire religions, nations, and countries such as the idea of the racialization of Islam, or of America; indeed even globalization has been viewed as racialization writ large.

Despite of all this, there is still some confusion about what exactly is meant by racialization in every instance where it is used, and what is being claimed in explanatory terms in the name of racialization. There is a feeling that the mere use of the term racialization has become a rather glib tag, which is sometimes made to stand as an explanation itself rather than being applied rigorously. There is also some uncertainty about what its status is. As Small says, racialization has been regarded as 'a problematic, a process, a concept, a theory, a framework and a paradigm' (Small 1994: 33). This lack of clarity extends across the field of teaching and research in the social sciences. To take the field of sociology, for example, a number of introductory textbooks in the United Kingdom refer to racialization, or indicate that it is a key concept or important in some way (e.g. Haralambos and Holborn 2000; Bilton et al. 2002). In introductory textbooks, Fulcher and Scott offer one of the fullest treatments when they say that: 'A race relations situation exists whenever ethnic relations have been racialized' (Fulcher and Scott 2003: 204); that is, when ethnic and group boundaries are defined in terms of race, understood as colour or biological difference. Both Fulcher and Scott (2003) and Bilton et al. (2002) refer to racialized discourse and the former also discuss racialized politics. Under this heading they mention the new right, racism in France, and Islamaphobia. Yet, curiously, it is rarely explained to students what the author(s) mean by it, or how others have used it, or precisely what its usefulness for discussing racial situations is. Dictionaries of sociology and of cultural studies vary in their approach; some do not contain a separate entry for racialization at all, and others provide a brief mention only. Naturally, more detailed coverage can be found in specialist dictionaries of ethnic and racial relations (unsurprising, as these are often written by some of the key figures who have used and developed the idea) covering the origins of the term, and the ways in which it can be used. Textbooks in ethnic and racial studies often provide more detailed examples that suggest how racialization occurs and the variety of ways in which it can be applied, though not always an account of why and how it is useful conceptually.

Because and in spite of its wide uses, a mini-backlash against the idea of racialization is noticeable. For Michael Banton, one of the first sociologists to use the term, there is a distinct lack of clarity about who and what is doing the racializing when it is argued that racialization is occurring. The very lack of clarity about racialization as a concept is why it is used so inconsistently, argues Carter (2000). David Goldberg suggests that the popularity of the concept of racialization is part of the success of the 'cultural turn' in the social sciences, the usefulness of which he thinks has run its course. In his book *The Racial State* he mentions, almost in passing, his feeling that racialization has become a cliché, too easily invoked and used in discussion and academic papers yet rarely explained or assessed rigorously. Goldberg (2002; see also Chapter 4, this volume) adds that it is one of the terms that he has taken to warning students against using in seminars, despite the rather shocked reaction it elicits from them. We return to these views in discussing the chapters by Banton and Goldberg in this volume.

Aims of this Book

It was in this context that we conceived of this volume. Individually, and like many others, we have found the idea of racialization useful for describing the processes by which racial meanings are attached to particular issues—often treated as social problems—and with the manner in which race appears to be a, or often the, key factor in the ways they are defined and understood. Racialization in this sense is the lens or the medium through which race-thinking operates (Malik 1996), or for Goldberg (this volume) it simply stands for any 'race-inflected social situations', a looseness that he finds unhelpful. For instance, the way in which post-war immigration into Britain became synonymous with black or Asian immigration, and associated with a range of social problems in housing, employment, policing, and social services, presents an example of the racialization of immigration through legislation and policy, media coverage, and various forms of political mobilization (Carter et al. 1987; Solomos 2003). Or, to take another example, in 1970s Britain a particular form of street crime, 'mugging', came to be seen as the actions of violent young black men. The ways in which a racial meaning structured other understandings of the causes and consequences of mugging presents one instance of the racialization of street crime. Since then, a number of other types of crime have been given a distinctive racial or ethnic spin. This indicates both the continuity and change in racialization processes, which can be seen through the persistent fixation with dangerous black masculinities. It also suggests the changing dynamic by which newer activities and cultural forms are grasped or explained in distinctively racial terms, or racialized (for applications of racialization to areas such as policing, public disorder, and the criminal justice system, see Holdaway 1996; Rowe 1998; Chan and Mirchandani 2002). In analyses such as these, race and racial meanings are sometimes manifest and sometimes they are inferred through other terms like ethnicity, culture, and the social problems approach. While this type of approach to racialization has provided a rich mix of studies it is the case that the increasing, common, and unelaborated uses of racialization as a problematic, a framework, or as a process has led to some rather frustrating catch-all uses of it descriptively, and a lack of development conceptually. It is not always clear what the race in racialization refers to—a specific and narrow discourse of biologically distinctive races, a process of cultural differentiation, or a code in which the idea or language of race is not manifest at all. Possible overlaps between these are not always closely analysed, with the unfortunate result that the uneven and differentiated ways in which racialization can occur is not brought to light. Consequently, racialization can sometimes be made to seem much more seamless and closed than the key emphasis on the construction of race that it contains should entail.

In seeking to push the agenda forward, we see this book as a set of theoretically informed studies that seek to explore the utility of the concept of racialization by providing both conceptual and empirical investigations of how it has been used and developed. We asked contributors to provide grounded analyses of how they use or have used the idea of racialization in their own work, or use their research to reflect upon the utility of the concept and its implications for thinking about race and racism. The chapters explore particular sites of racialization as a process in specific societies and historical contexts with the aim of providing routes for understanding and researching racialization in the future. Many of them show the utility of the idea in explaining identities and processes, in relation to young people, identities, social interaction, the media, whiteness, Jewish identities, autobiography, and political discourses. Other contributors draw upon the notion of racialization but stress their reservations to a greater extent. We have selected contributors who we think offer distinctive and indeed cutting-edge analyses of racialization, even though that sometimes entails a rejection of the use of the language and conception of racialization, and in other cases, arguments about the need for more refined and careful usage. There is no attempt to establish a 'party line' in this book, not that we believe that is either possible or desirable.

In the rest of this introduction, we aim to set the contents of this volume in context by providing a route map of the idea of racialization and of some of the main debates about it, though we deliberately do not recommend a linear reading between this and the following chapters. Although Barot and Bird (2001) offer a genealogy of racialization, the concept, our overview of it differs from theirs in providing a different way of narrating the uses of, and debates around, racialization. Our contributors sometimes connect with the existing themes around racialization but they also often go beyond them, signalling changing and sometimes new applications and understandings of racialization processes.

The dynamic and problematic nature of racialization is apparent in the opening chapter by Brett St Louis. The notion of racialization commonly draws attention to the constructed nature of racial categories and race-thinking processes, and contains a more or less explicit instance that race is not real, at least in any biological sense. Yet, as St Louis shows, the disputes about the 'reality' of race continue, though in rather circular ways which permit both the validation and invalidation of claims about biological race, such that he concludes: 'In short, attempts at definitive racial understanding have arrived at the following conclusions: race does/does not exist and we should/should not use the concept.' He considers how racialization occurs through contemporary biomedical research, and asserts the need for truth claims that draw on science and on an ethical framework to make judgements about ascribed and voluntary (self-) racialization. Avtar Brah touches on similar issues in Chapter 3, particularly through an assessment of what she calls the 'scienticism' of popular anti-racist texts, though in a rather different way to St Louis. Situating her chapter within the continuing debate about the categories of race and racism, Brah explores the 'contradictory relationships between author, text, and subject as constituted within and across social fields that include processes of racialization' through three significant texts. Her interrogation raises questions about what is consciously championed in these works and what is unconsciously disavowed, suggesting some of the shortcomings of racism as an explanatory tool and the limits of drawing upon that to advance deracialization.

Origins and Evolution of Racialization

In developing his own influential conception of racialization, Robert Miles traces its origins to Fanon (1967) and its development within sociology to Banton (1977). This version has been widely accepted, though Barot and Bird (2001) have recently supplemented the conventional history of the use of the term. As they point out, the *Oxford English Dictionary* traces its first use to 1899 and, 'On the whole, racialization is used in the late-nineteenth and the first half of the twentieth century and then disappears to re-emerge within the sociology of "race" and ethnic relations' (Barot and Bird 2001: 603). In its earlier incarnations in the fields of politics and anthropology, it was used mainly in the sense of deracialization, taken to mean the loss of racial qualities through increasing mixture. These early uses have not been widely taken up or influential in the academic literature. However, there are some significant points to be drawn from the nineteenth and early twentieth century uses of the word. One is that the occurrence of racialization/deracialization, even its earliest uses, has always been contested as Barot and Bird's discussion of the work of Sir Arthur Keith and Arnold Toynbee in the early twentieth century shows. A second is that the idea of deracialization appears at least as early as racialization, or perhaps even predates it. Consequently, there is not a linear process where racialization is followed by deracialization or reracialization; rather these moments or phases can often occur simultaneously and even in the 'wrong order'. And a third is that from its earliest history, its application has not been confined to academic writing and debates. One instance of its continuing resonance is a pamphlet by the Democratic Party (DP) of South Africa that complained about the ANC's policy of reracialization. In the 1990s, the DP complained that the ruling ANC's legislation and policy in areas such as higher education and employment, which favoured blacks and was justified as 'corrective action', was in fact a creeping reracialization of South African politics. The DP advocated a non-racial future, based on opportunity for all and treating all people with equal respect (Democratic Party 1998).

This advocacy of a non-racial future has found echoes in social policy and other fields. In recent times, and in the wake of the inquiry into the failure to bring to justice the killer of the black teenager Stephen Lawrence (Macpherson 1998; see also Chapter 8 by McLaughlin, this volume), there has been a call for 'colour-blind' approaches that treat individuals according to need rather than according to their 'culture' or race, or ethnicity. But what a colour-blind approach could mean, or how it can be operationalized seems far from certain, in a world often defined by race and colour divisions and where these bases of social differentiation operate as a modality of lived experience, albeit in uneven ways (cf. Winant 2001). Hence some of the same concerns have been registered against a parallel though more academic debate about post-race cosmopolitanism

(Gilroy 2000) which has kept alive the question of deracialization, even though the means to this end, and what a 'post-racial' world could look like, seems as far away as ever.

In the section on national culture in *The Wretched of the Earth*, Fanon (1967) mentions the 'racialization of thought' as the process by which colonialism erased differences among and within Africans and blacks in terms of racial categories such as Negro. For Fanon, such racial thinking in turn affects native intellectuals who adopt quasi-racial categories such as 'African culture', rather than proclaiming their own national culture. Fanon holds European colonialism responsible for this process or at least for beginning it, for 'colonialism did not dream of wasting its time in denying the existence of one national culture after another' (Fanon 1967: 171). He argues that responding to European domination by affirming Negro-ism is a political dead-end because the 'historical necessity in which men of African culture find themselves to racialize their claims and to speak more of African culture than of national culture will tend to lead them up a blind alley' (Fanon 1967: 172). Instead, Fanon advocated ways of looking beyond European models of thought and their influence, of which racialization, racial thinking, and racial categorization are examples that Fanon calls on anti-colonialists not to imitate. Anti-racism or anti-racialization in this argument rests not upon an assumed affinity between the national cultures of the colonized, but on the similar claims of colonized nations.

Fanon's quite brief remarks on racialization itself link it to European domination and to colonialism. Yet they contain the essence of the wider legacy of Fanon's work that draws attention to the relationship between the psychic and the social dimensions, and the ways in which subjugated identity positions can be internalized, even while they are in flux and being contested. His uses of racialization specifically has been underutilized, though Miles seems to suggest that his own conception of racialization may draw on it 'by highlighting the process of categorisation as one of attributing meaning to somatic characteristics, [it] presumes a social psychological theory which explains the nature and dynamics of the process' (Miles 1989: 75). The relationship between the psychic and the social has not been adequately explored in social–psychological and psychoanalytically influenced literatures on race although there are signs of advances being made (see Cohen 2002). In some cases, racialization seems to be used as a synonym for racism and as the process through which differences are naturalized and legitimated (Dalal 2002). For

Dalal, the structure of the psyche and the structures of society reflect and reinforce each other, so that if one is colour-coded, both will be.

Though Essed and Goldberg (2002) feel that the notion of racialization is now overused, they acknowledge Fanon's use of it and especially a distinction between it and an idea of 'humanization', to 'suggest the ways in which racial conceptions and structural conditions order lives and delimit human possibilities' (Essed and Goldberg 2002: 6). In this volume, we can see in both direct and indirect ways how a Fanonian approach reveals how lives are ordered and shaped by racism and racialization. In Chapter 5, Ann Phoenix draws on Fanon's legacy to examine racialization as a relational process. Using her own fieldwork on the social identities of black, white, and mixed-parentage young people, she develops Fanon's psychosocial orientation through the use of positioning theory, where, as she notes, racialization is itself a 'continuous process of positioning and identity construction'. The concept of racialization in this chapter is seen as offering a better way of grasping the dynamic and processual nature of identities, than the idea of race does. Thus, she has also recently argued (Lewis and Phoenix 2004) that racialization differs from race because, first, it emphasizes the social and psychological processes that puts people into racial categories; and second, it therefore entails that race is longer seen as fixed or natural, but as the outcome of particular ways in which people are classified and seen. The concept of racialization in this view does the same work as putting 'race' in quotation marks, in showing that race does not have a biological basis but that it becomes significant through social, economic, cultural, and psychological practices.

The other traces of Fanon in this volume are indirect and not always explicit. How people 'become racialized' and especially the role of childhood and place is the key theme of Vron Ware's use of autobiography to explore racial identity and the 'sinewy character' of racialization in Chapter 6. The psychobiographical tradition and the formation of identities that Ware connects with is reflected in a different way in Anoop Nayak's use of post-structuralist and psychoanalytical ideas in Chapter 7, which has theoretical links with Brah's view of racialization as a means to foreground the articulation between subjectivity and identity in Chapter 3. However, just as doubts have been raised about reading Fanon as a post-colonial theorist before his time (see Macey 2000), we should be careful about attributing all psychosocially influenced approaches to racialization to him. The main legacy of his work is the analysis of the mental states of the dominant and the subjugated and echoes of this are apparent in post-colonial studies. Although racialization itself has not been developed conceptually (cf. Wolfe 2002), such literatures provide historical and contemporary examples of the workings of 'race-making' and race-thinking processes.

As mentioned earlier, Michael Banton is credited with introducing the term racialization into sociology, initially in *The Idea of Race* (1977) where he discusses the racializing of the West and the racializing of the world. He writes that:

There was a process, which can be called racialization, whereby a mode of categorisation was developed, applied tentatively in European historical writing and then, more confidently to the populations of the world. (Banton 1977: 18–19)

Banton's view of racialization highlights the process by which, from the beginning of the nineteenth century, others came to be seen and defined in terms of biological differences, that is, that race came to be used to denote a physical category and not one that was to organize perceptions and ideas about differences. In Banton's *The International Politics of Race* (2002) he states that he introduced racialization in 1977 as a way of naming the modes of categorization through which people and nations came to be called races. For Banton, if the language of race was present then racialization occurred; if it was not there could not be any racialization said to be occurring. Banton's insistence that there has to be an explicit reference to or resort upon race is a position that he held consistently and formed the basis for disputes with others, as we discuss further below (see Miles 1993; Miles and Brown 2003). In Chapter 2, Banton updates and revisits the argument, presenting a case for the historical mode of racialization through ideas about race, and what he sees as the contemporary form of racialization through legislation and policy such as the Race Relations Acts in the United Kingdom. Like Banton, Carter (2000) also stresses the need for a boundary between social science and lay discourses when it comes to discussing race.

Banton's view that social scientists are often responsible for the very racialization that they claim simply to be trying to describe or depict finds an echo in Webster's argument about the racialization of America—'the systematic accentuation of certain physical attributes to allocate persons to races that are projected as real and thereby become the basis for analyzing all social relations' (Webster 1992: 3). Webster maintains that social scientists and legislators generate a racial order by their use of racial classifications in demography and official documents, in ways that give race a 'life of its own'. 'It is social scientists who classify persons racially, announce that race is a social reality, admit that race cannot be defined satisfactorily and claim to be dealing with the enigma of race' (Webster 1992: 3). Deracialization for Webster would entail the discarding of racial classifications, which he argues is what bedevils contemporary America, rather than race or racism.

David Goldberg sees racialization as vague as an analytical tool and instead develops an argument for examining 'regionally prompted, parametered, and promoted racisms linked to their dominant state formations' to distinguish between types and styles of racism (cf. Goldberg 2002). In Chapter 4, he looks at one particular type of racism that he calls 'racial Americanization'.

Neo-Marxism and Racialization

In the past two decades, Miles (1982, 1989, 1993; Miles and Brown 2003) has done most to develop the concept of racialization. His work has been influential, widely taken up, and much discussed. Initially, Miles' (1982) neo-Marxist analysis of race and class argued that migrant labour, as sections or fragments of the working class, became racialized through state policies and actions. In particular, the state's attempts to manage the contradiction between the needs of capitalist economies to have free movement of labour, and the competing need to define and regulate movement through national boundaries and legal citizenship, make racism the medium or the modality through which class is lived. For Miles, racialization indicated 'the existence of a social process in which human subjects articulate and reproduce the ideology of racism and engage in the practice of racial discrimination, but always in a context that they themselves have not determined' (Miles 1982: 177). Rejecting race as a basis of political organization and progressive politics, Miles sees race politics as distillations of class politics, the point for which he has been most criticized (e.g. see Solomos 2003), though it is a position he continues to advocate (Miles 1993; Miles and Torres 1999; Miles and Brown 2003).

Miles further developed the concept in several works, initially treating it as a synonym for racial categorization. Miles' approach rejects race and 'race relations' as analytical categories (for related arguments developed in France since the 1970s, see Guillaumin 1995) and instead uses racialization to examine the ways in which ideas about race are constructed, maintained, and used as a basis for exclusionary practices. His main definition of it is: 'those instances where social relations between people have been structured by the signification of human biological characteristics in such a way as to define and construct differentiated social collectivities' (Miles 1989: 75). Importantly, he goes on to make a point that is the basis for the disagreement with Banton. Miles adds that, 'The characteristics signified vary historically and, although they have usually been visible somatic features, other non-visible (alleged and real) biological features have also been signified' (Miles 1989: 75). Thus, for Miles, racism is more than a black and white matter and he shows, for instance, how Jews have been racialized through discourse and policy (Miles 1993; see also Kushner, this volume, Chapter 10). This broadening of the scope of racialization suggests that it refers both to ideological practices through which race is given significance, and cultural or political processes or situations where race is invoked as an explanation or a means of understanding. The latter has become the basis for the broader conception of racialization as expressing the ways in which social structures and ideologies become imbued with 'racial' meanings, so that social and political issues are conceived along racial lines. Among many issues that can be read in this way, Malik (1996) mentions class relations and poverty, especially in Victorian Britain, political discourse, and the idea of the Third World and North–South relations.

In this way, racialization has itself, arguably, been subject to 'conceptual inflation' in much the same way that Miles has argued about the concept of racism (which is the basis for his argument for a narrower use of racism as ideology, and not as an outcome or a practice). However, Miles has been accused of doing the same thing with racialization. Carter (2000) argues that Miles' use of racialization formulates a connection between an actor's beliefs and the social structure. That is, it entails an argument that shifts in signification have led to the world coming to be understood through a racial lens. From a 'realist' perspective (see also Rowe 1998), Carter (2000) argues that this is conflationary, because it refers both to social relations and the structuring of ideas about social relations. For Carter, it is not 'racialization as a signifying practice *itself* that structures social relations but those who employ this practice' (Carter 2000: 89). Miles' formulation, he argues, is unclear about whether racialization is an ideational or a structural phenomenon, or both (Carter 2000; cf. Goldberg, Chapter 4, this volume). In Carter's modified version, racialization 'rests on race ideas, is posterior to them and is a description of their popularity within the cultural system. Its effects on social structures and social relations is a matter of the analysis of social interaction' (Carter 2000: 91). Collins et al. also maintain that the main shortcoming of Miles' use of racialization is that it is treated as an ideological effect. Yet, they insist, racialization is 'not simply an issue of representation, but of social practices through which political, economic and social relations are structured' (Collins et al. 2000: 17). Racialization as it is used by them is a tool to examine the dynamic between structural relations of marginaliza-tion and the cultural representation of those relations. The broad use of racialization is for Goldberg (Chapter 4, this volume) sometimes ambiguous, and possibly vacuous. 'One cannot always tell, either explicitly or contextually, whether it is being invoked as a merely descriptive term or with deeper normative, critical thrust. Quite often it is put to work simply to suggest race-inflected social situa-tions, those informed or marked by racial characterization.'

As this suggests, both the narrow and broader versions of Miles' conception have been criticized by those who largely reject his approach as well as by those who accept its main thrust but modify or develop some aspects of it. The former camp includes Banton, as well as Cohen (1994). In a series of exchanges between them, Miles has recently been criticized by Banton again. Banton (2002) main-tains that Miles extended and expanded the usage of the idea of racialization, so that it could be seen as occurring whenever its effects can be observed. This is part of Banton's objection to the uses of racialization where race is seen as coded in statements but not explicitly mentioned. In the case of the (in)famous remarks about 'swamping' made by Mrs Thatcher in the 1970s (when she said that 'people are rather afraid of being swamped by those with a different culture'), which has commonly been taken as an instance of (coded) racializing discourse, even though race as such is not mentioned, Banton (2002) asks how race can be imputed when it is not manifest and when the imputation involves a claim that the reader knows the intentions of the speaker better than he or she does. Those doing so thereby lay claim to knowing what the speaker 'really' intended, Banton argues.

For Cohen (1994), the extension of the categories race and racism to a wide array of groups and phenomena through concepts such as racialization is dangerous and wrong. He maintains that anti-Catholicism, anti-Semitism, and anti-Irish prejudice were the main forms of group discrimination in Britain before mass Commonwealth migration after the Second World War. Racism, he argues, cannot retrospectively be applied to account for these. Similarly, he believes that more recent anti-Muslim feeling draws upon cultural and religious categories and not ideas about colour and descent. To call these instances of racism requires a degree of 'theoretical inventiveness' that, for Cohen, goes like this: 'of course the Irish, etc. are not a separate "race" (but we all know that "races" are artificial social constructs anyway), but as they are treated like a different race and alluded to in race-like ways, they are "racialized" and can thus be considered the victims of "racism." ' In short we can have "racism" without "race" (Cohen 1994: 194; on the racialization of religion, see Brah 1996; on the racialization of the Irish, see Malik 1996).

Miles' position has been amended and added to by Anthias and Yuval-Davis who are among those who make a case for the need to take greater account of gender relations (see also Guillaumin 1995) and of the intersection between ethnic, racial, gender, and class phenomena. Anthias and Yuval-Davis' (1992) approach opens the way to a broader conception of racialization because of their adoption of the notion of inferiorization. For them Miles' stance excludes migrants and refugees who are constructed as inferior in ethnic terms, though such inferiorization may not include racial categories or nomenclature. In their view, racism operates specifically through working on ethnic groupings: racism is 'a discourse and practice of inferiorizing ethnic groups. Racism need not rely on a process of racialization. We believe that racism can also use the notion of the undesirability of groups…this may lead to attempts to assimilate, exterminate or exclude' (Anthias and Yuval-Davis 1992: 12). This enables them to broaden the scope to include anti-Muslim racism, or 'Islamaphobia' as it is increasingly referred to.

This approach also opens the way for a parallel process of 'ethnicisation' that is sometimes used alongside racialization and as analogous to it (see also Essed 1991). For Lewis and Phoenix (2004) ethnicization works in the same ways as racialization in highlighting the contingent and constructed nature of differences, except that ethnicity as a cultural or national difference is invoked instead of race:

researchers on 'race' and 'ethnicity' have focussed on the *processes* they involve rather than identifying fixed characteristics of particular groups. 'Ethnicity' and 'race' are about the process of marking differences between people on the basis of assumptions about human physical or cultural variations and the meanings of these variations. This is what we mean when we say that individuals and groups are racialised or ethnicised…[such] identities are about setting and maintaining boundaries between groups.'

In a similar vein, Collins et al. (2000) indicate that ethnicization, rather than racialization, would be more appropriate for their work on the representation of ethnic youth gangs in Sydney, because ethnicity is the dominant motif of Australian debates. However, in the end they choose racialization because they believe that it provides a stronger sense of the attitudinal and institutional forms of racism involved in those representations (on institutional racism, see Macpherson 1998; Rattansi, Chapter 13, this volume). However, the relationship between ethnicization and racialization has generally not been explored systematically. In instances where racial and ethnic phenomena overlap and reinforce one another, there may be a case for looking at them together. The extent to which race and/or ethnicity is invoked may provoke inquires about the ways in which they are differentially invoked. The signification of ethnic and cultural characteristics may indicate that terms such as 'ethnicization' and, perhaps, 'culturalization' are more appropriate but the multiplication of terminology should be accompanied by an explanation of its utility, and with due regard for the ways in which ethnicization and racialization may or may not share common elements. In the updated edition of *Racism*, Miles and Brown (2003) draw upon Wallerstein (1995) to propose that ethnicization refers to the ways in which ethnic groups are constituted. Ethnicization is 'a dialectical process by which meaning is attributed to socio-cultural signifiers of human beings, as a result of which individuals may be assigned to a general category of persons which reproduces itself biologically, culturally, and economically. Where biological and/or somatic features (real or imagined) are signified we speak of racialization as a specific modality of ethnicisation' (Miles and Brown 2003: 99).

For Cohen (1994), the broadening of racialization processes in the way that Anthias and Yuval-Davis propose makes the definition so broad that a number of otherwise diverse phenomena—including nationalism and xenophobia—may be collapsed into one another, or subsumed within race or racism. Indeed, their approach does resuscitate the question of the relationship between what is specifically racial or racist, and other instances of 'othering' and inferiorization, which, following Edward Said's (1978) influential work on Orientalism, there has been a tendency to over-read. For Miles, racialization—'a process of categorisation, a representational process of defining an Other (usually, but not exclusively) somatically' (Miles 1989: 75)—is a dialectical process in which the defining of others necessarily entails the definition of a sense of Self (see also

Collins et al. (2000) for a view of racialization as othering; see also Pred 2000). Race and other axes of social differentiation do not exist apart from one another but that is not the same as claiming that they are only defined in and through each other. The precise nature of the relationship between race and class, or gender, or nationalism, is open to empirical investigation as are the links between racialization processes and other social processes (e.g. on class see Alexander and Halpern 2000, and Martinot 2003; on gender and sex Anthias and Yuval-Davis 1992, Brah 1996, and Eisenstein 1996). In their contributions to this volume Philomena Essed, Vron Ware, Anoop Nayak, Ghassan Hage, Eugene McLaughlin, and Ali Rattansi indicate some of the intersections, complexities, and articulations between racialization and gender and class. In Chapter 11, Essed uses the concept of 'cultural cloning' to explore the 'simultaneous operating forces of normalization, marginalization, problematization' that produces circles of sameness and exclusivity in a profession such as medical science. Her case study suggests that the application of the categories of race, racism, and racialization tend to produce a one-sided picture that does not wholly account for the complexity of the reproduction of sameness in professional cultures. Racialization, she maintains, 'emerges only through and in relation to notions of sex–gender–sexuality, physical and mental capacity, age, all of which are embedded and interwoven with into more general principles of modernization' (see Essed, Chapter 11, this volume).

In Chapter 9, Hage uses the idea of 'identity fetishism' to examine how white self-racialization occurs socio-historically among the Christian Lebanese. Locating his analysis within the colonial transformation of economy of Mount Lebanon, Hage shows how a white identity was 'intrinsically endowed with a causal power to generate the very capitalist social practices that produced it' through the 'magical qualities of fetishised collective identification', a fantasy that he has also explored in relation to whiteness in Australia (Hage 1998).

A sympathetic treatment of Miles can be found in the work of Stephen Small (1994). Like Miles, Small uses racialization to examine the signification of race, and as a way of rejecting the terms race and race relations (see also Bhattacharyya et al. 2002). For Small, race is a spurious idea while the category of race relations has to some extent legitimated the idea of race as a real and useful category by treating relations between racially defined groups as instances of race relations. Small argues that speaking of racialized identities and racialized relations offer better ways of discussing the power and influence of racial thinking without validating the idea of race itself. Furthermore, the racialization problematic that Small develops offers a way of unravelling patterns of racialized relations. He distinguishes between *the process of racialization* which is a 'process of attribution which has been unfolding historically and continues to unfold' (Small 1994: 33); and, by contrast, *the racialization problematic* which is a theoretical model or framework that allows the empirical data to be assessed against competing theories: 'The "racialization" problematic thus represents a paradigm within which competing theories can be advanced for an understanding and explanation of the creation and variations in racialised barriers, boundaries and identities in various socio-historical contexts' (Small 1994: 33). This, he insists, is more than a semantic issue. Rather the approach he advocates 'changes not just the language but also the framework and focus of the analysis, leading to a fundamentally different definition of "the problem" and to different types of policy and political proposals' (Small 1994: 34). In Chapter 10, Tony Kushner uses the racialization problematic to assess the racialization of Jews through science and culture in Britain in the twentieth century, and to draw some parallels between anti-Jewish racism and anti-black racism. However, the process/problematic distinction is not easy to maintain in practice, with Gabriel (1998), for instance, finding it useful to draw upon both the process and the problematic of racialization in his work, the former to examine the construction of white racialized identities, the latter to analyse cultural and media processes in the transformations of whiteness (cf. chapters by Nayak, McLaughlin, Hage, and Ware in the present volume).

Like the CCCS (1982) and Miles (1989), Small sees racialization as a means of redirecting the conventional gaze of race relations sociology away from the characteristics and actions of those defined racially and instead to focus upon the attitudes and motivations of more powerful social groups. In summary, Small's view of racialization to suggest 'that social structures, social ideologies and attitudes have historically become imbued with "racial" meaning [which are] contingent and contested and ... shaped by a multitude of other variables, economic, political, religious' (1994: 36) is akin to the broader view of racialization sketched by Miles.

Small's (1994) work on 'mixed race' identities (see also Bhattacharyya et al. 2002) leads him to define 'racialized harmony' as non-antagonistic relations between blacks and whites and he sees 'racialized parity' as denoting equal access to privileges. Both of these are similar in tone to Reeves' (1983) idea of practical deracialization.

It is however unlikely that Reeves' use of 'anti-racialization' as meaning the absence of race could fit with this, as Small's terminology indicates that groups racially defined in terms of blackness and whiteness would continue to be bases of collective self- and other-identification, though not antagonistically defined. Whether the language of race— or raciology as Gilroy (2000) refers to it—can preclude such non-conflicting relations is open to question at least. A further problem is that while it is understandable that Small's comparison of the United States and Britain leads to a focus on black–white relations, the scope of racialized relations is obviously far wider than this, with the racialization of South Asians and East Asians, among others (Rattansi and Westwood 1994; Brah 1996). Equally, there are fractures within whiteness where groups such as the Irish, the Italians, and Slavs have 'become white' over time, making racialization a complex and sometimes contradictory process (Warren and Twine 1997; Jacobson 1998; Bonnett 2000). Whether Jews can be regarded as white, or as a race, or as an ethnic or religious group indicates some of this, and there are both historical and quite recent examples of the uncertain locations of Jews in racial discourse (Miles 1993; Kushner, Chapter 10, this volume).

Racialization and Political Discourses

A rather different kind of analysis of racialization is to be found in Reeves (1983). In *British Political Discourse*, Reeves argues that racialization is a process through which race is adopted in situations in which it was previously absent. Racialization occurs in any case where race is increasingly used descriptively. This position introduces a temporal and historical dimension, indeed he even refers to 'historical racialization' as occurring when increasing racial elements are used where earlier there were less or absent, a prime example being the emergence of scientific racism in the nineteenth century. His main distinction is between *practical racialization*— this describes 'changes in the real world, in conscious or non-conscious social behaviour and physical and cultural characteristics'—and *ideological racialization*—'changes in the symbolic world in the way human beings choose to account for what they perceive and how they act' (Reeves 1983: 174). Although the latter is Reeves' main concern, he notes that practice and ideology may correspond when a group seeks to justify its domination, or to implement policies that maintain group boundaries and the rules of inclusion and exclusion. For Reeves, discourse is racialized when 'increasing use is made of some or all of the following: racial categorisations, racial explanations, racial evaluations, and racial prescriptions' (1983: 174).

Interestingly enough, Reeves also hints that racialization may be a means for political mobilization and necessary to address racially discriminatory practices. Raising the status and visibility of race may be necessary in situations where racial divisions operate without any willingness to do something about them. This racialization is an indication of groups' heightened awareness of, and a wish to reduce or remove, racial injustice and inequality. Reeves maintains that racialization here 'involves the recognition of race as a means to non-racial moral ends' (1983: 175) because a form of racial explanation is not used in an essentialist way in these cases but to highlight its superficiality, something that he calls anti-racialization. Others, however, are more doubtful about the degree of essentialism that such movements have entailed (Gilroy 2000). Tessman (2001) also recognizes the double-edged nature of the process, though Gilroy is a leading light in the shift from advocacy of race-based mobilization to increasing concerns about the ends to which race has been mobilized, especially in the United States. For Gilroy (2000), the uses of race in the twentieth century alone produce an urgent need for post-race imaginaries, sometimes in the name of cosmopolitanism. In his examination of urban politics and governance in London in Chapter 12, Michael Keith alludes to some of the shortcomings of the analytical lens of racialization, as well as political and urban theory, and social policy, for understanding such situations. He maintains that the lens of racialization suggests greater analytical certainty than is possible in understanding the formation of multicultural cities and instead draws upon cosmopolitan politics—or cosmopolitics—to advocate a more nuanced approach to issues of racial justice.

To return to Reeves' schema, *ideological deracialization* entails the attenuation, elimination, or substitution of 'racial categories in discourse, the omission or de-emphasis of racial explanation, and the avoidance of racial evaluation or prescription' (Reeves 1983: 177). This can take a synchronic or asynchronic form. In the former, ideological and practical deracialization occur at the same time, while in the latter, ideological racialization occurs alongside practical racialization. It is the latter that Reeves holds to be most useful for accounting for race relations in post-war Britain where although black migrants have practically experienced their structural and social position in racial terms, ideologically there has mostly been an avoidance of discussing these issues in racial terms. Reeves makes a further distinction between systemic ideological deracialization and self-conscious deracialization, a dualism that parallels a contrast between ideology and individuals. He further uses the notion of 'sanitary coding' to refer to forms of language or discourse that refer to race in a coded form but aim to avoid the clear expression of racism associated with the far right. Reeves' analysis provides examples of how this occurs through equivocation and mental imaging, though Banton (2002) is critical of claims about racial 'coding'.

Although Reeves presents one of the most developed accounts of the process of racialization and deracialization it is one that has, perhaps rather puzzlingly, suffered from limited impact. Other approaches to racialized discourse, especially those drawing upon Foucault, have been more influential (for instance, Goldberg 1993). The distinctions and methods proposed by Reeves have not been widely taken up or discussed and used as widely as Miles' work. Nonetheless, in revisiting the debate about race and immigration in post-war Britain, Ali Rattansi (Chapter 13, this volume) finds it useful to draw on Reeves' idea of 'discursive racialization'.

Cultural Processes and Racialization

The cultural turn in the social sciences and the impact of postmodernism and post-structuralism is one, though an important, influence behind the search for more nuanced analyses of racialization, though it does not have to be the only avenue through which this can occur. Such analyses tend to highlight the contingent, uneven, and unexpected features of the racialization process. Brah (1996) and Rattansi and Westwood (1994) are among those who have sought to explore the bases of differential racialization as a mode of power that defines 'others' in racial and/or cultural terms. For example, Brah considers the differences in the kinds of racism aimed at and experienced by blacks, South Asians, and East Asians in the United States as intersecting modalities of power, and relates these to social divisions such as gender, sexuality, class, and religion. She treats differential racialization as 'a concept for analysing processes of relational multi-locationality within and across formations of power marked by the articulation of one form of racism with another, and with other modes of differentiation' (Brah 1996: 196). Her analysis in Chapter 3 of this volume poses important questions about the cultural work that the texts examined do, as well as the articulation between power and knowledge. In Chapter 7, drawing on his own ethnographic work, Nayak uses post-structuralist and psychoanalytic ideas to examine racialization in two masculine youth subcultures, where despite apparent differences he finds similar patterns of 'cultural imagining of black bodies and subjectivities'. Embodiment is also a concern for Rattansi who argues for the articulation between modes of differentiation in Chapter 13, while in Chapter 8, the cultural construction of an 'ethnoracial imaginary' of white spaces is a key theme in the uneven process of racialization and deracialization in McLaughlin's reading of the news media's coverage of the five young white men suspected of the murder of Stephen Lawrence, which prompted an official inquiry (Macpherson 1998). These chapters connect with the more general wave of scholarship that has sought to explore various aspects of the 'cultural territories of race' (Lamont 1999).

Mac an Ghaill (1999) has welcomed the differentialist approach in his call for more complex accounts of racialization, the consequences of which he believes has not been explored sufficiently. Mac an Ghaill maintains that blacks continue to be the main object of inquiry in race relations sociology and says that, 'a main issue that has tended to be underplayed in the literature on racialization is the collective subject position of whites, which operates in a hegemonic logic in which "whiteness" is absent to the "racial majority" who assume that racialization is "something to do with blacks"' (Mac an Ghaill 1999: 69). Although we doubt the extent to which this characterization is valid, the fact is that in the time since this was written a whole subfield, or maybe even field, of whiteness studies has opened up (Bonnett 2000; Ware and Back 2002). The central role of whiteness in the racialization process has been widely explored, particularly in post-colonial histories (Stoler 1995, 2002) and in the contemporary United States (Jacobson 1998). The power of whiteness as well as its unevenness and contradictions is discussed at some length, and from a variety of angles, in the chapters by Ware, Hage, McLaughlin, and Nayak.

Racial Formation as a Process

Most of what we have considered so far has been used and discussed mainly in Europe and with applications to other situations like South Africa and Australia. The content and nature of the debate seems different in the United States, where the idea of racial formation seems to have been more influential. We consider this further in a moment and examine its links with racialization. First, it is important not to overstate the differences. There are US scholars who have engaged in the theoretical debate on racialization developed within sociology in Europe, most notably Goldberg (1993). Furthermore, there are numerous examples of the use of the idea of racialization in US academic literature within sociology, political science, cultural studies, literary theory, and post-colonial studies. Most of these are instances of the broader meaning of racialization as a lens or a perspective through which issues and debates become racially marked or signified (Williams 1998). For example, Zilber and Niven (2000) use it to examine the role of the news media in conveying understandings of contemporary racial inequality, especially in political representation in the United States where, they argue, whites receive more favourable coverage. Furthermore, they stress that racialized media coverage of black or African-American political candidates is the norm, rather than exceptional, as, if elected, such people come to be seen as minority officeholders. They regard racialized reporting as news coverage that portrays an inadequate and inaccurate image of African-Americans, who are over-represented as criminals and athletes. Sears et al. (2000) are also concerned with racialized politics in the United States but they explore this through public opinion about race and its effects on politics, particularly white attitudes to issues of racial difference and disadvantage. Through racialization, 'non-racial' issues such as targeted redistributive policies become sucked into racial politics and, thereby, racialized. In these works, racialization appears to mean either the ways in which race or blackness is implicated in news coverage (Zilber and Niven 2000), or the widening scope of race in political debates (Sears et al. 2000). In both cases, racialization appears sometimes to be a synonym for racial or racist meanings, or to suggest the process by which those meanings are made.

Another example is to be found in Kelley (2002) who examines racism in biblical scholarship, which he sees as pervasive and not incidental. In this work, racialization is used as akin to being 'infused with the category of race' (Kelley 2002: 4). In other cases, racialization is used to explore the race–gender nexus in literature (Najmi and Srikanth 2002), or political mobilization and black identity politics (Mostern 1999), or as a tool or method for grasping the racial order and racial projects for informing cold war period cinema (Noakes 2003). Another stream of literature uses the concept to understand the racialization and deracialization of Jewishness and Jewish identities (see Tessman and Bat-Ami 2001); in historical studies of labour and class in America (e.g. see Alexander and Halpern 2000; Martinot 2003); and in cultural geography (Pred 2000).

Another interesting contrast can be found in the idea of racial formation developed by Omi and Winant (1994). Barot and Bird (2001: 617) feel that Omi and Winant 'use the concept of racial formation as a perspective that is not fundamentally different from the concept of racialization as deployed in British literature in the 1980s'. The affinity or lack of it, between the influential ideas of racial formation and racialization is worthy of investigation and at first sight it seems that the two have a lot in common (see also St Louis, this volume). Omi and Winant maintain that race is an intractable and enduring feature of the United States. Racial meanings are pervasive and shape individual identities and collective action, as well as social structures. Although they see race as an 'unstable and "decentered" complex of social meanings constantly being transformed by political struggle' (Omi and Winant 1994: 68), they accept that it remains an organizing principle of social life. For them, racialization refers to a specific ideological process through which the shifting meanings of race are produced by the practices of various social groups. Winant (1994: 59) himself says that, 'The concept of racialization signifies the extension of racial meaning to a previously racially unclassified relationship, social practice, or group.' Racialization is the key process through racial meanings and identities are constructed in racial formation (Winant 1994). In other words, racialization is viewed as a way in which racial formation occurs, and not as equivalent to it. In both concepts there is a common emphasis on the process of race-making and race thinking and the ways that racial meanings are variable and differentially applied (cf. Winant 2001). In something that looks similar to Miles' formulation, for Winant (1994) racial formation theory suggests that: 'Although the concept of race appeals to biologically based human characteristics (so-called phenotypes) selection of these particular human features for purposes of racial signification is always and necessarily a social and historical process'. There are three implications of this view according to Winant. First, that racial meanings pervade social life; second, it helps us to grasp the expansion and intensification of racial phenomena in a globalizing world; and third, it produces a new and revised conception of racial time and history.

In some of his earlier work, Goldberg also appeared to see a connection between racial formation and racialization when he wrote that:

In using 'race' and the terms bearing racial significance, social subjects racialize the people and population groups whom they characterize and to whom they refer.... Conceived in this way, the concept that has assumed wide currency in characterizing the process by which human groups are constituted as races is *racial formation* (or, more awkwardly, *racialization*). Racial formation involves the structural composition and determination of groups into racialized form, the imparting of racial significance and connotation at given socio-structural sites to relationships previously lacking them. (Goldberg [1992] 1999: 375)

However, underneath this apparent affinity there are basic disagreements. Miles himself has argued that Omi and Winant's conception of racialization is underdeveloped and not used systematically. Miles and Torres (1999) object to Omi and Winant's idea of a critical theory of race because they maintain that such ideas are rooted in a race relations paradigm that reifies the idea of race itself. They argue that 'the process of racialization takes place and has its effects in the context of class and production relations and the idea of "race" may indeed not even be explicitly articulated in this process' (Miles and Torres 1999: 33). Thus, they maintain that the concept of racialization does contain a critique of all concepts of race, while Omi and Winant's defence of the race concept is 'a classic example of the way in which the academy in the US continues to racialize the world' (Miles and Torres 1999: 33).

Beyond the academic debates, both racialization and racial formation have been questioned in terms of their implications, with Tessman and Bat-Ami suggesting that they can entail the depoliticization of race: 'an analysis of racialization as the process of the social construction of race can lead theorists away from the possibility of race-conscious strategies for struggling against racism' (Tessman and Bat-Ami 2001: 5). As this suggests, what is at stake in seemingly academic debates about racialization are central questions about race, racism, and anti-racism and throughout this volume there is an ongoing debate about the extent to which racialization provides a better way of understanding these crucial issues. The answers provided in this book vary in their view, and among those who are most critical Barot and Bird (2001) also believe that the 'racialization problematic'—as a successor to the 'race-relations problematic' and the 'racisms problematic'—does not provide an adequate framework of analysis. Against that, there are in this volume and beyond a number of other perspectives about the value of racialization as a critical tool for studying how 'race-making' occurs.

The importance of racialization is underlined in the final chapter by Ali Rattansi, who we asked to provide a coda to this book based on his reading of the previous chapters. Rattansi argues for the indispensability of racialization and identifies at least two significant uses for it. First, drawing on Reeves (1983) and returning to the question of the racialization of immigration, he presents a picture of the multilayered and multidimensional character of racialization. Second, drawing upon Foucault, he argues that 'debates about colonialism, de-colonization, immigration, various aspects of domestic governmentality, foreign policy, and so forth have occurred within an overarching racialized unity and racial hierarchy which have privileged whiteness and its discursive links with varieties of "Western", "European", and "masculine" imaginaries'. This also leads him to stress the centrality of the 'race–nation–ethnicity complex' and its articulation with gender, sexuality, and class.

Conclusion

In this introductory chapter, we have endeavoured to cover most of the major writers and debates around racialization and to signal some of the ways in which the term is used and contested. We are convinced that there is much to be gained from a critical dialogue among scholars and researchers about key concepts and ideas as they are used to shape research questions. In this volume, we have sought to provide a basis for pushing ahead with some aspects of this dialogue by asking our various contributors to reflect on the rather different meanings that have attached themselves in the past two decades and more to the notion of racialization. It is of course necessary to link such debates to the realities of carrying out detailed empirical research within contemporary as well as historical environments, a point touched upon by a number of the contributors to the volume. It is also clear, however, that such empirically driven research needs to be carried out in dialogue with conceptual and theoretical debates if it is to help us to understand the changing dynamics of racial and ethnic relations in our contemporary environment. It is in the spirit of this dialogue that we offer this volume to a wider readership, in the hope that it will help propel us towards a more productive debate in the future.

REFERENCES

Alexander, P. and Halpern, R. (eds.) (2000) *Racializing Class, Classifying Race: Labour and Difference in Britain, the USA and Africa*. New York: St. Martin's Press.

Anthias, F. and Yuval Davis, N. (1992) *Racialized Boundaries: Race, Nation, Gender, Colour and Class and the Anti-racist Struggle*. London: Routledge.

Banton, M. (1977) *The Idea of Race*. London: Tavistock.

——(2002) *The International Politics of Race*. Cambridge: Polity.

Barot, R. and Bird, J. (2001) 'Racialization: The Genealogy and Critique of a Concept'. *Ethnic and Racial Studies*, 21 (4): 601–18.

Bhattacharyya, G., Gabriel, J., and Small, S. (2002) *Race and Power*. London: Routledge.

Bilton, T. et al. (2002) *Introductory Sociology*, 4th edn. Basingstoke: Macmillan.

Bulmer, M and Solomos, J. (eds.) (1999) *Ethnic and Racial Studies Today*. London: Routledge.

Bonnett, A. (2000) *White Identities: Historical and International Perspectives*. Hemel Hempstead: Prentice Hall.

Brah, A. (1996) *Cartographies of Diaspora: Contesting Identities*. London: Routledge.

Carter, B. (2000) *Realism and Racism: Concepts of Race in Sociological Research*. London: Routledge.

——Harris, C., and Joshi, S. (1987) *The 1951–55 Conservative Government and the Racialization of Black Immigration*. Coventry: Centre for Research in Ethnic Relations.

CCCS (1982) *The Empire Strikes Back*. London: Hutchinson.

Chan, W. and Mirchandani, K. (eds.) (2002) *Crimes of Colour: Racialization and the Criminal Justice System in Canada*. Peterborough, ON: Broadview Press.

Cohen, P. (2002) 'Psychoanalysis and Racism: Reading the Other Scene', in D.T. Goldberg and J. Solomos (eds.), A *Companion to Racial and Ethnic Studies*. Oxford: Blackwell.

Cohen, R. (1994) *Frontiers of Identity: The British and the Others*. Harlow: Longman.

Collins, J., Noble, G., Poynting, S., and Tabar, P. (2000) *Kebabs, Kids, Cops and Crime*. Annandale, NSW: Pluto.

Dalal, F. (2002) *Race, Colour and the Process of Racialization: New Perspectives from Analysis, Psychoanalysis, and Sociology*. Hove: Brunner-Routledge.

Democratic Party (1998) 'The Death of the Rainbow Nation—Unmasking the ANC's Programme of Re-racialization', photocopy available in the British Library.

Eisenstein, Z. R. (1996) *Hatreds: Racialized and Sexualized Conflicts in the Twenty First Century*. New York: Routledge.

Essed, P. (1991) *Understanding Everyday Racism*. London: Sage.

——and Goldberg, D. T. (eds.) (2002) *Race Critical Theories*. Malden, MA: Blackwell.

Fanon, F. (1967) *The Wretched of the Earth*. Harmondsworth: Penguin.

Fulcher, J and Scott, J. (2003) *Sociology*, 2nd edn. Oxford: Oxford University Press.

Gabriel, J. (1998) *Whitewash: Racialized Politics and the Media*. London: Routledge.

Gilroy, P. (2000) *Between Camps: Nations, Cultures and the Allure of Race*. London: Allen Lane.

Goldberg, D. T. [originally 1992] (1999) 'The Semantics of Race', edited extract in M. Bulmer and J. Solomos (eds.), *Racism*. Oxford: Oxford University Press.

——(1993) *Racist Culture*. Oxford: Blackwell.

——(2002) *The Racial State*. Oxford: Blackwell.

Guillaumin, C. (1995) *Racism, Sexism, Power and Ideology*. London: Routledge.

Hage, G. (1998) *White Nation: Fantasies of White Supremacy in a Multicultural Society*. Annandale, NSW: Pluto.

Haralambos, M. and Holborn, M. (2000) *Sociology*, 5th edn. London: Collins.

Holdaway, S. (1996) *The Racialization of British Policing*. London: Macmillan.

Jacobson, M. (1998) *Whiteness of a Different Color: European Immigrants and the Alchemy of Race*. Cambridge, MA: Harvard University Press.

Kelley, S. (2002) *Racializing Jesus: Race, Ideology and the Formation of Modern Biblical Scholarship*. New York: Routledge

Lamont, M. (1999) *The Cultural Territories of Race: Black and White Boundaries*. Chicago: University of Chicago Press.

Lewis, G. and Phoenix, A. (2004) ' "Race", "Ethnicity" and Identity', in K. Woodward (ed.), *Questioning Identity*. London: Routledge.

Mac an Ghaill, M. (1999) *Contemporary Racisms and Ethnicities*. Buckingham: Open University Press.

Macey, D. (2000) *Frantz Fanon: A Life*. London: Granta Books.

Macpherson, Sir William (1999) *The Stephen Lawrence Inquiry*. London: The Stationery Office.

Malik, K. (1996) *The Meaning of Race*. Basingstoke: Macmillan.

Martinot, S. (2003) *The Rule of Racialization: Class, Identity, Governance*. Philadelphia: Temple University Press.

Miles, R. (1982) *Racism and Migrant Labour*. London: Routledge.

——(1989) *Racism*. London: Routledge.

——(1993) *Racism After 'Race Relations'* London: Routledge.

——and Brown, M. (2003) *Racism*, 2nd edn. London: Routledge.

——and Torres, R. (1999) 'Does "race" matter?', in R. Torres, L. Miron, and J. Inda (eds.), *Race, Identity and Citizenship*. Malden, MA: Blackwell.

Mostern, K. (1999) *Autobiography and Black Identity Politics: Racialization in Twentieth-Century America*. New York: Cambridge University Press.

Najmi, S., and Srikanth, R. (eds.), (2002) *White Women in Racialized Spaces: Imaginative Transformations and Ethical Action in Literature*. Albany: State University of New York Press.

Noakes, J. (2003) 'Racializing Subversion: The FBI and the Depiction of Race in Early Cold War Movies.' *Ethnic and Racial Studies*, 26 (4): 728–49

Omi, M. and Winant, H. (1994) *Racial Formation in the United States*, 2nd edn. New York: Routledge.

Pred, A. (2000) *Even in Sweden: Racisms, Racialized Spaces, and the Popular Geographical Imagination*. Berkeley: University of California Press.

Rattansi, A. and Westwood, S. (eds.) (1994) *Racism, Modernity and Identity*. Cambridge: Polity

Reeves, F. (1983) *British Racial Discourse: A Study of British Political Discourse About Race and Race-related Matters*. Cambridge: Cambridge University Press.

Rowe, M. (1998) *The Racialization of Disorder in Twentieth Century Britain*. Aldershot: Ashgate.

Said, E. (1978) *Orientalism*. New York: Pantheon Books.

Sears, D., Sidanius, J., and Bobo, L. (eds.) (2000) *Racialized Politics: The Debate About Racism in America*. Chicago: University of Chicago Press.

Small, S. (1994) *Racialised Barriers: The Black Experience in the United States and England in the 1980s.* London: Routledge.

Solomos, J. (2003) *Race and Racism in Britain,* 3rd edn. Basingstoke: Macmillan.

Stoler, A. L. (1995) *Race and the Education of Desire: Foucault's History of Sexuality and the Colonial Order of Things.* Durham, NC: Duke University Press.

——(2002) *Carnal Knowledge and Imperial Power: Race and the Intimate in Colonial Rule.* Berkeley: University of California Press.

Tessman, L. and Bat-Ami, B. (eds.) (2001) *Jewish Locations: Traversing Racialized Landscapes.* Lanham, MD: Rowman and Littlefield.

Wallerstein, I. (1995) *Historical Capitalism; with, Capitalist Civilization,* new edn. London: Verso.

Ware, V. and Back, L. (2002) *Out of Whiteness: Color, Politics, and Culture.* Chicago: University of Chicago Press.

Warren, J. W. and Twine, F. W. (1997) 'White Americans, The New Minority?' *Journal of Black Studies,* 28: 200–18.

Webster, Y. O. (1992) *Racialization of America.* New York: St. Martin's Press.

Williams, P. J. (1998) *Seeing a Color Blind Future: The Paradox of Race.* New York: Noonday Press.

Winant, H. (1994) *Racial Conditions.* Minneapolis: University of Minnesota Press.

——(2001) *The World is a Ghetto: Race and Democracy Since World War II.* New York: Basic Books.

Wolfe, P. (2002) 'Race and Racialisation'. *Postcolonial Studies,* 5 (1): 51–62.

Zilber, J. and Niven, D. (2000) *Racialized Coverage of Congress: The News in Black and White.* Westport, CT: Praeger.

CHAPTER 1

Racialization in the 'Zone of Ambiguity'

Brett St Louis

> Few countries can be considered immune to a future tide of violence
> generated by intolerance, lust for power, economic difficulties, reli-
> gious or political fanaticism, and racialist attritions. It is therefore
> necessary to sharpen our senses, distrust the prophets, the enchanters,
> those who speak and write 'beautiful words' unsupported by intelligent
> reasons.
>
> Primo Levi (*The Drowned and the Saved*)

The circular disputes over the reality of race demonstrate the major
problem of assessing its conceptual and practical status. In the
absence of a clear consensus in the natural and human sciences as to
whether race exists or not there is a wide spectrum of affirmative and
negative statements on its veracity and subsequent usage. On one
hand, race *can* be identified as a *biological category* that distinguishes between population varieties in the human species (Sarich
and Miele 2004) or as a *syncretic category* that is formed (and continually reformed) at particular socio-historical junctures (Omi and
Winant 1994). On the other hand, race *does not* exist in any real
objective sense and instead is a *mythic category* that biologically mis-
represents existing ethnic groups (Montagu 1997) or is a *reified category* that conjures the fictive biological, social, and cultural unity of
arbitrary racialized collectivities (Appiah 1986). In turn, the categorical
existence/non-existence of race creates a series of corresponding
positions on its procedural efficacy. These range from its positivistic
value to epidemiological research and understanding evolutionary
history (Watts 1997); its strategic role as a form of social description
and source of political motivation (Brown et al. 2003); and its
absolute futility that invites the discontinuation of its formal and
informal use (Eze 2001). In short, attempts at definitive racial

understanding have arrived at the following conclusions: race does/does not exist and we should/should not use the concept.

On the face of it, this situation signals a descriptive and analytical impasse that obviates incontrovertible racial meaning and understanding. However, it is perhaps the quest for conclusive proof that is especially problematic. Arguments against the biological salience of race that assert its non-existence are simply contradicted by the counterclaims attesting to its existence, thus entrenching the impasse ever more deeply. This is not to abdicate the ethical responsibility entailed in mounting objections to naturalized notions of race and the gross abuses carried out in its name, but rather serves to state a point of logicality. When alternate facticities of race (the *qualities* of the fact of its existence or non-existence) confront each other, the basic didactic aim of establishing the *true* conceptual and practical status of race is unfulfilled. That one racial fact becomes more compelling than another is not solely due to its status as a fact but also the extent to which it represents a compelling moral ideal (St Louis 2004). Simply put, one either is or is not well disposed towards the biological notion of race in part because of a moral appreciation of its social connotation and implications. This quandary illustrates the problematic conceptual and practical status of race and the antagonism between realist and constructivist positions as well as those advocating its absolute inefficacy. Therefore, it is perhaps more profitable to confront this ever more firmly entrenched impasse by engaging what race *does* as well as what/whether it *is*.

This procedural focus is especially important given that the political use of the biological racial concept does not presuppose an acceptance of its actual existence. As perhaps its most notorious propagandist, Hitler acknowledged a means/ends expediency in his purely instrumental application of the biological race concept:

I know perfectly well, just as well as all those tremendously clever intellectuals, that in the scientific sense there is no such thing as race [...] I as a politician need a conception which enables the order which has hitherto existed on historic bases to be abolished and an entirely new and anti-historic order enforced and given an intellectual basis.... With the conception of race, National Socialism will carry its revolution abroad and recast the world. (Cited in Montagu 1997: 81)

In this case, objections to the biological concept of race based on its factual provenance and logical veracity are of limited use given that the appeal to race is not based on an understanding of its objectively true and scientifically valid status. Instead, what is central to the usefulness of race in the above example is a clear appreciation of its symbolic and political value that has always been the case—although seldom as transparent as in Hitler's private remark. Therefore, albeit oscillating between differing degrees of candour and opaqueness, the concept of race is and always has been, amongst other things, a political resource.

Accepting the existence of a circular logic that allows for the authentication *and* nullification of biological racial truth claims within competing scientific and political fields, this chapter focuses on the complex evolution of processes of racialization in order to consider the future of the biological concept of race. The chapter begins by outlining the ambiguities in the socio-cultural reification of a politics of difference that opens up different modalities for tacit biological racialization. I suggest that this presents specific dilemmas for analysing and critiquing biological racialization from an objectivist standpoint. The chapter then traces these conceptual and critical observations within a consideration of biomedical research into genetic disease frequencies as an example of contemporary racialization that resurrects the biological notion of race through a rhetoric of 'special' or 'target' populations. Ultimately, I argue for a more nuanced critique that moves beyond the normative pejorative sense of racialization and combines scientific truth claims with ethical assertions.

Racialization and the Politics of Difference

The normative scenario where the processes of biological racialization belie a regressive racial political project that can be clearly identified through their appeal to ideals of racial supremacy and inferiority is increasingly questionable. Of course, this is not to suggest that such racializing processes have been excised from the social sphere but rather to note their partial mutation into more palatable forms expressed through largely inoffensive sentiments. This transformation and the limitations of dominant conceptualizations of explicitly regressive racialization are transparent in Pierre-André Taguieff's (1990) admirable account of the framework and articulation of racism in contemporary France.

In pointing to the rehabilitation of right-wing racism through the development of a 'positive image' in an attempt to gain enthusiastic public appeal, Taguieff identifies a significant rhetorical shift.

Instead of launching the customary and expected negative attacks on inferior Others, the French right expresses its racist ideas through a 'differentialist argument' predicated on the foregrounding of positive statements on ethnic difference. Within this framework, 'true racism' is inverted as the attempt to suppress and eliminate ethnic difference through the enforcement of an untenable sameness as favoured by leftists and anti-racists alike. Against the nightmare of this monochrome idealism, the right—in a move ironically resonant of Jean-Paul Sartre's (1976) notion of Negritude as an 'anti-racist racism'—asserts its realist respect for the sanctity of difference as the true expression of anti-racism. As such, the right's praise of difference indicates a politically potent expression of anti-totalitarianism that resonates as a compelling articulation of freedom, independence, and autonomous thought.

The primary value of Taguieff's intervention lies in his penetrative focus on the sophistry and political dexterity of this racist programme that manages a reversal of classical anti-racist discourse. The right has, largely successfully, attempted to seize the respectable terrain of the 'reasonable' middle ground by appropriating the normatively desirable ideological values which has allowed it to force its anti-racist political adversaries onto the defensive. Within this political reversal not only does the right assume the mantle of the 'true anti-racists' but seeks to gain legitimacy through (re)presenting itself as the true guardian of authentic French positive social values. Although based on the specific example of French political culture, Taguieff's observation carries a grave implication for the possible formation of varieties of racialization and the differential discursive and political spaces that they are situated within. Taguieff notes that the right's anti-left stereotypes are constructed within what he terms 'zones of ambiguity' where 'New authoritarian projects are designated as "liberal," neo-racism is passed as "the right to be different," and nationalist currents rooted in anti-democratic traditions claim the idea of "direct" democracy as their own' (1990: 116).[1] This malleable discursive and political space is crucial in that the salience of the customary characterization of racialization as an external ascriptive form that is inherently regressive becomes severely limited. The exposé of this subtle appeal to the distinctiveness of group identity is laudable in demonstrating the fluctuating reference to and dependence on crude assertions of the superiority/inferiority axes within racist beliefs and practices. However, these 'zones of ambiguity' raise another perhaps deeper problem in that the regressive/progressive, racist/anti-racist universe that underpins culturalist and differentialist analyses of racism is increasingly difficult to identify and sustain as a point of departure for political critique.

The 'Special Problem' of Racial Critique

The discursive complexity of the novel and barely perceptible formations of racism is obscured within the (dis)ingenuous character of zones of ambiguity. This has a profound effect in that the project of countercritique is essentially revelatory; for example, it is based on the attempt to unveil the sophistry of the 'right to difference' through two key principles. First, the divisive intent of these (racist) discourses is obscured by their professed benign acknowledgement of objective racial difference which suggests that a clear distinction can be made between their *preferred* and *real* meaning. Second, following on from this, by focusing on the deceitful character of such apparently tolerant and respectful appeals to racial and cultural difference—which are in fact far from benign—a clear ideal–typical separation between politically progressive and regressive forms of racialization and racial formation is implied.

However, in addition to providing the discursive field wherein differentialist forms of racialization are constructed and enunciated, zones of ambiguity also produce and regulate racial meaning and understanding. Indeed, in Taguieff's estimation, as the 'progressive' discursive political space becomes increasingly ambiguous and open to instrumental manipulation, the successful right-wing conceptual and rhetorical appropriation of anti-racism radically alters the commonplace sectarian political certainties of what constitutes a progressive and anti-racist argument. This poses the problem of differentiating between separate and opposed modes of racial formation that share the same racial conceptual framework and rhetoric of cultural distinctiveness yet reflect morally opposed racial ideologies. Furthermore, this antagonistic symmetry makes it difficult to sustain the tacit political and moral judgements customarily associated with distinguishing regressive racial ideas and practices from their progressive opposite.

If this problematic threatens either an enveloping relativist inertia or the promotion of a sterile monologue amongst like minds, the conceptual resources to identify differential modes of racialization and advance critical judgements are available in a perhaps unlikely setting. In the first volume of his *Treatise on Social Theory*, W. G. Runciman sets out the analytical order for the emergence of sociological and social scientific understanding. His distinction between 'reportage', 'explanation', 'description', and 'evaluation' represents an invitation to understand given social phenomena through the sequential engagement of corresponding questions: 'what?', 'why?', 'what like?', and 'how good or bad?' (1983: 19). Runciman's ostensibly methodological concern with social scientific theoretical formulation and positivist sympathies aside, his schema is useful for understanding racialization—and its future possibilities—outside of the restrictions of its normative pejorative moral and political associations.

In raising the methodological and theoretical possibility of *reporting* what biological racialization is, *explaining* why it exists, *describing* what it is like, and *evaluating* it as good or bad, Runciman's framework enables us to imagine differential forms of racialization. Given the continued conceptual and practical impasse, his suggestion that the factual inaccuracy of a description need not prevent its articulation helps contextualize the circularity of debates on race and racism and the strongly disputed conceptual and practical status of the former and definition of the latter. And his central contention, that there is a 'special problem of explanation' but not of description in the social (as opposed to the natural) sciences, suggests that even when one identifies the correct description of a given social phenomenon the definitive scientific explanation of its causality is elusive.

If this appears as a naive paean to value-neutrality that tacitly and dangerously justifies regarding racism as a possible objective social fact external to partial judgement and moral assessment, Runciman's reminder of the entanglement of reportage, description, explanation, and evaluation—and the inescapable character of the last—should provide some solace. The unavoidable moral assessment of contentious social issues dictates that their analyst cannot necessarily be expected to suspend their affective response let alone prevent it from permeating their research. Although this is far from ideal for Runciman, it is acceptable if presuppositions are moderated through the process of 'theory-neutrality' (1983: 301–2). Given the fractious and impassioned tenor of debates on the status of race, Runciman's hope that such a process might be able to filter out the evaluative suppositions leaving behind unadulterated explanatory and/or descriptive content is perhaps wishful thinking. However, if one accepts, as Runciman does, the existing contingent relationship between moral and scientific values, the moral and political qualities of arguments against race cannot be erased. Therefore, instead of the decisive closure sought in the customary recourse to fact or truth, such attempts at an accurate description of the biological race concept ought to be supplemented by a transparent declaration of the attendant subjective investments that inform political prescription and moral disapprobation. In turn, this might better clarify the real political stakes and theoretical issues at hand in the all too often adversarial and opaque debates on race and racism that are further distorted within zones of ambiguity.

Biological Racialization contra Racial Formation

The objective impasse sketched above whereby race is both non-existent/existent and should not/should be used as category and concept is amplified by the subjective stakes generated by its associated affective dimension. For example, the implications of a perceived paradigmatic shift from materialist race-relations/civil rights concerns to a symbolic multicultural politics of representation—as well as the analytical and political purposes of characterizing such a 'break' given its inaccuracy—perhaps reflect larger social pressures. In the British context, for example, it might be a 'transruptive' sign of the dissonance encountered by the nation as it confronts (or circumvents) the messy task of managing the end of Empire, (ex)colonial immigration, and flows of migrant labour whilst forgetting its imperial past (Hesse 2000). Alternately, in the United States this shift is perhaps indicated in the taut project of including 'people of colour' within the historically all-white multiculturalist ideal (Glazer 1997). However, in terms of the perception of and objection to different conceptualizations of race, this shift towards a more (openly) affective cultural/identity politics also points to a fundamental conceptual contradiction. How is it that the moral disapprobation of free and frank discussion of race, real or imagined, is felt by those who both support *and* oppose its biological existence and accept *or* problematize its continued usage? Put differently, how do adherents to such divergent conceptual and political positions share an affective and discursive framework and what are the implications of this?

Subjective and affective responses to racial ideas notably inform a moral politics that is difficult to distinguish either as moral or political: politically, this problem is amplified by the difficulty of situating this moral politics coherently on an orthodox left/right, progressive/regressive spectrum. Again, this recalls Taguieff's argument that the fixed polarities of progressive/regressive and anti-racist/racist become asymmetrical as all sides claim affiliation to the more desirable progressive/anti-racist platform. But, it is important not to assume that the surreptitious importation of moral content within an ever more pliable political discursive field is the sole prerogative of reactionary conservatives and disenchanted leftists and liberals. Meaningful evaluative suppositions and moral assessments are also implicit within many positions that disavow the biological in favour of social and historical forms of racial description and explanation or reject race altogether in any form.

If race is non-existent in any real biological sense then, for many commentators, it follows that racist ideas and practices must be prefaced by a productive process in which the imaginary racial category is made real. Initially, this multifaceted project nominally includes specific processes of racialization where those objectified subjects (usually subaltern non-Europeans) who are not naturally racial are *made racial*, for example, through the application of bourgeois ideological principles (Césaire 1972; Miles 1982). The further significance of this biological constitutive process is its allusion to the *sinister and irredeemable moral taint* of racialization. This is suggestive of a contrast with the allied—yet altogether different—concept and process of racial formation that is irreducible to biological resources (cf. Gilroy 1991; Omi and Winant 1994). While racial formation is often understood in either a progressive or a regressive manner, that is to say the emergent racial group may reflect disparate historical backgrounds and political objectives, racialization customarily foregrounds the *external ascription* of given characteristics for the purposes of domination and subjugation (Miles 1989): the inferior racialized colonial subject is *made racial* by the colonizer and the authority emanating from the superiority of the latter (Fanon 1963). Racialization, therefore, primarily reflects a deterministic process that is externally enforced and lacks the voluntaristic and subversive Gramscian possibilities found within racial formation that may be organized in response to and against the dominant mode of racialization and racist power.

In addition, given the fallaciousness of the race idea, racialization reinforces the originary biological processes of constituting racial groups as real and establishing an iniquitous racial hierarchy. And although it has been suggested that the concept of racialization has sometimes been interchangeable with that of racial formation (Barot and Bird 2001), its biological variant carries an irreversible pejorative association that is important for the argument here in two key senses. First, in reflecting a set of originary processes, biological racialization re-establishes the naturalized racial reality that subsequent more explicitly social and political projects of racial formation encounter as a fait accompli. However, in contrast, racial formation projects face the choice of either reproducing or subverting the racial hierarchy laid down by processes of biological racialization. As such, biological racialization is the original racial sin that the actions of racial formation attempt to either redeem or compound. Second, while its dominant association with racist political projects marks biological racialization as irretrievably pernicious, racial formation (as separate from this historico-material basis) is able to exploit the conceptual slippage of race for the advancement of progressive as well as regressive political projects. And, more importantly, it is not simply that biological racialization is an intractable racist signifier, but that in distinguishing between regressive and progressive modes of racial formation according to respective racist or anti-racist motivation, there is a tendency to depict processes of racialization as inextricably linked to racist purposes and effects. Therefore, as the externally ascribed process by which people are involuntarily naturalized as biological beings that are brought into the social yet unreceptive to it in any formative sense, racialization is seldom referred to as a contextually specific and politically mobile concept. Instead, it is largely understood in a pejorative sense as a normative term that describes a pernicious social process.

This is not to mount a defence of biological racialization as the naturalization of racial groups. Rather, it is a means initially to highlight the problem facing analyses of the contemporary processes of racial formation that are often presented as signifying progressive political projects intimately tied to the promotion of social justice. As we will see below, some notable political examples of racial formation that are often presented as containing a corrective reaction to divisive racial ideals driven by restorative principles and oriented towards a more equitable redistribution of social resources and opportunities are linked to biological racialization. And in this political climate reinforced by the moral authority of cultural claims *à la* Taguieff, the orthodox analytical opposition between progressive forms of socially driven racial formation as based on corrective and restorative impulses and more regressive varieties of biologically based racialization reflective of racial subjugation and stratification agendas is woefully inadequate. For the want of better terms— although the inadequacies of the existing critical vocabulary in itself speaks volumes—the *true* 'true anti-racist' or committed cosmopolitan faces a difficult problematic. Even if never fully eradicated, the hitherto problematical biological processes of racialization are not only enjoying a renaissance, but are also being recuperated through elective voluntarism as well as external ascription. And considering the willing complicity of some racialized groups with their biological racialization alongside the expansion and appropriation of the normative progressive political ground, the development of a political and moral critique of racialization is increasingly complicated.

'Progressive' Biological Racialization 1—Racial Reportage and Description

To approach the problematic of biological racialization from Runciman's first stage of *reportage* is in itself revealing in that it is tempting to frame the project of naturalizing racial characteristics as a historical misnomer reflecting the mistakes of vacuous impressionism, weak inductive logic, and the malevolence of Nazi racial hygiene. However, despite much scientific evidence, political claims, and moral hopes to the contrary, the biological notion of race still enjoys robust health in certain quarters at the beginning of the twenty-first century. And although one might wish to dismiss the stubborn endurance of biological race as the domain of intuitive racism and ignorant curiosity, present-day biological formulations of race include 'acceptable' formal scientific hypotheses as well as commonsensical racial myths.

Again following Runciman, whether we agree with the biological race concept or not, its continued formal and informal salience confirms that competing racial understandings exist irregardless of whether they are valid truths or subjective speculations. For many ('professional' and 'popular') natural scientists, particular groups can be identified through their objective genetic distinctiveness but without the subjective intellectual and moral qualities spuriously imputed to races. Therefore, it is important to map this development without moralistic recrimination to understand how and why biological racial descriptions and explanations are (re)produced within a social sphere more sensitive to crude morphological racialization. It also emphasizes the complexities of advancing political evaluations within zones of ambiguity where biological racialization re-emerges through a novel rhetoric of 'special populations'.[2]

Leaving aside the explanatory question of 'why' an interest in the biological concept of race remains, the descriptive ('what like') character of contemporary genetic forms of racialization is significant in itself. The broad absence of a race concept and accompanying matrix of hierarchical ranking and moral judgement is a notable descriptive aspect of contemporary scientific processes of biological racialization where those interested in 'populations' often disavow any reference to race in favour of a declared interest in 'human biodiversity'. As such, a declaration of interest in 'population groupings'—that are *colloquially* (mis)understood as 'races'—for the strict purpose of gaining insights into human evolution, physical and physiological composition, and health and illness is neither uncommon nor unwarranted (Cook-Deegan 1994). The meticulous practised disinterestedness of proponents of this conceptualization of populations—and its dissimilarity from racial categorization—is supposedly transparent in that particular special populations can be identified and described only insofar as they share genetic markers that are primarily investigated as the basis for particular genetic disorders. Therefore, for example, 'Caucasians'/'Northern Europeans' might be identified as an ethnic group through their higher incidence of cystic fibrosis and similarly 'Chinese' and 'Southeast Asians' through alpha-thalassaemia (Burhansstipanov et al. 1987, cited in Duster 2003: 7).[3]

In the early 1990s, a key statement emerged on the distinctiveness of population groups identifiable through genetic characteristics that declared a politically progressive and sensitive approach to moral issues (Cavalli-Sforza et al. 1991). This proclamation has been regarded as a blueprint for the Human Genome Diversity Project (HGDP) that was touted as correcting the methodological limitations of the Human Genome Project (HGP) and its restricted donor sample that could only represent a fragment of human genetic history (Olson 2002). Conversely, the HGDP would build a comparative sequence from people throughout diverse regions of the world, which was all the more urgent considering the potential loss of much of the world's human biodiversity (Bowcock and Cavalli-Sforza 1991). Furthermore, the HGDP emphasized the urgent necessity of gathering blood samples from individual members of 'special interest' populations to form a permanent bank of DNA for anthropological and biomedical projects. This would enable a more accurate and expansive study of human history and, perhaps more importantly, provide a valuable biomedical resource for research into the relationship between genetics and disease.

This 'new' biological description of 'special/target populations' and human biodiversity notably constructs unique populations that are supposedly distinct from and yet run parallel to existing racial and ethnic groups. Therefore, even as the complex formation of populations supposedly renders the formal scientific category of races extinct, the informal possibility of a racial ideal is resuscitated through the rhetoric of 'populations of considerable interest' (Bowcock and Cavalli-Sforza 1991). This begs a key question: what is *really* of considerable interest, 'human biodiversity' *or* the population group, and why? This is not a semantic distinction given Naomi Zack's acute observation that 'the concept of a population could not take the place of the concept of a race *without presupposing and borrowing from the scientifically ungrounded racialist taxonomy that the population concept is supposed to replace*' (2002: 69, emphasis added). Even though Zack ostensibly makes this point in order to indicate the conceptual void between population and race, her reservation on the basis of a logical contingency is indeed prescient in that not all references to population are faithful to its conceptual ideal-type.

Joseph L. Graves (2002) recognizes this deviation within the popular misconception of a genetic predisposition towards particular diseases amongst racial groups as emerging directly from the definitional imprecision of special populations. Theoretically, the population group ought only to be of interest insofar as it demonstrates a given genetic marker. However, accepting that the concept of population is most cogent when the grouping in question has been demonstrably isolated for a relatively extensive period of time, in terms of hereditary traits population groups are best thought of as a *sum of individuals*. This supports Graves's point that the presentation of a correlation between a (racial) group and increased health risks, as practised, for example, by pharmaceutical companies in the labelling of their products, is fundamentally erroneous. Using an example warning of a higher risk of osteoporosis for particular groups in relation to the benefits of calcium supplements, Graves argues that the advice offered on diet and exercise should not have targeted particular constituencies as all groups have some risk of osteoporosis and the recommendations would have been useful for everyone (2002: 173–4).[4] For Graves 'all groups are minorities at the level of genetic variation' (p. 171) and attaching the prefixes 'special' and 'target' to populations can have the dangerous effect of reifying a human group composed of individuals as a biologically unified race.

'Progressive' Biological Racialization 2—Social and Political Explanation

If we turn to the 'special problem' of explanation it is possible to understand why the benign conceptualization of populations becomes problematical when prefaced by qualitative terms such as special or target. Despite using the now familiar ethical and humanistic refrain that an understanding of human species similarity is codependent on an appreciation of its differences, the HGDP was still subject to considerable criticism and objections on two key premises. First, various aboriginal groups argued that the HGDP would result in the theft of genetic material and cultural deracination and could inform genocidal impulses. Second, some activists and academics felt that the core notion of 'pristine' population groups of 'special interest' would trivialize the complexity of human genetic development and implicitly justify racist characterizations of 'primitive' aboriginal groupings (Harry and Marks 1999). Therefore, reflecting Runciman's contention that the social sciences face a special problem of explanation—that in this context is exacerbated by the political sophistry endemic to zones of ambiguity—it is unsurprising that those sensitized to the malicious spectre of biological racialization understand the social and political implications of special populations as problematizing the firm methodological separation between its descriptive form and explanatory function.

There is a simple, yet intricate, question here: if 'races' do not exist biologically but populations do then how can we *explain* the persistent conceptual slippage between the two categories and stubborn durability of the former? This invites comparison with two customary critical philosophical observations on science: first, that there is no necessary equivalence between conceptual and practical intent; and second, that scientific ideas and practices cannot be separated from the social context they emerge within. Therefore, it is worth considering the relationship of human biodiversity research to biological racialization in two related senses: first, the appropriation and/or distortion of biogenetic concepts—such as population—within a scientific process of racialization that disavows racial categories. And second, the political relationship between given populations or racialized 'communities' and 'the social' in its widest sense. At best there is a disjuncture between the ideal (the vaunted altruistic principles and aims of scientific inquiry) and the real (the manipulation of scientific procedure in accordance with socially embedded racial ideologies) that requires examination.

There is a foundational categorical discrepancy that makes the ongoing descriptive project of biological racialization through the population category controversial. It is not just that populations ought to be correctly considered as a sum of individuals, but that the very concept has been misappropriated to classify certain inherited genetic disorders as specific to given racial/ethnic/population groups. Even though for many analysts the 'evidence' for these tenuous associations is imperceptible if not non-existent, it does not prevent the popularization of inaccurate typologies; for example, the popular (mis)perception of sickle-cell as a 'black people's disease' (Duster 2003). This well-known 'fact' is disputed by the fact that 'sickle hemoglobin is found in a small Greek population at about double the rate amongst American blacks and . . . is not uncommon among Arabs, Sicilians, and other groups in the Mediterranean region' (Duster 2003: 47). Similarly, for Graves, the most significant association to be made with sickle-cell is neither race nor population but the presence of malaria which enhances its frequency; therefore, the vital causal link for sickle-cell is between environmental determination and genotypical fitness instead of popular perceptions of racial or population predisposition.

The conflict between the posited neutral health benefits heralded by genetic screening and hegemonic social and racial concerns cautions against accepting the notion of population-specific disorders as a simple classificatory error made in good faith with minimal or negligible injurious consequences. Troy Duster (2003) points to the significant disparities in the historical implementation of genetic screening policies of Jews for Tay-Sachs and blacks for sickle-cell anaemia in the United States despite sharing a common appeal to medical benefits. Duster's suggestion that the attention to securing the consent of the Jewish community for voluntary Tay-Sachs screening and the ongoing diligent processes of consultation and involvement in the development of screening practices was not replicated in the programmes for sickle-cell screening. As such, the more didactic public policies of sickle-cell screening were frequently compulsory and less concerned with securing the consent of the black community, informing it of the medical rationale, and dialogically developing a model of best practice. This dissimilarity in policy and procedure is, for Duster, indicative of the extent to which medical concerns and practices reflect the socio-economic stratification of racial and ethnic groups that is further manifest in a variety of ways including stigmatization and negative effects on job security and insurance coverage.

The biopolitical regulation of racial groups through the genetic screening of 'target populations' is an obvious example of biological racialization where the discursive processes have evolved yet the exclusionary principle remains. However, in addition to Taguieff's concern that differentialist racialization is expressed through anti-racist discourse, the conceptualization of biological 'population' groups is increasingly powerful in its capacity to produce *voluntaristic* modes of *self-racialization*. This profoundly disturbs the pejorative notion of racialization as a process where groups are naturalized and made racial through the external ascription of given characteristics. When framed in an ostensibly objective and value-free manner and placed alongside medical concerns, the edifice of biological groupness is not simply a descriptive marker but, as has always been the case with race, an important political resource. This importantly allows for a possible dual approach to racialization based on a pragmatic assessment of the propitious or harmful outcomes.

Historically, the figure of the heterozygote has sometimes been demonized as an infectious danger to the wider community.[5] In the case of the racialized heterozygote holding the recessive gene for a disease that is misunderstood as 'racial', the possible ensuing demonization may be attached to the entire group as individual uniqueness is a prime casualty of the totalizing logic of racialization. For example, Keith Wailoo (2003) recounts that the labelling of black sickle-cell heterozygotes as 'sick' that subjected them to stigmatization was also sometimes applied to successful heterozygote black athletes. However, Wailoo also points to alternative narratives that construct 'sicklers' (sickle-cell anaemia heterozygotes) as heroic figures that can serve as a source of pride. This attempt to subvert the stigma attached to sickle-cell demonstrates the perceived benefits of self-racialization as informing 'complex narratives of identity, achievement, and status' (Wailoo 2003: 247). In addition to these self-racializing narratives that operate as a form of cultural politics, Olson (2002) points out that various indigenous groups objected to the HGDP because of fears over possible abuses but not in principle as their involvement in biogenetic research trials would be acceptable under the correct conditions.[6] Drawing on the example of Native Americans and diabetes, Olson discusses a research study undertaken with the Oklahoma Apaches. This project is presented as an example of best practice through its cornerstones of 'informed consent' and 'community review'; the latter is especially important in instituting a dialogue for the initial design and future direction of the study. With these safeguards firmly enshrined within the project and given the debilitating problem that diabetes presents for many tribal members, participation in the research is presented as self-empowering for the tribe.

These examples of self-racialization return us to the notion of individuals as the composite of a population and genetic marker(s) as the primary unit of analysis instead of the group.[7] They also beg the question of whether biological racialization is acceptable and/or desirable when the political possibilities and social benefits are restructured in the favour of a given group. However, the subversive reversal of demonic characterizations of heterozygotes and racialized groups through narratives of historical strength is nevertheless an act of negation in response to unfounded racial panics; as such, they are a rhetorical strategy based on politically expedient grounds. Furthermore, the mobilization of the heterozygote as a source and symbol of racial pride dangerously legitimates the idea of racially naturalized traits as a conceptual resource, ontological epiphenomenon, and biological fact. Indeed, as Taguieff notes, abstract formulations of a politically inclusive and democratic cultural ontology, once inserted into concrete political situations, are neither necessarily authentic nor progressive despite their claims to the contrary. And, such democratic claims are also difficult to corroborate given the blurring of the customary political polarities of external determinism/internal voluntarism and regressive/progressive axes that group identity formation is generally understood to take place within. Therefore, given the elective and voluntaristic element outlined in the self-racialized adoption of the heroic narrative of the heterozygote as well as the objectivist and value-free humanitarian justifications underpinning research into special populations, the development of critical social and political explanations and evaluations of biological racialization is increasingly difficult.

Conclusion: Evaluating Racialization

The benevolence of an anthropomorphic science is a powerful yet flawed ideal. For Solomon Benatar (1999) modern advances in biotechnology such as the mass production of pharmaceuticals have not and will not benefit the African continent because of racist attitudes understanding African lives as less worthy of expensive intervention and the prohibitive cost to the biotechnological industry. However, if this testifies to the malevolence of science it also alludes to its promise. Accepting the direct link between rates of disease patterns, infant mortality and life expectancy, and levels of nutrition and wealth worldwide chronicled by Benatar, the idealized capacity of biomedical understandings of population groups to transcend ethnocentric and parochial national interest and affect global health change provides a compelling moral argument for its continuance.

In this chapter, I have suggested that the objectivist project to conceptualize race biologically cannot escape the miasma of analytical imprecision and ambiguity, affective imperatives and moral dogmas, and straightforward *realpolitik* that surrounds it. But, most importantly, these problems do not prevent attempts—both implicit and explicit—to use or invoke the biological race concept; instead, they provide an insight into the possibility of its progressive renovation. This recuperative racial project thrives within zones of ambiguity and is strengthened further by the inconclusive appeal to biological 'facts' suggesting its existence and the powerful validating force provided by the ubiquitous moral politics.

This leads me to restate the point I began with: namely that the unattainable quest for a universally acceptable biological truth adds fuel to the ongoing racial controversy. The factual basis of the non-existence of race is a starting point for a critique of biological racialization but insufficient as a singular strategy. The assertion that race is an unscientific concept and as such analytically untenable (Miles 1994) depends on a positivistic ideal of scientific validity that, in some contexts, is effectively disabled when confronted by alternative scientific facts falsifying that evidence and refuting anti-race arguments. Of course, this neither dismisses the simple proposition that one fact is correct and the other false nor negates the non-existence of race as a biological fact. Indeed, given the social authority of science it is crucial not to leave the scientific field uncontested and important to restate scientific evidence on the biological race concept as untenable as well as illuminating its conceptual imprecision. My wider concern, however, is to resist capitulation to a reductive scientific formalism where the veracity of facts are deemed self-evident and attendant moral issues can be simply resolved within a formal series of institutional checks and balances (Resnick 1999).

An excessive dependence on scientific logic not only invites a moral vacuum but also demonstrates how the project of racial/ethnic/population description inevitably slides into that of social and political explanation. The ideal of transparently describing racial difference has been shadowed by the explanatory corollary of whether its existence is utterly mundane or carries some larger—for example, moral, intellectual, and behavioural—significance. The inescapable interrelation of racial description and explanation as value-laden and socially meaningful further suggests that the posited non-existence/existence of race argued along (crudely speaking) constructivist/realist lines also demonstrates evaluative judgements. Indeed, the crux of Taguieff's argument is that, despite protestations to the contrary, the description of difference is never the benign recognition of something that 'just is'. Rather, such differences are (tacitly) evaluated, ranked, and ultimately interpreted as incommensurate and insurmountable which validates an exclusionary principle without reference to racial superiority or inferiority.

This suggests the critical usefulness of focusing on the rationale for the formulation of biological concepts and categories that serve a tacit racializing purpose; for example, questioning what generates the interest in populations of special interest if the unitary population is in itself an imprecise concept? Furthermore, if population differs from race and yet mirrors it, or biological racial differences exist in a pure descriptive sense but are supposedly devoid of significant evaluative content, then what exactly is meaningful about populations? In other words, if race has no meaningful scientific and substantive basis then why does this eternal fascination with biological racial difference persist?

This question is perhaps central to the circular debates on race and racism, which for all their scientific, analytical, and conceptual framing are profoundly political and affective. Many dominant perspectives such as the race relations orthodoxy and its critics in Britain have shared a commitment to eschewing the affective dimension of race and its effects on racial conceptualization in favour of a more positivistic approach. However, the thinly veiled impatience they share with less formalistic theorists and theorizations of race and racism emerge from their commitment to making clear, formal distinctions between racial description and explanation (Banton 1986; Miles 1994). If, as it seems to me, their (differing) distinctions contain certain evaluative judgements—for example, a diligent explication of misinterpretations of existing/non-existent racial groups as categorical and analytical *errors* driven by misplaced subjective investments—then it is as important to assess the qualitative basis for these assessments as it is their conceptual and analytical differences. Even though this hermeneutic task might be dismissed as speculative, Runciman's (1983) acceptance of presuppositions is useful here in suggesting the role of moral assessment within the *evaluation* of analytical description and explanation. Even if his commitment to theory-neutrality is untenable, it importantly lays the foundation for dispensing with veiled value judgements and making moral objections transparent. However, more significantly, it raises an important analytical protocol: the initial *separation* of racial description and explanation for the purposes of cataloguing—that is, the identification of different modalities of biological racialization as existing even if logically invalid—and their subsequent *reconnection* for purposes of racial evaluation and political assessment.

The local limitations of strict formalistic scientific approaches do not signal the futility of engaging race and racism; indeed, a refocusing of Anthony Appiah's (1990) notion of 'racialism' as a 'cognitive error' that misunderstands existing racial groups as having shared traits and tendencies is useful for developing a meaningful critique of biological racialization. While Appiah concentrates on understanding racist ideas and practices as emerging from separate moral assertions that perceive racial essences as having either *contingent* 'relevant qualities' or *intrinsic* 'significant qualities' that respectively give rise to 'extrinsic' and 'intrinsic' racisms varying in intent and intensity, one might view constitutive processes of biological racialization in a similar way. As a categorical and conceptual error, biological racialization is nevertheless formulated in different ways and on diverse predicates. A foundational appreciation of *intrinsically significant qualities* exhibits a foundational fascination with and belief in the profundity of phenotypical appearances and racial essences that can lead to the problematical residual existence of antiquated taxonomies within the supposedly transformative conceptualization of populations. Conversely, one might recognize alternate modes of biological racialization as indicative of *contingently relevant qualities* that emerge as a politicized response to dominant modes of intrinsic racialization. This amended formulation of racialism can explicate the different moral bases that inform the similar yet distinct scientific typological errors of biological racialization. Therefore, instead of distinguishing between the entrenched and flexible ideals of intrinsic and extrinsic racisms, one might alternately examine and interrogate the different political motivations for biological racialization on a case-by-case basis. Importantly, this would allow for a more dialogic approach towards forms of biological self-racialization based on an illumination of the dilemmatic usage of pragmatic and rhetorical strategies instead of a counterproductive patronizing and didactic position that may alienate potential allies.

Ultimately, this argument problematizes the normative pejorative associations of biological racialization and emphasizes the varieties ranging from external ascription to elective voluntarism as well as the synergy between the two. It is also prefaced by the need for a moratorium on the habitually antagonistic moral politics within studies of race and racism—but note this is not the suspension of moral preoccupation per se. Although the axiom advanced within some human biodiversity debates that an appreciation of difference is a prerequisite for understanding species similarity is largely an unreflexive ruse, it remains qualitatively pertinent. For those charged with identifying pernicious forms of racialization, biological and otherwise, a penetrative appreciation of the function of intrinsic right or extrinsic relevance as a qualitative basis of appeals to difference is crucial. This builds the capacity to question constructively the political and moral efficacy of assertions of biological group identification on the basis of contingently relevant qualities and reflect on the broader consequences and implications of pragmatic strategies of voluntaristic racialization. In such an undertaking, the *true* 'true anti-racists' and committed cosmopolitans might halt a potential descent into an introspective mode of auto-critique and advance the necessary dialogue to determine who else might be seated at the table of anti-racism.

NOTES

1. Primo Levi (1988: 41) uses the term zone of ambiguity to express the moral dilemmas faced by prisoners within the Lagers that he characterizes more broadly as the 'grey zone'.
2. This is not to suggest race and population group as interchangeable categories; biologically speaking, the former is based on a notion of hypo-descent while the latter is more broadly characterized as a multigenerational, interbreeding group (Zack 2002: 68).
3. Of course this remains problematical in a number of ways. First, it has been suggested that despite its stated focus on non-racial populations of special interest, the HGDP maintains archaic racial taxonomic categories in its reference to 'Caucasoids' and 'Mongoloids' (Harry and Marks 1999). Second, reference to some groups such as 'Chinese' refers to a mobile ethnonational category that is significantly dependent on sociolegal components such as citizenship. Third, the identification of broad groups such as 'Southeast Asians' attempts to naturalize a syncretic panethnic category that is cohered through strategic political alignments instead of biological cogency (cf. Espiritu 1992).
4. The case in point is a SmithKline Beecham product for indigestion relief that specifies 'certain ethnic, age, and other groups ... [as] at higher risk for developing osteoporosis, including Caucasian and Asian teen and young adult women, menopausal women, older persons, and those with a family history of fragile bones' (Graves 2002: 173).
5. The heterozygote is a person who carries the autosomal recessive gene for a particular disorder. In itself it is harmless to them but if they have a child with someone with the same autosomal recessive gene the resulting offspring has a 25 per cent chance of being affected by the disorder; alternately they may test positive for the trait (Duster 2003: 43–4). Wailoo (2003: 236) draws attention to this as informing ominous characterizations of the heterozygote as a 'carrier'.
6. The initial objections of indigenous groups to the HGDP included fears about negligible benefits for the group being tested; distortion of research findings resulting in possible public stigmatization; suspicions of 'biocolonialist' agendas within biomedical research; the incompatibility of logical empiricist research

principles and the alternative cultural and cosmological standpoints of groups being sampled; and a distrust of biomedical researchers' assertions of the minor commercial value of information about genetic variation given the patenting of cell lines and genes (Olson 2002: 212–14).

7. This point is all the more crucial given the multifactorial aspect of many disorders that emerge through a combination of genetic and environmental factors that interact in often unknown ways that are grossly misrepresented when presented simply as 'genetic disorders'. For example, the correlation sometimes made between specific populations and diabetes, heart disease, and cancer present genetic disorders that ignore contributory environmental factors such as poverty and diet.

REFERENCES

Appiah, K. A. (1986) 'The Unfinished Argument: Du Bois and the Illusion of Race', in H. L. Gates Jr (ed.), *'Race', Writing and Difference*. Chicago: University of Chicago Press.

——(1990) 'Racisms', in D. T. Goldberg (ed.), *Anatomy of Racism*. Minneapolis: University of Minnesota Press.

Banton, M. (1986) 'Epistemological assumptions in the study of racial differentiation', in J. Rex and D. Mason (eds.), *Theories of Race and Ethnic Relations*. Cambridge: Cambridge University Press.

Barot, R., and Bird, J. (2001) 'Racialization: The Genealogy and Critique of a Concept'. *Ethnic and Racial Studies*, 24, (4): 601–18.

Benatar, S. R. (1999) 'A Perspective from Africa on Human Rights and Genetic Engineering', in Justine Burley (ed.), *The Genetic Revolution and Human Rights: The Oxford Amnesty Lectures 1998*. Oxford: Oxford University Press.

Bowcock, A., and Cavalli-Sforza, L. L. (1991) 'The Study of Variation in the Human Genome'. *Genomics*, 11: 491–8.

Brown, M. K., Carnoy, M., Currie, E., Duster, T., and Oppenheimer, D. B. (2003) *Whitewashing Race: The Myth of a Color-Blind Society*. Berkeley: University of California Press.

Burhansstipanov, L., Giarratano, S., Koser, K., and Mongoven, J. (1987) *Prevention of Genetic and Birth Disorders*. Sacramento: California State Department of Education.

Cavalli-Sforza, L. L., Wilson, A. C., Cantor, C. R., Cook-Deegan, R. M. and King, M.-C. (1991) 'Call for a Worldwide Survey of Human Genetic Diversity: A Vanishing Opportunity for the Human Genome Project'. *Genomics* 11: 490–1.

Césaire, A. (1972) *Discourse on Colonialism* (J. Pinkham trans). New York: Monthly Review Press.

Cook-Deegan, R. (1994) *The Gene Wars: Science, Politics, and the Human Genome*. New York: W W Norton and Company.

Duster, T. (2003) *Backdoor to Eugenics*, 2nd edn. New York: Routledge.

Espiritu, Y. L. (1992) *Asian American Panethnicity: Bridging Institutions and Identities*. Philadelphia: Temple University Press.

Eze, C. E. (2001) *Achieving Our Humanity: The Idea of the Postracial Future*. London: Routledge.

Fanon, F. (1963) *The Wretched of the Earth*, C. Farrington trans. New York: Grove Press.

Gilroy, P. (1991) *'There Ain't No Black in the Union Jack': The Cultural Politics of Race and Nation*. Chicago: University of Chicago Press.

Glazer, N. (1997) *We Are All Multiculturalists, Now*. Cambridge, MA: Harvard University Press.

Graves, J. L. (2002) *The Emperor's New Clothes: Biological Theories of Race at the Millennium*. New Brunswick, NJ: Rutgers University Press.

Harry, D., and Marks, J. (1999) 'Human Population Genetics versus the HGDP'. *Politics and the Life Sciences*, 18 (2): 303–5.

Hesse, B. (2000) 'Introduction: Un/Settled Multiculturalisms', in B. Hesse (ed.), *Un/Settled Multiculturalisms: Diasporas, Entanglements, Transruptions*. London: Zed.

Levi, P. (1988) *The Drowned and the Saved*, R. Rosenthal trans. London: Abacus.

Miles, R. (1982) *Racism and Migrant Labour*, London: Routledge and Kegan Paul.

——(1989) *Racism*, London: Routledge.

——(1994) *Racism after 'Race Relations'*, London: Routledge.

Montagu, A. (1997) *Man's Most Dangerous Myth: The Fallacy of Race*, 6th edn. Walnut Creek, CA: AltaMira Press.

Olson, S. (2002) *Mapping Human History: Discovering the Past Through Our Genes*. London: Bloomsbury

Omi, M., and Winant, H. (1994) *Racial Formation in the United States: From the 1960s to the 1990s*, 2nd edn. London: Routledge.

Resnick, D. B. (1999) 'The Human Genome Diversity Project: Ethical Problems and Solutions'. *Politics and the Life Sciences*, 18 (1): 15–23.

Runciman, W. G. (1983) *A Treatise on Social Theory: Vol 1, The Methodology of Social Theory*. Cambridge: Cambridge University Press.

Sarich, V., and Miele, F. (2004) *Race: The Reality of Human Differences*. Boulder, CO: Westview Press.

Sartre, J.-P. (1976) *Black Orpheus*, S. W. Allen trans. Paris: Présence Africaine.

St Louis, B. (2004) 'Sport and Common-Sense Racial Science'. *Leisure Studies*, 23 (1): 31–46.

Taguieff, P.-A. (1990) 'The New Cultural Racism in France'. *Telos*, 83: 109–22.

Wailoo, K. (2003) 'Inventing the Heterozygote: Molecular Biology, Racial Identity, and the Narratives of Sickle Cell Disease, Tay-Sachs, and Cystic Fibrosis', in D. S. Moore, J. Kosek, and A. Pandian (eds.), *Race, Nature, and the Politics of Difference*. Durham, NC: Duke University Press.

Watts, E. S. (1997) 'The Biological Race Concept and Diseases of Modern Man', in E. N. Gates (ed.), *The Concept of 'Race' in Natural and Social Science*. New York: Garland.

Zack, N. (2002) *Philosophy of Science and Race*. London: Routledge.

CHAPTER 2

Historical and Contemporary Modes of Racialization

Michael Banton

In the nineteenth century, it was generally believed that either God
or nature had created races. In the twentieth century, social scientists
constructed a more complex account according to which humans
have always been engaged in processes of group formation, maintenance, and dissolution. Some large-scale groups, like nations inhabit-
ing territory with natural boundaries, display a high degree of
continuity. Smaller groups, like families, can be short-lived. Races
come in between. When intellectuals declared that certain categories
of persons constituted races (whether consciously or unconsciously),
they racialized these groups or categories. When the designations
race and *racial* were applied to them, this assisted processes of race-
making. Racialization was a process in the realm of concepts; race-
making and race-unmaking were processes in the realm of politics.
The historical mode of racialization was an attempt to account for
the unequal development of large human groups. The contemporary
mode of racialization is a way of claiming that the relative privilege
and disprivilege of such groups derives in part from earlier
misrepresentations of their biological distinctiveness.

Before I summarize the main features of the historical mode as I
have analysed it in earlier publications, the reader may like a personal
explanation. I started research into black–white relations in London's
East End in 1950 and have continued ever since to study what were
once called 'race relations'. This experience has bred in me a profound conviction that there was a momentous mistake when, in the
nineteenth century, what may be called 'the language of race' spread
in the English tongue. I refer to the use of the word 'race' to identify

population groups whose distinguishing characteristics are political and cultural, even if membership in them is signalled by physical features. Some uses of the word were unobjectionable, but others conveyed a seriously misleading conception of the nature of the groups and of the relations between them, and have contaminated the innocent uses. At no time has there been any consensus on a single correct use of the word. I have concluded that, in general, it is better not to use the words *race* and *racial* whenever there is an alternative; usually the alternative will be more accurate.

A common response to the difficulties created by the multiple meanings of *race* has been to maintain that there are separate concepts of biological and social race. I contend that it is better to distinguish two forms of language. One of them is the ordinary language of everyday life, which employs folk concepts and is fashioned to aid the solution of the practical problems of life in the society in question. The other is the language of science, which develops analytical concepts fashioned to help solve the problems of an international and transcultural field of study, be that zoology, genetics, or social science. Its vocabulary is constantly growing and undergoing internal revision as more knowledge is accumulated. Ordinary language sometimes learns from, and comes into accord with, scientific language, but realignment may take a long time. I conclude that while social scientists may properly try to correct ordinary language usage, this should be a lower priority than improving their answers to the questions that define their fields of study.

The Historical Mode

Use of the word *race* has a history in West European languages going back to the beginning of the sixteenth century. Originally, it was used to denote lineage, a line of descent, as in 'the race of Abraham', but often it was used very loosely. Then both French and British historians deployed it when interpreting their countries' histories as the outcome of relations between the indigenous peoples (Gauls in the case of France and Saxons in Britain) and the invading peoples (Franks and Normans, respectively). To call a group Gauls (or Saxons) was to use a collective proper name, one unique to the group so designated. This was an age in which most Europeans thought that the Bible offered a history of creation and of the peopling of the world. The Old Testament listed genealogies of groups as if this explained their distinctiveness. So, given the prevailing meaning of the word, it was not surprising that historians and others should have started to refer to Gauls and Saxons as races (Banton 1977: 16–19). Yet, because the word was acquiring new meanings, the naming of Gauls, Franks, Saxons, and Normans as *races* acquired an enhanced significance.

At the end of the eighteenth century some writers started to use *race* to denote a class of creatures with common characteristics, making it synonymous with either species or subspecies in modern classifications. Acceptance of this innovation gave the word a new dimension of meaning, to denote a class in the present, whatever its genealogy might have been. In the 1850s, just before Darwin's discovery of natural selection as the motor of evolution, some anthropologists in several Western countries advanced a theory of racial typology that represented human races as distinct species with different capacities and inherent antagonisms towards each other. Claiming that racial types were to all intents and purposes permanent, they offered a general explanation of the unequal development of the world's peoples. Some maintained that each racial type was suited to a particular province of the globe and that attempts to colonize other provinces were doomed to fail; others that races could be listed in a hierarchy of talent that was independent of environment (Banton 1998: 79).

In the United States, prior to the end of the eighteenth century, it was customary to refer to the three main groups as whites, Indians, and blacks or Negroes. Thomas Jefferson in his *Notes on Virginia* may have been the first to describe these three groups as distinct races (Jordan 1968: 489–90). This new vision of history was at first slow to catch on, primarily because the Bible was thought to declare all humans the descendants of Adam and Eve. For most white Southerners, the Bible contained a sufficient justification of slavery, while its description of creation discounted arguments from science. In opposition to the assumption that black–white differences stemmed from the less favourable character of the African environment, an intellectual minority held that blacks and whites were distinct types or species descended from different ancestors over a longer time period than was allowed for by the Bible. The theory of racial typology got a better hearing as the class of non-slave holding whites became more influential. After the civil war, the naming of groups as races gained official sanction in the 1866 Civil Rights Act with its declaration of the rights of all 'citizens of every race and color'.

The spread of typological doctrines vested the word race with a deeper meaning. To say that Gauls and Franks, or blacks and whites, were different races, was to equate their differences with those between lions, tigers, and leopards, different species within the genus *Panthera*, each with its peculiar capacities and behaviour patterns. These species maintain their distinctiveness of weight and body mass, not because the animals formulate and observe their own rules, but because nature keeps them distinctive through genetic inheritance. If the differences between Gauls and Franks, and blacks and whites, were permanent, political programmes needed to allow for them, either by compensatory measures or by acknowledging the limits to equality. For example, some deduced from such premises that in Ireland the descendants of seventeenth-century Protestant settlers from Scotland could never live in harmony with the indigenous Irish as members of one political unit.

As was apparent, when human groups came into contact they mated with one another, unlike lions, tigers, and leopards. Any distinctiveness of human groups was attributable, first, to the factors explaining variability within species, between what Darwin called 'geographical races, or subspecies'. Sub-Saharan Africans differed from north Africans because they were intrabreeding, geographically separated, groups. Second, the relevant differences between human groups were ones of their own creation. Differences of language, religion, and political organization were not caused by different genetic inheritance. When they come into contact geographical races can interbreed so that their variation is continuous. In humans this is outwardly manifest in varying shades of skin colour, but it is also characteristic of the distribution of many genes, like those determining blood types.

Darwin's conception of subspecies has been endorsed by subsequent biological science. There is no scientific objection to the use of the word race in the sense of subspecies, though if it is a synonym the word is redundant in science and its use best avoided because of the confusion it causes outside science. Any use of the words *race* and *racial* to identify categories other than subspecies constitutes racialization; it is a misrepresentation of the nature of the categories in question. Since racialization has no biological justification, it is best to restrict application of the concept to settings in which explicit use is made of racial nomenclature. This is an important restriction.

The typologists presented their notion of a racial type as an analytical concept that explained the underlying determinants of human grouping. Though it failed to do so, the usage reinforced the new meaning of the folk concept. Other writers, reasoning less rigorously, described ethnic groups as races without claiming that they resembled species. It is often impossible to be sure what late-nineteenth and early-twentieth century writers and speakers intended when they referred to race.

The typological argument could be turned on its head. Insisting that language was the best marker of racial distinctiveness, a combative historian of Anglo-Saxon England, E. A. Freeman (1877: 211, 225), contended that 'races which, in a strictly physiological point of view have no existence at all [nevertheless] have a real existence from the more practical point of view of history and politics' and that this had been shown in the rise of nationalism in the Balkans. Freeman maintained that the doctrine of race, which could work for good or for evil, was 'an inference from facts which the mass of mankind could never have found out for themselves' had they not been taught it, but, once learned, this doctrine could change the course of history. It asserted that popular allegiances to local communities were stretching outwards as people recognized linguistic and religious affinities; the sense of affinity was extending outwards from the nation 'to the whole race'. The map of Europe was being changed. The doctrine implied that everyone would have eventually to be grouped with others of the same race and governed as part of a homogenous unit.

Freeman did not use the word *race* in the sense of either species or subspecies. For him it was what sociologists belonging to a later generation would call a social construction. It was not a designation given to a group so much as one adopted by an elite within that group who used it to mobilize those whom they wanted as followers.

Other European writers, some influenced by Hegel, were writing to similar effect. They were trying to come to terms with what would now be called globalization. Thus, in 1885 the Polish sociologist Ludwig Gumplowicz interpreted the history of Europe as 'a process by which tribes became peoples, peoples nations, nations grew into races and developed themselves' as the outcome of 'the perpetual struggle between races for dominance, the soul and spirit of all history'. These writers thought that it was racial consciousness that was making races and racializing the world. They may have had their equivalents in other continents. For example, in 1903 a Chinese writer was explaining 'why races engender history' (Dikötter 2002: 501). The history of racial doctrine in the civilizations of the East has not yet been studied in much detail.

Globalization offers a context in which to appreciate the significance of the racializing and race-making processes. Humans were engaging in collective action to advance their shared interests in an expanding world. Conjecture about such matters must be unreliable, but, without any doctrine of race, blacks and whites would surely have lined-up in opposition to one another on grounds of colour, Europeans and Asians on grounds of culture, and Christians, Muslims, and others on grounds of religion. Globalization brought into contact groups at differing levels of economic development, creating what members of dominant groups perceived as a 'colour problem' or a 'race problem'. The former expression was the narrower: it could not be applied to relations between Gauls and Franks or Saxons and Normans. It singled out one variable only, one that identified categories but did not suggest what it was that made them distinctive.

The designation of groups as races encompassed all the dimensions of difference and represented that distinctiveness as an achievement of nature. The belief that physical differences generated group boundaries was a stimulus to mobilization, and to the maintenance of those boundaries. It had both functions and dysfunctions for the mobilizers. By providing a rationale for a kind of paternalism and by promoting white solidarity, it assisted relatively small groups of colonizers to dominate much larger groups of colonized people. Its prime dysfunction for the colonizers was that the colonized were bound, in reaction, eventually to develop their own forms of collective action that would be backed by superior numbers.

People who thought of themselves and others as belonging in races were said to be racially conscious. The spread of racial consciousness may have been related to the contemporary decline in the importance of inherited rank or status. Thus, in the last quarter of the nineteenth century in Britain, a time when individual social mobility was increasing, white attitudes towards blacks apparently became more negative. In the United States at the same time, opportunities were increasing for low-status people to invoke beliefs about racial difference to argue that members of other races should not be allowed to compete with them on equal terms. Democratic government is sensitive to short-term rivalries. The belief that inherited differences determined human capacities enabled democrats to close their eyes to the way that racial boundaries assigned benefits and costs to group members without taking account of their individual merits and demerits.

A high point of this first mode of racialization came in 1902 in a lecture entitled *The Relation of the Advanced and Backward Races of Mankind* by James Bryce, the brilliant professor of law who from 1907 to 1913 was a very successful British ambassador to the United States. Bryce concluded 'for the future of mankind nothing is more vital than that some races should be maintained at the highest level of efficiency... It may therefore be doubted whether any further mixture of Advanced and Backward races is to be desired'. The identification of certain kinds of group as races was thought to be a key that opened the way to an explanation of their unequal development. Some attempted racializations failed, such as the attempts on the fringes of British politics to present the Irish as a different, and inferior, race. A study of English representations of the Irish suggests that a few activists of extreme views could publish periodicals propagating such doctrines at times when English resentment of Irish nationalism was heightened (Douglas 2002: 54–8).

Nor was racial nomenclature adopted in official documents in Britain. When, in 1925, there was an addition to the 1914 Aliens Restriction Act, it was entitled the Special Restriction (Coloured Alien Seamen) Order. The idiom of colour was for many decades preferred to that of race. A study of 'the transformation in the thinking of British policy-makers on the race question' during the Second World War (Wolton 2000: x) indicates that the Colonial Office personnel who minuted the files and wrote such reports as have been archived only rarely used the word race, and then with reference to a presumed biological category rather than to a social construction. Their concern was with 'colour discrimination' and the problems that would arise if appointments were no longer restricted by a regulation that 'candidates must be of European descent'. For example, in 1938 the colonial secretary of one of the Malay states warned that 'if we at this end sent out a man who showed a trace of colour to a post normally filled by pure Europeans, i.e., a post for which no local man of colour would be recruited, there might be considerable discontent among people of the latter class...'. Officials identified groups by collective proper names rather than as races. From examination of what they wrote it is not possible to uncover their 'underlying assumptions about race'. To interpret their thought and actions in the terms of any later conception of race is to misrepresent them.

After the fall of Singapore, Britain worked hard to modify the desire of policy-makers in the United States who wanted a promise that after the war India and the colonies would become independent. Officials sought to oppose Nazi doctrine, react to the motivations that had led to colonial revolts, and devise a new political language suited to a post-war world in which Britain would need the support of the United States (Wolton 2000: 151). Imperialism was to be transformed into a partnership for promoting development and welfare, while the metropolitan power was to protect the minorities that might suffer were sovereignty too quickly transferred to representatives of the largest ethnic group. International politics changed colonial policy and placed questions of discrimination in a new framework.

Such testimony strengthens the conclusion that the language of race was not developed on the colonial frontier and then brought back to the metropolitan country. The evidence of racialization prior to 1939 is to be found in the ways that some intellectuals (of both left-wing and right-wing persuasions) wrote about groups and in the manner that some members of the public took up their ideas. *Race* featured in the law of the United States chiefly as an obstacle to the enjoyment of constitutional rights. US law engaged in a little race-making in order to combat racial discrimination.

Contemporary Race-making in the United States and Britain

In most parts of the modern world, humans do not categorize one another as belonging in races or treat one another differently on this account. In parts of Brazil, for example, people rank themselves and others according to skin colour, *branco* high up, *negro* low down, but they do not organize their social lives by reference to distinct categories. Almost half the world's population is in Asia, and the notion of race is foreign to most of its people. The belief that humans belong to races was an invention of the Anglo-Saxon Protestant West that has been spread wherever it had influence. In this sense, Westerners have made races.

The nature of the process was shown at its starkest in the United States. Using phenotypical differences, notably those of skin colour, white Americans constructed the categories black and white. There was no biological justification for counting as black rather than white someone who was of only one-eighth African ancestry. This shows that the two categories are social constructions, just as gender is socially constructed on the basis of the biological distinction of sex. *Black* and *white* are colour categories that become racial categories only when they are parts of a racial classification, though contemporary English-language usage elides the distinction between colour and race. It is not fanciful to imagine a society composed of three colour classes, black, coloured, and white; indeed, some societies in the Caribbean at one stage approached such mode of organization. *Black*,

Hispanic, and *Asian* can be collective proper names, like Nigerian or Muslim, denoting categories or groups. They too become racial names only when they are parts of a racial classification, and such a classification becomes important when it is a basis for unequal treatment. There should be no disagreement among sociologists that such ideas were used within the institutions that created the black, white, and Native American races. These institutions included not only the executive, legislative, and judicial branches of government, business interests, trade unions, the mass media, etc., but also political movements within the minorities. Just as they can all be seen as contributing to race-making, so in some measure they have contributed to race-unmaking. It is a complicated story.

It is intellectuals who produce the ideas and classifications in the first place. Often they begin by exposing errors in the prevailing ideas and by attempting to develop concepts that better represent the nature of the phenomena in question. Finding better concepts is a process of discovery. Yet, when they seek to persuade members of the wider public, intellectuals have to use a language the public understands and therefore they often employ, and thereby reauthorize, folk concepts, when they should be trying to supersede them. The notion that relations between blacks and whites were an example of *race relations* was developed in the United States in the 1930s and was taken up in Britain after 1945 when it was the more acceptable because, in the aftermath of the war, public opinion was shocked by the use the Nazis had made of racial ideology. This was an era in which anti-racist movements formed, though the expression *anti-racism* was little used before the 1970s.

In Britain, perhaps because of its imperial associations, nomenclature has been more varied than in the United States. A prime division in the 1950s was that between *white* and *coloured*, though particular groups were referred as West Indians, Jamaicans, etc. Government files from 1948 were first titled 'West Indian Migrant Workers in England', then referred to 'Coloured People' or 'Coloured Workers', before settling upon 'Colonial Immigrants' as a designation. Subsequently, members of the Caribbean and South Asian minorities were classified together as New Commonwealth Immigrants. The general public rarely used racial designations for the new groups, but there was a growing tendency, led by intellectuals, to prefer the language of race to that of colour. It is worth pausing over the comparison. It was better to describe a person by reference to his or her colour because colour is observable where race is not. To speak of colour differences is to recognize them as a form of continuous variation from individual to individual, but when designating groups or relations between groups it seemed better to follow US practice and refer to racial groups and racial relations. Oliver C. Cox (1948: 318) presented race relations as a subdivision of 'ethnic relations' and others spoke up for 'ethnic groups' as preferable to 'races', but anti-racists regarded the idiom of ethnicity as euphemistic.

The record suggests that black working-class people in Britain experienced much more discrimination before the Second World War than after it, and much more in the 1950s than in the 1960s or 1970s. At the outset, there was an assumption that the West Indian incomers were migrant workers, a source of labour that is usually complementary to the existing labour force rather than competitive with it. The West Indians were also colonials (unlike the South Asians). Many members of the white public believed that Britain benefited from having an empire and that it was the duty of the mother country to receive visits from colonials. Public opinion changed around 1958 when it became apparent both that the remaining colonies were set on the path to independence and that the colonials in Britain were more than visitors (Banton 1983*b*). Unlike the entry of persons from the Old Commonwealth, the entry of persons from the New Commonwealth was resulting in settlement. The increased white support for tighter controls on immigration over the years 1951–68 was a reaction to the end of empire and to concerns about settlement.

Everything changed towards the end of the 1960s. Whereas previously the adjective *black* had negative associations, the US Civil Rights movement redeemed it with its slogan of 'black pride'. In both the United States and Britain, the alternative adjective, 'coloured', was made to appear illegitimate. The movement accepted the whites' 'one-drop' rule because this helped it build a maximal constituency. If today there is any group whose members like to think of themselves as a race, it is African-Americans and those Afro-Caribbeans who favour the strategy that dominates the African-American political movement. African-Americans took the concept that nineteenth-century racial theorists had used to deny them equality, and, by turning it round, gave it positive connotations. They substantiated Freeman's forecast in a way he could never have anticipated. Responding to changes in power relations, Talcott Parsons argued that the polarization of black–white relations in the United States was 'more favourable to the resolution of the color problem' than the Brazilian grading of individuals by shades of pigmentation.

Accepting the folk concepts of the day, he asserted that in the USA race-making would lead to race-unmaking. The conditions under which it might do so were inadequately specified (Banton 1983*a*: 68–71).

The Civil Rights movement expanded the meaning given to the concept of racism, both in the United States and in Britain, as a basis for the impeachment of the socially privileged. Many whites, academics included, felt guilty about the way blacks had been treated. It was in this atmosphere that John Rex (1970: 12), seeking to distinguish 'the field of race relations', observed that the 'conceptual content of social relations' in some racially divided societies might 'consist of nothing more than stereotypes, proverbs, symbols, folklore and so on'. He and others maintained that 'functional substitutes' for biological doctrines could be as important as explicit theories in institutionalizing inequalities.[1] Robert Miles (1982: 121) likewise concluded that 'we must not restrict the application of the concept of racism to situations where people distinguish one another by reference to skin colour'. His claim that Irish as well as New Commonwealth immigrants had been racialized was supported by reference to the historical racialization of the Irish in nineteenth century mentioned earlier in this chapter.[2] This is straightforward, but his claim that hostility towards Irish migrant workers had been 'articulated in terms of race' as well as religion (1982: 150) is not substantiated. There was evidence that the attacks had been motivated by resentment of economic competition and that many English workers articulated their hostility in terms of anti-Catholicism, but none to indicate any distinct racial motivation. A few years later, he drew attention to 'a process of conceptual inflation' whereby more and more phenomena had been accounted racist (Miles 1989: 41), but his own writing stimulated a comparable inflation in the use of the concept of racialization.

The period following the arrival of the *Empire Windrush* in 1948 was interpreted by John Solomos (1989: 45, 50, 63) as one in which 'an increasingly racialised debate about immigration took place, focusing on the supposed problems of having too many black migrants'. Racialization was 'done through coded language', 'but "race" itself was not always mentioned as the central issue'.[3] The state and its institutions were said to have been heavily involved in defining the terms of a debate which continued apace in subsequent decades, the experience of urban riots being 'an example of the power of immigration as a political symbol even though there is no evidence of a causal relationship between the two processes'. When sociologists detect what they consider 'racial coding' they are laying claim to a better understanding of the reasons underlying the speaker's choice of words than the speaker's own. Any such reinterpretation needs to be carefully substantiated. Claims about racialization should specify what was done and by whom. The manner in which the riots were reported could well have strengthened a sense of racial division, but this is an empirical issue and the lack of evidence in its support should surely recommend greater caution in interpretation.

The main academic controversy concerning race-making in Britain has concerned the regulation of immigration, and, in particular, the reasons for the adoption of the 1962 Commonwealth Immigrants Act. William Deedes, who was a minister at that time, acknowledged that its 'real purpose was to restrict the influx of coloured immigrants'. Taking that as a datum, the controversy has centred upon the sources and motivations of the pressure for restriction. Did the white electorate oblige the government to introduce the legislation, or had the government earlier drawn a racial boundary to mark off the immigrants as people who did not belong to Britain? Were either the electors or the government motivated by a racial prejudice that defined the immigrants as people who could not form part of British society? Or was the government reforming antiquated legislation that entitled many millions of persons throughout the Commonwealth[4] to seek work in Britain irrespective of any resulting problems of employment, housing, and social services?

Such questions can be asked about the formulation of policy in other countries also, for the British debate about regulating immigration paralleled earlier discussions in the US legislature. Carter et al. (1996) reviewed the arguments over the adoption of the 1882 Act—by which the US Congress suspended Chinese immigration—and the US Immigration Act of 1924, comparing them with the exchanges that led to British legislation between 1948 and 1971. They concluded that in both countries the discussions were used to elaborate exclusivist doctrines of national identity, and that the state played an important part in the construction of images of migrants, thereby constraining their positions in the labour market and giving an enhanced significance to group differences. These are not ambitious claims. It would be surprising were not state institutions to some degree involved in the development of the relations between migrants and the majority population.

By contrast, a statement like 'immigration was essentially an issue of race' (Solomos 1989: 72) asserts a wide-ranging and complex proposition that cannot rest on a subjective judgement. It is necessary to distinguish the intentions of those who drew up the legislation from the effect of the legislation upon immigrants and upon the white public. Some have argued that the legislation was racist in intent because some of those responsible wished to maintain the racial homogeneity of the existing population. Some have held that the effect of the Act was to stigmatize New Commonwealth immigrants because, although its provisions applied to all Commonwealth citizens, its effects bore more harshly upon would-be settlers from the New Commonwealth. This leads on to the question of whether any change in white attitudes can be traced to the influence of the Act. If, and only if, it could be shown to have had a race-making effect, would there be sense in the claim that 'race is a product of racism' (Bulmer and Solomos 1998: 823).

In considering the views of the officials who advised the ministers, it is important to note the lack of agreement between different departments. Officials in the Colonial Office supported West Indian immigration and were critical of prevailing legislation because it permitted the entry of 'unskilled and largely lazy Asians'. The possibility of increased immigration from Asian countries had a significant effect in changing calculations about the numbers involved even if this received little explicit mention at the time. One Home Office official thought that no controls would have been introduced but for the possibility of increased immigration from India and Pakistan (Hansen 2000: 85). If a claim that immigration was an issue of race implies that either politicians or the public in general thought that immigration control was needed to protect the biological character of the British people, more evidence is required than the passage in the 1949 report of the Royal Commission on Population which stated that immigration could be welcomed only if the immigrants were of 'good stock'. A comprehensive examination of the archival evidence about the views of the various groups within, or consulted by, the government has concluded that academic support for the hypothesis that the Act was racially motivated has been based on a selective use of source material and a neglect of much contrary evidence (Hansen 2000).[5]

If there were race-making processes, they may have resulted less from racist attitudes within the government than from official measures to combat racial prejudices and discrimination, such as anti-discrimination laws and the collection of statistics intended for use in the promotion of greater equality. In the United States, the federal government had, by the end of the 1960s, recognized that the

processing of individual complaints of discrimination would never
be sufficient to remedy the systematic disadvantage suffered by
African-Americans. Federal action led to a programme of affirmative action that, by relying upon the ascription of individuals to
racial categories, strengthened race-making tendencies.

A further example of US race-making was the scheme of 'racial/eth-
nic categories' drawn up in 1975 to determine eligibility for benefits
under affirmative action. It encouraged a variety of immigrant groups,
such as those with origins in East Asian and South Asian countries,
and some Hispanic groups, to press for recognition as eligible
although they were of above-average income and were not disadvantaged. When ordinary members of the public look for cues about the
meaning given to the word race, they surely take leads from official
classifications such as this, from legislation, and from the census. The
US Census form of 2000 asked, first, 'Is this person Spanish/
Hispanic/Latino? Mark the 'No' box if not Spanish/ Hispanic/Latino'.
Then, second, 'What is this person's race? Mark *one or more races* to
indicate what this person considers himself/herself to be'. The first
question distinguished four Hispanic categories (Mexican, Puerto
Rican, Cuban, Others) from the non-Hispanic population; the next
question divided the latter, offering fifteen optional answers, starting
with White, Black... then Chinese, Filipino, Japanese... and ending
'Some other race—Print race'. The words italicized offered scope to
those who wished to acknowledge multiple origins. The form did not
describe the first set of categories as ethnic, nor the second set as
racial, though that is the way they are usually regarded. The scheme
as a whole was a compromise between logic and popular usage that
did not conform to the usual US tendency to see ethnic categories as
subdivisions of racial categories.

In Britain also, the enforcement of legislation against racial discrimination, particularly the 1976 Act, reinforced racial designations. It was also intended that the 1981 census in England and
Wales should invite everyone to state the country of birth of his or
her father and mother and then assign himself or herself to one of
ten 'racial or ethnic groups' identified by national names like
African/Indian/Pakistani, etc. Although it did not employ the then
contentious expressions 'white' and 'black' as names for categories,
its inclusion was nevertheless vetoed by the then prime minister. At
one stage it was announced that the 2001 Census in England and
Wales would ask persons to signify if they were 'Mixed Race', but
in the end the census included instead a question asking 'What is
your ethnic group?' and nowhere used the word *race*. References to

children as being of 'mixed race' are to be found in cases concerning adoption before the Court of Appeal from 1976. The expression is objectionable since it implies the existence of pure races.[6] Many, but not all, persons of mixed ethnic origin in Britain want a label that will express what they believe to be their identity. Many of those of partly African (or Afro-Caribbean) origin choose to identify themselves as black. Many favour 'mixed race', but others believe this unsatisfactory and either find some alternative that is suited to their circumstances or refuse to be classified in this fashion (see Alibhai-Brown 2001).

The number of children of mixed origin taken into care, placed in children's homes, or made available for adoption, was disproportionately high because many were not born into stable unions. At the end of 1970s this inspired a campaign in both the United States and Britain against what was called transracial adoption. It was an example of minority mobilization that secured the support of the social work establishment. In Britain, it appears to have been responsible for certain provisions in the Children Act 1989. Section 22(5) (c) of the Act declares that an authority in making any decision with respect to a child is to 'give due consideration to his religious persuasion, racial origin and cultural and linguistic background'. By January of the following year, the Social Services Inspectorate had second thoughts, and referred to 'ethnic origin' in place of 'racial origin'. To treat colour categories, or cultural differences, as racial, or to talk of racial identities, is to play the game of the racialists, bundling together criteria that are best distinguished.

Any comparison of race-making and unmaking processes in the United States and Britain has to examine the factors influencing the boundaries between groups in very many different spheres of life. In the United States in 1994, 3 per cent of blacks married someone of a different race or ethnicity. In Britain, blacks were ten times more likely to marry or live with a white person, while such unions were contracted much more often by persons who considered themselves to be of partly black origin (Banton 1997: 142–4). In one country the one-drop rule was being maintained, in the other it was almost forgotten. In both countries socio-economic status reflects average income differences as well as ethnicity or race, but there do not seem to be significant race-making tendencies in Britain in respect of housing, political organization, sports, or consumption. The strongest race-making institutions are in religious observance. In the United States it is possible to detect race-making as well as unmaking tendencies in all of these spheres of life.

Conclusion

The historical mode of racialization was an intellectual enterprise seeking to explain unequal development. Nations and other groups were represented as races as if this explained their character and achievements, but there is little evidence about the extent to which these representations were accepted by other people or whether they affected conduct and the course of events. In the contemporary period there is a process of racialization in a strict sense when words like *race* and *racial* are employed in policies to reduce discrimination. Some writers claim that racialization also occurs when groups are represented as having a racial character even though there may have been no explicit reference to race. By implication they reproach others for evoking misleading and dangerous associations. Those who write of racialization in this wider sense should specify more carefully who does the racializing and for what reasons. It remains unclear what standard of proof has to be met before a claim of racialization in this sense can be considered proven.

The source of all these difficulties lies in a mid-nineteenth century use of the word *race* which implied that the social characteristics of certain groups derived from their biological nature. The concept of racialization has been used to argue that those who called these groups *races* misrepresented the origins of their distinctiveness. This leads on to the question: if these groups are not to be called races, what should they be called? Any answer must first consider the purposes for which groups are to be named, recognizing the different functions of nomenclature in everyday and in scientific language.

In everyday language, changes in the naming of groups spring from society itself. As social alignments change, so does nomenclature. Some expressions within the language of race, like racial discrimination and incitement to racial hatred, have to be retained because they are essential to action against major social evils; other expressions are not essential and would be better discarded. That is not easily done. The report of a recent commission in Britain entitled *The Future of Multi-Ethnic Britain* (Parekh 2000: xxiv) explicitly avoided using the words *race* and *racial* in any sense that might imply that the human species consists of separate races, yet it was generally described in the British press as a 'race report' or a 'report on race'. There is no doubt that, in the short run at least, the mass media exert more influence than academics in deciding the names for groups to be used in everyday language.

In scientific language, changes in nomenclature spring from the discovery of theories that make possible better explanations of scientific problems. As social scientists improve their theories for explaining the formation, maintenance, and dissolution of social groups, so they will work out what, for their purposes, are the best names for the various kinds of group. That should be their priority.

NOTES

1. Subsequent publications about allegedly new forms of racism and of multiple 'racisms' have not advanced beyond Rex's argument in 1970 or tackled the main problem inherent in it, notably the claim to identify racism by the functions it supposedly serves. Any one stereotype, proverb, or symbol, etc. is likely to serve many functions. To prove that its racially exclusionary function is more important than its other functions may be impossible. There is also the difficulty of specifying the unit within which the stereotype, proverb, or symbol serves a function. The problems inherent in functional explanation cannot lightly be passed over.

2. Miles (1982: 168) states that the New Commonwealth migrants 'met with an increasingly negative political and ideological reaction, particularly in the 1960s and 1970s, which succeeded in applying the label of "race" to [them]'. The first whites to apply the label of race to the situation were academics like Kenneth Little and myself. As we were the anti-racists of our day, the suggestion that we were participating in a political and ideological reaction seems far-fetched.

3. Cf. Miles (1993: 145) where he asks whether the 1905 Aliens Act was racist. He notes that it made no reference to race or to Jews, but 'the Act legitimated this racist stereotype of Jews'. The Act presumably had many effects and this could have been one, but it is difficult to be sure that it had this effect for a significant number of persons and, if it did, that this effect preponderated over any effect it may have had in mitigating hostility towards Jewish immigrants from Eastern Europe. Trying to assess whether or not the Act was racist is an exercise of dubious value.

4. Introducing the Commonwealth Immigrants Bill, the Home Secretary stated that under the prevailing legislation 'one quarter of the population of the globe' was entitled to enter Britain (Hansen 2000: 111).

5. The interpretation of the lead-up to the 1962 Act to be found elsewhere (Banton 1985: 29–48) has been confirmed in its main points by this archival research. Its author concludes that the claims of the 'racialization school' are palpable nonsense (Hansen 2000: 63).

6. Between 1993 and 1996, I served on the Ethnic Minorities Advisory Committee of the Judicial Studies Board; since the Committee was advising courts and tribunals on the nomenclature it should employ in matters to do with ethnic minorities, I tried to persuade my colleagues that we should recommend that the use of 'mixed race' be discontinued, but without success. In January 1994, the Council of the Royal Anthropological Institute of Great Britain and Ireland adopted a motion in which it expressed concern 'at the increased use in Britain of the expression "mixed race" since this implies that there are pure races. The

Council believes that the expression "mixed origin," though not ideal, would be preferable' (see *Anthropology Today*, 1994, 10 (2): 26)).

REFERENCES

Alibhai-Brown, Y. (2001) *Mixed Feelings: The Complex Lives of Mixed-Race Britons*. London: The Women's Press.

Banton, M. (1977) *The Idea of Race*. London: Tavistock.

——(1983*a*) *Racial and Ethnic Competition*. Cambridge: Cambridge University Press. Reprinted Aldershot: Gregg Revivals.

——(1983*b*) 'The Influence of Colonial Status upon Black–White Relations in England, 1948–58'. *Sociology*, 17: 546–59.

——(1985) *Promoting Racial Harmony*. Cambridge: Cambridge University Press.

——(1997) *Ethnic and Racial Consciousness*. Harlow: Addison-Wesley Longman.

——(1998) *Racial Theories*. 2nd edn. Cambridge: Cambridge University Press.

Bryce, J. (Viscount) (1902) *The Relations of the Advanced and Backward Races of Mankind*. Romanes Lecture. Oxford: Clarendon Press.

Bulmer, M., and Solomos, J. (eds.) (1998) 'Introduction: Rethinking Ethnic and Racial Studies' *Ethnic and Racial Studies*, 21 (5): 819–37.

Carter, B., Green, M., and Halpern, R. (1996) 'Immigration Policy and the Racialization of Migrant Labour: The Construction of National Identities in the USA and Britain'. *Ethnic and Racial Studies*, 19 (1): 135–57.

Cox, O. C. (1948) *Caste, Class and Race: A Study in Social Dynamics*. New York: Monthly Review Press.

Dikötter, F. (2002) 'Race in China' in D. T. Goldberg and J. Solomos (eds.), *A Companion to Racial and Ethnic Studies*. Malden and Oxford: Blackwell, pp. 495–510.

Douglas, R. M. (2002) 'Anglo-Saxons and Attacotti: The Racialization of Irishness in Britain between the World Wars'. *Ethnic and Racial Studies*, 25 (1): 40–63.

Freeman, E. A. (1877) 'Race and Language'. *Contemporary Review*, 29: 711–41; reprinted in Michael D. Biddiss (1979) *Images of Race: A Selection from Mid-Victorian Periodicals*. Leicester: Leicester University Press, pp. 205–35.

Hansen, R. (2000) *Citizenship and Immigration in Post-war Britain: The Institutional Origins of a Multicultural Nation*. Oxford: Oxford University Press.

Jordan, W. D. (1968) *White Over Black: American Attitudes Towards the Negro*, 1550–1812. Chapel Hill: University of North Carolina Press.

Miles, R. (1982) *Racism and Migrant Labour*. London: Routledge.

——(1989) *Racism*. London: Routledge.

——(1993) *Racism after 'Race Relations'*. London: Routledge.

Parekh, B. (Chair) (2000) *The Future of Multi-Ethnic Britain: Report of the Commission on the Future of Multi-Ethnic Britain*. London: Profile Books.

Rex, J. (1970) *Race Relations in Sociological Theory*. London: Weidenfeld & Nicolson.

Solomos, J. (1989) *Race and Racism in Contemporary, Britain*. Basingstoke: Macmillan.

Wolton, S. (2000) *Lord Hailey, the Colonial Office and the Politics of Race and Empire in the Second World War. The Loss of White Prestige*. Basingstoke: Macmillan.

CHAPTER 3

Ambivalent Documents/Fugitive Pieces: Author, Text, Subject, and Racializations

AVTAR BRAH

In March 2003, I visited a Canadian university in order to give a lecture and participate in graduate seminars. In one seminar, the perennial issue, as to whether or not it is useful to characterize human variation in terms of 'races', came up again. Some of the students, including three of African and Asian ancestry, were cautious about the call in some academic literature, including my own, for relinquishing the use of the term 'race' for describing phenotypical differences. It was as though jettisoning the language of race would elide the very specificity of the economic, political, and cultural inscriptions through which racialized experiences have been inscribed. What did this concern amongst young people, who are already familiar with academic debate on the subject, represent? How are we to respond to it?

I believe that the kind of scepticism and anxiety expressed by these students can scarcely be dismissed through analytic fiat. But, how might we do it? There will of course be many different answers to this question but I would not wish them to entail reinstating the idea that human variation can be mapped according to a belief that humans comprise inherently different and discrete races. That narrative at least has long been discredited and I remain convinced by the arguments. But, in saying this I cannot claim an absolute truth. What I can lay a stake to, however, is that I hold a specific position within a critique of those modern discursive regimes that categorize humans into separate races. From the vantage point of this position, culturally constituted groups do indeed have their cultural specificities, and humans do indeed come in all different colours, heights, shapes and sizes, sexes, and social classes, but these 'differences' do not make us the bearers of some inalienable essential difference. The difficulty remains, however, that this 'anti-"race" perspective' has not succeeded in convincing even some committed anti-racists such as Ruth Benedict, architect of the term 'racism', and, in our own times, the geneticist Steve Jones, let alone the sceptics. We know that there is still no universal consensus even after the latest analyses of human genes have reaffirmed what has been known for decades, namely that individuals rather than groups are the repository of most human variation, with 90 per cent of such variation being attributable to differences among individuals. Yet, this continuing tenacity of a belief in the idea of some kind of inherent 'racial difference', despite evidence to the contrary, should not surprise us since biological discourses of race were, from their inception, imbued with value judgements about the groups whom they classified. The classificatory procedure itself was and remains a technology of power *independent of the intentions of those who deploy it.* Indeed, it is precisely because the cultural imaginary of race—drawing voraciously upon different and often disparate and conflicting fields of signification— continues to hold sway with devastating global effects, that ongoing analysis of twenty-first century processes that 'hail' us as differentially racialized subjects remain critical.

Given the complexity involved in the way human subjects have been deeply marked by consequences arising from social and cultural operations of the category race, the question remains whether the concept of racism which is often posited as a more analytically and politically useful alternative, is really adequate to the task of addressing the multifarious effects of 'racial' categorization? Relatedly, can the concept of 'race' be taken always and invariably to signify negativity? In this chapter, I wish to think through these questions by exploring the contradictory relationships between author, text, and subject as constituted within and across social fields that include processes of racialization, by addressing some themes in three influential and avowedly 'anti-racist' texts. I focus on these texts because it is instructive that such anti-racist texts are not denuded of contradiction/difficulties to which the student response noted above seemed to gesture towards. The three texts are 'Race and Racism', 'The Language of Genes', and 'Society Must Be Defended' by Ruth Benedict, Steve Jones, and Michel Foucault, respectively. All three books are written in a conversational, 'popular', and polemical mode, with the authors explicit about their position against racism. Since we are all psychosocial subjects who are in a sense at least partially opaque to others as much as to ourselves, such anti-racist claims raise interesting questions about the relationship between what is consciously espoused and unconsciously elided or disavowed. I am interested in teasing out some of these elisions and disavowals. Can a claim to an anti-racist position within a text in and of itself guarantee anti-racist textual effects? How is the idea of race, races, and racism used in these three texts? What textual and cultural work is performed by similar or different usages of these terms by these authors? What kinds of subjects are valorized, excluded, or disavowed in these works?

It is not my intention here to rehearse the long-standing important British debate on the concept of race and racism. As is well-known, there are different shades of opinion held by scholars in the debate. However, I trust that most would probably agree that racisms are inextricably linked with historically specific economic, political, cultural, and psychic dynamics associated with *varying and variable* discourses of 'race' in the context of a wide variety of projects, ranging from modern forms of slavery and colonialism, through fascism, socialism, democracy, to Holocausts and twenty-first century globalizations.

Race as Scientific Object, Racism as Dogma

I begin with the book *Race and Racism* by the American scholar Ruth Benedict, apparently the architect of the term racism. Hers is a passionate polemic directed against racist practices. It was written at a time when the Nazi regime in Germany was in the throes of using the idea of 'separate races' to exterminate all those whom they saw as degenerates threatening the 'purity of the German race'—Jewish groups, gypsies, gays, socialists, and so on. It was a period when white supremacists held sway in many institutional domains of the United States as, indeed, they continue to do, albeit differently under changed circumstances. As is now well-known, Benedict defines racism as follows:

Racism is the dogma that one ethnic group is condemned by nature to congenital inferiority and another group is condemned to congenital superiority. Racism is not, like race, a subject the content of which can be scientifically investigated. It is, like a religion, a belief which can be studied only historically. (Benedict 1983 [1942])

When we look at this definition, its strengths and weaknesses become immediately apparent. It is easy to concur with Benedict that racisms are seeped in histories that are complicit with attributions of superiority and inferiority based on a view that racialized bodies are the embodiment of some inherent and immutable difference, almost as if this difference was 'congenital'. Racisms do indeed naturalize socially constructed difference. They do so in and through processes that naturalize the imaginary of race. These processes include the emergence of modern scientificity and are generally signalled by the concept of racialization. But the Benedictian discourse predates the emergence of the concept of racialization. For Benedict, race is a pre-given 'fact', that can be scientifically investigated, whereas racism is a belief 'like a religion'. In saying this, her text reiterates the problematic binary—between a rationalist science and a non-rationalist, if not irrationalist, religion—that has dogged Western modernity for centuries. In the preface to the book, she explicitly remarks that 'to recognize Race does not mean to recognize Racism; Race is a matter for careful scientific study; racism is an unproved assumption of the biological and perpetual superiority of one human group over another' (p.vii). The confusion, she argues, resides in the 'facts of race and the claims of racism'. This revolving-turntable strategy in the text is altogether striking, not least because the first part of the book is devoted to debunking most of the claims that were the *raison d'être* of 'racial science'. For example, she systematically challenges the 'scientific validity' claimed by those who believe that intelligence tests can measure 'racial differences' in intelligence. But this does not lead her to question science as itself a culturally constructed discourse; rather she dismisses such projects as 'pseudo science', implying that there is a realm of objective and neutral science that can guarantee access to authentic truths. While she criticizes the notion of 'racial purity', she does not see any contradiction in her own simultaneously held belief that there is a domain of 'unsullied pure science'. Moreover, her understanding of 'what race is' can begin to sound frightfully like that which she critiques:

Race is not the 'modern superstition', as some amateur egalitarians have said. It is a fact. The study of it has already told culture-historians much, and further investigations, for which as yet science has not the necessary basic knowledge or tests, may even show that some ethnic groups have identifiable *emotional or intellectual peculiarities which are biological and not merely learned behaviour*: (p. 96, emphasis added).

Benedict would appear to be oblivious to the close resemblance between her own argument here and that of the advocates of intelligence testing!! While seeking to challenge hierarchies of superiority and inferiority, the text displays chronic anxiety about egalitarian claims that the idea of race is as much a 'dogma' as racism. According to this passage, the woolly analysis of cultural historians could seriously benefit from the insights of biologists, almost as if the academic discipline of biology exists outside culture. If one substitutes the word 'biological' with 'god-given', the Freudian 'repressed' begins to assume an identifiable shape. The text disavows the affinity of Benedict's own *belief* in science to that of religious *faith*. Such disavowals have been a recursive theme within many a meta-narrative of secularism. This particular Benedictine text sets up a dualism between race as exclusively a biological category (god-given) and racism as a social category, although even as a social category racism is analysed less as an immanent dynamic of culture than as an illogical fallacy embodied by the irrational faithful. Yet, importantly, Benedict remains alive to the global interconnections between racism, class, nation, and colonialism:

Racism did not get its currency in modern thought until it was applied to conflicts within Europe—first to class conflicts and then to national. But it is possible to wonder whether the doctrine would have been proposed at all as explaining these latter conflicts—where as we have seen, the dogma is so inept—if the basis for it had not been laid in the violent experience of racial prejudice on the frontier (of the USA and other colonies). (p. 111)

It is noticeable that she seems to regard racism as an 'independent factor' which is then *applied* to conflicts associated with class or nation whereas, in my view, all these dimensions are mutually constitutive. Bendict's book dramatically illustrates that an anti-racist stance can easily coexist with a belief in 'distinct races'. In her case, this operation is achieved through a splitting of race and racism across the modernist rational/irrational divide and by privileging a view of science as beyond cultural contamination. Such discourses tend to produce the racist as radical otherness: 'I could not, myself, possibly be racist/sexist/homophobic, class supremacist...'. Ironically, and perhaps not so ironically, self becomes the pristine realm but this 'purity' is projected on to that which is seemingly desired by the racist. As critics argued throughout the 1970s and 1980s, such anti-racist discourses produced their own 'moral panics' and spawned their own 'folk devils' as racism was regularly ascribed to the 'ruffians', the 'uneducated' or the 'misfits', or the 'vested interests'. We are still confronted with this legacy as when racist attacks in Britain are dismissed as the work of 'thugs', 'criminals', or 'loonies'. Racism is out there, rather than right here where we all become cultural subjects. At the time of writing, Kurdish Iraqi refugees in Wrexham, in northern Wales, were attacked with petrol bombs during the weekend of 21/22 June 2003. The eruption of such violence is not surprising given the current political climate when senior politicians such as the Home Secretary, David Blunkett, and other opinion makers describe minoritized groups, especially refugees and asylum seekers, as a major threat to British 'selfhood and security'. This is not to suggest a direct correspondence between Benedict and Blunkett. Rather, it is to invoke recursive elements of a discourse which is currently being reconfigured. The question of 'radical otherness' is at the heart of discourses which remain seeped in denial of the messiness of social, cultural, and psychic dynamics in and through which differentially constructed subjects are embodied by individuals and collectivities.

The Language of Genes

Fifty years after the publication of Ruth Benedict's book, Steve Jones, Professor of Genetics at London University, gave the prestigious BBC Radio Reith Lectures of 1992 entitled, 'The Language of Genes: Biology, History and the Evolutionary Future'. The book of the lectures was a runaway success and was awarded the Rhone–Poulenc Science Book Prize for 1994. A witty and accessible rendering of the scientific imagination, it has been reprinted several times with its revised edition issued in 2000, at a time when, as the author says:

Now everything has been transformed. *Homo Sapiens* is no longer the great unknown of the genetical world but has become its workhorse. More is known about the geographical patterns of genes in people than about those of any other animal...The three thousand million letters in the DNA alphabet have, at last, been read from end to end...The completion of the DNA map marks the triumph of genetics as a science. Its success as a technology—or, at least, as a medical technology—has yet to be established. (Jones 2000 [1993])

Like Benedict, Jones critiques the early studies of human inheritance and regards the field as 'the haunt of charlatans, most of whom had a political axe to grind'. He is categorical in his assertion that:

At last there is a real insight into race, and the ancient idea that the peoples of the world are divided into distinct units has gone forever. Separatism has gained a new popularity among groups anxious to assert an identity of their own, but they cannot call on genes to support their views. (op cit p. xi)

Like Benedict, Jones too has great confidence in the scientific procedure, but he is clear about its limits:

It is, though, the essence of scientific theories that they cannot resolve everything. Science cannot answer the questions that philosophers—or children—ask: why are we here, what is the point of being alive, how ought we have to behave? Genetics has nothing to say about what makes people more than just machines driven by biology, about what makes us human. These questions may be interesting, but a scientist is no more qualified to comment on them than anyone else. Human genetics has suffered from its high opinion of itself. For most of its history it failed to understand its own limits. Knowledge has brought humility to genetics, but its new awareness raises social and ethical problems that have as yet been scarcely addressed.... Genetics is more and more involved with social and political questions such as those of abortion, cloning, and human rights... At the time of my first edition,... the idea that animals—perhaps even humans—might routinely be cloned, or that lengths of DNA could be moved around at will seemed beyond belief. Now genetic engineering is a business worth billions a year. (pp. xi–xv)

Jones's attention to the limitations of what science can or cannot deliver; to its procedural reductionism; and to the centrality of politics, economics, and ethics in social relationships is clearly important. Like Benedict, he is fully committed to a non-racist world. Yet, his book too is replete with constructions, representations, metaphors, and narrative devices which, in effect, serve to inscribe what the author does not seem to intend. If the earlier generations of geneticists, according to Jones, were 'charlatans', to use his own term, the new geneticists emerge as the true purveyors of an authentic and disinterested science. In other words, this influential text unconsciously 'forgets' that scientific taxonomies—whether racial, sexual, or about social class—cannot escape the marks of their cultural histories. Jones notes that 'genetics is more and more involved in social and political questions' but how could it be otherwise when experts like him ascribe to 'genes' a far superior potentiality for furnishing accurate information about human pasts and futures than history itself. In a careful analysis of Steve Jones' text, Deborah Steinberg reveals complex ways in which the book's use of the metaphor of language and literacy imputes properties of narration to genes so that the 'gene' assumes a 'voice'. As a consequence, the gene is made to narrate 'race' and 'nation' through a *racialized* idiom even as the knowledge derived from the study of genes is represented as a 'proof' against racism. As Steinberg writes:

Thus, at the same time that Jones appears to reject 'race' as a meaningful category, it re–emerges, threading through the text in an uneasy countermotif.

LIVERPOOL JOHN MOORES UNIVERSITY
LEARNING SERVICES

Race, for example is a key analogy through which Jones explains the mechanisms of genetic inheritance…his claims for an anti-racist genetics produce a seductive image of a science harnessing nature in the service of democracy and social progress. Yet on closer inspection, we find a science proposed as an antidote for problems in which it remains foundationally embedded…. Jones's casting of contemporary genetics as a science no longer tainted by ideology or grandiose intentionalities constitutes an extraordinary denial of the putatively alternative ideological underpinnings of his own readings of the genes and of the power relations accruing to his claims for genetic literacy. (Steinberg 2000)

This does not mean, however, that Jones's anti-racism itself is in question. Rather, what is at issue is the author's *unawareness* of the text's own imbrication with regimes of power circulating through a discourse about a 'true' science as the rightful arbitrator of truth claims. Steinberg's analysis describes cultural and textual processes—of association, connotation, and metaphorical intimation—that combine to produce outcomes contrary to the author's stated intention. Today, we are confronted with a wide array of historical and contemporary meanings and power dynamics associated with the sign race—meanings that have become part of a certain kind of globalized 'commonsense' in Gramsci's sense of the term. The multifarious effects of these representational regimes, of which the language of genes (both the book discussed here and the textual strategy about genes which it, perhaps unwittingly, imparts to popular culture) can scarcely be mitigated by arguments which remain entangled within the very regimes of knowledge (e.g. the opposition between 'good science' versus 'charlatanry') which have been at the very heart of the idea of racial taxonomies. But the problem is not one that is simply about the shortcomings of a Manichean opposition that animates the texts by Benedict and Jones. It is a general problem about analytical and political strategies that: are reluctant to address 'science' and commonsense as relational *cultural* categories; continue to overemphasize the 'modernist' view that everything is knowable through 'rational' procedure; and disavow unconscious processes with little regard for the emotional life that is the basis of processes of subjectivity and identity.

Politics of Power: 'Race War' or Racism?

Michel Foucault is not well-known for his work on race, but in his 1976 lectures at the Collège de France he pays some attention to these issues, arguing that the idea of race and races is as an internal dynamic of European modernity. How does he conceptualize race and races? What role do these concepts perform in his text?

Race figures as a theme in his ruminations on the emergence of a specifically modern discourse on war. As we know, Foucault inverts the famous formulation generally associated with Carl von Clausewitz, that 'war is politics by other means'. In the aftermath of the Iraq War of 2003, this particular Clausewitzian aphorism still rings true. Similarly, Foucault's claim that 'politics is the continuation of war by other means' remains replete with significance for our time. In demonstrating this claim, Foucault introduces his concept of 'disciplinary power' as a new formation emerging during the sixteenth and seventeenth century as the opposite of the concept of power subsumed by the theory of sovereignty. As he says:

This new mechanism of power applies primarily to bodies and what they do rather than to the land and what it produces. It was a mechanism of power that made it possible to extract time and labour, rather than commodities and wealth, from bodies. It was a type of power that was exercised through constant surveillance and not in discontinuous fashion through chronologically defined systems of taxation and obligation. It was a type of power that presupposed a closely meshed grid of material coercions rather than the physical existence of a sovereign. (Foucault 2003 [1976]: 36)

We can recognize this as a form of power associated with the development of capitalism, transatlantic slavery, and colonialism. But Foucault, with his attention focussed almost exclusively on Europe, rather than with Europe's projects overseas, does not directly address the forms of power that worked on the enslaved body or the colonized body. As Spivak notes, this concept of power does not take on board the migration of old forms of 'directly coercive' power that Foucault associates with European feudalism, to the colonies (Spivak Chakravorty 1993 [1988]). In describing mechanisms of disciplinary power, Foucault is engaged in, among other things, a conversation with certain forms of liberal and Marxist tendencies during the 1970s which appeared to him to be positing a rather monolithic view of power, a view with which he disagrees:

Power must I think be analysed as something that circulates, or rather as something that functions only when it is part of a chain. It is never localised here or there, it is never in the hands of some, and it is never appropriated in the way that wealth or a commodity can be appropriated. Power functions. Power is exercised through networks, and individuals do not simply circulate in those networks; they are in a position to *both submit to and exercise this power.* They are never the inert or consenting targets of power: *they are always its relays. In other words, power passes through individuals. It is not applied to them.* (p. 29, emphasis added)

Aware that this view of power might be misunderstood as ignoring unequal power relations in which refusal to submit might not be a straightforward option, and acutely alive to the institutional mechanisms with which power is imbricated, Foucault explains that he is certainly not arguing the case that power is distributed evenly, democratically, or even in an anarchic fashion. Only that power is not monolithic or located in any one single centre from which it radiates to the peripheries. Rather, his analysis of power:

Begin(s) with its infinitesimal mechanisms, which have their own history, their own trajectory, their own techniques and tactics, and then look(s) at how these mechanism of power...have been and are invested, colonized, used, inflected, transformed, displaced and extended and so on by increasingly general mechanisms and forms of overall domination. (p. 30)

It is apparent that he is attempting to do away with monolithic scripts of 'victimhood' while recognizing the impact of subjugation and domination. Fundamentally, and this is important with regards to understanding racialized subjects, he is interested in the way human subjects are socially and culturally produced. The concept of disciplinary power attempts:

'To grasp the *material agency* of subjugation insofar as it constitutes subjects' and it seeks to '...discover how multiple bodies, forces, energies, matters, desires, thoughts, and so on are gradually, progressively, actually and materially constituted as subjects, or as the subject. (p. 28, emphasis added)

This power subjugates but it also produces agency. It is in thinking about a historically specific form of agency that Foucault makes the connection with race. Disciplinary power, according to him, underpins the emergence of the historical moment when the modern state acquires the monopoly on war. War becomes the centralized technical and professional responsibility of a controlled military apparatus leading to the emergence of an institutionalized military complex (See also Giddens 1985; Mann 1986). These changes are marked by the emergence of a discourse that *constructs peace itself as a coded war.* This discourse inscribes history as a power-filled heterogeneous space. It produces a subject who speaks of rights and who struggles to achieve them. This discourse of rights inscribes a notion of truth that is self-consciously partisan, paying homage to new knowledge but also to myth. This discourse of struggle or 'perpetual war':

is tied up with a knowledge which is sometimes in the possession of a declining aristocracy, with great mythical impulses, and with the ardour of the revenge of the people. In short, this may well be the first exclusively historico-political discourse—as opposed to philosphicojuridical discourse—to emerge in the West; it is a discourse in *which truth functions exclusively as a weapon that is used to win an exclusively partisan victory*. It is a sombre, critical discourse, but it is also an intensely mythical discourse; it is a discourse of bitterness [...] but also of most insane hopes. (Foucault 2003 [1976])

Significantly, Foucault describes this discourse as essentially one of 'race war', analysing its transformation in terms of two main types of 'transcription'. First, there is the explicitly biological transcription, pre-dating Darwin and borrowing its concepts and vocabulary from anatomical physiology. Supported by philology it spawns a theory of race in the historico-biological sense of the term. It is an ambiguous discourse easily harnessed to a variety of diverse, even disparate projects, used in nationalist movements and the struggles of different nationalities against the state, and subsequently in the service of colonization. Within this scenario, the social is seen as permeated by permanent struggle waged in terms of 'race struggle', where race operates as a synonym for groups attempting to secure 'partisan victories'. In the second transcription of this discourse of social war, beginning in the early years of the nineteenth century, the concept of racial conflict, Foucault argues, is recast as class struggle. If during the seventeenth century the discourse of race struggle was 'an instrument used in the struggles waged by decentred camps' it later becomes 'the discourse of a centred, centralized and centralizing power'. In this latter articulation the discourse assumes a different form:

It will become the discourse of a battle that has to be waged not between two races, but by a race that is portrayed as the one true race, the race that holds power and is entitled to define the norm, and against those who deviate from that norm, ... At this point we have all those biological-racist discourse of degeneracy, but also all those institutions within the social body which make the discourse of race struggle function as a principle of exclusion and segregation and, ultimately, *as a way of normalizing society.* (p. 61, emphasis added)

For Foucault, the earlier form of the discourse of race comprises a progressive intervention. He praises these early discursive formations and distinguishes them from racism:

I think we should reserve the expression of 'racism' or 'racist discourse' for something that was basically no more than a particular and localized episode in the great discourse of race war or race struggle ... Having said that to situate both the link and the difference between racist discourse and the discourse of race war, I was indeed praising the discourse of race war.

I was praising it in the sense that I wanted to show you—at least for a time, or in other words up to the end of the nineteenth century, at which point it turned into a racist discourse—this discourse of race war functioned as a counterhistory.

With this distinction between the discourse of race war and that of race, he comes to associate the former with the emergence of counterhistory. These counterhistories are seen as instituting a political consciousness that poses major challenges to the hitherto implicit identification of people with monarch and nation with sovereign. In this struggle against 'pre-modern' social relations, race becomes a code for recognition of heterogeneity and differences of social conditions. The discourse of distinctive races interrogates asymmetrical social relations so that it becomes possible to openly proclaim that:

The history of some is not the history of others...what looks like right, law, or obligation from the point of view of power looks like the abuse of power, violence, and exaction when it is seen from the viewpoint of the new discourse...Not only does this counterhistory break up the continuity of sovereign law that imposes obligation; it also breaks the continuity of glory, in to the bargain. (pp. 69–70)

Foucault's admiration for the early stages of the discourse of race war, most notably during the seventeenth and eighteenth centuries, is related to its performance as an oppositional force—galvanizing silenced, neglected, or marginalized groups, and enabling them to enter the stage as subjects of their own history. Whether they were distinguished by religion, language, or by 'barriers created by privileges, customs and rights, the distribution of wealth, or the way in which power is exercised' (p. 77), these groups mobilized the signifier of 'my race' to stake a claim to their own history as the basis on which to demand equity and equality. Foucault is dismayed by the changes that the discourse of 'race war' undergoes during the nineteenth century. The discourse bifurcates with the revolutionary impulse directed at human emancipation becoming translated in to the concept of 'class struggle', while the idea of race rapidly acquires connotations of inherent biological difference and is then used to rank groups across racial hierarchies of superiority and inferiority. At this point the theme of race struggle, according to Foucault, is replaced by that of racial purity, with the result that the discourse of *races in the plural is converted into race in the singular*. Racism, he suggests, is born at this juncture as an inversion of or an alternative to revolutionary discourse:

The connection between racism and antirevolutionary discourse and politics in the West is not, then, accidental; it is not simply an additional ideological edifice that appears at a given moment in a sort of grand anitrevolutionary project... Although they had their roots in the discourse of 'race struggle', the revolutionary project and revolutionary propheticism now began to take very different directions... Whereas the discourse of races, of the struggle between races, was a weapon to be used against the historico-political discourse of Roman sovereignty, the discourse of race (in the singular) was a way of turning the weapon against those who had forged it, of using it to preserve the sovereignty of the State, a sovereignty whose lustre and vigour was no longer guaranteed by magico-juridical rituals but by medico-normalizing techniques ... State sovereignty thus became the imperative to protect the race. (p. 81)

This, for him, is the basis for the genesis of state racism at the end of the nineteenth century which gets reworked in different directions during the twentieth century, becoming a distinctive feature of the Nazi, the Soviet, and the social democratic states, albeit it functions somewhat differently in these diverse forms of state racisms.

When asked where he would situate premodern genealogies of a phenomenon such as anti-Semitism, Foucault replies that he was not seeking here to 'trace the history of what it might have meant, in the West, to have an awareness of belonging to a race, or of the history of the rites and mechanisms that were used to exclude, disqualify, or physically destroy a race' (op cit p. 88). He explains that his primary objective in this instance has been to map the emergence in the West of a certain critical, political analysis of the state, its institutions, and its power mechanism during a specific historical period that later came to be identified as modernity. He wishes to show how a binarized discourse of race war figured as a constitutive dynamic within this analysis. This may be a perfectly reasonable answer in terms of the designate priorities of his particular set of lectures in 1976. Yet, I am nagged by Foucault's perfunctory response to the critical issue of how experience and processes of embodiment, including his own body, sensibilities, and desires, are racialized? His analysis of the transformation, even disintegration, of a discourse of race war into class struggle or 'social struggle' on the one hand, and race and racism on the other, is certainly illuminating. As is his genealogy of how these transformations feed differently and differentially into the constitution of certain historically specific forms of state racism. It is a narrative that has been traced by other scholars, albeit in somewhat different ways. The point, however, is that if the discourse of race war produces subjects endowed with a new awareness about the possibilities for liberation and emancipation, as Foucault argues, then how can he dissociate questions of experience from the emergence of these subjects? Is this a kind of conceptual formalism or a form of Freudian repression in Foucault? Why a reluctance to take on board theoretically the very processes by which racialized subject positions are created and embodied? Moreover, what does Foucault mean by 'a race' when he uses the phrase '...to destroy a race'? Is there an ontological reference here by a theorist who shuns ontologies? Is he using 'race' according to its early usage in the seventeenth century, almost as a synonym for a distinctive social group, or is his usage sub/unconsciously imbued with the word's more recent connotations? How is it that an intellectual whose immensely productive conceptual repertoire has opened up a whole new way of thinking about social phenomena remains perfunctory when it comes to explicating racism and colonialism's imbrications with the 'modern' power dynamics he so assiduously delineates? Which subjects are his own theoretical discourses unable to foster, and why?

Continuing Conversations

Such questions bring to the fore the long-standing vexed issue about the relationship between author/writer/agent (with all the apparent contradiction between, on the one hand, our intentionalities, priorities, and *sense* of agency *and*, on the other hand, the very impossibility of a wholly self-conscious and transparent knowing subject), text or in similar vein 'the social' (regulated by its own specific conditions of existence, including its own unconscious underground and its own forms of effectivity that cannot be reduced to or directly read from the author's intentionality), and individuals or collectivities who are culturally 'hailed' as (and into) subjects. The complex, uneasy, and never fully settled relationship between these three renders any neat heuristic separation between an analytic concept and commonsense understandings hugely difficult to sustain even though it is a distinction academics can scarcely do without. One cannot straightforwardly and unproblematically extrapolate from one to the other. The articulating temporalities and spatialities between the three are traversed by supplements, excesses, and remainders—many relational and contingent 'ifs', 'ands', and 'buts'—which continually interrogate moves of fixity and closure. It is precisely within their interstices that the irreducibility of the idea of race (or gender, class...) resides. We may decry belief in the idea of race or races from the perspective of a particular theoretical or political position, as I do. But the meanings associated with these terms are various and variable, spanning racist as well as anti-racist discourses and, as we have seen above, academic or scholarly anti-racist writing is far from free of these underpinnings. Indeed, the heterogeneity, multiplicity, polyvocality, and contradictory nature of the semiotic and psychic groundswell may serve as the commonsense of both types of discourses, permitting all manner of elisions, slippages, introjections, projections, transferences, proclamations, as well as disavowals. This may mean that we cannot settle this problematic once and for all. It is an open field of potential conflict as well as connectivity.

In texts such as that of Benedict and Jones, as I have already pointed out, there is the difficulty associated with scienticism. With all three, there is a tendency to underwrite a certain kind of rationality which disavows unconscious processes. For instance, Foucault's reservations about psychoanalysis are well-known. His otherwise productive conceptual repertoire is uneasy with un/subconscious emotional life that is so paramount in inflecting processes of subjectivity and identity. When he claims that 'Power is exercised through networks, and individuals do not simply circulate in those networks; they are in a position to *both submit to and exercise* this power (Foucault 2003: 29), he does not acknowledge that submission to power or the effects of its exercise cannot be reduced exclusively to conscious procedures. The discursive subject is 'hailed' not only by the social but also by the psychic. One ramification of the complex and continually changing discourses, practices, and histories of the idea of race is that the concept of racism may not itself be quite adequate as an explanatory tool. The undercurrents and unconscious ripples associated with discursive formations of race go wider and deeper than could probably be fully fathomed by the concept of racism. In other words, the act of mobilizing the trope of racism instead of race may not necessarily guarantee deracialization. The point is that race, racism, and anti-racism are not mutually exclusive terrains, as the growing importance of the concept of whiteness attests. Hence, such questions as the following remain relevant despite substantial debate concerning 'municipal anti-racism' of the 1980s: what is implicated in the historically specific relational operations of the category race, racism, and anti-racism? what kind of subjects are produced and through which modes of corporeality are they embodied? What kinds of pains and pleasures are experienced across the realm of ensuing social relations? Since we are differentially racialized, we are differently hailed as subjects, and are differently subjected to the power effects of racism. Correspondingly, we may have very different psychic or political investment in academic debate on race as a category of social differentiation, depending, *inter alia*, upon whether or not one belongs to a specific inferior-ized/subjugated/exploited/other category. The emotional and psychic onslaughts of racism, not directly experienced by those who are not subject to it, are as critical as the socio-economic and political out-comes of racial inequities, inequalities, and discrimination. Whether they are expressed in deepest subtlety or in crudest directness, the effects of racism are felt in the minutiae of daily experience. Hence, the question of 'experience' remains as critical today as it ever was, although, as Joan Scott—in a move against a notion of experience as unmediated transparency—argues: 'Experience is at once already an interpretation *and* is in need of interpretation' (1992: 37). It is easy to forget the implications of first part of the sentence for our lives and scholarly analysis.

Elsewhere, I have already emphasized the importance of addressing social relations, experience, subjectivity, and identity as mutually constitutive fields (Brah 1992, 2000). While this may call for a kind of multi/interdisciplinarity that is extremely difficult to achieve in practice, the concept of racialization, to my mind, is important in foregrounding processes through which these fields articulate, albeit in irreducible forms. As Foucault's notion of race war seems to sug-gest, certain discourses of race can prove to be productive for the groups who are so categorized, since the experience of belonging to a race can lead to political mobilization against racism and other forms of inequities and inequalities. As signifier of a sense of community and belonging in a given context, race may signal associations with the whole lifeworld of a group: its history, politics, symbolic and semiotic practices, cultural codes and rituals, its sensibilities, and its expressive cultures in the form of arts, dance, music, and literature. Hence, the injunction by academics to jettison the terminology of race could well sound as if one is being asked to deny one's history. In an attempt to valorize these broader aspects of life outside the imper-atives of racism, the term 'ethnicity' has come into increasing usage for this purpose. Important though this move has been, the concept of ethnicity itself is not devoid of the very same problems which have bedevilled the idea of race. It can be put to the same uses. So, the conundrum persists, as is evidenced by the three texts discussed above. There is much that 'refuses to neatly fit': much that touches body, mind, and spirit; that struggles with desires, losses, wounds, pain, pleasures, love, intimacy, antagonisms, conflict, memories of political battles won and lost; all experienced in and through multiplex domains of power, their effects registering with us differentially across our different positionalities.

What gives hope, however, is that the excess that refuses to fit neatly allows for fissures, openings, for interventions, conversations, and dialogues even in the most dire situations.

REFERENCES

Benedict, R. (1983 [1942]) *Race and Racism*. London: Routledge and Kegan Paul
Brah, A. (1992) 'Difference, Diversity, Differentiation', in J. Donald and A. Rattansi (eds.), *'Race', Culture and Difference*. London: Sage.
——(2000) 'The Scent of Memory: Strangers, Our Own, and Others', in A. Brah and A. Coombes (eds.), *Hybridity and its Discontents: Politics, Science, Culture*. London and New York: Routledge.
Foucault, M. (1975) *Discipline and Punish: The Birth of the Prison*. New York: Vintage.
——(2003) *'Society must Be Defended': Lectures at the College De France 1975–76* (D. Macey trans.). New York: Picador.
Giddens, A. (1985) *The Nation–State and Violence*. Cambridge: Polity Press.
Mann, M. (1986) *The Sources of Social Power*, Vol. 1. Cambridge: Cambridge University Press.
Jones, S. (2000 [1993]) *The Language of Genes: Biology, History and the Evolutionary Future*. London: Flamingo.
Spivak, G. C. (1993 [1988]) *'Can the Subaltern Speak?'*, in P. Williams and L. Chrisman (eds.), *Colonial Discourse and Postcolonial Theory*. New York: Harvester Wheatsheaf.
Steinberg, D. L. (2000) 'Reading Genes/Writing Nation: Reith, 'Race' and the Writings of Geneticist Steve Jones', in A. Brah and A. Coombes (eds.), *Hybridity and its Discontents: Politics, Science, Culture*. London and New York: Routledge.

CHAPTER 4

Racial Americanization

DAVID THEO GOLDBERG

Race is commonly assumed in the popular imagination to be an antique notion, a vestige of premodern or at least not adequately *modernized* social assertions and arrangements. I have written extensively against this understanding in earlier work. But in any case, we are now readily aware of the reformation and reformulation of contemporary racial conception. I want here to extend this frame of analysis by outlining a more or less recent turn in at least one regionally prompted, parametered, and promoted racism linked to its dominant state formation in the United States and its contemporary imperializing extension. This is part of a wider concern of mine elsewhere to outline a set of more or less recent typologies of regionally prompted, parametered, and promoted racisms linked to their dominant state formations.[1] I am suggesting regional models or really mappings rather than ideal types, broad generalizations as contours of racist configuration, each one with its own material and intellectual history, its prior conditions, and typical modes of articulation. They are often interactive historically, overlapping landscapes, but it remains nevertheless revealing to delineate them, to distinguish one kind and style as well as their conditions of possibility, expression, effects, and implication from another. Identifying these mappings in the name of the social places and spaces of their principal origination, historical manifestation, and regional articulations is not to limit the (partial) influence of their logics and effects on other places, spaces, and regions, which might not be readily identified with their coordinates of origination. Racisms have a history of travelling, and transforming in their circulation. What I register here as more or less discrete in order to identify their sociomaterial and intellectual conditions of emergence, logics, social manifestations, effects, and implications are in practice, in reality, interactive with each other at various times and places on the ground and across borders and oceans.

This way of putting it may be considered odd, may even look contradictory in a volume devoted to analysing 'racialization(s)'. For one, for some years now I have avoided using the very notion, both warning my students that 'racialization' has no purchase and refusing it as an analytic in my own work. I was recently asked by a colleague why this refusal. The usage of racialization so broadly in the literature is at the very least ambiguous, and may sometimes be vacuous. One cannot always tell, either explicitly or contextually, whether it is being invoked as a merely descriptive term or with deeper normative, critical thrust. Quite often it is put to work simply to suggest race-inflected social situations, those informed or marked by racial characterization. But lurking beneath the descriptive is often an implicit, unexplained, and almost invariably theoretically unmotivated critical rejection of the normative insinuation in the seemingly neutral description of the social arrangements being characterized as racial or in racial terms. The lack of specificity, the emergent ambiguities, blurs the line and so presupposes an answer to a question not even posed: namely, is racial characterization inevitably racist? All too often the use, if not the very conceptualization, of 'racialization' determines an answer in the absence of analysis. I want to insist, by contrast, on distinguishing between race and racisms, conceptually as much as politically—as objects and categories of analysis, as analytics or frames of analysis for different contexts, different if related geopolitical regions, as I put it below. To insist on the distinction even as their deep, complex, often tortured connections need disentangling acknowledgement.

In this scheme of things I identify five dominant mappings linked to different, if neither perfectly isomorphic nor absolutely discrete, spatio-historical conditions and expressions. These prevailing modalities include Americanization, Palestinianization, Brazilianization, Europeanization, and South Africanization of racism, and by extension of race. This order reveals what would otherwise be less noticed, that each represents a significance that is both historically resonant and politically dominant at specific global conjunctions, but also a logic of historical interaction. I am concerned in this chapter with a detailed focus on the historical logic of 'racial Americanization', as much for the way it comes to embody the emergence of 'born again racism' I have elaborated elsewhere as for its own historical significance. Racial Americanization projects itself as *the* model, the one to be emulated, the failure of which bears more significant costs than in each of the other, if related, instances. But though it insists on its exceptionalism, the globally interacting historical analytic on which I insist at once urges the interactive relation, and therefore influence, of other historically resonant modalities likewise on Americanization, thus indicating an exceptionalism disturbingly not too exceptional.

The oddity I am raising thus seems to come back to haunt me, the return of my own repressed even. How can I invoke the likes of racial Americanization in the face of my worry about racialization? The processes of signification and materialization I aim to reveal and elaborate below that are fabricated and fashion under the conceptual title offer social embodiment to racial characterization, a specificity produced out of its socially embedded milieu. The specificity, I am suggesting, comes less with the generalizability of 'race' or 'racisms' as concepts, as analytics; as concepts, after all, they are generalizations. Rather, the specificity derives from their embeddedness, from the particularities that count for sociospecific determinations. Racial determination, in short, is the multidetermination of social particularities, of socially embedded particularities resonant in racially related, racially conceived, racially significant terms.

Classic racisms were formed and fashioned in the contexts of European expansion, enslavement, and colonization. They were the racisms of self-proclaimed European superiority in pursuit initially of new sources of wealth, a servile labour supply, exotic goods, but over time this came to include expansive territorialization, settlement, globalizing dominance, and with them even new lives for the settlers and new forms of desire, dominance, degradation, even death for those thus made servile. The prevailing geographies of early modern racisms then—until at least the later eighteenth century—are projected as Europe's externality, the colonial outside, provincial extensions vested largely in the rural slaveries of plantation life. Here, the viciousness of the violent structures necessary to uphold the system were hidden just beneath the tranquil facade of settlement: wars, seizures, chains and whippings, deathly ships, disease, human auctions, but also the penning of dehumanizing rationalizations, Sunday sermons, and state edicts. In these classic expressions of racism, race was seen always as a disruption, as the invader, as outsider otherness asserting itself over or inserting itself into local homogeneity.

Racism's more modernizing modes in the wake of abolition and nineteenth-century industrialization, by contrast, are increasingly associated with urbanization and metropolitan life. Modern cities have traditionally been places of migratory attraction and moral repulsion. They have offered the lure of employment and recreational excitement, consumptive novelties and cultural development, radical possibility and intense anonymity. It is this radical heterogeneity that has served at once as magnet and threat, as appealing, even transgressive of conserving inhibition, and repulsive. The perceived threats to homogeneity, to the reproduction of sameness and identity, to the expected and the usual, to order and control, with which cities are associated historically prompted the institution of controls over urban space, restrictions on entry and movement, limits on access and acceptability. Thus, it is in cities that the perceived 'need'—the demand—for racial segregation was hardened, if not initiated, becoming the principal sites of formalized segregating institutionalization. Late in the nineteenth century, accordingly, urban space became the summary motivation and purpose of the drive by whites to segregate—namely, to restrict heterogeneity and hybridity, to delimit intercourse, to control interaction and relation. This was seen as especially compelling in the Anglo-settler societies, most notably America and South Africa, but also in Australia.

Segregation emerged as the dominant and formalized modality of racism in the United States as freed slaves moved off the plantations after abolition and into cities, first southern and then up the Mississippi and the east coast, and ultimately also westward. White politicians in the southern Democratic Party (DP) machine secured their political power by shielding the white urban working class from competition by newly emancipated blacks in the late nineteenth century just as the National Party came to power in South Africa in 1948 by securing the well-being of the white working and poor classes on the promise of apartheid. The ghettoized segregation widely associated with the height of American racism was a thoroughly urbanized post-Reconstruction development the full effects of which were realized in cities in the 1920s and 1930s, by which time it was being thoroughly contested by black social movements.

If what we have come to recognize as standard American racism took the cruel form of a constitutionalized segregation (accompanied by the cultivating ethnocide of assimilating what was left of American Indians), contemporary racial Americanization has informalized apartness, rendering it the effect of privatized preference schemes rather than explicitly institutionalized legalities. Increasingly today, members of different ethnoracially constituted groups—whites, blacks, Latinos, Chinese, Vietnamese, Cambodian,

Indian, and Arab Americans—have come 'by choice'—principally the choices of whites—to occupy discrete urban spaces, at first different neighbourhoods but now overwhelmingly different municipalities, different cities. The choices have been shaped by policy and law to order social opportunities for some while closing them down for others, streaming access in the former case while plugging it up in the latter. This reveals how preferences are moulded even as that discriminate sculpting is obviated, rendered obscure and indiscernible in the name of its claimed obsolescence.

Black migration from the south coincided with European immigration to cities like New York, Philadelphia, and Chicago. But it was coterminous as well as with Chinese and Japanese settlement especially in San Francisco, and Chicago migration to southern California and later across the southwest to join those already long settled as a result of earlier American territorial annexations. But as racial interaction began to increase as a result, African-Americans, Latinos, and Asians were becoming progressively segregated within cities. The more black urbanization expanded, the more their racial segregation and restriction within cities was extended. Thus by 1930, the spatial location of segregation already had transformed perceptibly from regional to neighbourhood divides. Until the late 1800s, nearly 90 per cent of black Americans lived in southern rural counties while almost that proportion of whites lived in northern cities. By 1930, 40 per cent of black urban residents tended to live in wards 40 per cent black. From 1890 to 1930 black residence in New York surged nearly tenfold from 36,000 to 328,000, in Chicago over twenty fold from 14,000 to 234,000. Chicago neighbourhoods just 10 per cent black in 1900 were swept by the cold wind of segregation into neighbourhoods 70 per cent black just thirty years later. By 1950, a majority of African-Americans had become city folk, and by 1960 a greater percentage of blacks than whites lived in cities. Between 1920 and 1980, blacks living on the land and working in agriculture declined 96 per cent, and by 1981 this figure had almost disappeared to 1 per cent.

Already in 1940, ethnic white neighbourhoods were far from uniform in their ethnic composition. Neighbourhoods in which blacks or Latinos lived tended much more to be overwhelmingly black and Latino. Identifiably 'Irish' areas of cities included just 3 per cent of the total Irish population, and most of New York's Italians did not live in Little Italy, for instance. By contrast, 93 per cent of blacks lived in neighbourhoods that in the categorical formation of race in the United States can be characterized as majority black. The construction and containment of Chinatowns within major metropolitan centres at precisely the same time reinforces the ethnoracial logic at work here. Thus, the conditions for the reproduction of European immigrant ghettoes have never existed in the way they did in the twentieth century for African-American and Chinese ghettoes. European immigrant segregation ebbed as their migration flow waned, while black segregation within the boundaries of confined black and Chinese space increased not primarily as a result of black housing preferences but of conscious white avoidance, as manifested in the use of physical violence, intimidation, and the creation of a dual housing market by way of racial covenants and the like. So white exposure to blacks was still self-determinedly minimized through ensuring black isolation in urban ghettoes. Cities became instruments for European immigrant group advancement, but blocks especially for blacks not only residentially but educationally and economically also. Chinese entrepreneurship was left to flourish within the strict confines of Chinatowns, linked as it was to external sources of capital formation in Asia, opportunities definitively denied black ghetto dwellers.

The post-Second World War period saw the emergence of nationalized desegregating efforts—in the army, the courts, on the streets, in buses and schools—prompted not only by moral and internal political imperatives but also by geopolitical cold war competition and assertive local mass mobilization. The 'national interest' and foreign policy demands necessitated public commitment to race-neutral governmentality. On the face of it, the federal government also made a huge commitment to producing much needed urban public housing, in 1949 authorizing 810,000 new units over six years. In fact, the federal government became principally engaged in reproducing segregation. In the post-war modernization boom fuelling the economy, federal policy initiatives regarding mortgages and taxes promoted the suburban housing explosion for middle and working class whites, while federal property appraisal policies rendered possible bank and mortgage company redlining of inner city property purchase and development. Government, national and local, massively promoted private (re)development and gentrification of CBDs by underwriting loans; incentives to redevelop inner cities by building housing for the urban poor were almost wholly absent. By 1962, only 320,000 of the public housing units promised in 1949 (roughly 40 per cent) had been constructed. Much more inner city housing in fact was bulldozed away in terms of the 1949 federal housing law than was actually built: premonitions of 'group areas' apartheid

South Africa. From the end of the Second World War until 1960, less than 2 per cent of new housing financed by mortgages guaranteed by federal insurance went to black homeowners. From about 1950 on, then, segregation across and not just within cities began to increase. By the 1980s, this trend had become evident: increasingly members of ethnoracially defined and identified groups, and not only blacks, tend to live not just in different neighbourhoods from whites but in different cities. Their children likely attend overwhelmingly segregated schools in different school districts, growing up literally not knowing each other beyond the stilted stereotypical images they glean from television.

At the very time there was growing desegregation in the public sphere, one could say there was publicly subsidized resegregation in the private. Desegregation never stood a chance. By 1980, Massey and Hajnal (1995) have calculated, blacks living in cities found themselves in municipalities on average 35 per cent black; if black and white residents were to be evenly distributed across municipalities, 50 per cent of blacks in cities would have to switch places of residence with whites. It is revealing to note that such calculations somehow are invariably made on the dislocating assumption that blacks, not whites, should move, Owen Fiss (2003) being simply the most recent to promote such a plan. The suburban explosion that pulled whites out of the cities transformed the countryside into sprawling suburbs. These suburbs eventually became small self-governing cities, the effect as much of the desire to be politically and fiscally autonomous from deteriorating old black-identified cities as of some purely administrative rationality.

In 1950, there were no central cities in the United States that were overwhelmingly or even largely black. No city with a population larger than 100,000 had a majority black population. Forty years later there were fourteen such cities including Atlanta, Baltimore, Detroit, Gary, New Orleans, and Washington, DC. Eleven more cities had black populations between 40 and 50 per cent, including Cleveland, St Louis, and Oakland. Among cities larger than 25,000 in 1950 just two had majority black populations, a number that had exploded to forty by 1990. Interestingly, the increase in segregation after midcentury is characteristic only of larger cities with large black populations. There was a noticeable decline in segregation in small cities with small black populations. In the latter cases African-Americans found themselves assimilated into dominant white space with little if any noticeable effect on prevailing urban arrangements or culture. By the end of the Civil Rights era, in contrast, geographic isolation of blacks

in larger urban settings—the overwhelming majority of black folk—
was nearly complete.

In a provocative thought experiment in 1971, Thomas Schelling
exemplified the segregating implications effected through personal
preference. (Schelling used a checkerboard with dimes and nickels
though I think the colouring of the chess pieces more provocative.)
Take a chessboard: fill 10 per cent of its spaces with black pawns;
fill 70 per cent of its spaces with white pawns. Assume each black
pawn wants at least one neighbour to be a black pawn, and each
white pawn wants at least one neighbour to be a white pawn.
Segregation sets in within a couple of moves (try it). If each wants
both neighbors to be like itself, segregation is produced all the more
quickly. So, rational choice theorists to the contrary, preferences are
not naive, discursively unstructured, simply given, or unchanging.
Preferences are *ordered* by the dominant discursive culture and
terms. In the case of the preference for segregated space, segregation
is discursively (re)produced and ideologically massaged. White
Americans of all class stripes reportedly prefer to live in neighbourhoods which are at least 80 per cent white; black Americans prefer
to live in neighbourhoods which are 50 per cent white (which is to
say 50 per cent not white). Given that those classified white make up
over 70 per cent of the population, that leaves vast areas of possibility for all white areas. The age of late twentieth century deregulation
prompted a more widespread segregation, one less formally imposed
than the more formal attempts of the old activist segregation but
produced via the informalities of private preference schemes.

Nancy Denton (1994) has demonstrated the debilitating effects of
such segregation thus. Take a city, not unrealistically, that is 25 per
cent black or Latino with a white poverty rate of 10 per cent and a
black or Latino poverty rate of 20 per cent. Absent segregation, the
neighbourhood poverty rate is 12.5 per cent (whites make up three-
quarters of the population). Where segregation is complete, the
neighbourhod poverty rate for blacks or Latinos becomes 20 per
cent. Where class segregation intersects, the multiplier effect on the
neighbourhood poverty rate of poor blacks or Latinos doubles it to
40 per cent. In the face of economic downturns, the black or Latino
poverty rate jumps from 20 to 30 per cent. The black or Latino
neighbourhood poverty rate then would double to 60 per cent. That
means almost two-thirds of the people in the black or Latino neighbourhood would live in poverty. The same logic applies to predominantly segregated towns or cities. This perhaps is a major
underlying reason why, according to a *Los Angeles Times* report,

two-thirds of new immigrants to the United States claim to be 'white' on the US census no matter what their ethnoracial background. White, it turns out, is thought to identify what it means to be American, with the assimilative logic of 'fitting in', that is, with opportunity and access, with getting ahead and succeeding. If California is the leading edge of trends in the United States, the desert communities stretching from east of Los Angeles to the Arizona border exemplify these divides. The areas west of Palm Springs are home to retired whites living in gated communities on artificial lakes spending their days on golf courses kept green by water piped in from the Colorado River dividing California from Arizona. East of Palm Springs, the terrain dries quickly into dusty desert sand, garbage dumps, toxic sewage cesspools, and is home to a population overwhelmingly of Mexican immigrants not yet citizens, barely out of their teens and speaking little if any English whose drastically devalued labour makes possible the lifestyle of those to the West.

Prompted by a mix of fear, restricting potential competition, and cementing power, whites could enthusiastically embrace the ideological shift at the middle of the last century from assimilation to pluralism. Pluralism is experienced as the commitment not only to different histories, cultural values, and practices but also to the ideological cliché of 'live and let live'. This made conceivable and legitimated contrasting urban conditions, and by the same token the abandonment of certain city spaces. The libertarian licence to 'live and let live' is stressed so long as one does not get in the way of institutionalized Americanization, at home or abroad. Racial Americanization in this context includes nominal commitment to liberty, individualism, market economies, private property, and profit, but also historical denial of or disregard for others' suffering and concerns, of one's own privilege and self-assertion.

Old segregationist racism, from post-Reconstruction to *Brown* (1954), thus was an *activist* segregation produced for the most part by an active intervention in politics, economics, law, and culture self-consciously designed to produce segregated city, town, and neighbourhood spaces. To combat this activism, the Civil Rights Movement likewise found itself called to action in every dimension. The period from post-Second World War to the 1970s, by contrast, was one of tension and contradiction, promise and projection, expectation and elevation, denial and dashed hope. It was a period of desegregating commitment and the seeds of a resegregating mobilization. The logic of the old segregation supposedly was swept aside—only to be replaced by the whisper of the new, the subtle and silent, the informal and insidious. This newly expressed segregation, the newly privatized segregation at the heart of what I am characterizing as the model of racial Americanization, is one no longer activist (at least at home) but conservative, a segregation in the literal sense conservationist.

Racial Americanization thus proceeds not simply by reducing the social to the preferential, the state to (in)civil society. Preferences are not expressed, enacted, and experienced in a political and institutional vacuum. Rather, public spheres—and the state especially—structure the conditions of possibility in which choices are to be made, preferences pushed, and indeed in some cases punished. State structures channel, shape, and mould both the boundaries and terrain of choice-making and implication; and preferences expressed and enacted reinforce existing state formation even as inflecting and colouring them.

This conservationist segregation, the model of *racial Americanization*, proceeds by undoing the laws, rules, and norms of expectation the Civil Rights Movement was able to effect, attacking them as unconstitutional, as the only sort of racial discrimination with which we should be concerned today! Racial Americanization embraces *race neutrality* even as it licenses 'limited' racial profiling for purposes of security maintenance, targeted policing, and medical research as legitimate for combating the moral panics of terror, socially or naturally initiated. In the absence of the Civil Rights spirit, and now in its active undoing, accordingly, the present period *conserves* (and deepens) the hold of racial preference schemes historically produced *as if they were the nature of things*. So racial Americanization is produced by a mix of doing nothing special, nothing beyond being guided by the presumptive laws of the market, the determinations of the majority's personal preferences, and the silencing of all racial reference with the exception of racial profiling for purported purposes of crime and terror control. This silencing fails to distinguish between exclusionary racist designs and practices, on the one hand, and redressive or ameliorative racial interventions, on the other, reducing the latter to the former as the only contemporary racist expressions worth worrying about. The libertarian pluralist motto of 'live and let live' at once licenses a surplus of possibility and opportunity for the affording few at the expense of the impoverished many. It might more accurately be replaced with the New Hampshire state motto, 'live free or die,' implying that those who cannot afford the freedom will be left to perish. Histories forgotten, activist interventions restricted (save for pointed exceptions), the racial status quo (re)fixed in place, at home and now increasingly abroad.

In this mode, the current commitment by fundamentalist fiscal radicals to defund social programmes such as education, health care, popular culture, and the arts through extreme forms of tax reduction while increasing military and prison budgets brings public funding to the point of bankruptcy. And as with personal or corporate bankruptcy, it forces a radical restructuring of public programming and state governmentality. The immediate implication is to redistribute wealth upwards with the social effect not that social spending ends completely but that in being redirected into private hands it is fashioned by the social and political interests of those with capital. So private (toll) roads, the recent emergence of private electrical grids in the face of blackouts, privatization of funding for radio stations, policing functions (at least supplementally), certainly schools and in some instances such as Philadelphia entire school districts, hospitals, and universities (even public ones) are thrown increasingly into the hands—and so at the discretion of—those who can afford and choose to support them. The effect is not that all funding support for public programming ends but that funding for almost anything other than explicit behavioural control programmes becomes pointedly privatized, thus directed by and so serving the supposed interests of the wealthy with disposable income or investment capital.

Now the elevated factions of social class in a racial state like the United States have traditionally been white, or more precisely representing the interests of those occupying the structural class position of whiteness (and men). The US Census Bureau reports that in 2000 the top 5 per cent of white wage earners received wages almost double those of the top 5 per cent of black wage earners. Unsurprisingly, the largest contributors by far to political campaigns are white men. Under this mandate of radical privatization, funded institutions, programmes, and activities accordingly become dramatically less diverse both in their programming, scope, and commitments, and notably, in their employment patterns. Hence, the fundamentalist conservative outrage expressed by the likes of Abigail Thernstrom, Ward Connoly, Linda Chavez, and the Center for Individual Rights regarding the Supreme Court's recent upholding in *Grutter v. Bollinger* (2003) of law schools' limited affirmative action programmes for the sake of maintaining a diverse student body. Neoconservative critics committed to a 'race-free' America (note, not *racist* free) have blasted the diversity commitments of the Court's majority as 'tortured' (Ward Connoly), as 'diversity drivel'

(Michael Greve), and discriminatory (Linda Chavez), indeed, even 'racist' (Abigail Thernstrom). If it is no longer possible to restrict demographic diversity, the culture wars can be won by defunding progressive cultural commitments, by shrinking the cultural horizons of heterogeneity.

Implicit in this model of *racial Americanization* thus is a set of barely stated assumptions, its circle of presuppositions. First, homogenized apartness is taken as the deracialized norm, the assumed, the natural, the given. Integration, or at least desegregation, comes over as unnatural, literally absurd, and irrational in the prevailing order of things, requiring intervention by the state at the cost of liberty (the freedom to choose where one lives or is educated, who one hires or works with, where one hangs out, worships, or may be laid to rest). Second, standards are represented mainly as white, that is, those associated with the structure of whiteness, which are assumed as the norm, as the criteria of judgement, as representing excellence—as what everyone else should aspire to. Third, whites are projected as the real victims of anti-racist excess (of leftist anti-racist racism, of political correctness, of liberal soft-headedness, of the ideology of egalitarianism). And finally, those committed to affirmative action, those against the undoing of anti-racist protections and for vigorously heterogeneous public culture, are chided by the agents of rational choice and unfettered individual preference—by racial americanists, in other words—as the cultural elites (the very terms Bob Dole used to knock Democrats in his acceptance speech for the Republican nomination in the 1998 Presidential election), out of touch with the 'real' concerns and interests of real, everyday, working—that is, street wary and weary white—people.

But racial Americanization is not simply a movement looking to local conditions. Where it is self-conscious, racial Americanization has come to combine domestic with foreign design. In the wake of 9/11, Americanization became exportable to those ethnoracially conceived countries or (sub)continents deemed to threaten its security. The conservationism of domestic racial Americanization has been supplemented by an activist agenda regarding externalities, one that has redounded on the fragilities of the domestic mandate in unsettling ways. Domestically, as we have seen, the commitment is supposed to be homogenizing racelessness as the rejection of 'diversity drivel', where the civilizing standards are those of heteronormative, homogenizing whiteness. By extension, ethnoracial rationalization as civilizational superiority is readily invoked in the war on terror and exported as the neolibertarian imposition of 'living free.' Living free means buying (into) the American dream: privatizing (i.e. corporatizing) national industries, cut-throat competitiveness, a culture of possessive individualism, the freedom to choose (ultimately to starve), of unsettling the status quo and putting in place US-friendly puppets. The foreign extension of racial Americanization returns racial configuration to externalities internalized, to race as the outside threat of heterogeneous diversity, as the perceived activist need to reinvent a segregationist logic on an ethnonationalized global scale. Rogue states, those premodern avatars of repressive unfreedom or chaotic anarchy, are the new targets of opportunity. Until the American Dream of 'living free' is internalized in those civilizational places most resistant to it—notably societies seen to be ordered by the terrors of assertive Islam—they need to be quarantined, segregated into containable and controllable cantons, movement of human and economic capital to and from them constrained and conditioned, filtered and sterilized lest they infect the land of modern liberty.

Muslims are the new niggers of this globalizing racial Americanization. And given that transnational flows are less readily containable and conditioned than they were a century ago, this newly necessitated activism has redounded back on the American 'homeland' (how much more an ironically inverted historical invocation of racially conceived place can one get?). The circulation of terror today knows no borders or boundaries. The dictates of national security have been internalized in the form of 'homeland security', at once identifying the transnational uncontainability of an ethnoracially conceived people elsewhere (Muslims everywhere, all two billion, worldwide) into a more strategically manageable grouping (Arabs), geographically locatable in a single, if extended, region (the Middle East). The transmutations of geostrategic national and localized homeland securities into each other have a double dictate: on one hand, wherever they might be, the terrorists must be eradicated, no matter the collateral damage, or failing that at least kept at bay (though given the need to protect global interests, American presence in any bay has become a vulnerable target). Collateral damage, as Mahmood Mamdani has pointed out, is 'not an unfortunate byproduct of war; it was the very point' ... of terrorizing the general population into submission, a logic destined to bite back the hand that feeds it, as the Iraqi debacle of 'Operation Enduring Freedom' is illustrating on a daily basis. That freedom is to be 'endured' reveals something of the ironies at work here. It reveals, on the other hand, that the uncivil must be civilized, educated where at all possible in the virtues of the American way, all the while keeping them at arm's length lest they bite back, which they invariably do. The logic of domination, of enduring freedom, dictates it.

This ambivalence between embracing and distancing, between paternalistic rule and the segregative security state, is mirrored by the ambivalence towards racial profiling. Prior to 9/11, racial profiling in the United States especially by the police was being rolled back in the face of widespread public consensus that it was unworkable and unjust. Post-9/11, public opinion had swung dramatically, 70 per cent now supporting profiling as a means to effect security in the homeland. One-third of people polled in the United States responded that all Arab Americans ought to be interned as a bulwark against potential terrorism. Think of it: sixty years after the Second World War, every third non-Arab American one might come across in a random public place in America wants to round up their Arab American compatriots in a concentration camp. Paul Gilroy is right at least in this: the resonances of fascism die hard. President Bush's executive order clarifying his administration's policy on racial profiling seeks to capitalize on these tensions. Banning profiling by federal law enforcement agents for 'routine law enforcement investigations', the order nevertheless enables the use of race and ethnicity in 'national security' (including all border) considerations as well as in cases where 'trustworthy information' exists identifying specific criminal activity or membership of a criminal organization. So while police cannot target a neighbourhood because of its racial composition, border patrols can stop a person on the basis of a racial profile, race can be used to 'identify terrorist threats, and stop potential catastrophic attacks', and federal agents can stop racially identified suspects in a particular crime where they claim to have clear evidence that the perpetrator fits the racial profile. Clearly, this executive order on racial profiling will have no diminishing effect on the racially driven rates of incarceration in America where people of colour, barely totalling 30 per cent of the general population, make up more than 70 per cent of the spiralling prison population. Racially driven incarceration, in fact, is a cornerstone of the logic of born again segregation. The almost random rounding up of Arabs is a predictable extension of this logic. The president's profiling policy thus exemplifies the logic of racial Americanization perfectly well: appear to strike racial reference from formal public dictate while endorsing its covert extension, in private and public interactions, especially in cases of national security.

In terms of the institutionalization and reproduction of racial Americanization, these new forms of segregation have managed to *informalize* what used to be formally produced, both to *realize* and *virtualize* segregative exclusions. Race continues to define, globally as domestically, where one can go, what one can do, how one is seen and treated, one's social, economic, political, legal, and cultural, in short, one's daily experience. Global circulation, like local city space, is increasingly contradictory: as there is greater heterogeneity and multiplicity so segregation is refined; as visible openness and accessibility are enlarged exclusionary totalization is extended; as interaction is increased access is monitored, traversal policed, intercourse surveilled. As boundaries and borders become more permeable, they are refixed in the imaginary, shifting from the visible to the virtual, from the formalized to the experiential, from the legal to the cultural at a time when the cultural, economically and socially, has become dominant.

National security has become the abiding insomnia of American paranoia. Where segregation has been privatized along with much else in American life, its logic has come to dominate United States foreign policy. Segregation was never about the complete dislocation of one racially conceived group from another, a final solution of another sort, so much as it was conceived as a logic of ongoing control. Blacks were to be externalized from the social life of whiteness for all purposes other than menial services, demeaning labour, and sometimes sexual experimentation or satisfaction. The logic in the case of the Middle East, and indeed now Africa, is of the same order. We will interact with you only insofar and for as long as you service national interests. But the history of segregating others reveals that it necessarily entails more or less extensively isolating oneself. Hence the lure to whites of Harlem at the heights of segregating America or of Sophiatown or District Six in apartheid South Africa. Racial Americanization is about unilateral Americanism, a new global politics of going it alone because, in elevating oneself above all others, one is reduced to the paranoidly assertive insecurity of rendering oneself too sensitive to touch, thus literally untouchable. Targets of opportunity turn on their paternalists, once they figure out there are no free opportunities. This shrivelling of possibility reduces the plaintive cry of freedom to turning the self-proclaimed father figure of America into targets. Racial Americanization externalized is the fuel of terrorism internalized.

NOTE

1. David Theo Goldberg (2006) *The Death of Race* (Oxford: Basil Blackwell).

REFERENCES

Brown v. Board of Education, 347 U.S. 483 (1954) U.S. Supreme Court.

Brown, M. et al. (2003) *Whitewashing Race: The Myth of a Colorblind Society.* Berkeley: University of California Press.

Denton, N. (1994) 'Residential Segregation: Challenge to White America'. *Journal of Intergroup Relations*, XXI (2): 19–35.

Dudziak, M. (1995) 'Foreign Policy and Desegregation' in R. Delgado (ed.), *Critical Legal Studies*. Philadelphia: Temple University Press.

Fiss, O. (2003) *A Way Out: America's Ghettos and the Legacy of Racism.* Princeton: Princeton University Press.

Grutter v. Bollinger et al. No. 02-241. Argued April 1, 2003; decided June 23, 2003. U.S. Supreme Court.

Gumbel, A. (2003) 'Pentagon Targets Latinos and Mexicans to Man the Front Lines in War on Terror'. *Independent.* London, 10 September.

Hirsch, A. (1993) 'With or Without Jim Crow: Black Residential Segregation in the United States' in A. Hirsch and R. Mohl (eds.), *Urban Policy in Twentieth Century America.* New Brunswick, NJ: Rutgers University Press, pp. 65–99.

Los Angeles Times (2002) 'The Great White Influx', July 31, p. 1.

Massey, D. and Denton, N. (1993) *American Apartheid: Segregation and the Making of the Underclass.* Cambridge, MA: Harvard University Press.

——and Hajnal, Z. (1995) 'The Changing Geographic Structure of Black–White Segregation in the United States'. *Social Science Quarterly,* 76 (3): 527–42.

'The Michigan Decisions' (2003) *The Chronicle Review, Chronicle of Higher Education.* July 4, pp. 10–12.

Mohl, R. (1993) 'Shifting Patterns of American Urban Policy since 1900' in A. Hirsch and R. Mohl (eds.), *Urban Policy in Twentieth Century America.* New Brunswick, NJ: Rutgers University Press, pp. 1–45.

CHAPTER 5

Remembered Racialization: Young People and Positioning in Differential Understandings

Ann Phoenix

Fanon (1967*a,b*) documents how colonizers and colonized are inextricably linked in the relational process of racialization. According to Fanon, the category 'white' depends for its stability on its negation, 'black'. Neither exists without the other. Historically, both come into being with imperial conquest and the colonizer/ colonized relationship is normalized in the psyche. These ideas (of process, relationality, psychological and social impact) have sedimented into the academic discourses of those who study 'race' and ethnicity (e.g. Omi and Winant 1986; Miles 1989; Brah 1996; Lewis 2000; Solomos and Back 2000), who emphasize that race is socially constructed, involves power relations, and becomes socially significant through social, economic, cultural, and psychological processes.

Yet, as the term 'racialization' has become more widely used, it is often unclear what processes are being invoked or that relationality is at the heart of the process. Thus, while the diversity of uses of the term are not in themselves problematic (and are arguably a welcome advance on other ways of theorizing race and ethnicity) there is a need to specify the ways in which it is employed and to clarify what it adds to the understanding of everyday practices. This is particularly the case since the idea of race has long been critiqued (e.g. Banton 1977), 'raciology' and 'compulsory raciality' have been challenged (Gilroy 2000), and yet 'post-race' thinking has to engage with the ubiquity and durability of racisms (Rattansi 1992; Ali 2003). Racialization as a concept can, arguably, accommodate these apparently contradictory perspectives.

This chapter uses a study of the social identities of black, white, and mixed-parentage young people's social identities to examine young people's accounts of the first time they became aware of their colour. Those accounts contribute to a non-essentializing understanding of racialization and demonstrate the utility of the concept of racialization in providing a more nuanced and dynamic picture than the concept of race does. This is because young people who are constructed as belonging to the same race report different experiences of becoming conscious of race and have varied interpretations of their experiences. They can thus be said to be differentially racialized both within and between socially constructed races. Such differences highlight the significance of Fanon's theorization of racialization as involving psychic as well as social processes since the differential racialization of young people constructed as belonging to the same race arises both from their varied experiences (and so different histories) as well as different emotional investments in their positioning in relation to race. Fanon's approach fits with psychosocial approaches which are concerned with both psychic and social processes and so demonstrate how different people interpret the same events differently depending on their current as well as past social positioning (e.g. Hollway and Jefferson 2000). Interpretation is thus central to the construction of identities. Middleton and Hewitt (1999), for example, suggest that identities are accomplished as part of the social practice of remembering. Far from being a neutral process, psychologists and those engaged in psychosocial research recognize that memory changes over time, is selective and (re)constructed—often for emotional reasons (Brace and Roth 2002).

The chapter focuses on the young people's retrospective accounts of whether they recall first becoming conscious of colour and/or racism and, if so, what led to that new consciousness. It would, however, negate the conceptualization of racialization as a process if one time point were to be privileged as the only key to understanding a process. Such an approach would also ignore notions of lifelong development and of identities as continually negotiated and produced. Instead, therefore, the focus here is on such memories as part of the lifelong process of racialization that demonstrates relationality and gives insight into the processes involved. It is not being suggested that young people's accounts document the 'reality' of their first experiences related to colour and/or racism (remembered sometimes years later). However, the retrospective construction of a founding moment of racialized consciousness in itself constitutes a resource, around and against which narratives of racialized identities can be articulated. Omi and Winant (1986) suggest that racialization signifies the extension of 'racial meaning' to the previously 'racially unclassified'. The chapter examines this extension at the microlevel of young people's identities.

A focus on the earliest memories of awareness of colour can demonstrate the utility of the concept of racialization by showing that these are socially produced, relational, and assume significance because racialization is a continuous process. In the examples provided below, whether or not young people identify particular experiences (which may have been puzzling and upsetting at the time) as significant is dependent on their subsequent experiences and understandings. The chapter first discusses the concept of positioning and then briefly describes the study that informs the chapter before examining young people's recollections of their first experiences of racialization.

Analysing Positioning

Increasingly, researchers interested in identities and subjectivities are using the notion of 'positioning' to conduct analyses that recognize that people are not fixed in social locations (as suggested by the metaphor of role) (Davies and Harré 1990). Instead, the concept of positioning constructs people as engaging in dynamic social relationships in which each participant creates and makes available positions for themselves and others to take up, ignore, or resist. Positioning theory provides a way to capture both continuous personal identity and discontinuous personal diversity. In order to do this, it focuses particularly on the exchanges produced in conversation. 'It is one and the same person who is variously positioned in a conversation. Yet as variously positioned we may want to say that that very same person experiences and displays that aspect of self that is involved in the continuity of a multiplicity of selves' (Davies and Harré 1990). People position themselves and others as they explain, defend, abandon, or entrench their own positions and resist or take up the positions others produce for them to occupy (van Langenhove and Harré 1999).

Positions only become 'subject positions' if people take up a particular position as their own—whether for a moment or for longer periods. In other words, people make particular positions their own through repeatedly taking up particular positions in conversations. Once they have done this, they see the world from that perspective and are more likely to act in accord with it, be emotionally invested in it, and take on the moral responsibilities, rights, and duties with which it is associated. The taking up of particular positions is part of their 'identity projects'—that is, part of the process of trying to become who/what they envisage themselves as being (Foucault 1977).

Being a 'subject', with the emotions and self-reflection that this entails, results from all the subject positions that someone experiences and their history of having been in multiple positions and engaged in different forms of discourse (Davies and Harré 1990). Of course, this leaves open the question of how and why we take on particular subject positions. Althusser (1971) used the concept of interpellation to mean the way in which we come to be 'hailed' by particular discourses in the process of being constituted into cultural/social subjects (Brah 1999). Woodward (1997) suggests that interpellation can explain the process by which we are recruited into subject positions by recognizing ourselves—'yes, that's me'—through an unconscious process that has potential for explaining the situatedness of subjectivity and positioning. Davies and Harré (1990) also argue that positioning has unconscious elements in that people are not always conscious of the positions that they set up for themselves and others, or of the subject positions they take up.

The accounts people give allow insights into their identity projects and how they are positioning themselves. Riessman (1993, 2001) suggests that an important impetus for our accounts is to justify ourselves. Stories are told in particular ways for that purpose. Conversations, however, are not only interactions with other people who are present. The stories we tell ourselves equally serve to position ourselves and others. Similarly, conversations are not asocial, but are always socially located so that their complexity includes positioning in relation to the social context as well as interpersonally. Positioning is always, then, psychosocial—being necessarily relational and both social and personal. In other words, it always involves negotiation between the positions that other people expect someone to take up and what they do take up. It follows then that the storylines that develop in conversation can produce a social order that allows the claiming of particular identities, specific ways of negotiating the social world, and anticipations of future identities (Wetherell 2003). For this reason, many theorists now see identities and subjectivities as locally situated, accomplished in social interaction, and performative (Riessman 2001).

There is a general agreement that the local accomplishment of positioning means that each interactional situation allows the possibility of different positioning. This is partly because people will have experiences of various other people attempting to position them in very different ways. Since people are not 'social dopes' or ciphers, but practised at social interaction, each interaction allows opportunities for taking up, ignoring, or resisting particular positions. This opens up the possibility of contradictions in positioning with people being positioned differently in different interactions and, sometimes, at different points in the same interaction. It also means that people sometimes find themselves in 'troubled' subject positions as they negotiate conversations (Wetherell 1998).

Racialization and positioning are complementary and mutually reinforcing theoretical concepts in that racialization can be seen as positioning in relation to race. According to positioning theory, what race, ethnicity, nationality, or religion mean for identity is not fixed, but flexible, shifting, and contested. The spatial metaphor of position allows recognition of flexibility (rather than fixity) in location and the possibility of negotiating (including accepting and contesting) the ways in which people are positioned by others and position themselves in relation to discourses of race. Racialization, in turn, involves differential positioning. A consideration of young people's retrospective accounts of racialization may thus help to illuminate how they construct subject positions and identities that are part of the process of becoming racialized and that allow them to negotiate current experiences of racialization.

There is ample evidence that young people are well aware of how they are positioned within society. For example, Archer and Yamashita (2003) found that working class fifteen- and sixteen-year-old Londoners who were not doing well at school incorporated the notion that they were 'not good enough' and that they 'knew their limits' into their identities. The counterpart of that is that those who are doing well include in their identities aspirations for the future that are not limited. Similarly, in the United States, Laura Abrams (2003) found that 15–18-year-old young women were acutely aware of women's subordinate social position, but their experiences and their strategies for dealing with this varied according to whether they went to a wealthy, suburban school in a white community or a working class, urban, ethnically mixed school. In a study of young people living in Brixton, London, Caroline Howarth (2002) found that 12–16-year-olds from a range of ethnic groups recognize how they are stereotyped because of the area from which they come and develop a range of strategies to deal with this. Back et al. (1999) and Räthzel and Hieronymus (2000) also found that geography differentiated young people's racialized experiences and identities. In all these examples, young people are demonstrating the importance of relationality—how their strategies for dealing with their positioning of themselves involve comparison with the ways in which others are positioned and their understandings of how those others position them. They also demonstrate that, just as social class and gender (as well as other social positions) intersect to produce multiple positions, so they intersect to produce diverse possibilities of racialized positioning.

The ways in which young people discuss their earliest memories of racialization can, arguably, contribute to an understanding of their positioning by allowing insights into their autobiographical accounts of 'becoming racialized'—a mode of self-fashioning also discussed in this volume by Vron Ware. This chapter complements Ware's chapter in being an analysis of accounts of racialization produced in interview conversations, rather than in published autobiographical accounts. Published accounts present thoughtful, reflexive, and considered retrospective accounts—often of well-worn stories, or stories that are carefully worked out as they are written. However, interviews allow the possibility of making visible negotiations, collusions, contradictions, and contestations as well as the taking up of subject positions and the production of accounts that may not previously have been given about racialization, but are worked out and developed because the questions asked help to generate new accounts.

The rest of the chapter examines how young people negotiated discussions with interviewers about consciousness of colour and the positions they took up in those discussions.

The Study

The data on which this chapter is based come from an interview study jointly conducted with Barbara Tizard on the social identities of 248 14–18-year-old black,[1] white, and mixed-parentage young Londoners, young women and young men from different social classes, who attended fifty-eight schools (twenty-nine state and twenty-nine private).[2] The interviews with the young people were semi-structured and were conducted at school (some of their parents were then interviewed at home). In most cases, black young people were interviewed by one of two black women interviewers (including the author), white young people were interviewed by one of two white interviewers, and just over three quarters of the young people of mixed-parentage were interviewed by two black women, with just under a quarter being interviewed by two white women. The interviews were conducted in the early 1990s, but continue to provide unique insights into the racialization of a large number of young people from diverse backgrounds and a wide variety of schools.

First Consciousness of Colour[3]

It is important to note that eight of the 248 14–18-year-olds interviewed said that they had never been conscious of colour (one black young person, seven white young people, and none of mixed-parentage). While the numbers involved are very small, this raises the question of what it means, given that colour is one of the most visible differences between people, and since studies of very young children would suggest that they are conscious of people's colour by the time that they are about three years old (e.g. Holmes 1995). One possible explanation may be that some children refuse to name or discuss colour because, confusingly, they have been told that it does not matter by adults who take a 'colour-blind' approach and have learned that it is not acceptable, or is painful, to talk about (Williams 1997). Alternatively, van Ausdale and Feagin (2001) found that young children do not necessarily want to discuss race in front of adults. This may well be an early version of the denial of being racist (Billig 1991; van Dijk 1993)—an explanation that may well hold for at least some of the seven white young people who said that they had never been conscious of colour. 'Not noticing' differences forestalls possible accusations of treating people differentially on the basis of colour. In an interview situation, it may result from ways in which identities are accomplished and performed in locally situated, social interaction (Riessman 2001). The first example that follows illuminates the intersubjective processes at work in the interview in which the young woman participant offered her account. She immediately backtracked the moment that she started to admit that she has noticed, but ignored, differences in colour between people.

Q. Can I ask if there was ever a time when you became conscious of people's colour?
A. I don't know, just sort—I never really took much notice. I just sort of take people as they are and just ignored it if they are a di—I've never noticed!
Q. So there was no time when you were conscious at all?
A. No (092; white young woman).

While the young woman above does not produce a narrative of a specific event, this short account demonstrates emotional tone in that she clearly does not want to give the interviewer the idea that she notices colour differences and abruptly interrupts her account when she seems about to do so. The question has certainly touched sensibilities about colour (in the British context relating to black, white, and Asian people) that serve to reveal her defensive anxieties about the issue—in this case, about potentially being positioned by the interviewer as racist. Instead, she takes up a position as so non-racist that she does not notice colour differences.

For the one black young man who said that he had never been conscious of colour, denial of consciousness was related to the production of discourses which suggested that he was not obsessed with issues of colour and felt no need to dwell on them. Here again, the interview as a relational context is likely to have affected the discourses produced in that, while he was interviewed by a black interviewer, the notion that black people have 'chips' on their shoulders constitutes enough of a discursive formation for some young black people to want to defend themselves against a possible charge by an adult whose views they do not know. This may be the product of resistance to what Gunaratnam (2003: 112) identifies as 'assumptions about the inherent centrality of "race" and ethnicity to the identities of minoritised research participants'. Resistance of this kind helps to produce racialized positions as not being defined by 'race'.

Whatever the reasons for a denial of colour consciousness for the seven white young people and the one black young man who produced them, such accounts aimed to empty race of its social meaning through resistance to producing discourses of it. This operates as prolepsis (Billig 1991) in that it defends them in advance from charges of racism or being obsessed with race. These young people produced discourses of themselves as deracialized subjects in a racialized society. Contrary to what appears to be the intended function, such discourses serve to position them as 'protesting too much' in relation to race. They demonstrate relationality both intersubjectively (with the interviewer) and in concert with societal strictures against racism and against sensitivity to noticing racism (for those from minoritized groups).

What do the Young People Mean by Early Consciousness of Colour?

The majority of young people from all three groups that we interviewed (82 per cent) said that they were conscious of people's colour by the time that they went to secondary school at age eleven years. Indeed 60 per cent of the whole sample reported that they had been conscious of colour when they were in infant school—by the time that they were seven years old. However, it was only a minority of the young people who gave accounts indicating that they recalled being conscious of colour before they entered school at four or five years of age.[4] For most of the young people then, their accounts are at odds with work indicating that most children are conscious of race by three years of age (Milner 1983). This may be because of differences in methodology. This study relied on retro-spective accounts and these are known not to produce accurate information on timing of events (Brace and Roth 2002). In addition, memory is a constructive process that works best when memories are rehearsed and discussed (Billig 1999).

The importance of these accounts, however, does not lie in the accuracy of their recall and recounting of the age at which they became conscious of colour. Instead, they indicate when and how the young people constructed themselves as becoming racialized. The sections that follow explore further the different ways in which young people reported that they had come to consciousness of colour and what this means for the understanding of racialization as a relational process as well as differences in the way young people were positioned in relation to race. There were four main ways in which the young people reported that they came to consciousness of colour: 'non-racializing recognition of difference'; 'racialized dis-junction caused by recogniton of numerical minority status'; 'other indirect observations that produced racialized consciousness; and 'racialization through being directly positioned in relation to racism'. The sections that follow focus on two of these: 'non-racializing recognition of difference' and 'racialization through being directly positioned in relation to racism'.

Non-racializing Recognition of Difference

The analyses presented in this chapter are informed by questions that ask the young people when they first became conscious of colour. As in any conversation (including interview conversations) the questions asked affect the terms of the answers produced. In this case, the answers given did not only focus on a black–white binary in that they included black, mixed-parentage, and white people. Nonetheless, the introduction of the notion of colour meant that at this point in the interview (but not others) racialized markers other than colour were not mentioned.

Given that all the young people we interviewed attended schools in or around London, it is not surprising that they had generally seen people of other colours. Since a great deal of effort is often expended in teaching children colour names, it is equally not surprising that some reported that they could 'always' pick out colour differences between people. Thirteen per cent of the young people said that they had 'always known' about colour differences, so that recognition of, or consciousness of, colour was not the result of a specific incident.

Q. When did you first become conscious of people's colour?
A. What do you mean by that?
Q. Any time that you noticed it?
A. Well it's just really they look different. That's all really. It's just never really occurred to me that they're different—that's it (white young man).

As in the account above, some of the young people who did pick an age in early childhood as a time when they recollect first noticing people's colour also discussed this first consciousness as something that had no personal meaning for them. Such accounts indicate a similar performance of not being either racist or too sensitive to race as do the accounts of the eight young people who disclaimed consciousness of colour and are, of course, also produced within the relational context of the interview. So, for example, asked 'When did you first become conscious of people's colour?' the young man above asks for clarification of the question and, when it is rephrased, ends by rebutting the notion that people of different colours from himself are different—a question that has not been asked. This defensive rebuttal of what has not been asked gives a clue that colour is a socially marked issue for him and, as Billig (1991) argues, the norm against racism is so strong that it is necessary for him to position himself as someone who does not assume essential differences between people of different colours.

A quarter (25 per cent; 62) of the young people asked, said that no particular incident had triggered their awareness of colour. Given that they were less likely to have been subject to racist name-calling or other racism, it is perhaps not surprising that white young people were less likely than others to recall an incident that had made them conscious of racism (35 per cent of white young people, 16 per cent, black young people, and 22 per cent of mixed-parentage young people could not recall such an incident). According to these accounts, skin colour was not significant when first consciously noticed.

Q. Okay, if you think back to your childhood, when did you first become conscious of people's colour?

A. I don't know. About—I don't know—I would only kind of notice it if I was—notice it and not kind of think anything of it, just notice it just like I saw a new tree or something and it wouldn't—I wouldn't really—when I kind of—when I was small I wouldn't really attach any significance to it. I would just notice, but I wouldn't think anything of it. I can't actually remember noticing it at all. I can't actually remember a difference from being young and old—and older like now..., (white young man).

A. Um I think it must've been when I was about five. When I did this picture of a white man and a black woman or something. I don't know exactly but two a black and a white person holding hands. I suppose it must have been around then.

Q. Right, so what made you conscious? Was it doing the picture?

A. I suppose it was just purely aesthetic, that some people have dark skins and some people have light skins.

Q. So it was no particular incident or anything that brought it home to you?

A. No.

Q. Right what did you feel when you were first conscious, can you remember?

A. Not really, I just suppose I accepted it. Like some people have brown eyes and some people have blue eyes.

Q. And were you always conscious of colour after that?

A. Not really. I've never been *that* conscious of it (mixed-parentage young woman).

'Non-racializing' here refers to the fact that young people who gave accounts such as that above spoke of their recognition of differences to do with race as socially insignificant—just one of many inconsequential differences between people. Accounts such as those above do important moral-political work in that they allow young people to position themselves as not preoccupied with race and not racist. It is, of course, possible that young people categorized here had neutral feelings about difference. However, the complexity of analysing racialized positioning is indicated in the above example by the emphasis of the mixed-parentage young woman, who does not say 'I have never been conscious of it', but that 'I have never been *that* conscious of it'. Her wording and emphasis supports an interpretation of denial of preoccupation with race since she does not entirely deny that she is conscious of race but uses prolepsis (defends herself in advance) against the charge of being too conscious of it. Paradoxically, non-racializing accounts involve the taking of a racialized position in the denying of race as important.

Racialization Through Being Directly Positioned in
Relation to Racism

Some of the young people reported that their first consciousness of colour involved recognition of being positioned in relation to an episode of racialized discrimination. Some mixed-parentage, black, and white children all reported this but, as with their recognition of being positioned with regard to race (as opposed to consciousness of it that did not include awareness of positioning in relation to it) black and mixed-parentage young people reported different experiences from white young people. For the following white young man, racism was so salient that he positioned himself in relation to it by launching into a discussion of race when asked about his father's feelings about people from a different social class to himself—leading the interviewer to switch to asking questions about consciousness of colour at that point.

A. He doesn't like Indian people. He likes some of them but he don't like the way they—what they are doing over here in this country, what they think they can do—same as my mum I suppose.
Q. When did you first become conscious of people's colours?
A. About the age of seven.
Q. What happened then?
A. I just gone off most Indian people, blacks, just don't like them.
Q. When you were seven what happened? Why...?
A. I just don't like what they are doing over here, staying in the country and getting in the way in the streets and they don't move... (white young man).

An account that addresses the same theme, but takes up an entirely different position is provided by the following young white woman.

I couldn't honestly tell you. My mum said apparently I went through a stage when I was six or seven when I didn't like coloured people, but I can't actually remember that, but apparently I didn't—although I mean there were people around me who were coloured. I didn't make any racial discrimination at all. I just—inside I was a bit wary of them. (white young woman).

These two young white people (both interviewed by a white woman) were asserting that when they were about six or seven years old, they were conscious of not liking black people—that is, of being positioned in opposition to black people. The second account (from the young woman) constructs this as a transient period (two to three months), heralded by nothing that she can remember. The young man, on the other hand, reports a more static picture, saying that he still does not like black or 'Indian' people and that this is consistent with his family's dislike of Indian people.

Neither of these two young people described themselves as having (had) racist feelings towards black people or of *being* racist. The discourse they chose instead, of not liking black people, is arguably a more legitimate one at a time when most people disavow racism (Barker 1981; Billig 1991). Aboud (1988) and Hirschfeld (1996) argue that it is a natural part of cognitive development that white children should be wary of black people up to the age of seven because, for example, of associations of blackness with danger, etc. However, in the study discussed here, very few white young people reported memories consistent with this. The notion that racialization produces a range of possible positions to be occupied or resisted provides more analytical purchase here in that the two white young people quoted above document their inscription into racialized discourses that were self-consciously racist, but indicated different trajectories through the racialization process and, possibly, different family positions.

By contrast, no black or mixed-parentage young people described coming to consciousness of colour *because* they suddenly recognized that they did not like white people. Instead, they gave a variety of examples of incidents that they considered had led them to this consciousness:

Discrimination from Adults

Altogether, 7 per cent of young people (17) said that they became conscious of colour as a result of racism other than name-calling. All but two (both white young people who observed racist incidents that did not involve them) were black or of mixed-parentage.

A. I think in junior school I was aware of it. There were quite a few black children in my junior school, but I remember—I think it was in the second year—I had quite a racist teacher. At the Easter I had been to Jamaica with my parents and family and I remember coming back and we used to have to write in pencil and when I came back, everyone had started writing in pen but you had to like practice in pencil and to show that you were good enough to write in pen. And I remember I was kept back for writing in pen. And also I was very good at maths and I was kept back because—I don't know, but I did have—she was racist, a racist teacher and my mum had to go up and see the headmaster (black young woman, state selective school).

This episode was exceptional in that the very few young black children and children of mixed-parentage who mentioned that they felt their teachers had discriminated against them mainly attended private schools. They reported incidents like being given stereotypical parts to read; having a golliwog placed in an art room; and being called names by teachers. In the above example, it is not at all surprising, given its enormity, that this event marked a turning point in this young woman's understanding of her own racialization.

Some young people explained that they became conscious of colour not through school, but in their neighbourhoods. For example, the following young black man is rare in the sample in claiming that he always knew about colour differences because he was conscious that some of the people on his estate 'did not like black people'. While the example he gives is likely to relate to his recent past in that it was generally when they were of secondary-school age that black boys reported that white women began to demonstrate fear of them on the streets, he nonetheless constructs the process of racialization as lifelong positioning—starting from much earlier in his life.

A. I have always been aware of it. Always—because there is people in my estate that don't like black people.

Q. On your estate? Is that where you have always lived?

A. Yes and they don't really like black people. They don't say it, but they make it sort of obvious that they don't.

Q. Like how?

A. They see you coming and cross the road, or if they see you they grab up their handbag like you are going to thieve them or something. I have got nothing like that in mind. I would never thieve from anybody.

Q. Okay, so you were conscious of that right from when you were small?

A. Yes (black young man).

For the above young black man, racialization may well have become part of his identity project since he reports that he both has always been conscious of colour and has notions of what he is like that resist common constructions of black people in his locality. However, recognition of racialization was no guarantee that it would become part of young people's identity projects. The following quotation, from a black young man, demonstrates this differential racialization in that he acknowledges that colour 'always came up', but his discourse of 'never really thought about it' is explained by his saying that 'it never really bothered me'.

Q. After that, did colour sort of fade from your mind for a while and then come back or was it something that you were always conscious of after that?

A. It always came up around here. I never really thought about it. It never really bothered me (black young man).

While the young man quoted above does not deny the ubiquity of racism, he does eschew its power to define his racialized identity as 'bothered'.

Racial Harassment and Attack

Racial harassment and attack were obviously more serious and dangerous than other forms of racism but, from the young people's accounts, it was thankfully exceptionally rare. Not surprisingly, such accounts were dramatically racializing.

A. I don't know. Just like the way you see people treated as well in a way and like—it's like when we used to live on our old estate and there was these National Front people that used to live opposite us and one day like when they came chasing after me. He was coming after me with a chopper and that.
Q. How old were you then?
A. I was pretty young actually. I was about seven, six or seven (black young man, state boarding school).

Theoretical Understanding of Racism/Anti-Racism

It was equally rare for the process of racialization to be dated from events that produced theoretical understanding of racism. Nonetheless, just as Troyna and Hatcher (1992) found that some white junior school children were avowedly anti-racist, a few young people in this study gave accounts that indicated that they became consciously racialized through gaining theoretical understandings of racism and/or anti-racism. One white young woman mentioned that she became conscious of race because she had a very anti-racist friend in primary school.

A. When I was seven or something.
Q. What in particular happened?
A. Well, I had this friend who was very very anti-racism you know. She thought that blacks and whites should be equal and things like that ... And I didn't really think of it before. And then when I saw things on the news about it—that was the only time I really thought about racism anyway (white young woman, independent school).

Although this example is unusual, it demonstrates that some young white people position themselves or others as having been opposed to racism since early in childhood and suggests that this influences other children. The espousal of anti-racist discourses meant that black, mixed-parentage, and white children were not *necessarily* divided from each other in the process of racialization by their experiences, and discourses, of race and racism.

Theoretical understanding of racism and the possibility of being positioned against it is likely to be extremely rare in young children, but another young person (a black young man) reported that he first became conscious of race when he went to primary school because he was told about racial oppression in various countries.

A. Um, when I—there used to be—most of the time when I started primary school. They used to tell—tell you about slavery in the 1960s in America, um racism, Ku Klux Klan and that's when I really got conscious of colour. Then South Africa.
Q. How did you feel when you first became conscious of colour in primary school?
A. Well, I hated it...(black young man).

It must not be assumed that attempts to introduce a theoretical understanding of racism in primary school necessarily either led to greater understanding or was much appreciated by children. One young white woman, for example, reported resentment that people who came into the school to talk about racism had separated black children and white children to different sides of the hall. She complained that she considered that this was racist in itself. From her account, it produced racialization in emphasizing difference in relation to children of other colours and a positioning of herself in opposition to anti-racism.

Name-calling Leading to Consciousness of Racism

Racialized name-calling can be viewed as a liminal event in relation to awareness of colour and awareness of racism. On the one hand, it can be used (and taken) as a joke (Back 1996) or as an interactional strategy devoid of racist intent (Troyna and Hatcher 1992). On the other hand, it can signal racist intent. As such, it positions young people with regard to racism, not simply race or colour.

It was more common for young people who mentioned that a specific incident had led them to become conscious of race to cite an incident of name-calling than to cite anything else. Just under half of the young people of mixed-parentage (46 per cent) and a third of black young people (31 per cent) identified name-calling as leading to their consciousness of colour (cf. two white young people). This provides a further indication of how black and white young people were generally differentiated in the processes of racialization.

For the black and the mixed-parentage young people, name-calling in childhood led to consciousness of racism (although they did not necessarily call it that) and so of how they were positioned in relation to racism. It thus led to awareness not just of being positioned in relation to race, but to consciousness of the social significance of race.

In a lifecourse perspective, name-calling could lead to a turning point in young people's racialized careers because it led to race acquiring emotionally marked social significance.

A. About six, five... Oh I was in (other school) when I was six and then I—you know, people used to call me names and I asked my mum what that meant and they told me. That's what I really found out—and I wondered, you know—about the different colours.
Q. What did you feel...?
A. I felt a bit annoyed and then I thought that it didn't make any difference. You know, it wasn't bad.
Q. Were you always conscious of colour after that?
A. Yes (mixed-parentage young man).

Concluding Thoughts: Negotiating the Process of Racialized Positioning

The young people interviewed in the study reported here were colour differentiated according to whether they reported that they stayed conscious of colour after first becoming aware of it. Fewer white young people than black or mixed-parentage young people reported an incident that had made them conscious of colour. If, however, they did report such an incident, white young people were *slightly* more likely than black young people to say that they always remained conscious of colour afterwards (two-thirds of white young people compared with three-fifths of mixed-parentage young people and half of black young people). At first sight this seems paradoxical. However, it must be remembered that more white young people had no such incident to report and so less than half of the sample of white young people considered this question relevant to them. Those who did consider it relevant may thus be unusual. In addition, since many black and mixed-parentage young people said that the incident that led to their first consciousness of colour was emotionally upsetting, their answers may indicate that they did not continue to feel as emotionally upset or angry as initially they had been.

Whatever the explanation the fact that a substantial minority of mixed-parentage, black, and white young people said that they did not continue to be conscious of colour after first becoming aware of it, alerts us to the psychosocial complexity of how racialized positioning becomes part of young people's identity projects or is eschewed. Being able, retrospectively, to relate an experience that made them conscious of race, even where they claim recognition of racialization, is no guarantee that racialization will straightforwardly become part of young people's identity projects.

According to positioning theory, language provides a key site for negotiating the multiple positions that are made available (by people themselves and others) in interactions (Davies and Harré 1990) and for people to make particular positions their own through repeatedly taking them up as part of their 'identity projects' (Foucault 1977). Many of the young people's accounts in this study equally allow insights into how language can facilitate the refusal of particular identity projects and the positioning associated with them.

Young people's reports of their experiences of 'race' and racism demonstrate that they are positioned unequally with respect to racialized power relations. All the young people in the study reported here were racialized, but in different ways (both within and between colour groups). For many black and mixed-parentage young people the first memory of awareness of racism centred on being the object of racialized name-calling. This was generally reported to be a shocking and painful experience that marked a turning point in their way of looking at the world. In the white young people's retrospective accounts, there was usually no mention of a specific incident which had jolted them into consciousness of colour. Their positioning frequently demonstrated Billig's (1991) 'norm against racism' in that their accounts could be seen to be structured in ways that served to defend them against potential charges of racism.

A focus on the earliest memories of awareness of colour demonstrates Omi and Winant's (1986) notion that racialization signifies the extension of racial meaning to the previously racially unclassified. It also demonstrates the analytic purchase of the concept of racialization by showing that these are socially produced, relational, and assume significance because racialization is a continuous process of positioning and identity construction. This dynamism is not captured in the concept of race.

NOTES

1. This study was particularly concerned to address issues of identity relevant to the 'transracial adoption' debate. As a result, black here was confined to young people of African descent with two black parents of African descent. The term

'mixed-parentage' was used to refer to people who, in the study described here, have one black and one white parent. The racialized categorizations applied to the young people in the study were ones they agreed with, even if, particularly for those of mixed-parentage, they used other nomenclature to refer to themselves or, particularly for white young people, said that they did not use any colour terms to refer to themselves.

2. In Britain, private schools are fee-paying schools and state schools are free to the recipients. Those parents who choose private schools for their children generally do so because they tend more reliably to produce higher levels of attainment than do state schools.

3. At this point in the interview it was left open for the participants to discuss what they understood by the questions relating to consciousness of colour. In other parts of the study, the young people were asked about whiteness as well as blackness, mixed-parentage, and people of other ethnicities.

4. The figures for this were 16% overall (40); 24 % mixed (14); 19 % black (16); and 10% (10) of white young people.

REFERENCES

Aboud, F. (1988) *Children and Prejudice*. London: Basil Blackwell.

Abrams, L. (2003) 'Contextual Variations in Young Women's Gender Identity Negotiations'. *Psychology of Women Quarterly*, 27: 64–74.

Ali, S. (2003) *Mixed-Race, Post-Race: Gender, New Ethinicities and Cultural Practices*. Oxford: Berg.

Althusser, L. (1971) 'Ideology and Ideological State Apparatuses: Notes Toward an Investigation', Translated by Ben Brewster, in L. Althusser (ed.), *Lenin and Philosophy and Other Essays*. London: New Left Books, pp. 121–73.

Archer, L. and Yamashita, H. (2003) ' "Knowing their limits"? Identities, Inequalities and Inner City School Leavers' Post-16 aspirations'. *Journal of Education Policy*, 18 (1): 53–69.

Back, L. (1996) *New Ethnicities and Urban Culture*. London: UCL Press.

——Keith, M., and Cohen, P. (1999) *Between Home and Belonging: Critical Ethnographies of Race, Place and Identity. Finding the Way Home*. Working Paper 2, Centre for Urban and Community Research and the New Ethnicities Unit, London.

Banton, M. (1977) *The Idea of Race*. London: Tavistock.

Barker, M. (1981) *New Racism: Conservatives and the Ideology of the Tribe*. London: Junction Books.

Billig, M. (1991) *Ideology and Opinions*. London: Sage.

——(1999) *Freudian Repression: Conversation Creating the Unconscious*. Cambridge: Cambridge University Press.

Brace, N. and Roth, I. (2002) 'Memory Structure, Process and Skills', in D. Miell, A. Phoenix, and K. Thomas (eds.), *Mapping Psychology*. Milton Keynes: Open University.

Brah, A. (1996) *Cartographies of Diaspora*. London: Routledge.

——(1999) 'The scent of memory: "Strangers," "Our own" and "Others"'. *Feminist Review*, 60: 4–25.

Butler, J. (1993) *Bodies that Matter*. New York: Routledge.

Davies, B. and Harré, R. (1990) 'Positioning: The Discursive Production of Selves'. *Journal for the Theory of Social Behaviour*, 20 (1): 43–63.

Fanon, F. (1967*a*) *Black Skin, White Masks*. New York: Grove.

Fanon, F. (1967*b*) *The Wretched of the Earth*. Harmondsworth: Penguin.

Foucault, M. (1977) *Discipline and Punish*. London: Allen Lane.

Gilroy, P. (2000) *Against Race: Imagining Political Culture Beyond the Color Line*. Cambridge, MA: Harvard University Press.

Gunaratnam, Y. (2003) *Researching 'Race' and Ethnicity: Methods, Knowledge and Power*. London: Sage.

Hirschfeld, L. A. (1996) *Race in the Making: Cognition, Culture, and the Child's Construction of Human Kinds*. Cambridge, MA: MIT Press.

Holloway, W. and Jefferson, T. (2000) *Doing Qualitative Research Differently*. London: Sage.

Holmes, R. (1995) *How Young Children Perceive Race*. Thousand Oaks, CA: Sage.

Howarth, C. (2002) 'So, you're from Brixton?: The Struggle for Recognition and Esteem in a Stigmatized Community'. *Ethnicities*, 2 (2): 237–60.

Lewis, G. (2000) *'Race', Gender, Social Welfare*. Cambridge: Polity.

Middleton, D. and Hewitt, H. (1999) 'Remembering as Social Practice: Identity and Life Story Work in Transitions of Care for People with Profound Learning Disabilities'. *Narrative Inquiry*, 9 (1): 97–121.

Miles, R. (1989) *Racism*. London: Routledge.

Milner, D. (1983) *Children and Race: Ten Years On*. London: Ward Lock Educational.

Omi, M. and Winant, H. (1986) *Racial Formation in the United States: From the 1960s to the 1980s*. New York: Routledge.

Räthzel, N. and Hieronymus, A. (2000) 'The Hamburg Story: The Everyday Lives of Young People in a German Metropolis', in *Finding the Way Home*, Working Paper 6, Centre for New Ethnicities Research, University of East London.

Rattansi, A. (1992) 'Changing the Subject? Racism, Culture and Education', in J. Donald and A. Rattansi (eds.), *'Race', Culture and Difference*. London: Sage.

Riessman, C. K. (1993) *Narrative Analysis*. London: Sage.

——(2001) 'Positioning Gender Identity in Narratives of Infertility: South Indian Women's Lives in Context', in M. C. Inhorn and F. van Balen (eds.), *Infertility around the Globe*. Berkeley: University of California Press.

Solomos, J. and Back, L. (eds.) (2000) *Theories of Race and Racism: A Reader*. London: Routledge.

Troyna, B. and Hatcher, R. (1992) *Racism in Children's Lives: A Study of Mainly-White Primary Schools*. London: Routledge.

Van Ausdale, D. and Feagin, J. (2001) *The First R: How Children Learn Race and Racism*. Lanham, MD: Rowman and Littlefield.

Van Dijk, T. A. (1993) *Elite Discourse and Racism*. London: Sage.

Van Langenhove, L. and Harré, R. (1999) 'Introducing Positioning Theory', in R. Harre and L. van Langenhove (eds.), *Positioning Theory*. Oxford: Blackwell.

Wetherell, M. (1998) 'Positioning and Interpretive Repertoires: Conversation Analysis and Post-Structuralism in Dialogue.' *Discourse and Society*, 9: 387–412.

——(2003) 'Paranoia, Ambivalence and Discursive Practices: Concepts of Position and Positioning in Psychoanalysis and Discursive Psychology', in R. Harré and F. Moghaddam (eds.), *The Self and Others: Positioning Individuals and Groups in Personal, Political and Cultural Contexts*. New York: Praeger/Greenwood.

Williams, P. (1997) *Seeing a Color-Blind Future: The Paradox of Race*. New York: Noonday Press.

Woodward, K. (ed.) (1997) *Identity and Difference*. Milton Keynes: Open University Press.

CHAPTER 6

The Power of Recall: Writing Against Racial Identity

Vron Ware

> I wrote it because I had to find out what life in a segregated culture had done to me, one person; I had to put down on paper these experiences so that I could see their meaning for me. I was in dialogue with myself as I wrote, as well as with my home town and my childhood and history and the future, and the past. Writing is both horizontal and vertical exploration. It has to true itself with facts but also with feelings and symbols, and memories that are never quite facts but sometimes closer to the 'truth' than is any fact.
>
> (Smith 1963: 3)

In a powerful essay that was to provoke new directions in feminist discourse, the poet Adrienne Rich spoke of her place of birth as a site that already marked her existence as a product of a particular social order (Rich 1986: 215). Born in 1929 under the apartheid rules of Jim Crow America, she identified her own primary location within a cruelly unjust system. 'White, female; or female, white. The first obvious, lifelong facts. But', she continued, 'I was born in the white section of a hospital which separated black and white women in labor and black and white babies in the nursery, just as it separated black and white bodies in the morgue.' Even as she took her first breath, her body was claimed as white before it was identified as female. First published in 1984, this essay called on anti-racist feminists first to recognize and then to take responsibility for their own processes of racialization if they were to help create an inclusive, 'de-Westernizing', global movement for change.

Rich's intervention was made at a time when many feminists, black and white, were treating those 'obvious, lifelong facts' as a fixed, even rigid, basis for political action. Those who were more hostile to identity politics interpreted her plea as a demand for a more complex, intuitive effort that was both a highly individual matter and, at the same time, necessarily part of a collective conversation about the fluidity of all socially constructed identities. Twenty years later, asking a different question about the relationship between where and what we are born, and what we choose to become, I am curious about the way that children who are brought into the world as racial subjects learn to refuse, or certainly be confused by, the precepts of racial hierarchy. I am specifically interested in stories told by adults where they recall the first time they became uncomfortably aware of being positioned within a racial, social order that required compliance and defied explanation. I suggest that attention to this autobiographical voice can provide valuable insights into the way that racial identities are learned, and more importantly than this, how they are also transformed or even rejected altogether.

Introducing their essay on the role of self-narrative in post-apartheid identity politics, Sarah Nuttall and Cheryl-Ann Michael wrote:

The autobiographical act in South Africa, more than a literary convention, has become a cultural activity. Memoir, reminiscence, confession, testament, case history and personal journalism, all different kinds of autobiographical acts or cultural occasions in which narrators take up models of identity that have become widely available, have pervaded the culture of the 1990s and have spread into the new century. (Nuttall and Michael 2000: 298)

Their discussion of a range of texts suggests ways of interpreting this 'cultural activity' as a profoundly useful insight into formations of racial community, and what they call 'shifting registers' of discourse during a period of revolutionary transformation. As the above extract shows, they offer strategies for evaluating autobiographical writing in the context of particular time and space, searching for resonant themes that help to extend dialogue with self into broader conversations about local and national identities.

Stanley Cohen offers an example of the moment when he was first aware of his own participation in a system founded on privilege, injustice, and racism (Cohen 2001). Aged about twelve or thirteen, and living at that time in Johannesburg, he suddenly noticed the old Zulu nightwatchman huddling over a charcoal stove while he was preparing to slip into his warm bed inside the house. The questions that flooded through his mind filled him with a profound sense of guilt. Years later, in the preface to his extraordinary book *States of Denial*, Cohen reflected on his 'bedroom epiphany', convinced that this was his earliest memory of becoming politically aware, the beginning of what was to become an obsession with the study of denial as a social process: 'But later, even when I began to think sociologically . . . , I would still return to some version of that early psychological unease. I saw this unease—correctly, I believe—as arising from a sense of knowing that something was deeply wrong, but also knowing that I could not live in a state of permanent awareness of this knowledge' (p. ix). This fleeting autobiographical disclosure is offered at the start of his book on knowing about atrocities and suffering not because it is out of the ordinary, nor from an impulse to legitimate the author, but because it alerts the reader to the ultimate ramifications of not cherishing those personal, individual, childish sensibilities. The discussion that follows provides a window on to the mechanics, as well as the ethics, of recovering that sense of unease from the overwhelming social and political forces that seek to obliterate it.

This essay explores the significance of childhood and place in autobiographical accounts of 'becoming racialized', that is, of learning to think and act both within, and especially in defiance of, racial terms. It entails reading different kinds of 'autobiographical acts' where the authors reflect on the significance of spatial barriers that marked the lines of segregation in their home environment, and contemplate, with hindsight, the possibilities of their transgression. I will limit my argument to mainly American writers in the second half of the twentieth century, focusing on the narratives of women and men who were raised to think of themselves as white but who came to see themselves as race traitors. I am particularly interested in the ways that these writers evoke a structure of feeling for place, not as a passive witness to emerging social consciousness, but as an active component in producing certain foundational truths (or falsehoods) about racial identity. In short, I am asking for a reading of the autobiographical text that explores the ethics of 'assembling' the anti-racist self (Rose 1997: 225): looking for qualities such as ruthless honesty with oneself, a sense of morality, a readiness to admit heresy, and a poetic sensibility to location and, in particular, to being estranged from one's surroundings. Zygmunt Bauman expresses it better in his observations on the creative possibilities of exile, which he defines as: 'the refusal to be integrated—the determination to stand out from the physical space, to conjure up a place of one's own, different from the place in which those around are settled, a place unlike the places left behind and unlike the place of arrival' (Bauman 2000: 208).

Stressing that the state of exile does not necessarily entail physical dislocation, he continues:

The resolute determination to stay 'nonsocialized': the consent to integrate solely with the condition of non-integration; the resistance—often painful and agonizing, yet ultimately victorious—to the overwhelming pressure of the place, old or new; the rugged defence of the right to pass judgement and choose; the embracing of ambivalence or calling ambivalence into being— these are, we may say, the constitutive features of 'exile'.

Autobiography has been exhaustively studied as a literary form, and there is certainly a rich literature on place, memory, and first-person writing which needs to be acknowledged before I go much further. Dolores Hayden writes, 'place is one of the trickiest words in the English language, a suitcase so overfilled one can never shut the lid' (Hayden 1995: 15). My focus on early childhood means that I am dealing with an understanding of place always reconstructed in the past tense, that is, places of growing up as they are remembered in adult life. As Yi-Fu Tuan describes in his cross-cultural reflection *Space and Place*, it is rare for young children to be haunted by memory, and most do not yet have the faculties to comprehend their interactions with their environments. 'The child not only has a short past, but his eyes more than the adult's are on the present and the immediate future. His vitality for doing things and exploring space is not suited to the reflective pause and backward glance that make places saturated with significance' (Tuan 1977: 33). The techniques of writing about the self at an early age demand both a selective recovery of one's own history, as well as an interpretation of the past that draws on the present. Recollection of place, meaning situation as well as location, is then an integral part of the processing of memory.

The Sense-making of Children

C. Wright Mills once defined the sociological imagination as the intersection of biography and history. He surely meant that biography included, even took for granted, the effects that place has on perception, identity, and behaviour. Experience of home, for example, and then the reasons for leaving or staying; lives spent in corners of particular cities, regions, or the nation as a whole: all these scales of dwelling constitute place in some shape or form, and are arguably relevant to social interaction of all kinds. Unlike most of the work that passes for sociology today, however, autobiographical writing, in common with creative fiction, is freer to speculate on the contingent and haphazard routes to self-awareness. Where ethnographic interviews and oral histories are legitimate within the disciplinary rules of ethnography, the practice of self-narrative is often considered an indulgence and of questionable value, beyond adding a personal, even poetic voice. For instance, as a practising sociologist, Dalton Conley warns his readers of the inherent unreliability of memoir as opposed to social science. In the epilogue to his own memoir of an unconventional childhood in New York, he comes close to apologizing for not meeting the requisite standards of evidence. There are compensations, however:

The greatest of these is the depth of understanding attained when one is more participant than observer—that is, when one spends many consequential—even formative—years of one's life in a social setting, rather than swooping in from afar to gather data for a time before going home to dinner and one's real life. (Conley 2000: 229)

Echoing Tuan's point that children are not sensorily equipped to analyse the significance of their daily lives in relation to their social environments, he points out that his book 'is as much about what is not understood as it is about what is grasped. It is about the sense-making of children more than professionals. In short, it is about literary truths, not scientific ones'.

These 'literary truths', however, have a habit of capturing the imagination in ways that science is rarely able. In a recent edition of the journal *Souls*, a panel of writers, including Conley himself, assembled for an improvised discussion on 'white identity' and 'white privilege,' first in the context of New York, and second in relation to the country as a whole. The attention to the city already suggested a focus on the local, and indeed, the personal. The edited transcript begins with a series of questions posed by the chair, Manning Marable:

When were you born and when you were growing up, what did it mean to be white? Dalton and Ann (Douglas), when did you first realize you were white, or what whiteness was? Robin (D. G. Kelley), as an African American, when did you first realize that there was something called *whiteness*? (Conley 2002: 74)

Faced with this challenge to identify earliest memories of racial self-consciousness, each member of the group described the place characteristics of their childhood homes. Ann Douglas offered her recollection of growing up in 'an upper-class rural community outside Manhattan'. The location, both geographical and social, suggested complex hierarchies of ethnicity, gender, and class that held the place together and gave it a unique, though typical, character: 'This was fox-hunting territory, high-finance territory, and so needless to say, it was not a mixed population of equals. All the men in my family worked in Manhattan.' Douglas continued to give an unflinching critique of the social relations of her household that included an anecdote about acting too familiar with a black female servant. When she was about three years old she held her arm next to the arm of her grandmother's companion, of whom she was very fond, and asked her, 'Why are you darker?' The sharp reprimand, rather than explanation, that she received from her mother drew her attention to the powerful attraction of something taboo, sowing the seeds for the future rebellion. Looking back, she recalled that the incident prompted her eventually to ask questions about the values underpinning her parents' home: 'I wasn't happy in the world in which I was raised. I didn't seem to fit in.'

Her awakening sense of what it meant to be racialized as white grew partly from close observation of and sensitivity to the ways that ethnicity dictated who was excluded from this community, who was accepted, and what jobs they performed. Although she does not elaborate further on the physical characteristics of this place where she learned these lessons, her reply demonstrates the ecological nature of human development: children can only become aware of becoming marked by social, economic, and cultural difference in the context of particular environments. When recalling the feelings and memories evoked by talking about one's childhood, it is hard to separate the dynamics of family life inside the home from the people and the spaces that surround it. Once again, this turn to the past is unhelpful unless it is anchored in historical time. Interestingly, it is only later in the conversation, however, that Douglas reveals she was born in 1942, a fact that immediately anchors her 'upper-class, rural community' in a particular time as well as space.

Moved by Douglas's recollection of the sharp reaction to her spontaneous and relatively innocent act, and the lessons it taught her about the unspoken racial codes that held her childhood universe in place, Conley relates a story of his own. It is an anecdote that he tells in the opening chapter of his autobiography, *Honky*, and a formative episode in his emerging sense of self, also as a three-year old. Desperate for a baby sister and frustrated by his parents' seeming indifference to his pleas, he found a suitable candidate in the playground one day, and pushed the baby carriage over to his mother, jamming the stroller against her leg in an act of defiance. Her embarrassment that he had kidnapped someone else's child was less mortifying than the reprimand that she could not be his sister because she was black, a factor that had been of no significance to the young boy up to that point. This story can only make sense once it is placed in the wider context of where this family lived, as well as the year in which it took place (Conley et al. 2002: 75).

The abiding value of Conley's autobiography is that he experienced the first part of his life as a minority, growing up in the early 1970s in a mostly Puerto Rican and African-American neighbourhood on the Lower East Side. As a young teenager he crossed Manhattan to attend a 'white school' in Greenwich Village, moving, as he puts it, between 'two racial worlds'. In this same conversation in *Souls* he recounts further stories of how he figured out what whiteness might mean as he learnt about power and authority in relation to the spatial organization of the city. The unconventional lived experience that he recounts through the interpretive gaze of the sociologist contains all kinds of potentially useful insights into racialization as a process that is at once individually specific and inescapably social. To downplay this 'cultural occasion' as a form of literary rather than scientific truth does an injustice both to literature and to science in my opinion. The memories are selective, to be sure, and the author is allowed to present his own analysis first. But once they are in the public domain they can acquire the characteristics of authentic ethnography, if that is what is needed to take them seriously.

A fly buzzes round the window interrupting my chain of thought. It is a distinctively English sound, startling me into a different frame of mind. Of course, there are flies in Connecticut where I now live, but there are also screens on every window to prevent them from entering the building. The intermittent noise returns me to another time, another place, where flies seem to hide behind the curtains all winter, bumping lazily into life when spring comes round again. I feel a pang of homesickness, and this disjunction makes me wonder: how do we recall those first moments when we felt at odds with our surroundings; or identify that sudden sense of not belonging, not feeling part of the crowd, or wondering if our parents could be right about everything? How rare, but how valuable, are the stories that can connect those qualms of doubt to the incipient awareness of being an exile in one's own country.

Situating Whiteness

Ruth Frankenberg's foray into what she terms the 'racial social geography of race' offers a theoretical model, if one is needed, for writing ethnographies of growing up 'white' (Frankenberg 1993: 44). In a broader investigation of the social construction of whiteness, she asked her interviewees, all female, to remember how they conceptualized and related to the people surrounding them as they grew up. 'To what extent, for example, did they have relationships of closeness or distance, equality or inequality, with people of color? What were they encouraged or taught by example to make of the variously 'raced' people in their environments?'(p. 44). The material gathered from individual respondents is not treated as representative so much as colours in a larger picture. Frankenberg uses it to 'begin the process of "defamiliarizing" that which is taken for granted in white experience and to elaborate a method for making visible and analysing the racial structuring of white experience'. As the women reminisce about the lessons on social differentiation absorbed in the spaces of childhood, the sociologist's ear listens for clues indicating how their environments were shaped by social, political, and economic forces.

The skilful ethnographer elicits the autobiographical voice from his or her informants. If their words are allowed to breathe on the page, they too can speak for themselves. Although anthropologist of whiteness John Hartigan did not invent the concept of the 'racial situation', he used it with good effect to argue for an ecological approach to analysing social conflict (Hartigan 1999). His project provides another way of reading autobiography as a dialogue between self and place, history and politics, past and future, compliance and resistance. Taking his theoretical cue from Michael Omi and Howard Winant's influential *Racial Formation in the U.S.*, he set out to complicate the historical and political processes involved in defining, contesting, and interpreting racial categories and their meanings in the context of a very particular place, and among people of differing class identities. Detroit, in his view, provided the perfect setting to investigate the social ecology of what he calls 'racialness' since 76 per cent of its inhabitants are black and the 22 per cent white inhabitants, who range from rich to very poor, are therefore in a minority. His substantial fieldwork in different neighbourhoods allowed him to explore the 'interpretive repertoires' of race that emerge from highly complex but well-documented dramas of urban life, sensitively conveying the intricacies and contradictions of individual and collective response.

Throughout his interviews and conversations with mainly white Detroiters living within the distinct spatial order of the city, Hartigan was guided by two simple questions: what does race mean to these people, and how do they decide if a situation is racial? Linking his project to a broader literature on racialization, Hartigan suggests: 'There are copious distinctions between the ways, in general, whites and blacks are racialized—the social and political ramifications are hugely different. But by examining how whites are racialized—always unevenly, always following the contours of class distinctions—we can think more clearly about the way racial identity varies by social and geographic location' (p. 13). Within the context of global, national, and regional histories of white supremacy, Hartigan's ethnographic detective work among ordinary people in the streets where they live is a useful reminder that race can also be 'a local matter':

Instead of drawing generalized assertions and summary judgements about race, I suggest that the economy of racial explanations and analysis needs to be oriented towards a greater dependence on and retention of the particular situations and settings where race is at work. That is, by considering the specific circumstances of racial situations, we can counter the allegorical tendencies that render people's lives as abstractions, such as 'white' and 'black'. (p. 282)

The focus of both these writers on the sites and settings of white racialness represents a new body of work influenced by feminism's insistence on the 'politics of location'. Before going any further, however, I want to emphasize that my interest in autobiographical accounts of 'becoming estranged from whiteness' does not presume that this is automatically the best, or even the only, point of view that reveals how whiteness operates. In the same way that feminism has exhaustively debated different theories of 'situated knowledges', this recent attention to the social construction of white identity reiterates the question: from what angles, or standpoints, do we learn most about the intricacies of racial power and the myriad forms of resistance that emerge in response? Writing about Primo Levi's discussion of 'ordinary virtues' in the practice of bearing witness to the dehumanizing effects of racism, Robert S. C. Gordon observes:

Practical intelligence in Levi entails looking at and understanding the world responsively, flexibly, critically: it is a form of 'good' or 'right' looking, looking at the world anew. And such quality of vision depends, among other things, on where one is looking from and on knowing where one is looking from: in other words on perspective. (Gordon 2001: 149)

Levi returns again and again to the role of the eyewitness as the agent of testimony, confirming his belief in the importance of *seeing*, the language of the visual. As Gordon elaborates: 'The eye-witness has seen an event or an action from a position of proximity but also, most often, of personal detachment (or at least a presumed lack of complicity). At the same time, however, the specificity of any single perspective is as much as a guarantor of subjectivity as of objectivity'. Reading Levi's philosophical reflections on eyewitness accounts of the Holocaust is profoundly affecting, and I borrow his terms in order to link the unspeakable histories of white supremacy to the more mundane racial situations that I have described so far. Moving away from the abstractions and generalizations so often invoked as racial explanation, Levi's work is a reminder that, first, paying attention to personal testimonies entails listening to multiple points of view, and, second, that their significance and value depend on whether we can identify a 'right' way of looking at the world, however partial.

The White Environing World

In the same way that autobiographical acts articulate new modes of identity within post-apartheid South Africa, so the testimonies of African-Americans from Frederick Douglass onwards have helped to define what it has meant to become American in different historical periods as well as offering powerful communication across the vortex of racial terror, ignorance, and complete indifference. Although in this essay I am giving preferential treatment to the significance of place in memoirs of those racialized as white, this work means less without reference to those who are made to learn about whiteness from a distance that is more forcefully imposed. Douglass' account of his first conscious exposure to the inhumane cruelty of white power stands out. The episode comes at the beginning of his *Narrative*, and is described twice on the same page. He first recalls his master's propensity to whip his slaves to a bloody pulp; one such victim was Douglass' own aunt, whose heart-rending screams would wake the young boy at dawn. One day he witnessed this event, and he searches for words to describe the effect that this had on him:

I never shall forget it whilst I remember any thing. It was the first of a long series of such outrages, of which I was doomed to be a witness and a participant. It struck me with awful force. It was the blood-stained gate, the entrance to the hell of slavery, through which I was about to pass. It was a most terrible spectacle. I wish I could commit to paper the feelings with which I beheld it. (Baker 1982: 51)

Douglass follows this passage with a detailed report of what he actually saw. As he writes, he relives the episode in his mind, sharing with his readers the perspective of both witness and participant as he leads them into the same kitchen where the flogging took place, and then to the dark closet where he fled in terror.

Almost a hundred years after Douglass's autobiography was first published, W. E. B. Du Bois explained how he derived his sociological analysis of American racism from his personal experience of growing up in a society founded and organized on the principle of white supremacy:

Much as I knew of this class structure of the world, I should never have realized it so vividly and fully if I had not been born into its modern counterpart, racial segregation, first into a world composed of people with colored skins who remembered slavery and endured discrimination; and who had to a degree their own habits, customs, and ideals; but in addition to this I lived in an environment which I came to call the white world. (Du Bois 1986: 653)

The theory of double consciousness that Du Bois developed through living in, and being exiled from, these two worlds simultaneously is well known, but it is worth repeating his account of how he was conditioned and constrained by 'the white world' from early childhood:

I could not stir, I could not act, I could not live, without taking into careful daily account the reaction of the white environing world. How I traveled and where, what work I did, what income I received, where I ate, where I slept, with whom I talked, where I sought recreation, where I studied, what I wrote and what I could get published—all this depended primarily upon an overwhelming mass of my fellow citizens in the United States, from whose society I was largely excluded.

Du Bois' observation of his transition from birth to adulthood is rooted in a sense of place mattering at every move. Attempting to transgress the physical and symbolic boundaries of racial segregation was not only almost inconceivable, but often fatal. This brief extract reveals once again how racism relies on a spatial logic that is not always visible to the naked eye. The ecology of white supremacy in early twentieth-century America meant that most people positioned across the colour line had entirely different notions of what life 'on the other side' might be like. 'Of course', continued Du Bois, 'there was no real wall between us'. He knew since childhood that 'in all things in general, white people were just the same as I'. However, one big difference was that whites did not have to take 'into careful daily account' the reactions of the people who lived across the colour line. Whites did not automatically, out of necessity, develop an intimate sense of their black 'prisoners' that was passed down from one generation to another. The way in which the two groups perceived each other was as asymmetrical as their relationship to power and privilege.

This passage was written shortly before Ann Douglas was born into the pre-Civil Rights household of servile servants that provided her first useful lessons of estrangement. Quite probably, Du Bois' outrage that white Americans simply failed to see beyond the walls they had constructed around their privileged and fearful environs must have spurred many would-be race traitors to interrogate their own imprisonment. In a literary review of what he calls 'the white southern racial conversion narrative' Fred Hobson notes that, 'The outburst of white southern autobiography driven by racial guilt, beginning shortly before mid-century, would continue for three decades, indeed still continues to a great degree' (Hobson 1999: 15). Attributing this phenomenon to the emerging 'southern party of guilt', Hobson identifies the 'religious impulse' as the factor that spurred a new generation of whites to take social action against southern racial divisions. That same decade, Lillian Smith became the first American writer to embark on her autobiography as a psychological analysis of white racism. An investigation into the mental and social structures of segregation, *Killers of the Dream* was published in 1949, and later reissued with a new prologue in 1963. As Smith explained in the extract that begins this essay, 'I wrote it because I had to find out what life in a segregated culture had done to me, one person.' Her motives were not, of course, as narrow as this comment suggests; the very first paragraph of her book evokes the terror of growing up in a community vibrating with the ominous rhythms of self-destruction. 'Even its children knew that the South was in trouble. No one had to tell them; no words said aloud. To them, it was a vague thing weaving in and out of their play like a ghost haunting an old graveyard or whispers after the whole household sleeps—fleeting mystery, vague menace to which each responds in his own way' (Smith 1963: 15).

Tangled Dreams and Anxieties

As an internationalist, Smith consciously wrote her book against a background of murderous fascism in Europe and militant struggles for decolonization throughout the world. Anxious to reveal connections between all forms of racial terror, she chose to explore the systematic structures of racial segregation from childhood to the grave, returning repeatedly to her own life to describe the lessons she imbibed with the very air of her home town:

In this South I lived as a child and now live. And it is of it that my story is made. I shall not tell, here, of experiences that were different and special and belonged only to me, but those most white southerners born at the turn of the century share with each other. Out of the intricate weaving of unnumbered threads, I shall pick out a few strands, a few designs that have to do with what we call color and race... and politics... and money and how it is made... and religion... and sex and the body image... and love... and dreams of the Good and the killers of dreams. (p. 16)

This is the autobiographical act of a race traitor, one who throughout her life urged disloyalty not just to the southern traditions within which she was raised, but to civilization itself. The book requires a longer discussion of its contents and conclusions, and Smith herself a more thorough evaluation than she has hitherto enjoyed[1]. Here, however, I want to draw attention to the powerful structure of feeling that emerges from her descriptions of the geographic contours of racism. She draws repeatedly on the affective lineaments of southern ecology, her vocabulary rich with allusions to a teeming natural world polluted by years of enslavement, forbidden desire, and hatred:

The physical setting for these tangled dreams and anxieties, the place we lived, was a backdrop to our Deep South childhood that seemed no more than a giant reflection of our own hearts. Back of our little town was the swamp, tangled green, oozing snakes and alligators and water lilies and sweet-blooming bays, weaving light and shadow into awful and tender designs, splotching our lives with brightness and terror. (p. 95)

It was not simply the natural, living landscape that mirrored the fatal contradictions between Christian love and inhuman cruelty: 'Every little southern town is a fine stage-set for Southern Tradition to use it as it teaches its children the twisting, turning, dance of segregation. Few words are needed for there are signs everywhere. White... Colored... White... Colored...' (p. 80). And where there are no words, she continues, there are still signs: 'big white church on Main Street, little unpainted colored church on the rim of town; big white school, little ramshackly colored school; big white house, little unpainted house...'. Repeating the theme of the seductive dance, muscles moving in step with no interference from head or heart, Smith weaves a visceral sense of her own entanglement in a way of life that was at once profoundly unsettling but also self-perpetuating. Yet why was her integration not complete, and what allowed her to resist the sheer pressure of the place?

A few pages into the book Smith asks herself this same question. She learned the southern way of life as a child, absorbing its lessons 'by closing door after door until one's own mind and heart and conscience are blocked off from each other and from reality' (p. 19). But

one day, she continues, 'they began to open again'. As a writer interested in the deep psychological recesses of the human mind, Smith
remains unwilling to identify a 'cause' that explains everything;
nevertheless she turns to one experience in particular that she
believed 'pushed these doors open a little', showing 'glimpses of the
world beyond, of that bright thing we call "reality"'. Just as both
Douglas and Conley interpreted one particular situation from their
childhood as a significant shift in consciousness, Smith recalls an
episode that was less a moment of trauma than 'a symbol of buried
experiences that I did not have access to'.

The incident took place when the young Lillian was about six years
old. A small scandal erupted when a fair-skinned girl of roughly the
same age was seen playing in the yard of a household in the coloured
part of town. When she was removed, or kidnapped as her own family saw it, Smith's mother agreed to adopt her. The two girls became
friends for the three weeks in which the newcomer lived in her house.
Then as suddenly as she was introduced she was returned to her
black family when it was discovered that, contrary to her appearance, she was a Negro. Although she was allowed to give one of her
dolls, Smith's questions and protestations were silenced and all further reference to the episode were banned. There are other details
that Smith later recalled with tremendous guilt and pain. Shortly
after the event, however, she forced herself to forget and for more
than thirty years, she later wrote, 'the experience was wiped out of
my memory' (p. 27). But then, as she eventually returned to lance the
internalized wounds of childhood, she found her way back to
the unanswerable questions that were stifled with the removal of
the girl. Turning in her mind to dress the sores that still remained
after years of deference to a system that virtually crippled the psychic development of all its adherents, Smith reflected: 'As I sit here
writing, I can almost touch that little town, so close is the memory
of it. There it lies, its main street lined with great oaks, heavy with
matted moss that swings softly even now as I remember' (p. 28).

Compiled a decade before Bachelard explored the notion of 'topo-
analysis' in *The Poetics of Space*, Smith's analysis of the repressed
guilt experienced by southern whites entails a walk back through
'the streets of one's own childhood...the town where one was
born'. Fascinated by the development of the child's mental universe
within the dimensions of the interior of the house in which it comes
to consciousness, Bachelard wrote later, 'memories are motionless,
and the more securely they are fixed in space, the sounder they are'
(Bachelard 1964: 9). By making the landscapes of her childhood

articulate the choking nightmares of racial segregation, Smith helped to reveal the psychological costs of maintaining that 'white environing world' from within.

Our Grasp on the World

Although Lillian Smith was not comfortable with being called a feminist, her work has had enormous influence of subsequent generations of southern women writers. In the mid- to late-1980s, Mab Segrest, who was born in Alabama, worked as an organizer against the far right in North Carolina where she lived. Her autobiographical project *Memoir of a Race Traitor* began as a documentary account of what she thought of as 'objective' facts recording both random and routine racist crimes. 'I did so', she wrote, 'out of the certainty that, in the face of evil, good people do not respond because they can pretend they do not know' (Segrest 1994: 1). Like Smith, whose words form a powerful epigraph on the opening pages of her book, she locates herself at the very start as southerner born and raised in the same soil that had produced the neo-Nazis and Klansmen. But her attempts to be detached, to shape 'the procession of crisp black letters across the empty page', gradually induced a kind of madness. After she manifested both physical and mental symptoms of distress, she was forced to quit work 'to find again "subjective" language, what poet Muriel Rukeyser called "unverifiable fact" ' (p. 2). Searching for a different register, Segrest walked back down the streets where she was born, determined to locate and face up to the sources of her terror and fury. Her memoir is not so much a dialogue with her home town as a confrontation with her family history, knowing that in the white household where she was raised, 'themes of race permeated our family interactions'. Her extraordinary book manages to investigate the pathologies of deep-seated racism within southern culture by showing a link between this personal life and the barbaric, systemic violence of white supremacy.

Segrest's perspective as an anti-racist witness is inseparable from her politics of gender and sexuality, and her memories of growing up at odds with a dysfunctional white family are enriched by her adolescent remonstrations at all kinds of discrimination and injustice. The southern tradition within which she continues to write was transformed by feminism barely two decades after Smith completed *Killers of the Dream* in 1949. That same year, Simone de Beauvoir, also attentive to black struggles for self-determination throughout the world, had offered a view of gender politics that was to radical-ize a new generation. 'The body is not a thing', she observed in *The Second Sex*, 'it is a situation: it is our grasp on the world and a sketch of our projects' (Beauvoir 1989: 34)[2]. While reminding us that the sociological process called racialization is about so much more than race, this wise and enduring claim also directs us to adapt Adrienne Rich's fruitful question for feminists, posed nearly forty years later: 'Where, when, and under what conditions have women acted and been acted on, as women?' (Rich 1986: 214). The sinewy, slippery tentacles of racialization appear in sharper relief if we give more space to the autobiographical act; if we allow the poetic narratives of self-critique to offer their uncomfortable honesty; and if we demand accountability from the self-imposed exiles who can expose the absolute hollowness of racial power.

NOTES

1. See Hobson (1999) for a fuller discussion of *Killers of the Dream* as a conver-sion narrative (pp. 18–50); I have discussed Smith's other writings in chapter 4 of Vron Ware and Les Back *Out of Whiteness: Color, Politics, and Culture* (Chicago: University of Chicago Press, 2002).
2. For a contextualized discussion of de Beauvoir's statement, see Toril Moi *What is a Woman and Other Essays* (Oxford: Oxford University Press, 1999: 59).

REFERENCES

Bachelard, G. (1964) *The Poetics of Space*. Boston: Beacon Press.
Baker, A. J. Jr. (ed.) (1982) *Narrative of the Life of Frederick Douglass, An American Slave (1845)*. Harmondsworth: Penguin Books.
Bauman, Z. (2000) *Liquid Modernity*. Cambridge: Polity Press.
Beauvoir, S. de, (1989) *The Second Sex* (H. M. Parshley, trans.). New York: Vintage Books.
Cohen, S. (2001) *States of Denial: Knowing, About Atrocities and Suffering*. Malden, MA: Blackwell Publishers.
Conley, D. (2000) *Honky*. Berkeley: University of California Press.
——Douglas, A., Kelly, R. D. G., and the Editors (2002) 'Circling the Wagons: Whiteness in New York City and Beyond'. *Souls: A Critical Journal of Black Politics, Culture, and Society*, 4(4, Fall), 73–81.
Du Bois, W. E. B. (1986) 'The White World', in *Du Bois Writings*. New York: Library of America.
Frankenberg, R. (1993) *White Women, Race Matters: The Social Construction of Whiteness*. Minneapolis: University of Minnesota Press.
Gordon, R. S. C. (2001) *Primo Levi's Ordinary Virtues: From Testimony to Ethics*. Oxford: Oxford University Press.

Hartigan, J., Jr. (1999) *Racial Situations: Predicaments of Whiteness in Detroit*. Princeton: Princeton University Press.

Hayden, D. (1995) *The Power of Place: Urban Landscapes as Public History*. Cambridge, MA: MIT Press.

Hobson, F. (1999) *But Now I See: The White Southern Racial Conversion Narrative*. Baton Rouge: Louisiana State University Press.

Nuttall, S. and Michael, C. (2000) 'Autobiographical Acts', in S. Nuttall and C. Michael (eds.), *Senses of Culture: South African Culture Studies*. Oxford: Oxford University Press.

Rich, A. (1986) 'Notes Toward a Politics of Location', in *Blood, Bread, and Poetry: Selected Prose 1979–1985*. London: Virago Press.

Rose, N. (1997) 'Assembling the Modern Self', in Roy Porter (ed.), *Rewriting the Self: Histories from the Renaissance to the Present*. London: Routledge.

Segrest, M. (1994) *Memoir of a Race Traitor*. Boston: South End Press.

Smith, L. (1963) *Killers of the Dream*. New York: Anchor Books.

Tuan, Y. (1977) *Space and Place: The Perspective of Experience*. Minneapolis: University of Minnesota Press.

CHAPTER 7

White Lives

Anoop Nayak

The idea of race is one of the most persistent and seductive fictions of the twenty-first century. The belief that human populations can be divided up into discrete 'races' with identifiable characteristics is an enduring myth, not yet fully displaced by the plethora of scientific reports and detailed research undertaken in the social sciences, arts, and humanities that vigorously proclaim otherwise.[1] So why, in a predominantly post-colonial age, has the fallacy of race held such lasting appeal?

Here, the seemingly permanent signs of racial authenticity inscribed most potently by way of skin colour—black, white, yellow, red, or brown—have tended to be regarded as purely chromosomal distinctions that conceal the innate truth about immutable human difference. Rarely, outside of academic discourse and the politics of anti-racism, is the sign of colour emphasized as spatially and temporally variable, taking on different meanings and new signification according to situation and context. As much recent work has shown, racial identities are, above all, *social constructions*: there is no 'inner truth' to their status, only a set of socially ascribed attributes or deficiencies. So called racial 'characteristics' are, then, only given meaning as they unfold in the act of representation. The process of racialization, that is the application of imagined racial 'essences' to everyday phenomena, enables race to operate as a 'sticky' sign that magically adheres itself to bodies, places, and a whole host of social activities. Most commonly this is articulated discursively, elaborating upon popular understandings of nationhood, ethnicity, or colour. For example, when one speaks of a 'Gallic shrug' or 'black crime' it may appear that these acts are racially identifiable phenomena set apart from, and in contradistinction to, other less-marked gestures or misdemeanours.

In short, this everyday discourse is part of the invisible grammar through which racialization is commonly articulated. In this way racialization, in its negative sense, may operate as both a form of social ascription and a marker of difference used to divide up the world and its peoples into seemingly homogenous imagined communities. Robert Miles deploys this definition when he asserts:

The concept of racialization therefore refers to the historical emergence of the idea of 'race' and to its subsequent reproduction and application. Furthermore, the racialization of human beings entails the racialization of the processes in which they participate and the structures and institutions that result. (1989: 76)

For Miles racialization is a negative force, a product of capital that colours the field of migrant labour. In this tightly bound definition, there is little scope for transgressing race logic, as the act of racialization (attributed to employment, the public housing stock, health, or other state provisions) inherently invokes the notion of race. He goes on to describe racialization as 'a dialectical process by which meaning is attributed to particular biological features of human beings, as a result of which individuals may be assigned to a general category of persons which reproduces itself biologically' (p. 76). Racialization is then transformed into a thoroughly *essentialist* project, in this case used to divide up sections of the working class.

Significantly, in such materialist analyses racialization carries with it the oppressive inscriptions of power that are 'structurally determined, politically organised and ideologically inflected...within positions of domination and subordination' (Green and Carter 1988: 23). The regulatory effects of racialization are apparent in the meticulous research conducted by Stuart Hall et al. in *Policing the Crisis: Mugging, the State, and Law and Order* (1979). The work explores the crisis or 'moral panic' around street crime interrogating, 'why and how the themes of *race, crime and youth*—condensed in the image of "mugging"—come to serve as the articulator of the crisis, as its ideological conductor' (1979: viii). As we shall find, the racialization of black youth and their associations with crime and the culture of the street have yet to disappear (Westwood 1990). Indeed, the materialist emphasis on unequal relations of power continue to be of importance in an age where debates on immigration or law and order are all too easily read through the lens of colour.

Racialization, then, remains a powerful and necessary tool for grasping the production and proliferation of racial divisions in society. In particular, materialist scholars have emphasized the social basis of racialization and its connections to capital and power. However, if racialization is fundamentally a regulatory device in these accounts, for cultural writers influenced by the French post-structuralist critic Michel Foucault, such forms of power are rarely absolute. Power is not the possession of institutions, structures, or dominant groups for Foucault, but comprises a dynamic 'multiplicity of force relations' (1978: 92) that operate 'as a productive network' (1980: 119). This idea that 'power is everywhere' (p. 93) complicates the materialist conception of racialization as an ideological imposition from above that converges across a black/white racial binary. Instead, power is conceptualized as productive rather than negating, 'it doesn't only weigh on us as a force that says no, but... it traverses and produces things, it induces pleasure, forms of knowledge, produces discourse' (1980: 119). Moreover, in Foucaultian analysis power is not something white subjects have and black subjects lack, but rather, the nexus of relations implicates each and every one of us—'Where there is power, there is resistance' (1978: 95).

Recognizing that racialization is not only about institutional polic-ing and regulation, but may have a series of unanticipated effects has led a number of writers to return to the concept and argue that it 'offers several strengths' (Small 1994: 29). I will now consider some of these possibilities by drawing upon recent post-structuralist and psychoanalytic perspectives on racialization that have developed in the aftermath of the 'cultural turn' (see Bonnett and Nayak 2003). In particular, I will use this new thinking on identity to reveal how racialization as a negative sign is being economically, politically, and culturally 'redescribed'. Furthermore, I would venture that the ascendancy given to competing interpretations of racialization—as either inherently biological, or explicitly social—will no doubt deter-mine the future value it holds as a node of theoretical exchange and political currency in the field of race and ethnic studies.

Representing Racialization: Theory and Politics after the 'Cultural Turn'

There are two central questions we must ask of the new literature on racialization. First, how can we begin to fashion a productive notion of racialization that moves beyond the category of race? And second, can a critical use of racialization really challenge the power of white supremacy as evidenced in materialist accounts?

In order to address these issues I will explore ideas that have arisen in the wake of what is popularly termed the 'cultural turn' (see Ray and Sayer 1999). Within the arts, humanities, and social sciences this 'turn to culture' has seen a once stalwart reliance upon older class-based models of power give way to new, arguably more sophisticated ways of thinking, writing, and understanding. In particular, this has seen the emergence of striking new theories (e.g. Actor Network Theory, Queer Theory), the exploration of hidden spaces (bodies, cyberspace, the night-time economy), and the enunciation of hitherto marginal identities (new ethnicities, dissonant sexualities) come to the fore. By investigating issues of cultural identity and representation racial theorists have elaborated upon the earlier, materialist analysis of 'race relations' tied to market forces, state institutions, and global capital (Rex 1970; Miles and Phizacklea 1979; Rex and Tomlinson 1979). In the past decade we have witnessed an explosion of new thought and practice on race and ethnicity, perhaps most evident in the flourishing cultural sphere of literature, music, film, and art. Recent examples of this new politics of representation can be found in contemporary British popular culture as evidenced in Zadie Smith's novel *White Teeth*, the music of Talvin Singh, or Keith Piper's artistic installations of Black-British cultural identity. In this rich and dense constellation of experimental ideas, theories, and politics we are now seeing increasingly complex processes of racialization refracted through a prism of culture (Bradley and Fenton 1999).

These cultural insights have deepened our understandings of race, power, and subjectivity, engendering a more theoretically reflexive understanding of racialization. Moreover, through *post-structuralist* methods it is now possible to engage in a detailed, critical deconstruction of the signs, symbols, motifs, and myths that constitute the social category of race. Here, it is shown that race does not prefigure discourse, but rather, is produced and feverishly kept alive in and through the multiple, if at times conflicting, discourses of racialization. Through successive iterations these discourses are made to appear intelligible and over time may congeal to purvey the illusion of substance, embodied in the aforementioned Gallic shrug, or other culturally inscribed performances we habitually inhabit. In this sense, there is no presocial racial identity, no stable racial core or locus of agency from which various actions follow. Recent post-structuralist work has then been keen to emphasize racialization as a type of process, an activity that has the power to deconstruct racial categories and reveal their historical making. Deploying the idea of racialization as a mode of deconstruction not only uncouples it from the concept of race but also enables the critique of racial categories to occur. Thus, according to Stephen Small, racialization actually 'questions the existence of "races," looks at how groups not previously defined as "races" have come to be defined in this way, and assesses the various factors involved in such processes' (1994: 30).

An example of the post-structuralist 'undoing' of race, through a renewed understanding of racialization, is present in the work of Avtar Brah who, amongst others, favours a notion of 'differential racialization' (see also Cohen 1988; Phoenix 2001):

I argue against positions that conceptualise racism through simple bipolarities of negativity and positivity, superiority and inferiority, inclusion or exclusion...I point to the ways in which racism simultaneously inhabits spaces of deep ambivalence, admiration, envy and desire. The changing forms of a plurality of racisms are analysed with the aid of the concept of *differential racialization*. This idea is an important component of my conceptual framework, interrogating binarised forms of thinking, and exploring how different racialised groups are positioned differentially vis-à-vis one another. (1996: 18)

Thus, rather than viewing racialization as an inherently negative sign, absent of power for those subjects it is said to oppress, post-structuralists point to its multidiscursive and polysemic value across a number of sites. The sign of blackness which has historically been equated with evil, death, sin, and so forth, in post-structuralist writing is then given a semiotic multiaccentuality. In changing global times the elastic sign of blackness is stretched so that it may also come to be ascribed more positive associations, such as 'urban cool' or any number of contradictory signifiers that elicit admiration or envy. Although the notion of blackness as ambiguous is nothing new, and dates back at least to early ideas of the 'noble savage', new communication technologies have intensified the proliferation of such fractured images. However, the newer set of representations do not entirely eclipse the older; they overlap and coexist in a field of shifting relations that allow the sign of blackness to convey multiple meanings, subject to context and situation. In these readings blackness is split, marked by an ambivalence that does not necessarily equate with 'powerlessness' (as presumed in the old anti-racist statement that racism = power + prejudice). Instead, the process of racialization may render visible minorities more powerful in certain arenas and less powerful in others, and in turn create 'a plurality of resistances' (Foucault 1978: 96).

A post-structuralist use of racialization, then, recognizes the productiveness of power, its uneven distribution, and the need to disband with simplistic racial dualisms (Hall 1992; Cohen 1994; Rattansi 1994). In doing so, it opens us up to the possibility that there are different types of racialization—some of which may be 'positive', if still problematic—and that their effects are not always predictable. Greater attention is also given to the multiple configurations of race and the criss-crossing that occur as class, gender, age, and sexuality interact with, and so inflect our understandings of, racialization. Moreover, the materialist use of racialization as an imposition of the ideological state apparatus has tended to imply that certain groups, institutions, or organs of the state have ownership over power while others do not. In doing so, this may underplay the numerous sites and interrelationships that enable power to be effected. In particular, the role of human agency and the countless nodes of resistance may tend to be overlooked. In contrast, in a post-structuralist Foucaultian reading, 'The individual is both an effect of power and the element of its articulation' (Smart 1985: 79).

A further way to interrogate productively the category of race through racialization is to deploy *psychoanalytic* forms of cultural analysis. Of particular importance is that psychoanalytic frames not only reveal how racialization is experienced at a discursive level but investigate how it is lived out in the mental gymnastics and spectacular acrobatics that take place in the Imaginary. Some of the most interesting examples are the unconscious emotions articulated in dark colonial fantasies, Othering, and the strange voodoo of racial fetishism. For it is here that we gain an insight into the contradictory dimensions of racialization. Indeed, it is within the landscape of the Imaginary that barely suppressed, archetypal images of race can be found vaulting, pirouetting, and somersaulting their way through our unconscious. The concept of racialization can then extend beyond the material world of labour markets or immigration policies to incorporate a subterranean psychic economy, those unspoken, 'hidden narratives in theories of racism' (Cohen 1994: 62).

Thus, psychoanalytic studies of race indicate that the process of racialization effects not only those who are subjected to the exigencies of its power but also those who are implicated in the racializing of Others. This process of displacement not only constitutes the identity of the Other but also becomes a means of producing one's own identity in relation to these imaginary Others (Said 1978). Moreover, this symbolic, internal act of splitting is not a neat surgical excision, as the Other may return to 'trouble' the subject in unconscious fantasies and unspoken desires. As an act of projection racialization involves spinning a psychic web of sensation—fear, envy, and desire—intricately woven across, and thereby binding, the bodies of racialized Others in a silvery thread of white anxiety. These unspoken perspectives take us beyond the perception of racialization as simply a by-product of capitalism. They also transcend the rationalist model of enquiry that conveys 'nothing has any meaning outside of discourse' (Foucault 1972). Indeed, Phil Cohen critiques such rationalism on the basis that the 'rationalist model ignores the deeper reaches of the racist *imagination*, the structures of feeling and phantasy which are embedded in even the most rationalized forms of racist argument and action' (1994: 82). Understanding how social and psychic processes interact, and the 'structures of feeling' they elicit, may lead us to a more complex if less clear-cut appreciation of racialization.

Despite a plethora of important accounts on racialization, undertaken by both materialist and culturalist writers in the field, there has been an assumption that racialization is somehow a 'black thang'. The vast majority of studies on racialization have then tended to omit or at least underplay the racialization of ethnic majorities, especially those individuals deemed 'white' (Bonnett and Nayak 2003; Nayak 2003*a*). The inability to appreciate that white people live racially structured lives, even if this places them within ever-mobile systems of privilege, is something of an historical conceit. For it allows whiteness to escape racialization and maintain its position as dominant, normative, and transparently set apart from the question of race. Recent research on whiteness is now helping to displace this misguided assumption by demonstrating that its hegemonic status is accelerated through the deracialization of 'white' as a racial signifier (Dyer 1997; Bonnett 2000; Levine-Rasky 2002). Understanding how the articulation of one racial identity is always dependent upon the production of others, discloses the interconnectedness of all socially constituted racial demarcations. This in turn may enable us to implode racial binaries altogether through the production of new 'cultural geographies of racialization' (Bonnett and Nayak 2003: 300) that illustrate the historical and geographic making of race concepts.

In view of the paucity of detailed investigation into the racialization of whiteness I will now go on to utilize insights that have developed in the aftermath of the cultural turn, applying these to ethnographic illustrations of my own. These perspectives will highlight the interconnections, contradictions, and multiple subject positionings that arise in and through the practice of racialization amongst white youth. The ethnographic vignettes explore the practice of racialization within two masculine youth subcultures. At first glance, each of these cultures appears diametrically opposed to one another. The Pale Warriors, a Skinhead subculture in the English West Midlands, espouse overtly racist opinions and openly admit to being perpetrators of racist violence.[2] The B-Boyz subculture, on the other hand, display a strident affiliation with black culture to such an extent that they are construed as 'race traitors' within the parochial and ostensibly white region of the northeast of England. However, as each of these subcultural case studies will elucidate, both masculine peer group formations are implicated in the 'discursive formation' of race through the cultural imaginings they attribute to blackness, whiteness, and the lexicon of other racialized tropes. To illustrate these processes the ethnography will draw upon recorded interviews, observations, and 'thick' description of people and place. The analysis reveals that racial identities are not only discursively constituted but are embodied, performed, and endowed with a corporeal significance that makes them appear 'as if real'. Furthermore, the ethnography will demonstrate how the practice of racialization is itself deeply contradictory in young lives, to the extent that at least some of the power and prestige ascribed to whiteness may simultaneously be undermined.

Pale Warriors

The Pale Warriors all lived on the Kempton Dene estate, a quintessential white suburb located at the edge of Birmingham in the West Midlands, UK. Built in 1952, the estate emerged as part of a postwar reconstruction policy to relocate the English working classes in outer-city areas. At the time of the research there were 4182 people living on 'The Dene', 98 per cent of whom were classified as white.[3] The suburb was regarded as a 'white space', a 'no-go' area for ethnic minorities and outsiders. At a macropolitical level this cartography of racialization was partially achieved as a consequence of economic transformations in the region, 'white flight' from the city, and local city council housing policies that sought to disperse minority groups throughout the conurbation. However, the construction of the Dene as a white space was further secured at a micropolitical level through intimidation, harassment, and the perpetuation of racist graffiti (see Back and Nayak 1999). The ward also has a history of far-right voting patterns in local elections. Moreover, there are deeply felt class resentments between those who have lived in the locality for successive generations, those from neighbouring areas, and any 'newcomers' to the estate. This tension is compounded by the social geography of the estate where one side looks out on to open fields and farmland, while the other corners border the affluent town of Chalk Vale. Nearly 50 per cent of properties on the estate are classified as owner-occupied households, a legacy of a Conservative administration that encouraged aspiring working class individuals to become house owners and purchase what was previously Council property. As mortgage interest rates increased, repossession, redundancies, and crime set in. It is within this context that Skinheads and racist activity have become pronounced.

The Pale Warriors subculture was made up of around ten young men aged 13–16 years. All identified as white English, with the exception of Calvin and Leonard who had English mothers and African Caribbean fathers. Significantly, the young white males heralded from large families who had lived on the West Midlands outer -city estate of Kempton Dene for a number of years. Moreover, there was evidence that certain family members had previously voted for the British National Party and the National Front during elections. These families had notorious reputations within the community and were feared by many residents. It was rumoured that most of the criminal activities that occurred on the estate were attributable to one of three families to which the young men all belonged. At the time of the research, the young white men interviewed were either unemployed, about to leave school, or, in the case of Daniel, had been expelled for 'paki-bashing'. None of the respondents were in permanent employment and had fragmentary work experience at best, gained from temporary manual labour helping out their fathers when situations arose. Consequently, they spent long stretches of time out on the streets but during evenings occupied a local youth club where interviews were undertaken.

The prevailing economic situation appears to have left the Skins without a secure work-based identity where investments in specific styles of whiteness became a substitute for the masculine-affirmative process of manual labour. Arguing for the protection of white jobs was an expression of a wider 'rights for whites' discourse. Here, the young men discuss the issues of immigration and employment at local and national scales:

Daniel (white): It's our country, not theirs.
Leonard (mixed-heritage): Yeah, they don't belong in our country.[4]

Daniel (white): Fuck 'em off. They've got all the jobs, like me and Mark could be working now but fucking two pakis [*referring to local Asian shopkeepers*] have jumped in our place haven't they?

The sense of ownership over the nation ('our country') and the labour market ('our place') is illustrative of the silent racialization of the nation-state as white. It also reflects the subculture's inability to relinquish white privilege in a period of widespread socio-economic transformation. In his analysis of youth training schemes in the region, Hollands also reflected upon the plight of working class males and the racialization of the labour market. Many 'have a strong interest in maintaining "white identity" in the context of the present economic crisis, because', he maintains, 'they are in a declining position, even if this has nothing to do with the presence and activities of black people' (1990: 171).

The Skinhead hairstyle and clothing may itself be seen to articulate multiple masculine fantasies of existence related to manual labour, militarism, prison identity, and 'hardness'. Although the cut connects up with elements of working class manual work, significantly, none of the young men interviewed were actually in employment at the time. Thus, it was the *fantasy* of the macho style that was particularly attractive. Cohen (1972: 25) has accurately described such 'machismo' as 'the unconscious dynamics of the work ethic translated into the out of work situation'. Here, the Skinhead haircut is consciously emblematic of working class identifications and a broader, bourgeois social alienation. It is also a look which encapsulates a 'geometry of menace' (Hebdige 1982), symmetrically choreographed to invoke the collective presence of a 'gang' or paramilitary force. The appearance then conveys the spirit of white masculinity as aggressive, lumpen, and fiercely nationalistic. This body styling display, which in other contexts may signify a gay or even anti-racist identity (see Healy 1996), held less obvious ambiguity in Kempton Dene. Here, the cut operated as a cultural register for deindustrial England, revealing only a certain naked vulnerability: the bald truth of a bleak future.[5]

Bodies of Evidence: 'Acting your Colour'

In being of mixed-parentage, the position of Calvin and Leonard within this ostensibly racist peer group was inevitably precarious. It was essential that they were seen to 'act white'. 'I've mixed in half with the crowd that are NF and they know I'm alright', remarked

Calvin, 'It's like if I didn't mix in with them they'd give me "assle" '. Each of these young men spoke at length to explain how they had 'whitened' their dress style, language, and comportment when they had moved to the Dene to fit in with the Skins. According to their new peers, Calvin and Leonard could be carefully distinguished from other black youth in what in friendship terms amounts to an act of 'cultural refencing'. Here, the borders of the peer-group are restaked without significant alteration to the values of the group and the broader subcultural ethos of racism:

Robbie (white): [Pointing to Leonard] He hasn't got an attitude. He don't go round like sucking his teeth and talking.
Leonard (mixed heritage): Yeah.
Mark (white): He did in that prison, remember? Flared your nostrils.
Leonard (mixed heritage): That bloke had bad breath!
Anoop: What does that mean, an 'attitude'?
Darren (white): He don't act like a black person really.

For the Kempton Dene Skins 'acting black' is a thoroughly embodied activity. It meant flaring your nostrils, wearing 'black' clothes, speaking in patois, having a pronounced walk, 'sucking' or 'kissing' your teeth. Blackness is then read through the register of the body and was encapsulated by the term 'attitude'. According to Mark, blacks who had 'bad attitude' tend to 'walk past ya, kiss their teeth, flare their nostrils at ya'. However, deeper questioning revealed that all blacks regardless of their disposition were despised, 'attitude' was merely a rationale for further outrage and discrimination. Soon after the youth club interviews had taken place, Calvin and Leonard parted company with the Kempton Dene Skins. One of the unintended consequences of this ethnographic 'race talk' may have been to render their position untenable within the group.[6] A local youth worker explained, 'I think what happened was that you confronted all the contradictions in that group and as a result they couldn't paper over the cracks anymore, or go on like they were just one of the lads.' The Skins regarded the departure of Calvin and Leonard as further evidence that the youth were, in the final instance, 'just like the rest of 'em'; that is, quintessentially black. The act of 'cultural refencing' that had extended to incorporate certain black (or at least mixed-heritage) youth was now being retracted. The issue of 'acting' in accordance with accepted racial stereotypes was also a means of confirming and preserving ideas about the 'white race'. I pursued this theme in discussions with the Skins by asking: what do you mean by the phrase 'act your own colour'?

Mark: We act like we act, and get all the black people like walking, swing-
    ing their fucking arms like fucking apes.
Darren: We wear jeans. Niggers wear cuts in their jeans. Pakis wear pyjamas.
Daniel: And fucking towels.

Here, the different practices of racialization are laid bare. African
Caribbeans are akin to animals engaged in spectacular bodily displays, 'swinging their fucking arms like fucking apes'. This process of
racialization is intertwined with gender and sexuality to the extent
that, 'fear and desire double for one another and play across the
structures of otherness, complicating its politics' (Hall 1992: 256).
Here, the hidden desires embedded in the white fantasy of black
machismo are displaced and instead come to depict blacks as primitive, savage beasts. Consequently, we are informed, 'niggers wear cuts
in their jeans', locating African Caribbean identities as urban, streetwise
ethnicities that are potentially threatening and dangerous, indeed,
ape-like. The racist articulation of blackness creates a *hyper-mascu-
line* image of African Caribbeans. The passage alludes to bodily
boundaries where choreographed actions are seen to attribute directly
from the supposed race of individuals. This 'unspoken', yet secretly
admired black identity is (mis)recognized by the Skins and selectively
evoked through the stereotype of the macho, urban, American male.

The racialization of South Asians is also criss-crossed through a
nexus of sex/gender relations. In contrast, Asians are constructed as
a *feminized* people, secured through the discursive production of
identifiable stereotypes. The feminization of Asian masculinities was
evident by the fact that there was no systematic equivalent to paki-
bashing when it came to African Caribbean youth. Indeed, the
Warriors portrayed African Caribbeans as potential aggressors
(hypermasculine) though this did not curtail a series of violent interactions between each of these different youth cohorts. In contrast,
Asians were regarded as 'asking for it' on the basis of an assumed
passiveness and a perceived unalterable cultural difference. Paki-
bashing in school, the street, and also the corner shop was a regular
occurrence. The (imagined) Asian body was also subject to a deeply
racialized encoding. Here, their 'subordinate' masculinities are produced through the tropes of 'towels' (turbans) and 'pyjamas' (sal-
waar-kameez). In contrast to the 'ruff', cut-up denim dress of African
Caribbean youth—a style that brazenly exposes black skin—Asian
clothing appears modest, concealing, and covering up the body.
Moreover, these items connote softness and domesticity, when juxtaposed to the outdoor labouring clothing of denim allegedly donned
by whites, and the subversive streetwear of black youth. Although

there is evidence to suggest that contemporary representations of Asian youth are now shifting (Alexander 2000), at the time of the research in the 1990s the Skins appeared to have deep investment in producing them as feeble, weak, and feminized.

It is also worth considering the deracialized construction of whiteness through this strategic encoding. Indeed, a key mechanism for enacting whiteness is to assert the cultural difference of racialized Others. The comments about 'acting your own colour' suggest an inherent way of 'being' white which involves an intrinsically different body schema than those adopted by African Caribbean or Asian youth. In contrast, whiteness is supremely ordinary, 'We act like we act', and as commonplace as denim, 'we wear jeans'. In this sense whiteness appears to escape racialization, a transparent quality that is found in 'emptiness, absence, denial' (Dyer 1993: 141). As such, the (dis)embodiment of whiteness is a process that relies upon recognition with racialized Others to define itself. In so doing, the practice of 'differential racialization' situates the socio-sexual position of all cultural identities, including white. Post-structuralist insights inform us how 'Structures of class, racism, gender and sexuality cannot be treated as "independent variables" because the oppression of each is inscribed within the other—is constituted and constitutive of the other' (Brah 1992: 137). And yet the ethnography reveals precisely how racialization can entail the freezing and reification of difference. The displacement and ambivalence is further underscored as the responses concerning 'pakis' in pyjamas were made to me, a British Asian researcher who dressed in jeans throughout the ethnography. It is then through the filter screen of blackness that a flickering sense of whiteness at last becomes intelligible at the superficial level of representation.

The B-Boyz

The Tyneside conurbation in the northeast of England is a post-industrial area, once associated with coal mining, ship building, and heavy engineering. More recently, the locality has witnessed severe economic restructuring and has been characterized as 'a region in transition' (Tomaney and Ward 2001) with the cessation of its mineral-based coal economy. The descaling of industry that led to a substantial increase in masculine unemployment rates has more recently been accompanied by the emergence of a new service sector economy. This has seen a rise in female employment, part-time labour, fixed-term contracts, and more 'flexible' patterns of work. In place of the pit, shipyard, and factory are now to be found a growing predominance of table-waiting jobs, telephone call centre work, and insecure employment linked to 'footloose' multinational organizations that maintain their headquarters elsewhere (Nayak 2003*a*, *b*). Indeed, it has been argued that in the contemporary period young men are more likely to be 'learning to serve' (McDowell 2000) than 'learning to labour' (Willis 1977). The turn from production to consumption is also illustrated by the global corporate leisure industries in the region that have heralded a new night-time economy, dominated by standardized nightclubs, cafes, restaurants, and waterfront bars (Chatterton and Hollands 2002, 2003).

Today the northeast remains an ostensibly white region, a point starkly reflected in the 2001 census which classifies 97.6 per cent of the population as white. However, this includes some longstanding Jewish, Scandinavian, Irish, Scottish, and East European settlers. There are also small migrant groups including Arabs, Indians, Pakistanis, Bangladeshis, and West Indians, though these numbers hardly compare to those located in most British multicultural centres (Nayak 1999). Recently, the British National Party has been actively campaigning across the region in places such as Teesside, Sunderland, and Durham. Indeed, a government Home Office report for 1999–2000 indicates that the county of Northumbria has the highest levels of racially motivated attacks outside of London (1159 assaults or 2.15 per 1000 of the population). In Newcastle alone Northumbria Police documented an increase in racist incidents from 460 to 690 during the period of April 2000–March 2001.[7] It is within this cultural milieu of post-industrial transformation and white chauvinism that the B-Boyz are trying to forge new urban ethnicities.

The B-Boyz formed a masculine subculture whose enthusiasm for basketball had encouraged a partial and ambivalent affiliation with black culture. The appellation 'B-Boyz' was replete with multiple meanings. Some youth said it was a sporting reference (B)asketball-Boys; others that it was a musical epithet where the 'B' could symbolize break-dancing, bee-bop, or even the Bronx; and a few subcultural members even reclaimed the sign in an assertion that they were '(B)adass-Boyz', implying they were 'cool' or 'hard'. Nevertheless, despite this struggle for the sign, a number of other white youth declared that the B-Boyz and their ilk were aptly named since they represented that most contentious of social groups, (B)lack-Boyz. However, though this identity was initially much disparaged, towards the end of the research there was growing evidence that the negative epithet B-Boyz could be transformed into a positive signifier of identity and collective social belonging.

Basketball, Racialization, and the Black Body

In the mainly white preserves of Tyneside, basketball offered a symbolic gateway into black culture. For a number of B-Boyz the sport offered the first real opportunity of meeting other black youth. 'Most of the professional team was black', trilled Chris, a member of the local under-17s team. 'The best players on it was black, and like my coach was black! So I associated with them, and all.' The B-Boyz had developed a deep respect for the infectious exuberance of their black American coach. It was a respect that gradually reached out to other black players they met on travels when playing opposing teams in different cities. The sport encouraged them to become increasingly aware of their own conservative white dress style as they slowly adapted it in accordance with new found peer groups, global youth styles, and, of course, one another. They explained the connections between sport, clothing, and racialization to me:

Chris: There was a few people into it [basketball], there's loads [now], we all got together and started listening to the music that seemed to fit with the sport.
Anoop: What music was associated with the sport?
Chris: Well Rap music, I suppose, with basketball. I dunno why but it just does, it just seems right. And it's also black culture, in basketball there's a lot of black culture. The best players are black in general.

For the Boyz there appears a stylistic 'fit', or what Willis (1978) terms an 'homology', between basketball, hip hop music, and black culture. Indeed, the flamboyant dress code evokes a global outlook that reaches across the 'Black Atlantic' (Gilroy 1993) for its inspiration:

Anoop: Is there a link between basketball and Hip-Hop then?
Sam: Well it's American.
James: It is. It's like American and basketball's baggy stuff and dead long t-shirts.
Sam: Cos everyone that plays basketball listens to Hip-Hop.

The baggy streetwear of the B-Boyz is suggestive of their looser ties with white Englishness and their desire to experiment with a global multiculture. The dress style also symbolizes the '"shaggy", hybrid identities that are a feature of postmodern youth cultures. Such global youth cultures may be less likely to draw their influence from cultural happenings at a neighbourhood, regional, or even national scale. Indeed, the effects of a global consumer culture were most evident in the dress styles of the B-Boyz. 'There's normally baggy clothes for Hip-Hop', explained Sam, 'I normally wear baggy clothes and caps and everythin': basketball tops and jeans, big jackets and everythin'. This act of racialized embodiment also included the adoption and adaptation of black hairstyles through the deployment of 'dreads', tramlines, braids, and beading. Thus, Sam informed me he was about to get dreadlocks, while other young men were drawn to the elaborate sculpted patterns sometimes shaved into the heads of black urban youth:

James: I like the bricks me. You get all of it shaved off to a No.2 or 3 or something, then you get a step shaved in a No. 1. Y'na bricks.
Anoop: Bricks?
James: Aye, like little rectangles shaved in with a step.
Michelle: With lines.

At least at the level of style, then, the Boyz were able to parade as race traitors, white mavericks who appeared to be challenging the meaning of whiteness in the locality through corporeal techniques of consumption and display.

But to what extent does a stylistic transgression of whiteness equate with a genuine anti-racist politics of transformation? And why did the Boyz show little interest in making links with the largest visible minority group in the region, South Asians? Such questions call for a rethinking of the radical potential of cultural hybridity to unsettle racial binaries in ways suggested by contemporary post-colonial theory (Bhabha 1995). Indeed, at its most extreme, it appeared some B-Boyz expressed an unremitting desire to 'be' black (whatever that meant) and had chosen to embrace the full blazonary of black style. As this was a high-risk display that frequently resulted in verbal insult or physical abuse from what remains a predominantly white, conservative, and localized youth culture, I was keen to enquire if there were any advantages to blackness.

Chris: Well from an athletics point of view I think that there are. They're good at most sports [...]. When it comes to sprinters, stuff like that, blacks seem more powerful.
John: There's more power thrusting you see.
Chris: The black basketball players can jump higher than the white basketballers. I dunno why, maybe they've got more explosive legs or something. Sprinting, jumping, both things—explosive legs!
Suzanne: Then there are blacks who aren't that athletic at all, same as whites.
Chris: Yeah, but when you look at the athletic whites and the athletic blacks, the blacks are more athletic than the athletic whites.

Although the Boyz celebrate aspects of cultural fusion, then, there continues to remain a belief in fundamental, corporeal differences between blacks and whites that is not dissimilar to the discourse of racialization deployed by the Pale Warriors. Their comments also reveal the cultural imaginings of blackness and demonstrate how the production of whiteness is reliant upon the depiction of racialized Others. The transformation of blacks from subhuman—as recounted by the Warriors—to superhuman as endorsed by the Boyz, reveals the tensions entrapped in the discourse of racialization. This racial ambivalence is neatly expressed in Fanon's (1970) compelling psychoanalytic couplet, *'fear/desire'*. The belief that black subjects embody anatomical qualities that are frustratingly out of reach to white youth was a recurring feature in B-Boyz accounts which focused upon blacks as having explosive, power-thrusting legs which made them majestic jumpers and lightning runners.

Indeed, the cultural imaginings of black bodies by white youth vibrated with a potent sexual urgency. As Richard Dyer (1997) has expressed in his study on whiteness, the myth that 'white men can't jump' is a racialized fiction that has masculine reproductive connotations related to leaping spermatozoa. In contemporary youth cultures black men, in particular, are imagined as 'hypersexual'. As Paul disclosed, 'I'd like to jump as high as 'em in basketball, it'd be great! I could jump through the hoop!' Such deeply racialized impressions turn the black body into a symbol of phallic assertion. It springs into action, is dynamically thrusting, and penetrates hoops in what is ultimately an orgasmic, extra 'explosive' performance. In this moment, Fanon reveals, 'the negro is eclipsed. He is turned into a penis. He *is* a penis'. (1970: 120). This 'doubling' of fear and desire in the accounts of B-Boyz was evident when they spoke about the sporting prowess of black athletes and ratified the belief that they were good 'movers-'n'-shakers'. As Paul, an established B-Boy and ardent hip hop fan declared, 'D'ya know what I really hayut about blacks? They're all such good dancers!' That blacks are simultaneously admired and 'hated' exposes the double-edged nature of racialization. At the same time, black masculinity is reduced to the body which is transformed into a type of 'racial fetish, a juju doll from the dark side of the white man's imaginary' (Mercer 1994: 184).

The 'dark side' of racialization alluded to above, became all too apparent when the B-Boyz drew a critical distinction between black and white sporting attributes. For example, the Boyz reflected upon the success of the white British Olympic triple jumper Jonathan Edwards who hails from the locality. They used a curious 'racial logic' to explain how his physical dominance in the field in recent years is not necessarily undermined by his whiteness.

Chris: Depends on what you need for the sport. Long jump is just a burst, one burst of power to push yourself. But triple jump you've got to have balance and er...

John: You've got to measure your jump so you don't do big jumps, and then you can't do a massive one.

Even amongst the Boyz, black sporting superiority is a partial, tenuous, and often contradictory discursive repertoire. Black sporting success is related to physical differences, the muscular ability to make explosive leaps or bounds. In contrast, white success is attributed to superior 'technique' that can prevail over raw bursts of power in certain situations. Where qualities such as balance, strategy, or other functions associated with the mind are required, white superiority wins out. Thus, the timing and precision needed to 'measure' jumps is said to place the black athlete at a strategic disadvantage when s/he can no longer rely on a primitive 'burst of power' but has to calculate the point of departure. The racialization of black athleticism on the sports track or basketball court is, then, a profoundly ambivalent metamorphosis. The bodily schema means their sporting success is rarely attributed to hard work, strategy, technique, or timing—these remain the mind zone of the white man and serve to freeze the black individual out of subjective experience. According to the spurious logic of racialization, white men can jump it seems, but they do so in ways that are intrinsically different to their black counterparts.

Concluding Remarks

In what is a rapidly changing world the certainty attributed to race may appear to offer a measure of security, however illusory this may be. The accounts of young people suggest that the salience of racialization has extended into the post-colonial era and can form a compelling rubric from which to interpret difference. However, these responses also indicate that there are multiple forms of racialization: 'positive', 'negative', and many evidently ambiguous. What is more, is that the racialization of black and brown bodies is implicitly tied to an unspoken understanding of whiteness. It is here that I have shown how the new, cultural approaches to racialization can be most revealing.

The ethnography illustrates how racialization crystallizes in the material, social, and psychic habitus of young white lives. In particular, masculine peer groups are seen to engage in a practice of racialization that is profoundly ambivalent and marked by dissonance, rupture, and incoherence. Here, blacks may be positioned simultaneously as savage apes or super athletes as each of these images become super-imposed—time and again—upon one another. Indeed, the speed and immediacy of global media technology may have encouraged the acceleration of the image to such an extent that a distorted version of blackness is readily available for consumption in advertisements, film, and music videos (Nayak 1997). In such mesmerizing repres-entations the black body is often found leaping headlong through our fibre-optic cables, satellite linkups, computer laptops, and digit-ally enhanced screens. Although these racialized images are con-nected to a broader economy of signs, produced through the machinery of corporate capital, they are also interpreted at symbolic and imaginary levels.

However seductive the image of race may seem, tattooed upon our inner minds, it is undoubtedly worth recalling that the mirage of racial difference can only be sustained by an excessive amount of mental labour—fantasy, projection, sublimation, displacement, dis-avowal, and dissimulation. It is through a critical reading of these displays that we may begin to map whiteness and displace it from its invisible, deracialized mantle. In doing so, it seems such acts of racialized projection and psychic expulsion are never complete as the phantasmal representation of blackness, as image or imago, returns to haunt white subjects, reminding them of their physical insecur-ities, sexual anxieties, and disembodied sense of 'lack'. This leaves us with a curious sense that the doing away of race may yet come to be as much of a relief to white lives as it does to black subjects who have long struggled to escape the exigencies of racialization. This realization may engender a greater willingness from young people to challenge the archetypal descriptions that underpin all racial cat-egories. Until whiteness is also located in this process the concept of race may continue to persevere as a dark 'regime of truth' (Foucault 1980) in a globalized post-colonial world.

NOTES

1. There is also, it should be noted, a slew of early pseudoscientific research that has continued to propagate the idea of race as composed through immutable biological differences. However, this work has either been largely discredited or has come under rigorous critique from other scientists (see for example Rose et al. 1984).

2. I would like to thank Les Back for allowing me to use some of the material from our study on perpetrators of racist violence (ESRC 000234272).
3. From the 2% of ethnic minority residents, numbering 86 people, 42% were African Caribbean and 43% were Asian (heralding from India, Pakistan, and Bangladesh).
4. Directing venom against an Asian Other was one way through which the mixed-heritage males, Calvin and Leonard, could insert themselves into a white racist group and claim Britain as 'our country'.
5. This underlying vulnerability may be better understood when we consider that the shaven appearance is also associated with babies, wasted drug-users, and patients undergoing chemotherapy. It was also alleged to be a style taken up by the Luddites, skilled artisans who destroyed nineteenth-century industrial machinery as they feared it would make their labour redundant.
6. Les Back and myself have considered this at length and feel uncertain as to our possible role in facilitating the situation. This example is evidence of the sensitive dynamics researchers encroach upon when conducting ethnographic work with young people. On one level we were concerned that we may have upset the existing peer group relations, while on the other we were aware that this may have been a first step in challenging racism among these young people by encouraging the individuals to make personal choices. At the same time, Calvin and Leonard may have left for reasons unbeknownst to us.
7. These figures may also reflect better reporting mechanisms by the police in the wake of the Macpherson Report (1999). However, Newcastle City Council have also identified increased racial tensions aimed at asylum-seekers in depleted urban areas who are seen to be competing for ever scarcer resources with poor, unemployed, white families.

REFERENCES

Alexander, C. (2000) *The Asian Gang: Ethnicity, Identity, Masculinity*. Oxford: Berg.
Back, L. and Nayak, A. (1999) 'Signs of the Times? Violence, Graffiti and Racism in the English Suburbs', in T. Allen and J. Eade (eds.), *Divided Europeans: Understanding Ethnicities in Conflict*. The Hague: Kluwer Law International.
Bhabha, H. K. (1995) *The Location of Culture*. London: Routledge.
Bonnett, A. (2000) *White Identities: Historical and International Perspectives*. Harlow: Pearson Education.
———and Nayak, A. (2003) 'Cultural Geographies of Racialization—The Territory of Race', in K. Anderson, M. Domosh, S. Pile, and N. Thrift (eds.), *Handbook of Cultural Geography*. London: Sage, pp. 300–12.
Bradley, H. and Fenton, S. (1999) 'Reconciling Culture and Economy: Ways Forward in the Analysis of Ethnicity and Gender', in L. Ray and A. Sayer (eds.), *Culture and Economy after the Cultural Turn*. London: Sage, pp. 112–34.
Brah, A. (1992) 'Difference, Diversity and Differentiation', in J. Donald and A. Rattansi (eds.), *'Race', Culture, and Difference*. London: Sage, pp. 126–45.
——— (1996) *Cartographies of Diaspora: Contesting Identities*. London: Routledge.
Chatterton, P. and Hollands, R. G. (2002) 'Theorizing Urban Playscapes: Producing, Regulating and Consuming Youthful Nightlife City Spaces'. *Urban Studies*, 39(1): 95–116.
——— (2003) *Urban Nightscapes: Youth Cultures, Pleasure Spaces and Corporate Power*. London: Routledge.

Cohen, P. (1972) 'Subcultural Conflict and Working-class Community'. *Working Papers in Cultural Studies,* 2: 5–51.

——(1988) 'The Perversions of Inheritance: Studies in the Making of Multi-racist Britain', in P. Cohen and H. S. Bains (eds.), *Multi-Racist Britain.* Basingstoke: Macmillan, pp. 9–118.

——(1994) "It's Racism what Dunnit": Hidden Narratives in Theories of Racism' in J. Donald and A. Rattansi (eds.), *'Race', Culture and Difference.* London: Sage, pp. 62–103.

Dyer, R. (1993) 'White', in R. Dyer ed., *The Matter of Images: Essays on Representations.* London: Routledge.

——(1997) *White.* London: Routledge.

Fanon, F. (1970) *Black Skin/White Masks.* London: Paladin.

Foucault, M. (1972) *The Archaeology of Knowledge.* London: Tavistock.

——(1978) *The History of Sexuality: An Introduction.* Harmondsworth: Penguin.

——(1980) 'Truth and Power', in C. Gordon (ed.), *Power/Knowledge: Selected Interviews and Other Writings 1972–77.* Brighton: Harvester Press.

Gilroy, P. (1993) *The Black Atlantic: Modernity and Double Consciousness.* London: Verso.

Green, M. and Carter, B. (1988) ' "Races" and "Race-Makers": The Politics of Racialization'. *Sage Race Relations Abstracts,* 13: 4–30.

Hall, S. (1992) 'New Ethnicities', in J. Donald and A. Rattansi (eds.), *'Race', Culture and Difference.* London: Sage.

——Critcher, C., Jefferson, T., Clarke, J., and Roberts, B. (1979) *Policing the Crisis: Mugging, the State, and Law and Order.* London: Macmillan.

Healy, M. (1996 [1989]) *Gay Skins: Class, Masculinity and Queer Appropriation.* London: Cassell.

Hebdige, D. (1982) 'This is England! And They Don't Live Here', in N. Knight (ed.), *Skinhead.* London: Omnibus Press.

——(1987 [1979]) *Subculture: The Meaning of Style.* London: Methuen.

Hollands, R. G. (1990) *The Long Transition: Class, Culture and Youth Training.* Basingstoke: Macmillan.

Levine-Rasky, C. (ed.), (2002) *Working Through Whiteness: International Perspectives.* Albany: State University of New York.

Macpherson, W. (1999) *The Stephen Lawrence Inquiry.* Cm. 42621, London: HMSO.

McDowell, L. (2000) 'Learning to Serve? Employment Aspirations and Attitudes of Young Working-Class Men in an Era of Labour Market Restructuring'. *Gender, Place and Culture,* 7 (4): 389–416.

Mercer, K. (1994) *Welcome to the Jungle: New Positions in Black Cultural Studies.* London: Routledge.

Miles, R. (1989) *Racism.* London: Routledge.

——and Phizacklea, A. (eds.) (1979) *Racism and Political Action in Britain.* London: Routledge and Kegan Paul.

Nayak, A (1997) 'Frozen Bodies: Disclosing Whiteness in Haagen-Dazs Advertising'. *Body and Society* 3 (3): 51–71.

——(1999) 'White English Ethnicities: Racism, Anti-Racism and Student Perspectives'. *Race Ethnicity and Education,* 2 (2): 177–202.

——(2003a) ' "Ivory Lives": Economic Restructuring and the Making of Whiteness in a Post-industrial Youth Community'. *European Journal of Cultural Studies* 63: 305–25.

Nayak, A (2003b) 'Last of the "Real Geordies"?: White Masculinities and the Subcultural Response to Deindustrialisation'. *Environment and Planning D: Society and Space,* 21: 7–25.

Phoenix, A. (2001) 'Racialization and Gendering in the (Re)production of Educational Inequalities', in B. Francis and C. Skelton (eds.), *Investigating Gender: Contemporary Perspectives in Education*. Maidenhead: Open University Press, pp. 126–38.

Rattansi, A. (1994) 'Changing the Subject? Racism, Culture and Education', in J. Donald and A. Rattansi (eds.), *'Race', Culture and Difference*. London: Sage, pp. 11–48.

Ray, L. and Sayer, A. (1999) *Culture and Economy after the Cultural Turn*. London: Routledge.

Rex, J. (1970) *Race Relations in Sociological Theory*. London: Weidenfield and Nicolson.

——and Tomlinson, S., with Hearnden, D., and Ratcliffe, P. (1979) *Colonial Immigrants in a British City: A Class Analysis*. London: Routledge and Kegan Paul.

Robins, K. (1991) 'Tradition and Translation: National Culture in its Global Context', in J. Corner and S. Harvey (eds.), *Enterprise and Heritage: Crosscurrents of National Culture*. London: Routledge.

Rose, S., Lewontin, R. C., and Kamin, L. J. (1984) *Not in our Genes*. Harmondsworth: Penguin.

Said, E. (1995 [1978]) *Orientalism: Western Conceptions of the Orient* Harmondsworth: Penguin.

Small, S. (1994) *Racialized Barriers: The Black Experience in the United States and England in the 1980s*. London: Routledge.

Smart, B. (1985) *Michel Frucault*. London: Tavistock.

Tomaney, J. and Ward, N. (2001) *A Region in Transition: North East England at the Millennium*. Aldershot: Ashgate.

Westwood, S. (1990) 'Racism, Black Masculinity and the Politics of Space', in J. Headen and D. Morgan (eds.), *Men, Masculinities and Social Theory*. London: Unwin Hyman.

Willis, P. (1977) *Learning to Labour: How Working Class Kids get Working Class Jobs*. London: Routledge and Kegan Paul.

——(1978) *Profane Culture*. London: Routledge and Kegan Paul.

CHAPTER 8

Recovering Blackness/Repudiating Whiteness: The *Daily Mail*'s Construction of the Five White Suspects Accused of the Racist Murder of Stephen Lawrence

Eugene McLaughlin

Reflecting on the complexity of entanglements of issues of 'race', racism, and anti-racism in the early 1990s, Solomos and Back (1996) were of the opinion that neither the race relations problematic of the 1970s nor the racisms problematic of the 1980s was capable of explaining what was happening to 'the social' in contemporary Britain. Since then there has been renewed critical discussion of how 'racialization'—the social processes that actively construct and reconstruct race and 'racial difference' as having self-evident meaning—'works'. But questions remain about how racialization is expressed, who exactly it is that is *doing* this racialization, why it works, and what its limits are.

Two developments are pertinent to the focus of this chapter. First, there is the acknowledgement that racialization processes, in their various articulations, are intimately connected to the 'norming' discourses and practices of gender, sexuality, and class formation. Bhattacharyya et al. (2002: 17) have argued that these discourses and practices do more than just coexist. Their interrelationality allows a complicated, sometimes academically inexplicable interplay that can both 'strengthen each other's grip on popular consciousness and cement social relations across a range of axes' and erase each other.

In principle, there is no limit to the number of determining factors that can generate racialized relationships. Second, the analytic framework of racialization has also to identify the processes through which racial meaning can be ascribed to social relations, practices, and groups that have been previously 'unraced'. There is increasing recognition, for example, that 'whiteness' profoundly problematizes our understanding of how the processes of racialization work (see Delgado and Stefancic 1997; Fine et al. 1997; Nakayama and Martins 1998; Rasmussen et al. 2001; Rockquemore and Brunsman 2002; Roediger 2002; Swain 2002; Ware and Back 2002).

Stuart Hall (1982: 35) has famously argued that the media is not only a powerful source of ideas about race, 'they are also one place where these ideas are articulated, worked on, transformed and elaborated'. The media is not unbiased or neutral: it provides the connecting words, ideas, and images out of which we fashion 'our very identities, our sense of selfhood; our notion of what it means to be male or female; our sense of class, of ethnicity and race, of nationality, of sexuality, of "us" and "them." Media images help shape our view of the world and our deepest values. Media stories provide the symbols, myths and resources through which we constitute a common culture and through the appropriation of which we insert ourselves into this culture' (Kellner 1995: 25). To be sure, it is virtually impossible to prove the effects of media coverage on what the public thinks and does about race. However, there is evidence that print and broadcast news media discourses are a constitutive part of everyday family and communal conversational interactions.

Consequently, an understandable place to start to address the tricky question of how and whether racialization works is to probe how the media's 'boundless appetite for racial image and narrative is crucial to its capacity to signify' (Torres 1998: 4). Numerous research studies have demonstrated how the racialized images and representational tropes circulating in the news media can transform complex human identities and social issues into one-dimensional, colour-coded stereotypes and caricatures (see Martindale 1986; Dates and Barlow 1990; Gray 1995; Wilson and Gutierez 1995; Gabriel 1998; Hunt 1999; Entman and Rojecki 2001; Jacobs 2000; Law 2002). However, to date researchers have paid scant attention to exploring the few moments when mainstream journalism and prime time television news decide to address whiteness explicitly (see Neal 1999; van Loon 1999).

I have elected to situate my discussion of how the racialization of whiteness works with the *Daily Mail's* role in the campaign to bring the murderers of Stephen Lawrence to justice. The *Daily Mail* is one of the United Kingdom's most successful and politically conservative mass circulation newspapers. When it chooses to do so, this mid-market tabloid can embrace more than two million readers, via headline stories, editorials, opinion essays, and human interest features, in a heated conversation on the changing nature of race relations in the United Kingdom. Put bluntly, what we might describe as its working within whiteness 'race work' does more than tell its readers *what* to think about race; it also uses well-established reportorial cues and structures to tell its readers *how* they might want to think about race. Although several broadsheet newspapers and independent television companies had investigated the Stephen Lawrence murder, it was the *Daily Mail's* high-profile campaign that set the agenda for the terms of the public debate about who and what was responsible for the killing. Never before had a racist murder been so graphically and repeatedly described and condemned by a right-wing newspaper in the United Kingdom. Equally importantly, this newspaper campaign offered 'Middle England' the possibility of thinking differently about both the racial injustices of everyday life and the reasons why a young man could be murdered on a suburban street because of the colour of his skin. In the Stephen Lawrence case, I will attempt to demonstrate how the *Daily Mail's* produced what is best described as a psychopathological version of whiteness that made the racist murder comprehensible to the ethnoracial imaginary of Middle England.

This chapter is divided into the following sections. First, I sketch how the *Daily Mail's* racialization processes constitute the ethnoracial imaginary of Middle England. In the next section, I examine how the newspaper first of all assimilated Stephen Lawrence into Middle England and then psychopathologized the whiteness of the five suspects. Finally, I consider the implications of the *Daily Mail's* willingness and ability to engage in multicultural race work for our understanding of racialization.

The data are drawn from a qualitative analysis of the *Daily Mail's* coverage of the Stephen Lawrence case between 1993 and 2003. They are supplemented by material gleaned from observational research of the Macpherson inquiry into the murder and documentation acquired in the course of writing the report on racial stereotyping that was submitted to the inquiry on behalf of the legal team representing Stephen Lawrence's friend Duwayne Brooks (see Hall et al. 1998).

Before proceeding, I need briefly to remind readers of the basic details of this notorious stab-and-run murder that continues to define debates on British race relations. On the night of Thursday, 22 April 1993, Stephen Lawrence, an eighteen-year-old black student, was stabbed to death by a group of young white men in the southeast London semi-suburb of Eltham. Stephen and his friend Duwayne Brooks had been waiting for a bus to take them home. He did not know his killers and his killers did not know him. According to Duwayne the only words uttered on that fateful night were 'what, what, nigger?' In the years to follow, the remarkable campaign organized by his parents Doreen and Neville Lawrence to bring the murderers of their son to justice transformed yet another unsolved racist murder with limited newsworthiness into a national conversation on race and justice. In a news media frenzy, on the 24 February 1999, the report of Sir William Macpherson's public inquiry into the murder declared that professional incompetence, institutional racism, and a failure of leadership within the Metropolitan Police had allowed the murderers to escape justice. Against a backdrop of blanket news media coverage, Prime Minister Tony Blair and the then Home Secretary, Jack Straw, declared that the Macpherson report would serve as a watershed to British society's attitudes to racism. Despite the media frenzy, there has been a relative lack of critical commentary on the news media's coverage of this extraordinary moment in the post-war history of UK race relations (see Cathcart 1999; Alibhai-Brown 2000; Cottle 2000; Law 2002). This is particularly the case concerning what I would argue is the racialized framing of those held responsible for the murder of Stephen Lawrence. These five young white men are in effect a taboo topic for scholars, their racist words and violent actions to be condemned rather than analysed.

Working Within Whiteness: The Daily Mail's Ethnoracial Imaginary of Middle England

Since the 1980s, the *Daily Mail* has played a pivotal role in constructing the potent political imaginary of self-reliant, aspirational, family-centred, socially conservative, self-evidently whiter-than-white Middle England. The idealized suburbs, towns, and villages constitutive of this ethnoracial imaginary are places separate from but also deemed to be under constant assault and threat from the shameful end of the nation, that is the violent, decaying, inner city and peripheral council estates inhabited by a morally degenerate, welfare-dependent, multiethnic underclass (Bywater 1998). The newspaper has been remarkably consistent in its 'what the order of things should be' editorial sensibilities: it both pinpoints the social, cultural concerns and personal anxieties that make the inhabitants of Middle England uneasy and upholds the core moral and political values that can keep what it views as the forces of disorder and cultural degradation at bay. The influence of the *Daily Mail* may well have something to do with current destabilization of virtually every aspect of British society: its complex patterns of signification work to restabilize, restore, and revalue. It is not afraid to air its views on controversial social issues such as homosexuality, HIV/AIDS, divorce, and illegitimacy. It has also taken on the responsibility for governing the terms of the public debate about race relations in the United Kingdom, supporting a strident assimilationist stance. Fearing the cataclysmic change this might bring, during the 1970s and 1980s the *Daily Mail* took the lead in demanding both that 'coloured' immigration be tightly controlled and that immigrants be socialized into and taught to observe the distinctive value system that gives British national and cultural identity its coherence and meaning. Boldfaced front pages and editorials have consistently highlighted the failures of post-war immigration policies in the United Kingdom and warned of the intractability of the 'race problem'. In this context, it gives undue coverage to conservative minority ethnic academics and commentators who argue that the main source of black underachievement in the United Kingdom (and the United States) is not white racism but dysfunctional family and cultural norms. To reinforce this point, the newspaper has also made periodic efforts to create a place in Middle England for successful 'new citizens' and 'model minorities' by, for example, acclaiming the 'respectable' Asian family and 'spicing' up its celebrity profiles with lifestyle stories of a few favoured black stars.

Crime is an emblematic issue for the *Daily Mail*, fostering fear and anger among readers. It provides graphic coverage that enables its readers to discuss the causes and solutions to the United Kingdom's crime problem within a racialized 'something-must-be-done' framework. It also has the resources to crusade around what we might define as 'sign of the times' crimes, particularly if it can hang the initial story on 'ideal' victims who have been subjected to heinous criminality. In doing so, it is of course making value judgements about the relative 'newsworthiness' of a human tragedy. At the same time, an innumerable number of crime problems receive little, if any, coverage in the newspaper. Most controversially, it stands accused of systematically under-reporting racist violence. The *Daily*

Mail's coverage of racist violence is premised upon the notion that tolerance and fair play are defining features of British society. Overt racism is not a part of Middle England and racist incidents are exceptional events perpetuated by fringe neo-fascist and white supremacist groups or almost the inevitable result of inner city racial tensions. It is therefore a 'switch off' issue for Middle England. However, in addition to strategic omission and/or distancing, the *Daily Mail* is also capable of 'reality check' stories that seek to turn public discussion of 'only whites can be violent racists' on its head. The newspaper periodically declares that an unspoken aspect of racist violence in contemporary Britain is one of anti-white street crime perpetrated by predatory young black men. It also condemns what it defines as the politically correct criminal justice and media establishment for suppressing or attempting to explain away the extent and seriousness of black-on-white criminal violence. The dramatic visual imprinting of 'black crime' stories on the public imagination, has led critics of the newspaper to accuse it of racially coding the United Kingdom's crime problem. Equally provocatively, the *Daily Mail*'s reporting of racist violence is intimately linked to its animosity towards anti-racist and multicultural initiatives. The paper implies that the introduction of US-style colour conscious affirmative action and racial preference strategies will generate white resentment, racial polarization, and cultivate an atmosphere within which incidents of racist violence can occur. In the next section of the chapter, I attempt to demonstrate how the *Daily Mail* completely bewildered its critics by deciding to revise its 'default mode' on its reporting of racist crime and black youthful masculinity and designating a young black man as an innocent victim deserving of the newspaper's support.

Recovering Blackness: The Assimilation of Stephen Lawrence

The *Daily Mail*'s initial reporting of the murder of Stephen Lawrence was true to form. On 8 May 1993, a 'news in brief' story noted that three white teenagers were being questioned by the police about the killing of Stephen Lawrence. There was 'no front page on the horror of it all. No shouting headlines or a demand for an end to racial injustice. No mention of the fact that it could even be a racially motivated attack. Just one short news story' (Ahmed 1999). However, two days later the newspaper spotlighted the murder as 'a family tragedy' to which many of its readers could relate. As it turned out, the *Mail* was in the process of not just putting faces to names but testing whether Stephen Lawrence and his family might be worthy of the support of Middle England. According to the news story and the associated editorial, Stephen Lawrence was a devout Christian and a hard-working sixth-former who wanted to train as an architect. His parents, Doreen and Neville Lawrence, were decent, moderate people who had encouraged his ambitions and were proud of his achievements. The Lawrences assured the newspaper that they had had brought their son up to respect the law and not to see colour as an issue. Indeed, they went so far as to declare that neither they nor their children had experienced racial harassment, let alone violence.

The paper was therefore able to draw a categorical distinction between the Middle England values of the Lawrence family home and those of the anti-racist and 'rent-a-mob' groups who had taken to the streets in the aftermath of the killing and were talking of reprisal attacks. The editorial line was clear:

Racism is abominable. Those of the neo-nazi persuasion who preach and provoke it should be condemned. But is there not also something contemptible about professional protestors who capitalise on grief to fuel confrontation? Such street agitators of the right and left need each other. Most of us in Britain—whatever our colour—need them like the plague.

A follow-on exclusive interview with Doreen and Neville Lawrence which the newspaper ran on 12 May provided more intimate details of the strain placed on this ordinary family by the murder of their eldest son who had passed seven GCSEs and was studying for four A-levels with the intention of becoming an architect. The grieving parents once more distanced themselves from the extremists who were trying to hijack the murder of their son for political ends. As the first arrests were made and court appearances took place, the *Daily Mail*'s representation of Stephen Lawrence as the innocent victim of a racist attack was consolidated:

Stephen, an A-Level student who hoped to become an architect, was killed on April 22 at a bus stop in Eltham, South-East London. He was waiting with a friend for a bus to return to his home in near by Plumstead when he was stabbed by a gang of between 4 and 6 white youths who had apparently made racist remarks. (*Daily Mail,* 22 December 1993)

The newspaper had little to say about the collapse of the public prosecution case against the suspects and the subsequent decision of the Lawrence family to launch a private prosecution in April 1996. However, the emotional scenes accompanying the collapse of the

LIVERPOOL JOHN MOORES UNIVERSITY
LEARNING SERVICES

private prosecution in April 1996 and the reconvening of the inquest of February 1997 allowed the paper to remind readers of what had happened and who was involved. Although the photographic and discursive image of Stephen Lawrence's innocence and the quiet dignity of his parents was by now firmly established in the public imagination, because of legal restrictions very little information was available about the young white men accused of his murder. However, all this would change as a result of the *Daily Mail*'s frame-breaking decision to invest its moral authority, political clout, and considerable investigative resources in a high-profile crusade to bring the murderers of Stephen Lawrence to justice.

Repudiating Whiteness: The Psychopathologization of the Five Suspects

In a blaze of publicity, on 13 February 1997 the five suspects reluctantly presented themselves at the reconvened inquest to be cross-examined about their alleged involvement in the murder of Stephen Lawrence. The decision by the suspects to exercise the legal right to refuse to answer any question that might incriminate them frustrated and infuriated all involved in the inquest process. It also most likely contributed to the inquest verdict that Stephen Lawrence had been killed 'in a completely unprovoked racist attacks by five white youths'. The following day, the *Daily Mail* recorded a journalistic first in the United Kingdom, attracting approval and condemnation in equal measure for printing a front page banner headline— 'Murderers: The Mail accuses these men of killing. If we are wrong let them sue us.' The most significant factors in the *Daily Mail*'s decision to print the names and the photographs of the prime suspects seem to have been that the extensive Metropolitan Police investigation and various unsuccessful court hearings confirmed that Stephen Lawrence was the victim of an unprovoked racially motivated attack: he did not have a criminal record, was not associated with drug dealing or a member of a street gang. He had been stabbed repeatedly and left to die because of the colour of his skin. The newspaper's preliminary investigations into the murder also confirmed that Stephen's parents were 'ordinary', 'decent', and 'dignified' people who had refused to allow race extremists to make political capital out of their son's death. The newspaper was also concerned that the suspects' manipulation of the legal process and the atmosphere of fear and intimidation surrounding the unresolved murder were threatening to lock Middle England into a racial crisis comparable to anything that had been seen in the United States in the aftermath of the Rodney King case.

In a complicated double movement, the *Daily Mail's* subsequent 'Justice for Stephen Lawrence' campaign repeatedly acclaimed the Lawrences as a grief-stricken family that had been left with the knowledge that a grave injustice had been allowed to prevail. In the process, Doreen and Neville Lawrence were transformed into a couple of extraordinary moral authority and respectability and their son Stephen idealized as an icon for Middle England. He was the gifted black schoolboy whose dream of becoming an architect had been brutally ended on a south London street in April 1993. These images would stand in pointed contrast to the *Daily Mail's* depiction of Neil Acourt, Jamie Acourt, Gary Dobson, Luke Knight, and David Norris, as the five white 'racist savages', the 'pack of bigots', the 'gang of evil killers', the 'moronic thugs' 'overflowing with hatred' who were 'walking free and smirking at the thrill of getting away with it'. In conjunction with its own investigations, the newspaper used the evidence that had emerged in earlier court hearings as the basis for its relentless hounding of the prime suspects. As a result, they would be transformed into a portrait of white psychopathological savagery that threatened all that Middle England stood for.

Acting it Out I: Video Footage of Natural Born Racists

The newspaper's overall construction of the suspects was based on police video evidence showing the five men expressing extremely violent racist views. In December 1994, as part of the Metropolitan Police investigation, a camera and a microphone had been hidden in a rented flat occupied by one of the suspects. The blurred footage with its 'yob culture' background 'of loud music, blaring TV shows and foul and racist language' provided *Daily Mail* readers with an insight into the private lives and thoughts of the suspects. It reveals 'a group of violent depraved men almost insane with hatred of people they called "Pakis and coons"' and 'a soundtrack of sickening racist obscenities'. The *Daily Mail*, along with the other newspapers and broadcasters, would subsequently make extensive use of this 'reality TV' footage as it illustrated 'the gang's love of knives and violence', predilection for 'racist thuggery', and 'psychopathic hatred of blacks'. And there is no doubt that the raging, racialized anger, and paranoia articulated in this video makes for disturbing viewing and listening. Throughout, the suspects brandish knives and practice stabbing moves and shout racist abuse at black entertainers and athletes as they are watching television. A couple of the suspects attempt to outdo each other in their stream of consciousness fantasies about the extreme violence they want to enact on 'fucking niggers' and 'Pakis' who they hold responsible for their predicament and all the ills of contemporary multiculturalized Britain.

What exactly is being acted out in this edited videotape, as well as why, has generated heated discussion. The suspects always claimed that they knew that the flat had been bugged and that they had used extreme language deliberately and acted provocatively both to undermine this supposedly covert police operation and express their anger about being unfairly hounded for a crime they did not commit. It therefore proved nothing. Indeed, on the video, they go to strenuous lengths to deny any involvement in the murder and distance themselves from the neo-fascist groups operating in the locality. However, for the *Daily Mail* the video footage provided incontrovertible evidence that the suspects were foul mouthed, uneducated, hardcore racists who glorified in the doing of extreme violence. These were the sort of 'natural born racists' who could have murdered Stephen Lawrence for no reason other than because of the colour of his skin. In the following months, the repetition of the contents of the video footage across the newspaper and the rest of the news media magnified the identikit racist views and transparent guilt of the five suspects.

The Murder Scene: The Racist Badlands of South London

Equally significantly, the *Daily Mail* produced expansive investigative reports on the disconcerting racial dynamics of the 'sprawling' working class Brook council estate in Eltham, that tightened its representational grip on the 'natural born racists'. These 'heart of darkness' and 'badlands', 'be grateful you do not live here', reports from the murder scene tapped into and voiced local gossip and rumour about the murder of Stephen Lawrence. They implanted the notion that the murder was not a random act of mindless violence but the outcome of a geographically isolated white working class culture of racism. This was a murder waiting to happen. Other newspapers and television programmes had already run investigative features on the semi-suburban locality identifying it as 'a smouldering cauldron of race hatred' and the 'race hate capital of Britain'. Now the *Daily*

Mail confirmed that the five suspects and the 'white place' they lived in were mutually constitutive:

If you ask decent law abiding residents questions about the Stephen Lawrence murder you will 'taste the fear' in this locality. This is because the Brook council estate is also home to a group of aggressive young men who delight in calling themselves the Firm. Violent and racist, they rule the area 'like cockerals'. In one of the very few uncared for houses lives Neil and Jamie Acourt, the uneducated, 'jobless brothers' who modelled themselves on the Kray Twins. This group exulted in their title. For several years the Firm had 'strutted the streets, drinking heavily and spending freely' in the pubs, clubs and bars of south London. (*Daily Mail,* 14 February 1997)

The gang had known each other since childhood. In their early years they were regarded by classmates as 'wimps, useless at football and academically poor'. However:

they transformed themselves, by a kind of group osmosis, into fearsome young thugs who both used and allegedly dealt in soft and hard drugs. They were tutored in this by some members of their families, at least one of whom has been involved in major crime.

Only Norris and Knight have ever held jobs since leaving school, and then only briefly. Yet they always have large amounts of money which they enjoy flashing around. On the estate where most vehicles are second hand, they are seen driving expensive cars.

They enjoy buying fashionable clothes. For night clubs four-buttoned tight suits and narrow ties, like the anti-heroes from the film *Reservoir Dogs*. For days spent wandering the parks, drinking and smoking cannabis, they wear Polo shirts and Hugo Boss jeans. (*Daily Mail,* 15 February 1997)

The disreputable value system that permeated this white working class estate was the reason why the police investigation had run into a 'wall of silence' even though many law-abiding residents were disgusted by what had happened.

The Acourts' personal terror campaign against black residents was the reason why the Brook estate was predominantly white. Although the *Daily Mail* could not find evidence that they were members of local neo-fascist groups, it was in no doubt that the primary focus and pleasure in the five's otherwise pointless unemployed lives involved seeking out young blacks and Asians and deploying their 'vicious brand of designer racism'. For the 'innocent and unfortunate Stephen Lawrence, whose family had until that day four years ago never experienced serious racism in Britain, the Firm's sick pleasure exploded into murder outside the doors of Eltham Parish Church'.

The reports also found evidence of their love of violence. One resident informs the newspaper that the suspects enjoyed flashing the knives they routinely carried. 'I always had a feeling they were all acting out some kind of movie in their heads. Because they were so fast in their movements. And because they were either drunk or drugged up most days, they were scary kids.' Neil Acourt is identified locally as the 'completely fearless' and 'on the very edge of extreme violence' leader of this tightly bonded gang.

Neil with his close cropped hair and permanent half smile, was widely feared by other gang members because of his mood changes. He was the most ferocious racist in the group and was said to be involved in several vendettas against other youths, mostly black, on the rival Ferrier estate.

On 16 March 1998, the newspaper revisited Eltham, the by now, 'grimy', 'desolate' southeast London suburb 'which earned unwanted notoriety when the studious black teenager Stephen Lawrence was killed by a gang of white thugs'. Sitting outside multicultural London this is an area 'blighted by racism, sometimes crude and violent, sometimes casual and unthinking, but always lurking there like a malignant cancer'. Away from the High Street with its chain stores and McDonald's many of the shops have closed down and are smeared with graffiti and the area has experienced some of the worst racist violence in the country. Blacks and Asians avoid the area after dark. The reporter encounters John, '6ft tall, built like a tank with shorn hair, rippling muscles and several tattoos' who aggressively denies there is racism in the area and a nervous elderly Asian shopkeeper 'wearing an immaculate grey suit who does not want to get dragged into a discussion about racism'. The cause of this racism was identified:

There are lots of single mothers around here, and many of the kids have problems. When they finish school, they find there are no jobs, so many of them turn to crime or racism. Lots of them hang around and get their kicks trying to intimidate you.

Investigating the locality further the reporter also identified the rougher estates

My first stop, the Ferrier Estate, surrounded by a 5ft high wall, reminded me of a prison. Nonetheless, I made my way inside. Its long corridors were deathly quiet and the air was oppressive. Two hard faced youths approached me and gave me such a cold, sustained stare that I turned on my heels and left. It was a terrifying hint of menace that even I, as a white person, would be foolish to ignore. And it gave me a chilling glimpse of the daily nightmare of life faced by so many decent families in these badlands of south London just because their faces don't match the required colour. Clearly, even now, five years after a pointless stabbing shocked the nation, little has changed in Eltham.

Readers were left in little doubt that the intrinsic violently racist culture of the semi-suburban racist working class estate that had bred the five suspects was a place at odds with not just nearby multicultural London but Middle England.

Acting it Out II: The Public Inquiry

At the end of June 1998, one of the most eagerly anticipated news media events of the year took place at the public inquiry into the murder of Stephen Lawrence. The appearance and performance of the uneducated, unemployed, lower class white suspects who had expressed such extreme racist sentiments delivered the most dramatic episode of the inquiry. They also created the definitive visual images that have been reproduced and commented upon on countless occasions. An atmosphere had been created that bore a remarkable resemblance to a racially charged show trial. Fighting broke out among protestors and police as the five suspects made their way into the inquiry. At one stage, during the first day of cross-examination of the suspects, police officers used tear gas when members of the Nation of Islam demanded to be admitted to the already packed inquiry. The exit of the five from the public inquiry sparked public disorder in the surrounding streets.

Rather than breaking under concentrated questioning the suspects toughed it out, refusing to account for their whereabouts on the night of the murder and denying that they had murdered Stephen Lawrence. They also repudiated the assertion that the racist words and violent actions detailed on the police videotape evidenced their pathological hatred of black people. Neil Acourt, for example, admitted using the word 'nigger' but denied this attested to his racism: 'Black people call each other niggers, so why does it matter if white people say that?'. He declared that the language he had used in the video was the result of the stress and harassment he had suffered after being accused of the murder. He had been stupid to react as he did. He also drew a distinction between words and actions. He was just going through the motions: 'It is not as if I'm going to do it, is it? I've been through a lot and when you have been through a lot you say things you don't mean.' In addition, 'when you watch the video you can see laughing and joking going on ... it's a joke ... everybody makes jokes about everyone else ... when your young at that stage and you are angry and you are laughing and joking, you say things, you don't mean them'. The other suspects put their performance down to immaturity and being very angry about being accused of a murder they did not commit.

Intense news coverage was given to what was defined as an outrageous performance of white working class defiance and arrogance. The *Daily Mail* (30 June 1998) reported on how the suspects, in their sharp suits, crisply ironed shirts, greased hair, and sunglasses, had 'strutted into the emotion-charged inquiry' past a chanting mob to resist all attempts to implicate themselves in the murder of Stephen Lawrence. Gary Dobson, 'a crew cut young white man gazed back at the learned QC with impudence in his eyes. He had nothing to fear unless he lied in court, and most of the time he wasn't able to lie because he "couldn't remember" ... His use of the word "cannot" instead of can't was fascinating. It was the one piece of standard English in a sea of cockney. Who could have taught him that one wondered?'

The newspaper also provided details of the suspects' family members who had the audacity to show up to support their murderous offspring. Again its description reinforced a powerful image of 'white trash' culture. 'Teresa "Tracy" Norris ... wore a blue blazer and check shirt. A blue velvet band held back her bottle-blonde hair ... Luke Knight's mother was also there, another bottle blonde in brown leggings, suede jacket and gold bangle earrings.' The *Daily Mail* also made much of the 'flash lifestyle' of Clifford Norris, the well-known south London criminal who was supposed to have protected the suspects. On the chaotic scenes that erupted as the suspects made their final departure from the inquiry, the *Daily Mail* commented:

Their faces were contorted with hatred as they lashed out at anybody within reach. These were the five men named by the *Daily Mail* as the murderers of Stephen Lawrence as they came face to face with a riot yesterday. Greeted by a baying mob and a hail of bottles, bricks, stones and punches outside the public inquiry into the black teenager's death, the sullen contempt they had shown earlier vanished and was replaced by anger. Undaunted by two days of questions and accusations before a hostile audience, they shouted racist abuse at the crowd and revelled in the conflict as they made their getaway. They even fought with the policemen there to ensure their safety.

What also concerned the newspaper was the descent into racial mayhem exemplified by what it viewed as the choreographed appearance of the Nation of Islam. For the newspaper, the 'burlesque sense of menace' was like something out of 'the sinister race pantomime played out in Tom Wolfe's devastating novel *The Bonfire of the Vanities*'. The Nation of Islam, with its espousal of black supremacism, was 'in many ways a mirror image of the white racism of the National Front, an equally repellent organisation'. The *Daily Mail* noted that the Lawrence family 'reacted with great dignity to this deplorable attempt by extremists to hijack the inquiry into the killing of their son'.

In the aftermath of the publication of the report of the public inquiry, the *Daily Mail* tracked the unremitting police attempts to bring a fresh case against the five suspects. In September 2002, Neil Acourt and David Norris were convicted on charges of launching a racially motivated attack on an off duty black police officer in Eltham. The case provided the newspaper with the opportunity to celebrate the jailing of the 'sneering and swaggering' pair who had 'cheated justice over the murder of Stephen Lawrence'. It also reminded readers of the defining characteristics of Acourt and Norris, highlighting their criminal aspirations and connections and lack of visible means of support. The description of Acourt declares that 'Like many criminals, he dresses in the manner of a man with money to burn. Only the best designer labels will do'.

In April 2003, the *Daily Mail* ran three double-page, fully illustrated tenth anniversary pieces on 'the legacy of the racist murder that shook Britain'. The articles updated readers on the lives of Neville and Doreen Lawrence. Among other things, the articles told of the disintegration of their marriage in the aftermath of the murder of their son and Neville's decision to return to the West Indies. Later in the year, the Lawrences, 'an ordinary hard-working couple who emigrated from Jamaica in the early 1960s', would receive OBEs for their campaigning work on behalf of talented black youngsters. In the course of the interviews, the parents ruminated on the type of man Stephen would have turned out to be if he had lived. His father had an image of 'a tall, confident 28-year-old architect striding into his office, suit sharply pressed, briefcase swinging by his side' while his mother thinks constantly about 'what kind of father and husband he might have become'.

The articles on Doreen and Neville Lawrence also provided readers with details of what had happened to the 'gang of hate-filled white racists', the 'would-be white supremacist god fathers' whose 'blind hatred...motivated them to encircle and slaughter [Stephen Lawrence] like some deep south lynch mob'. The 'gloating killers' continue to 'swagger around their south London manor with sickening arrogance. Though they have no discernible employment, they drive smart cars, dress fashionably and are usually to be found surrounded by cronies in local pubs'. They are still protected by 'a complex web of friends and relations in the south London underworld'.

The final substantive *Daily Mail* article focused directly on what was happening in the 'sordid lives' of the suspects and the 'menacing white-dominated suburb' of Eltham. Readers were reminded of what the five men were like:

They wore dark glasses, greased their hair back, Fifties style and dreamed of ruling their manor through fear—and purging the nation of black people in the process. Who can forget the police surveillance video, shot covertly as the four lolled around in a cannabis fogged flat discussing their stomach churning ambitions and rehearsing knife-thrusts, chillingly similar to those which sliced through Stephen's main arteries.

The piece provided snippets of the 'foul-mouthed racist views' of the suspects before updating readers on what had happened to them:

Pathetically, if predictably, the junior branch of the Eltham mafia—still bound together by bigotry—have drifted into a life of petty theft and social security benefits. They flit between scruffy, welfare-subsidised homes, kept by 'starry eyed molls' who breed their hapless children.

The article also detailed the role played by the 'overbearing and fearsomely protective mothers' in their violent racist, petty criminal lives. A follow-up opinion piece 'What have we learned from Stephen's death?' reassured readers that the state of race relations in Britain was:

certainly not typified by the south London thugs who murdered Stephen Lawrence. They are said to be celebrated in some of their local pubs and clubs but, disagreeable though that thought is, we should not assume that these misfits represent anything more than an aberrational minority...His killers though free, are freakish outcasts on the edge of society, reviled by almost everyone. (23 April 2003)

The piece concluded with the declaration that there was significantly less racism in Britain in 2003 when compared with the 1960s. Now 'young blacks and young whites are increasingly seen in each other's company without giving it a second thought. A quiet revolution has been going on, and will continue'.

Conclusion

The main purpose of this chapter was to re-emphasize the need to conduct case study research on the role played by the news media in racializing public debate. The vanguard role played by the *Daily Mail*, the self-declared guardian of Middle England, heightened the public profile of the racist murder of Stephen Lawrence and armed the Lawrence family with the moral authority and political clout to persuade the incoming New Labour government that it was politically safe to establish a judicial inquiry. The newspaper's decision to embrace the Lawrence family can be seen as part of a highly complex and volatile reworking of the coverage of race relations in the UK news media. 'Black Britons' are no longer homogeneously the 'alien other' or quintessentially 'different' because of their 'non-whiteness'. Rather the *Daily Mail*, in accepting the integratedness of Doreen and Neville Lawrence, is involved in redefining the conventional ethnoracial imaginary of Middle England. In memorializing Stephen Lawrence the newspaper broke out of its knee jerk framing of young black men as 'muggers' and 'yardies'. This particular young black man moved from being just another violent crime statistic to being one of the most powerful images of end-of-the-century Middle England. Hence, the newspaper was making its own conservative readjustment to the multiculturalism and cosmopolitanism that was transforming post-colonial British society.

However, important aspects of the *Daily Mail's* split-screen, double click racialization strategies in the Stephen Lawrence case deserve closer examination. First, what we might describe as the *Daily Mailization* of Doreen and Neville Lawrence as members of Middle England glosses over uncomfortable facts that did not fit the preferred narrative of the newspaper. In the course of the *Daily Mail's* attempt to invest the campaign with universal human interest and the moral claim to 'one of us' sameness a process of erasure occurs, that is, 'race' is made to matter less and less and to some extent is even written out of the script. Readers, irrespective of race, could identify with a grief-stricken family trying to come to terms with the emotional devastation instigated by the murder and the sense of injustice that is the essence of the Stephen Lawrence case. This deracialization process manifests itself in a variety of ways. For example, the iconic photograph of Stephen Lawrence looking reproachfully at the viewer also appears to feature him making a clenched fist salute. However, in the 'locking' of this iconographical representation this is rarely, if ever, noted and while there is no way of knowing whether it was intended as a 'Black power' salute or streetwise gesture, the fact that it can have this association clearly makes it uncomfortable for sections of the news media. Similarly, the representation of Neville and Doreen Lawrence avoided conventional black stereotypes and inner city references. Instead their blackness was marked culturally through references to their traditional West Indian values.

In the process of distancing them from its dominant discourse of 'problematic blackness', some extremely hard-hitting statements on the state of British race relations by Doreen Lawrence were disregarded. She declared, for example, that the murder was the inevitable result of decades of racial discrimination and the failure of the authorities to act against racist violence. Her statements and views had to be silenced because they did not fit in with the assimilationist ways in which the newspaper wanted to represent Stephen Lawrence.

Second, the newspaper's racialization of the suspects was built up layer by layer via a well-established discourse that blamed many of Britain's ills on lawless white underclass masculinity, obsessed with designer clothes, lacking in the work ethic and having no respect for authority, and capable of extreme violence. The *Daily Mail* had already condemned problematic male whiteness associated with the 'white riots' of the early 1990s, football violence, and more generally with 'yob culture' on similar terms. In addition to the video footage that *visualized* the problematic whiteness of the suspects, the newspaper's you-are-here reports also *localized* white racism to what it viewed as an unrepresentative disreputable place in the nation, landlocked between multicultural London and Middle England. Hence, white racism continues to be presented as an exceptional and spatially specific rather than routine or commonplace experience for a significant section of the population. These twin processes of underclassing and localizing racism also exonerate Middle England of any responsibility for the murder of Stephen Lawrence.

We can also see this in the newspaper's response to the findings and recommendations of the Macpherson report. The *Daily Mail* was pleased that the report's psychopathological depiction of the prime suspects bore a remarkable resemblance to its own master script. However, along with the rest of the right-wing press, the newspaper was furious, that despite all its hard work to ring fence the suspects, the report had concluded that 'institutionalized racism' was responsible for the police not bringing the killers of Stephen Lawrence to justice.

The newspaper found it almost impossible to work out how the report had managed to racially responsibilize the whole nation. A series of angry 'state of Middle England' commentaries and editorial pieces endeavoured to dismantle the politically correct lie that 'white Britons' are a 'nation of racists'. The general tenor was that the brutal murder of Stephen Lawrence by a gang of racist thugs in a disreputable south London suburb shamed every law-abiding

Briton, irrespective of race. The enormity of this crime against Middle England cried out for justice. The *Daily Mail* accepted that the government needed to deal with racist officers in the Metropolitan Police and reform the criminal justice system to ensure violent racists such as the suspects were brought to justice. It was even willing to concede that in immediate post-war period, 'Britain was a largely racist society, with a white population that had naturally inherited the superior racial attitudes of the age. For most of that age, very few non-whites were their equals' (23 February 1999). However, the 'unthinking racism' which had greeted many immigrants was part of the past. Britain, unlike Sir William Macpherson, Eltham, and the five white suspects, had moved on. It would do no service to the memory of Stephen Lawrence if, as a result of the Macpherson report, 'a fundamentally decent and harmonious society' fell into the grip of what the paper defined as a chilling 'racial McCarthyism'. The murder was nothing to do with Middle England and to claim otherwise would 'destroy that edifice of tolerance which the rest of us have built up over the years'. The *Daily Mail*, in conjunction with the rest of the right-wing press, subsequently mounted a campaign to pressurize the government to distance itself from the more 'politically correct' recommendations of his report.

This illustrates both ability and willingess of the *Daily Mail* to engage in densely and complexly layered multicultural race work which both pluralizes and diversifies its Middle England ethnoracial imaginary and allows it to redraw boundaries. It is capable therefore of presenting a multiplicity of perspectives on race and ethnicity. However, virulent exclusion and condemnation can continue under the appearance of inclusion and appropriation. For example, victims of racist violence who do not fit the newspaper's deracializing and sanctifying construction of the 'ideal victim' of Stephen Lawrence should not expect to see positive representation in the paper. In addition, the *Daily Mail* is also equally prepared to engage in continually and mercilessly parading fear- and anger-inducing depictions of highly racialized threats. The newspaper has continued to run a stream of 'racial violence cuts both ways' stories as well as persist with its 'street crime is race crime' headlines. It has also taken a key role in mobilizing public opinion against the 'flood' of 'bogus' asylum-seekers that it holds responsible for draining the British welfare state of scarce resources. It remains to be seen whether its conservative multicultural twisting and turning not only complicates and nuances its racialization discourses and practices but fundamentally impacts on its ability to signify its ideologically potent ethnoracial construction of Middle England in place.

REFERENCES

Ahmed, K. (1999) 'Lawrence Inquiry: How Murder Became a Media Event'. *Guardian*, 25 February.

Alibhai-Brown, Y. (2000) *Who do We Think We Are? Imagining the New Britain*. London: Penguin.

Bhattacharyya, G., Gabriel, J., and Small, S. (2002) *Race and Power: Global Racism in the Twenty-First Century*. London: Routledge.

Bywater, M. (1998) 'A Land Where Immigrants Peddle Drugs and Molest your Daughter, While Single Mothers Cheat the State and Beggars Live in Luxury. How very . . . English'. *Observer*, 14 June: 20.

Cathcart, B. (1999) *The Case of Stephen Lawrence*. London: Viking Press.

Cottle, S. (ed.) (2000) *Ethnic Minorities and the Media: Changing Cultural Boundaries*. Buckingham: Open University Press.

Dates, J. L. and Barlow, W. (1990) *Split Image: African Americans in the Mass Media*. Washington, DC: Howard University Press.

Delgado, R. and Stefancic, J. (eds.) (1997) *Critical White Studies; Looking Behind the Veil*. Philadelphia: Temple University Press.

Entman, R. M. and Rojecki, A. (2001) *The Black Image in the White Mind: Media and Race in America*. Chicago: University of Chicago Press.

Fine, M., Weiss, L., Powell, L. C., and Wong, L. M. (eds.) (1997) *Off White*. New York: Routledge.

Freedland, J. (1998) 'In Search of Middle England'. *Guardian*, 18 June, G2: 1–2.

Gabriel, J. (1998) *Whitewash: Racialised Politics and the Media*. London: Routledge.

Gray, H. (1995) *Watching Race: Television and the Struggle for 'Blackness'*. Minneapolis: University of Minnesota Press.

Hall, S. (1982) 'The Whites of their Eyes: Racist Ideologies and the Media', in G. Bridges and R. Brunt (eds.), *Silver Linings: Some Strategies for the Eighties*. London: Lawrence and Wishart.

——McLaughlin, E., and Lewis, G. (1998) *Report on Racial Stereotyping* (unpublished).

Hunt, D. M. (1999) *OJ Simpson Facts and Fictions: News Rituals in the Construction of Reality*. Cambridge: Cambridge University Press.

Jacobs, R. N. (2000) *Race, Media and the Crisis of Civil Society*. Cambridge: Cambridge University Press.

Law, I. (2002) *Race in the News*. Basingstoke: Palgrave Macmillan.

Kellner, D. (1995) 'Cultural studies, multiculturalism and media culture', in G. Dines and J. M. Hamez (eds.), *Gender, Race and Class in Media*. Thousand Oaks, CA: Sage

Macpherson, Sir W. (1999) *The Stephen Lawrence Inquiry: Report of an Inquiry by Sir William Macpherson of Cluny*. London: The Stationery Office, Cm 4262.

Martindale, C. (1986) *The White Press and Black America*. New York: Greenwood Press.

McLaughlin, E. and Murji, K. (1999) 'After the Stephen Lawrence Report'. *Critical Social Policy*, 19(3): 371–85.

Nakayama, T. K. and Martins, J. (1998) *Whiteness: The Communication of Social Identity*. London: Sage.

Neal, S. (1999) 'Populist Configurations of 'Race' and 'Gender': The Case of Hugh Grant, Liz Hurley and Divine Brown', in A. Brah et al. (eds.), *Thinking Identities: Ethnicity, Racism and Culture*. Basingstoke: Macmillan.

Rasmussen, B. B. et al. (2001) *The Making and Unmaking of Whiteness*. Durham, NC: Duke University Press.

Rockquemore, K. A. and Brunsman, D. L. (2002) *Beyond Black: Biracial Identity in America*. London: Sage.

Roediger, D. R. (2002) *Coloured White: Transcending the Racial Past*. Los Angeles: University of California Press.

Solomos, J. and Back, L. (1996) *Racism and Society*. Basingstoke: Macmillan.

Swain, C. M. (2002) *The New White Nationalism in America*. Cambridge: Cambridge University Press.

Torres, S. (ed.) (1998) *Living Color: Race and Television in the United States*. Durham, NC: Duke University Press.

van Loon, J. (1999) 'Whiter Shades of Pale: Media Hybridies of Rodney King', in A. Brah, M. Hickman, and M. Mac an Ghaill (eds.), *Thinking Identities: Ethnicity, Racism and Culture*. Basingstoke: Macmillan.

Ware, V. and Back, L. (2002) *Out of Whiteness: Color, Politics, and Culture*. Chicago: University of Chicago Press

Wilson, C. C. and Gutierrez, F. (1995) *Race, Multiculturalism and the Media*. Thousand Oaks, CA: Sage

CHAPTER 9

White Self-racialization as Identity Fetishism: Capitalism and the Experience of Colonial Whiteness

Ghassan Hage

In the early twentieth century, when Australia's selection of its immigrants was based on the racial 'White Australia policy', many Christian Lebanese, who had began immigrating to Australia in the 1880s, were often shocked to learn that they were classified racially as 'Asians' (based on Mount Lebanon being part of Syria and the Ottoman Empire at the time). In 1911, a Lebanese migrant already living in Australia sent a letter to the prime minister objecting to the classification and arguing that the Lebanese were 'Caucasians and they are as white a race as the English. Their looks, habits, customs, religion, blood, etc., are those of Europeans but they are more intelligent' (in MacKay and Batrouney 1988: 667). In fact, the belief in the Christian Lebanese's whiteness/Europeanness on the basis of 'looks, habits, customs, religion, blood, etc ...' had began developing in the mid-nineteenth century with the spread of capitalist social relations in the Lebanese mountains almost exclusively among the Christians. From a mode of identification that primarily stressed religious difference from a largely Muslim environment, the Christians' identity (especially the Maronite Catholics') was transformed into a racialized world view that saw difference from Muslims in terms of cultural hierarchy and culminated in the Christians' self-perception as more 'European' than 'Arab', and as 'white'. In this chapter, I want to examine this socio-historical process of white self-racialization, what it entails, and how it can best be understood. I will argue that an essential part of the process is what I will call 'identity fetishism': a process whereby 'the products of the human brain appear as autonomous figures endowed with a life of their own' (Marx 1976: 165).

Although Marx's analysis of 'commodity fetishism' is often considered as embodying his most complex theorization of ideology, as far as I know, it remains unutilized in the analysis of the ideological formation of identities. In this analysis Marx aims to show how certain social products that appear on the capitalist market 'detach' themselves, so to speak, from the social relations that produce them, and are experienced as having powers of their own. In much the same way as a 'fetish' is experienced as having an intrinsic power over a tribe, even though the tribe must have initially produced it and given it such power, commodities under capitalism are experienced as having a life and social powers in themselves and in abstraction from the social relations that continue to give them such power. At the core of Marx's analysis is that this experience of an inversion of power between product and producer is not the result of some 'mental or intellectual deficiency' on the part of people. It is not because they are not thinking properly about it that they perceive commodities from such an inverted perspective. Rather, the perception is the product of their practical experience. As Maurice Godelier famously put it long ago, 'it is not the subject that deceives himself, it is reality that deceives him' (Godelier 1975: 337).

In much the same way, I examine below how, in its emergence in the midst of the colonial transformation of the economy of Mount Lebanon, Christian Lebanese identity was experienced by those identifying with it as European and white, and as intrinsically endowed with a causal power to generate the very capitalist social practices that produced it. I conclude by showing what this identity fetishism can tell us about the relationship between colonial white racialization and class.

The Maronites and the Transformation of Mount Lebanon's Economy

When in 635, the Muslim tribes of the Arabian Peninsula invaded the Christian Fertile Crescent, the Christians and the Jews, being 'people of the book', were considered under the Islamic Shari'a law to be the 'dhumma', or those to be tolerated and protected. Practically, these laws marginalized the non-Islamic communities. The latter were to suffer in certain circumstances 'outbreaks of intolerance on the part of the

Muslim mob' (Rodinson 1981: 8). It was most probably in times like these that the majority of the Maronites, followers of Saint Maron of Antioch, fled northern Syria to settle in the northern parts of Mount Lebanon, seeking the protection of its rugged mountains (when exactly is a hotly debated issue—see Beydoun 1984). The southern part of the mountains gave refuge to the Druze, followers of a secretive offshoot of Shiite Islam originating in Egypt at the end of the Fatimid era.

In their early days of settlement, the Maronites were an over-whelmingly peasant community working under the rule of Shi'a Muslim overlords (*muqata'jis*) within a quasi-feudal system known in Mount Lebanon as *iqta'*. The Maronite peasants lived 'either as landless serfs or metayers, or combined their primary labour as metayers with the cultivation of their own small parcels' (Saba 1976: 1–2). The Shi'a overlords were later replaced by the Druzes who were seen by the ruling Muslim authorities as having valiantly fought against the Crusaders. Furthermore, in the seventeenth century, important demographic changes occurred when the Maronites began to spread south into central Lebanon and to the southern Shuf Mountains with the encouragement of Druze muqata'jis. The Chevallier D'Avrieux who lived in the Mountain during that period noted that in the villages where they lived with the 'unfaithful', the Christians, 'had the entire liberty to openly practice their religion, to build churches and monasteries...The unfaithful who are the masters allow them everything to keep them, so as to extract from them the sums of money they have to pay to the Ottoman Porte' (in Chevallier, Dominique 1982: 12). Beside the Maronites' geographic spread and increase in numbers, of equal importance was that they, like other minorities within the Empire, virtually monopolized marginal economic activities such as commerce and craft. When they moved into the Druze districts they were seen as coming 'to perform tasks Druze thought degrading' (Polk 1963: 216). This Christian quasi-monopoly over trade and crafts became increasingly significant as the economic developments of the late nineteenth century tended to make these initially marginal and 'degrading' activities increasingly central and led to the rapid growth of Christian villages.

An important example of this change was the Christian village of Dayr el-Qamar (Smilianskaya 1972: 16), which developed into a major trading town for silk as the Mountain witnessed a growth in the cultivation of the mulberry tree due to 'a growing demand for raw silk on the Egyptian market' (Saba 1976: 3). It also witnessed a growth in handicraft production which extended to other Christian towns in the central Mountain. These developments furthered the spread of money transactions among the Christians, 'enlarging the scope for small accumulation among peasants and artisan producers, and a growing involvement of these or of other individuals in the slowly widening sphere of trade and exchange' (Saba 1976: 3). Furthermore, the Maronite monks, who had earlier 'demonstrated to everyone that they were hard workers and could actually increase the country's productivity and hence the revenue of the muqata'jis' (Harik 1968: 114), were by the turn of the century slowly becoming big landowners in their own right. This new landowning role challenged the power of the Druze muqata'jis, even though, initially, the politics of the Mountain remained largely in their hands. Inevitably, however, signs of dissatisfaction with the existing political order emerged as Christian merchants and craftsmen, along with the Maronite Church, yearned to free themselves and their activities from the muqata'jis who had set out to benefit from the new economic developments by taxing mills, local trade, crafts, and the weighing of silk (Harik 1968: 64). The Christians, however, lacked the military power that could allow them to overthrow the iqta' system. This military power was to be provided later by the French who were already intensifying their colonial competition with Britain for the control of the disintegrating Ottoman Empire.

By the beginning of the nineteenth century the signs of the Ottoman Empire's end were many. The emergence of industrial capital in Europe had already set the Empire on the road of underdevelopment, destroying the local industries the Porte was unwilling or unable to protect (Mouzelis 1978: 12). The power of the central state was all but gone, and the control of the expanding capitalist activities in the region were increasingly seen by some of the local rulers as a source of enrichment. They set out accordingly to 'modernize' the state and their district, basically improving the infrastructure necessary for the penetration of capital. Thanks to the protection of its surroundings by the Prince of the Mountain, a Druze who significantly had by now converted to Christianity, Beirut became increasingly viable as a port for the export of Lebanon's silk to France. From 1833 to 1836 the silk exported through the port increased more than threefold (Polk 1963: 171–2).

Until the early eighteenth century the dominant European presence in the Empire was that of English and French merchant capital. The effect of this presence on the existing productive practices was minimal. For 'merchants do not make their profits by revolutionising production but by controlling markets, and the greater the control they are able to exercise the greater the profit' (Kay 1975: 96).

However, by the early 1800s, industrial capital began to emerge as a significant social force thanks to France's involvement in the development of the local silk industry, parts of which had been integrated in the circuit of French merchant capital since the seventeenth century (Smilianskaya 1972: 14).

As the Lyon silk industry developed, France aimed at increasingly monopolizing the Lebanese silk produce. Towards 1835, 25 per cent of the Mountain's silk production was exported to Lyon; by 1861 more than two-thirds were (Dubar and Nasr 1976: 53). In buying silk for French industry and, more importantly, in employing wage labour the French were speeding the development of capitalist practices within the Maronites' social sphere and integrating their economy within the capitalist system of production and exchange like never before (Chevallier 1982: 220). Of equal importance was the attempt at controlling production itself. In 1810, an industrialist from Lyon established France's first local spinning mill employing local labour (Labaki 1984: 79). The introduction towards 1830 of vapour heating into the spinning mills permitted their transformation from a family business to a capitalist industry 'that knows the division and mechanisation of work' (Labaki 1984: 79). By 1851, seven French silk mills were operating in the Mountain (Raccagni 1980: 364).

The increase in this activity accelerated the rise of an embryonic Lebanese Christian bourgeois class active in various sectors of the economy. The Beirut Christian bourgeoisie was mainly formed by the established local merchants who attached themselves to European capital. Already in 1827, the French consul in Beirut had reported that 'of thirty four commercial firms dealing with Europe, fifteen belonged to local Christians and six to Turks' (Issawi 1966: 71). By 1839, there were sixty-seven commercial houses of which thirty-four were Lebanese (Dubar and Nasr 1976: 57). These local merchants 'served as intermediaries between the European wholesaler and the local retailer, whose language they spoke and whose needs and tastes they knew...' (Fawaz 1983: 86). In the Mountain's interior another group of intermediaries operated between the Mountain's silk producers and the Beirut houses (Chevallier 1982: 234).

The rise of silk as a crop transformed the peasant economy and weakened the dependency of the peasant on the muqata'jis, substituting it with dependency on the market (Polk 1963: 173). A class of rich Christian peasants emerged, buying land and employing daily workers, lending money to embattled muqata'jis as well as renting villas to rich Beirutis (Smilianskaya 1972: 25). The Maronite Church itself continued to amass riches and was establishing itself as the biggest landowner in the Mountain. Furthermore, the monks had in education, the production of silk, olive oil, and wine another source for accumulation of wealth (Chevallier 1982: 254–5). Furthermore, '(t)he merchants and artisans of the new Christian market towns of Zahle and Dair al-Qamar', writes Hourani, 'were no longer willing to accept the lordship of the local Druze families. The cultivators were establishing a direct link with the silk merchants of the ports, who gave them advances or loans; they were less willing to give their ancient lords the traditional services and share of the silk crop, because they were no longer so economically dependent on them' (Hourani 1966: 21). This climate of communal tension soon degenerated into open conflict in 1841 when a series of small incidents developed into a civil war. Christian towns were refusing to pay taxes to the muqata'jis' collectors. As the Druze population rallied around their muqata'jis, the Maronites rallied around the Church (Churchill 1973: 50). The contradictions between the two socio-economic sets of relations was played out in the form of a religious conflict. Thanks to their continuing military superiority and organization, and with the help of the British who were always happy to undermine French control, the Druze lords managed tenuously to retain their political supremacy over the mountain. But this supremacy had become totally anachronistic with their socio-economic significance and it was only a matter of time before the conflicts flared again.

Indeed the victory of the Druzes in the 1841 war did nothing to slow the economic transformation of the Mountain. The value of imports through Beirut continued to increase: from 22 million francs in 1845 to 46.5 million in 1862 (Dubar and Nasr 1976: 54). The integration of the Lebanese silk sector in the French economy underwent a qualitative change, timidly begun in the 1830s, as French capitalists began to exert control over the quality of the silk produced in the Mountain to make it more suitable for the use of the Lyon industrialists. French spinning mills were set up in the Mountain, mulberry tree plantations were purchased (Raccagni 1980: 347), and breeders began to use imported eggs (which carried several diseases and ended up destroying the indigenous breed) (Labaki 1984: 32). Furthermore, the merchant class of Beirut continued to grow in strength and expanded its comprador function through newly established financial institutions (Sharara 1975: 89). The Mountain merchants, following the installation of the French spinning mills, began to invest themselves in such productive ventures. In 1846, five mills were financed by local capital (Labaki 1984: 103). There was limited local capital involvement in the setting up of many French mills as

well as two English ones (Labaki 1984: 86). By the 1850s, thirty
mills had been established employing an average of seventy to eighty
workers (Saba 1976: 13). The Mountain merchants expanded their
control over silk prices by expanding their money-lending network
among the peasant growers (Smilianskaya 1972: 20). Likewise, the
Maronite Church also continued to grow as a landowner, and
strengthened its links to French capital through the selling of silk to
the local French industry (Sharara 1975: 85).

Beside widening the scope of accumulation for the local bourgeoisie, the European industries increased the uneven development
between the Druze and the Christian communities. Of nine localities
in which mills were established, only one (an English mill) was in a
totally Druze district (Labaki 1984: 102). Therefore, capitalist social
relations were continuing to develop almost exclusively within the
Christian community, as the latter provided the majority of the mills'
wage labour (Sharara 1975: 85). By the late 1850s, some Druze
muqata'jis were sending their men to attack various Christian towns
to try and reassert some semblance of taxing power over them but
these attacks were now effectively attacks on the French capitalist
interests in the towns. The French silk manufacturers explicitly
requested the intervention of their government (Labaki 1984: 87).

As the situation degenerated into another communal civil war in
1860 with another Druze military victory, French troops were sent to
Mount Lebanon and an international commission was set up to find
a solution to Mount Lebanon's 'political' crisis. The latter came in the
form of what became known as the *Règlement Organique* (Spagnolo
1971: 26), which brought to an effective end iqta' practices and the
feudal powers of the Druzes and effectively replaced it with the
colonial power of the French silk industry. As Raccagni puts it:

The Règlement Organique of June 1861, recognising the autonomy of
Mount Lebanon, indirectly gave the Lyonnese industrialists all they had
wished: Lebanese autonomy from Constantinople presented a better guarantee for foreign investments, while the abolition of feudal privileges and
the setting up of a land register enabled Maronite farmers to adapt the cultivation to suit export needs. (Raccagni 1980: 366)

The confessional delineation of the process of socio-economic
domination and the fact that it was accompanied by equally confessional religious conflicts facilitated a general experience of this social
change as a process of dominance of Christians over Muslims *tout
court*. It is this experience that is reflected in the changing mode of
Maronite identification that accompanied those transformations.

The Racialization of Maronite Identity

The Muslim Shari'a's differentiation of Christian minorities on the basis of their religious identity, and both their collective tolerance and persecution on the basis of this identity, have led the Maronites to become permanently conscious of their status as a religious minority in a Muslim-dominated region. This has created a constant impetus for internal cohesion. When the Maronites settled in Mount Lebanon, the need for cohesion was further strengthened by their collective subjugation, as an overwhelmingly peasant community, to the exploitation and sometimes tyranny of Shi'a Muslim overlords. Throughout that period, the struggle to maintain unity was mostly carried out by the Maronite Church (Sharara 1975: 59).

The writings of the Maronite historian Ibn el-Qilai (b.1450) clearly reflect the tendency for unification in the face of many divisive issues whether of a religious doctrinal, or of a more explicitly political, nature (in Daou 1977, part VI, chapter 2). Ibn el-Qilai treats the Maronites in most of his writings as a united communal subject, divisions being a deviation from the norm. He also gives us a clear image of Maronite aspirations in his depiction of a golden past:

But histories tell us of what happened in our home countries and to those who were before us the inhabitants of Mount Lebanon.

They were united in the religion all working for it the rich as well as the poor obedience and love with faith.

Heretics they did not have and no Muslim lived among them and if a Jew was found his grave was soon covered by crows. (in Daou 1977: 282–5)

Whether such a past existed is, of course, doubtful. What is important, however, is its glorification: 'God lived among them...' Such glorification indicates what was perceived as desired in the present, and what the Maronite leadership, the clergy, to whom Ibn el-Qilai belonged, was struggling to maintain: namely, unity, and a purely Maronite Mountain, free from the presence of Jews and Muslims (Dib 1973: 102).

To strengthen the necessity of unity, the golden past is contrasted with a time of division which brought the defeat of the Maronites at the hands of the Muslim Mamluks, who were still ruling the Mountain when Ibn el-Qilai was writing:

The devil father of all tyranny saw the people of Maron happy he envied them and sunk them in sorrow through two men who were monks.

They said Jesus had no spirit or nature that suffers and feels and 'we shall not obey Peter's see because it believes otherwise'.

Evil spread and became two parties and there was a split because of the two

King Barkuk heard of this a closed door opened to him he sent armies up and down to besiege Mount Lebanon. (in Daou 1977: 536)

Because of the Church's dominant role within the community, one can assume that the aspirations and fears of Ibn el-Qilai were common among the Maronites. As such, his writings give us a rare glimpse of the nature of Maronite identity at the time.

Within this Maronite identity, the 'other' was political (defined as a military threat) and/or religious (in the strict meaning of the term). Among all the 'others' (the Jew, the Muslim, and the heretic), the Muslim is undoubtedly the central one. This is not due, however, to any special inherent antagonism between the Muslim and the Maronite identity that did not exist between the Maronite and the Jewish identity, for instance. The Muslims are central for the obvious fact that they constituted the most powerful and the most immediate danger. They are not only enemies of the faith, but also oppressors who aimed at and were capable of subjugating the Maronites. One is permitted to speculate that such a Maronite identity reflects also, albeit in a primitive form, the class position of the Maronites as a mainly peasant community, involved in identical practices determined by an identical and collective subjugation to Muslim overlords. At no time, however, does the Maronite identity articulate meanings of cultural differentiation. That is, in no sense does it try to differentiate between Maronites and others in reference to cultural practices. It is important to stress this point to appreciate the significance of later changes. As pointed out by Chevallier, Ibn el-Qilai wrote his history in an Arab dialect, and in a popular Arab poetic form. This shows that the Maronites had by that time 'abandoned their Aramian idiom and integrated in Arab culture' (Chevallier 1982: 17). This remained the case under the Ottomans.

Like the writings of Ibn el-Qilai, the writings of the Maronite historian, Bishop Istphan el-Duwaihi (1630–1704) during the early period of Druze domination, are also concerned with Maronite religious orthodoxy and unity in the face of Muslim domination (Harik 1968: 132). Those writings also show signs of the Maronites' integration in Arab culture for they bear the influence of Arab historical methodology as set out by el-Tabari (Kawtharani 1981: 68). However, from the mid-nineteenth century and with the spread of mercantile- and silk-related capitalist practices the meanings

articulated to the Maronite identity began to undergo certain transformations. This is clearly seen in the writings of Bishop Niqula
Murad in the 1840s who, while like Ibn el-Qilai and Istphan
el-Duwaihi emphasized the unity of the Maronites, aimed at *culturally*
differentiating the Maronites from the Muslims in general, and more
specifically the Druze. That is, the practices Murad invokes to
explain the distinctiveness of the Maronites are no longer strictly
limited to the religious sphere or to the portrayal of the other as a
political/military threat. In Murad's opinion, Harik tells us:

The Druze...are inferior in all respects. They are religiously confused and
socially backward, generally lazy with no skills or trades other than tilling
the ground...Except for a few of them who have intimate contact with the
Maronites...the Druze can neither read nor write. Beside they are dependent on the Maronites, for 'they cannot live without the Christians of the
country who are familiar with all the occupations prevalent in Europe'.
(Harik 1968: 139)

We can see here the importance of stressing that identities on their
own, whether black and white, or, as is the case here, Christian and
Muslim, are never 'natural' ways of delineating cultural differences.
These differences are always the product of the historical articulation
of cultural differences to identity differences. As we shall see, this
articulation is crucial for an understanding of the historical process
of racialization. We can see above, in the case of Murad, how a new
basis of difference, a difference based on socio-economic practices:
the 'occupations prevalent in Europe' as opposed to 'tilling the
ground', is now explicitly emphasized along with the element of religious differentiation. This new differentiation reflects most clearly
the Maronite experience of the spread of capitalist and capitalist-
related practices among them. It is important to stress here, however,
that what the Maronites experienced was not simply a change in their
economic productive and mercantile practices. These could not but
induce a further and more general transformation of their 'way of life'.
Polk, for instance, shows that what accompanied the intensification of
capitalist penetration was 'a change in tastes' based on the domination
of 'Western goods' (Polk 1963: 164). A further change in their way of
life was also reflected in the second difference emphasized by Harik:
the Druzes, unlike the Maronites, 'cannot read or write'.

This difference based on reading and writing skills was as much
the product of the new reality generated by the capitalist transformation as were the differences in economic practices mentioned by
Murad. Already, since Pope Gregory XIII opened the Maronite college in Rome in 1584, many of its graduates returned and opened

Maronite schools in the area (Dib 1973: 42). More important was the army of French missionaries that were established in the Maronite regions in the wake of the French penetration of the region. These missionaries, belonging to various French congregations, initiated a veritable boom in schooling as they competed for students and influence. The competition between the Jesuits and the Lazarites was most notable (Chevallier 1982: 260–5). This education was not unrelated to the economic developments in the area. The Lazarites, for instance, explained that they had opened the Ayntura College in 1834, to educate the French children living in Syria and the 'young Maronites destined to become tax collectors, shop owners, clerks and interpreters' (Chevallier 1982: 264). The French traveller Volney remarked that 'the most solid advantage which resulted from these missionary works, was that the art of writing became more common among the Maronites' (in Salibi 1977: 13). In much the same way as they remained marginal to the capitalist development of the Mountain, the Druzes were also marginally affected by the educational developments that accompanied it. Educational practices were experienced by the Maronites as specific to their community and part of what gave them a distinct identity.

An equally crucial aspect of Murad's new mode of differentiation is its hierarchical understanding of the cultural differences between Maronites and Druzes. While for Ibn el-Qilai and el-Duwaihi the Muslims were seen as different and as enemies, for Murad they also become inferior. This is of course closely linked to the perception of the Maronites as part of a different civilization based on 'the occupations prevalent in Europe', reading and writing and the Western commodity. This is where we begin to get a clearer hint that this change in the mode of self-identification is a process of internalizing the racialized outlook that shaped European colonialism. Indeed, from that point onward, the Maronites increasingly saw themselves in the image of the Europeans, responsible for what their ideologues referred to, in a direct identification with the French colonialists, as a 'mission civilisatrice'. This identification developed to the extent that by the turn of the century, a Christian Lebanese lawyer and a leading nationalist ideologue could simply claim that since the epoch of the crusades 'the Maronites had become the first French people of the Levant' (in Sassine 1979: 61).

This identification with France which emerged when the French took on the role of 'protectors' of the Maronites during the rule of the Ottomans was not merely an idiosyncratic intellectual affair but a deeply felt popular sentiment. When, in 1870, the regime of Napoleon III and the Second Empire ended, this was experienced by

the Maronites as a catastrophe since it was the imperial government
that helped them in 1860. The people of the village of Damour
thought themselves capable of influencing the course of events in
France by marching in the streets and singing: 'Either Napoleon is
reinstated or the village will revolt' (in Karam 1981: 183).

It is interesting to note that in this process of self-Europeanization
and racialization, the language of whiteness and race is hardly ever
used. This is because, as has often been argued (see Frankenberg
1993; Dyer 1997) with the rise of Western colonial hegemony, colonial whiteness is subconsciously internalized as a norm of what it
means to be 'human' and does not usually manifest itself in speech
and writing except in times of crisis. This is somewhat like the identity 'being human'. We hardly ever go parading it as ours. We take
it for granted for as long as everyone else around us does. But when
this humanity is challenged, such as when we feel dehumanized by
someone, this is when we make the explicit identity claim: 'I am a
human being.' It is this same logic that governs the discourse of
white identification. That this logic is part of the process of Maronite
identification is amply demonstrated by the fact that whiteness *does*
emerge in writing and speech whenever its normality is threatened
and questioned such as in the Australian example we began with in
the introduction. Interestingly, it was during the period of the French
mandate over Lebanon, following the European powers' carve up of
the Ottoman Empire after the First World War, that the 'racial
threat' was at its most acute.

Having grown to believe that they represented the embodiment of
Western civilization in the Levant, the Christian Lebanese found it
hard to reconcile this belief with the idea of being themselves colonized by the French. No one has expressed the sentiment generated
by this process like Farjallah Hayek, a popular Christian intellectual
at the time:

France has come to stay here with the Mandate's text in its pocket, and a
colonial experience in its mind . . . the Lebanese elite, the Lebanese clergy, the
Lebanese peasant have welcomed the Mandate with a sentiment of security
and an enthusiasm that no ink in the world can express . . . (But the French)
have spoken too much of a civilising mission. We do not need to be civilized
. . . More than anyone else France knew our degree of evolution. Less than
anyone else can it be forgiven for confusing things. (in Sassine 1979: 155)

It is in this state where 'things are confused' that the language of
race and whiteness emerges. Hayek's attempt at making things less
confused is remarkable. The Lebanese, he asserts, are 'white, white

to the bones, of an unalterable white, authentic, that leads to no ambiguity; a fanatical white in opposition to the Moroccan, the Algerian or the Senegalese' (in Sassine 1979: 296). And he benevolently adds: 'We owe a lot to our brothers of the black and yellow race. We regret being superior to them. Nature might be unjust but what can we do about it' (in Sassine 1979: 297).

Similarly, in the 1930s and in the early 1940s, when the Christians perceived themselves to be threatened by an 'Arab/Muslim' drive to eradicate the Christian specificity of Lebanon, a series of Christian intellectuals assiduously set out to prove that the Lebanese differed racially from their Arab environment, often linking them to the Phoenicians or what became jokingly known as 'nos ancêtres les Phéniciens'. This culminated in the writings of Michel Chiha who is considered a founding father of the Lebanese Republic. In 'Liban d'aujourd'hui', a seminal lecture he gave in 1942 (in French, of course), Chiha moves to 'prove' beyond reasonable doubt that Lebanon is distinct from its Arab environment and that the Lebanese cannot be Arabs. This is first apparent in the country's landscape. 'Lebanon of today covers a surface of 10,500 sq. km., almost the quarter of Switzerland' explains Chiha (1984: 24). Immediately, in this innocent comparison he removes Lebanon from its Middle-Eastern environment and repositions it in Europe. But the difference between Lebanon and its environment is much more concrete: 'The Lebanese landscape possesses the most characteristic features of southern Europe. It particularly resembles that of the big Mediterranean islands' (Chiha 1984: 23). In opposition to this peaceful resemblance, Lebanon 'contrasts violently with the nearby landscapes, offered by the oasis, the steppe and the desert' (Chiha 1984: 23).

If Lebanon's landscape makes it so different from its Arab environment, the Lebanese are even more different. Like others before him, but more 'scientifically', Chiha moves to demonstrate the Lebanese link with the Phoenicians. As importantly, Chiha informs his audience, that the Phoenician alphabet is today used by 'the quasi-totality of the white race'. 'To which we belong', he hastily adds (Chiha 1984: 38). Reviewing the many people that had invaded Lebanon, he takes a special interest in reminding us that of the 'thousands of Westerners who came from Europe, without forgetting the Scandinavians [!!], many never went back' (Chiha 1984: 32). He goes through considerable pain to show that after those westerners many other non-Arab people came and stayed. The 'racial proof' that the Lebanese are not Arabs accumulates ... To end with, Chiha injects into the Lebanese more of his favourite sperms: 'And let us remember a fact that we cannot neglect. Only in the last twenty-five years, the mixed marriages between Lebanese and Westerners have produced thousands of children...' (Chiha 1984: 34).

Immediately following this revelation concerning the sexual prowess of the Europeans in Lebanon comes the question whose answer had become obvious to any scientific reader who cares about facts: 'After all this, is it going to be said that the Lebanon of today is Semitic? Are we going to say that it is Arab?' (Chiha 1984: 34).

Faced with this occasional discourse of whiteness we have to ask the question: given that for all practical purposes, and like most Mediterranean and Arab people, the Christian Lebanese come in a variety of colours and shapes, how did they come to perceive themselves exclusively as white? Do people like Nujaym above develop some kind of paradoxical colour-blind racial ideology? And if not, *where* does the prevalent whiteness he perceives reside? But this question does not need to be asked only in relation to the white component of the Maronite identity. It is also relevant to all the components we have examined above (the feeling of superiority based on acquiring a variety of practices, skills, and tastes 'similar to those in Europe'). Although we have clearly shown that this mode of differentiation had a definite basis in the reality of the Maronites, it should be remembered, however, that with the capitalist transformation of the Mountain, the Maronite community was composed of a variety of classes who benefited unequally from the spread of capitalism. Consequently, it would be ludicrous to think that capitalism had transformed every single Maronite into a new subject practising a 'European occupation', capable of reading and writing, and with a developed taste for Western commodities. Many Maronite peasants remained just what they were under iqta'. Even if engaging in capitalist-related practices, such as working in a silk mill, it is hard to imagine how this in itself could form the basis for a Maronite to feel superior to a Druze peasant let alone a muqata'ji. Yet, the identification with the new way of life and the hierarchical view depicted by Murad was by no means just the single view of an extremist Bishop. It was a widespread feeling among most of the Maronite population. Colonel Charles Churchill, the well-known witness and contemporary of the stormy period of the 1840s and 1860s, also points out that for the Christians in general, the Druze had become 'hewers of wood and drawers of water' (1973: 105).

As I will now conclude by arguing, it is only if we capture the identity fetishism that was part and parcel of this process of racialization that we can understand why both the dark skinned and the light skinned, the poor and the rich, the educated and the uneducated Maronite could all identify themselves with European whiteness and feel superior to the hewers of wood.

Identity Fetishism and the Formation of Racial Fantasies

Following a small-scale military confrontation in 1841 leading to yet another military defeat for the Maronites, Bishop Murad wrote to France asking for its help, wondering 'whether the most advanced people of European civilisation will, without pity, allow my community to be throated by barbarians and even worse kind of people. My community, whose only crime is to be invincibly attached to the faith of its forefathers...' (in Attallah 1980: 184). Beside the recurrence of the racist opposition between 'the most advanced people of European civilization' and the Druzes who had in five years graduated in Murad's thought from 'backward' to 'barbarians and worse kind of people', what is significant about Murad's appeal is that he locates the basis of the conflict solely ('whose *only* crime') in the Maronites' attachment to 'the faith of their forefathers'.

Murad is certainly aware of the many socio-economic changes embodied in the Maronites' identity which reflect the practical substance of their conflict with the Druzes. He is also aware of the French's awareness of this practical dimension of the crisis. Yet, he locates the roots of the conflict solely in 'the faith of the forefathers'. That is, rather than stating that the conflict is based on what being Christian has come to mean in the specific historical circumstances, he sees the Druzes as attacking the Maronites for the simple fact of being Christian. It should be made immediately clear that Murad's discursive tournure is not simply the case of the category Christian playing the role of the signifier of those historical circumstances. By talking about the faith of the forefathers he gives the category a historical continuity. That is, he essentializes and dehistoricizes the category of identification, Maronite. If it is argued that the Maronites 'only crime' was to be Maronites in the same way as their forefathers, and if there is an implicit admission that the issue is about the historically articulated content of the Maronite identity, then, what is being argued is that the Maronite category of identification has the same meaning it always had throughout history. Consequently, these meanings are not seen as historical products but as an intrinsic aspect of the category of identification, Maronite. It is precisely this aspect of the process of identification that constitutes the fetishism of identity. The Maronites did not simply experience their identity as symbolizing the new occupations, skills, and tastes they acquired. Rather, they experienced it as their ultimate cause: it was *because* they were Christians that they could do what they were doing. As stated above, to stress the fetishism underlying this process of identification is to stress that it was not the product of a misinterpretation of reality. It was simply the way reality appeared to the Maronites.

In many ways, this fetishism of religious/confessional identity was ensured by the very confessional exclusivity of their experience: if those who engaged in the new practices are almost exclusively Christian, it becomes obvious that being Christian or Muslim is an important factor in establishing the kind of practices one is likely to be engaged in. To that extent, saying that one has become a silk merchant or an employee in a silk factory *because* one is Christian, for example, reflects a definite aspect of reality. Identity fetishism lay in the Maronites not experiencing the relational reality behind their process of identification: that the powers acquired by the Maronite identity were the product of the capitalist relations of dependency established by France and the class relations underlying it.

The permeation of religious ideology through the new social relations and the role of the Maronite Church in mediating the existence of the new practices, were important in consolidating such an experience of identity. It was through the Church's institutions, for instance, that the Maronites learned to read and write. Furthermore, as Chevallier points out, in the nineteenth century it was still common to seal various economic associations in a church under the watchful eyes of the Holy Virgin (Chevallier 1982: 131). The role of religious ideology and the Church in the silk industry was even more pronounced and important. Sharara rightly indicates that local industry was not faced with the 'naked arms' of those who had nothing to sell but their labour power. Most of the labour was drawn in fact from the peasantry, which was employed on contractual basis, often through the intermediary of a religious authority (Sharara 1975: 86). The role of the Church in providing labour for the industry reached somewhat un-Christian proportions as it proceeded to open, in association with the industrialists, religious orphanages next to the silk mills transforming them into an important source of cheap labour (Labaki 1984: 101). Often clergymen were employed as foremen in the mills (Sharara 1975: 85). These Church practices undoubtedly reinforced the experience of the Maronite identity as the intrinsic cause of the new social practices. The physical presence of the Church (the custodian of identity) as the mediator or the supervisor of the new practices stood metonymically for the causal power of the identity itself.

However, the question with which we ended the previous section remains: how can and how does a Maronite individual experience his or her identity as causing the 'superior' practices that the Maronites, in general, are perceived to be engaged in when this particular individual does not have access to these practices? That is, how can this experience of identity happen across classes and across 'skin colours'?

Here we come face to face with the magical quality of fetishized collective identification. This magic begins from the moment the individual acquires the capacity to think the collective identity: We Maronites. For one of the most enjoyable powers of the collective 'we' lies precisely in its capacity to make an 'I' experience what the 'I' by itself cannot possibly experience. 'I' can be uneducated and yet can confidently claim that 'we are highly educated compared to the Muslims'. 'I' can be a peasant but can proudly boast that 'we are a very sophisticated people'. 'I' can speak only in Arabic but can proudly claim 'we have always spoken French'. Likewise 'I' can be poor but can note that 'we are a rich community'. And finally in much the same way 'I' can be dark skinned and say 'we are white'.

What actually happens that allows the 'I' to 'get away' with this? I would like to suggest that this can only be explained by understanding the nature of the fetishized identity as a fantasy. This fantasy is at the core of all white processes of racialization.

Let's go in a slightly more microscopic way into the working of the racist mind that thinks something like: 'I belong to the Christian/White/European race who are familiar with the superior occupations prevalent in Europe. The Druze/Muslims are inferior non-white people, hewers of wood.' Now when some Maronites make such a statement, when they think 'I belong to the race of developed superior people', *who* exactly do they imagine in their mind as the 'superior people'? The white people who are most likely to be invoked in their mind will not be a group of smelly French drunken destitutes sleeping under the bridge. When the white racists think of 'their people' they immediately think of those who are conceived as superior beautiful people among their people. That is, the images that dominate their imaginary are fantasy images of white people rich in economic, aesthetic, and/or cultural capital (defined according to the various conceptions of national culture): people who within their communal milieu represent the best of the best.

But with this process of 'positive' selection comes another necessary process: repression. The person represses precisely those images that undermine the aestheticized image invoked by thinking 'My people are superior people.' That is, racialized thinking requires the suppression of the unpleasant images of 'underdeveloped' members of one's own group, a classification that has class at its very core. We can see that although colonial racism tried to undo class racism in favour of other biological or cultural forms of racism (see Miles 1993, particularly chapter 3; Todorov 1989), it is still haunted by the imaginary of the underdeveloped, smelly, brute underclasses, and therefore constantly works at repressing their images from the collective conception of the 'racialized community' even when parts of a 'neat' working class culture are included in the racial imaginary.

But this is not enough to understand this class imaginary of colonial racialization. For along with the positive aestheticization of the self comes the process of negatively aestheticizing the other, the one who is being racialized as inferior. That is, our white colonial racists will engage in exactly the opposite process where the colonial other is concerned. When the Maronites think that the Druze are inferior people, they do not start thinking of a refined and maybe even cosmopolitan Druze muqata'ji's son; they start thinking of wretched people, hewers of wood, etc. That is, they invoke and collapse the other into the very class images that they have banished from their definition of themselves and their white people. Likewise with skin colour: one systematically represses the whiteness of the other and the non-whiteness within the self to end up with a white self and a non-white other. I would suggest that what makes the Maronites peculiar 'white people' is not that they are colour-blind as opposed to European white people. It is more that they make the paradoxical colour-blindness that is part of *all* processes of white colonial racialization more obvious. This also shows how, through this selective aestheticization, racialized thought manages to create a sense of absolute difference between self and other.

Just as importantly, once the racialized and aestheticized collective 'we' is constructed it is also transformed into a fantasy: something one feels entitled to aspire to. The person uttering 'we Maronites are superior because we speak French and we are familiar with the professions prevalent in Europe' has already set himself or herself on the road to 'trying to be a superior Maronite.' The imagined 'we', in a kind of noblesse oblige, *actually* becomes causal in influencing the capacity of the person who is trying to be what their 'we' is. What the fetishism of identity implies is precisely the access to this causal fantasy. The internal logic of the fantasy goes something like this: 'I am a Maronite; I can't speak French and I am hewer of wood; but we Maronites are superior, speak French and have access to the sophisticated practices prevalent in Europe; and since I am a Maronite I can aspire to have access to these practices prevalent in Europe, etc...; this is unlike my next door neighbour, a Druze, who like me is also a hewer of wood but he is not Maronite; as such, he is deprived of the potential that my Maronite identity gives me.' The causality attributed to the racialized and fetishized identity is therefore conceived in terms of a potential. This is why it can act as an equalizer: not all Maronites have access to the occupations prevalent in Europe but all Maronites can potentially access them from the mere fact that they are Maronites.

It is often argued that one of the mystifications of communalism is that it blurs social divisions within the community. For Benedict Anderson, for instance, one of the reasons why nations are 'imagined communities' is because 'regardless of the actual inequality and exploitation that may prevail in each, the nation is always conceived as a deep horizontal comradeship' (1983: 16). Yet, given that inequality within a nation is obviously visible and is the subject of internal struggles, it seems necessary to explain why the feeling of 'horizontal comradeship' overrides the perception of 'vertical differences'. This is what a theory of identity fetishism allows us to do. It stresses that the feeling of horizontal comradeship among so much inequality is not a simple mental emotional illusion. It has its material base in what is perhaps the only thing that a 'community' distributes equally among its members distribution: the 'potential' to be what the idealized best of the community are.

Finally, one should note that once a racialized and fetishized identity emerges, the very logic of fetishism entails that it becomes immunized from the very social conditions that gave rise to it. It is not that once the differential socio-economic conditions between the Maronites and the Druzes stop existing the Maronites' identity is transformed once again. Rather it develops a kind of conatus of its own: a striving to persevere in its own being.

REFERENCES

Anderson, B. (1983) *Imagined Communities: Reflections on the Origin and Spread of Nationalism*. London and New York: Verso Press.
Attallah, D. B. (1980) *Le Liban, guerre civile ou conflit international?* Beirut: A B M Attalah.

Beydoun, A. (1984) *Identité confessionelle et temps social chez les historiens libanais contemporains*. Beyrouth: Publication de l'Universite Libanaise.

Chevallier, D. (1982) *La société du Mont Liban à l'époque de la révolution industrielle en Europe*, 2nd edn. Paris: Librairie Orientaliste Paul Geuthner.

Chiha, M. (1984) *Visage et Présence du Liban*, 2nd edn. Beyrouth: Editions du Trident

Churchill, C. H. (1973) *The Druzes and the Maronites Under Turkish Rule, From 1840 to 1860*. Reprint. New York: Arno Press.

Daou, p. (1977) *The Religious, Political and Cultural History of the Maronites* (Arabic). Beirut: Publisher unknown.

Dib, P. (1973) *L'Eglise Maronite*, 3 vols. Beyrouth: Editions La Sagesse.

Dubar, C. and Nasr, S. (1976) *Les classes sociales au Liban*. Paris: Presses de la fondation nationale des sciences politiques.

Dyer, R. (1997) *White*. London and New York: Routledge.

Fawaz, L. T. (1983) *Merchants and Migrants in Nineteenth Century Beirut*. Cambridge, MA: Harvard University Press.

Frankenberg, R. (1993) *White Women, Race Matters: The Social Construction of Whiteness*. Minneapolis: University of Minnesota Press.

Godelier, M. (1975) 'Structure and Contradiction in Capital', in R. Blackburn (ed.), *Ideology in the Social Sciences*. London: Fontana/Collins.

Harik, I. F. (1968) *Politics and Change in a Traditional Society, Lebanon, 1711–1845*. Princeton: Princeton University Press.

Hourani, A. H. (1966) *Minorities in the Arab World*. Oxford: Oxford University Press.

Issawi, C. (1966) 'Economic Development and Politics', in L. Binder (ed.), *Politics in Lebanon*. London: John Wiley & Sons.

Karam, G. A. (1981) *L'opinion publique libabaise et la question du Liban (1918–1920)*. Beyrouth: Publications de l'Université Libanaise.

Kay, G. (1975) *Development and Underdevelopment: A Marxist Analysis*. Basingstoke: Macmillan.

Kawtharani, W. (1981) 'The Christians, from the Mullah System to the Modern State' in E. Khuri (ed.), *The Christian Arabs* (Arabic). Beirut: Arab Research Institute.

Labaki, B. (1984) *Introduction a l'histoire économique du Liban: soie et commerce exterieur en fin de période Ottomane (1840–1914)*. Beyrouth: Publications de l'Universite Libanaise.

MacKay, J. and Batrouney, T. (1988) 'Lebanese Immigration since the 1970s', in J. Jupp (gen. ed.), *The Australian People: An Encyclopedia of the Nation, its People and their Origins*. North Ryde: Angus and Robertson.

Marx, K. (1976) *Capital, A Critique of Political Economy*, Vol 1. London: Penguin Books.

Miles, R. (1993) *Racism After 'Race Relations'*. London and New York: Routledge

Mouzelis, N. P. (1978) *Modern Greece: Facets of Underdevelopment*. New York: Holmes & Meier.

Polk, W. R. (1963) *The Opening of South Lebanon, 1788–1963: A Study of the Impact of the West on the Middle East*. Cambridge, MA: Harvard University Press.

Raccagni, M. (1980) 'The French Economic Interests in the Ottoman Empire'. *International Journal of Middle East Studies*, 11.

Rodinson, M. (1981) *Marxism and the Muslim World*. London: Monthly Review Press.

Saba, P. (1976) 'The Creation of the Lebanese Economy: Economic Growth in the Nineteenth and Twentieth Century', in R. Owen (ed.), *Essays on the Crisis in Lebanon*. London: Ithaca Press.

Salibi, K. S. (1977) *The Modern History of Lebanon*, 2nd edn. New York: Caravan Books.

Sassine, F. (1979) *Le Libanisme Maronite: contribution à l'étude d'un discours politique*. Paris: Thèse Ronéotée (IEHEI).

Sharara, W. (1975) *On the Origins of Confessional Lebanon* (Arabic). Beirut: Dar al-Tali'a.

Smilianskaya, I. (1972) *Peasant Movements in Lebanon, the First Half of the Nineteenth Century* (Arabic). Beirut: Dar al-Farabi.

Spagnolo, J. P. (1971) 'Constitutional Change in Mount Lebanon, 1861–1864'. *Middle Eastern Studies*, 17: 1, 25–48.

Todorov, T. (1989) *Nous et les Autres: La reflexion française sur la diversité humaine*. Paris: Éditions du Seuil.

CHAPTER 10

Racialization and 'White European' Immigration to Britain

TONY KUSHNER

The academic study of anti-Semitism and anti-black racism have followed similar patterns. Until at least the late nineteenth century, the assumption of Western scholars, reflecting as well as reinforcing the dominant belief structures in the world around them, was that prejudice and hostility against Jews and blacks was normal. Its existence was to be explained by the nature of these minorities (either their natural inferiority or inherent and unsavoury difference) and was not because of any subjective bias emanating from majority culture, society, and politics. Pre-Holocaust, for example, the Anglican clergyman and activist James Parkes (1939: 248) was almost unique and isolated, even within the relatively liberal atmosphere of inter-war Britain, in arguing that anti-Semitism was 'a measure not of Jewish failings, but of Gentile failure'. The reflection on the genocide and ethnic cleansing of the Second World War stimulated not only a reassessment of the validity of 'race science' but also a slowly evolving critique of the nature and origins of racism itself (Barkan 1992).[1] An extensive literature developed on the history of anti-Semitism, and, further stimulated by decolonization and post-colonial studies, the origins of anti-black racism in Western culture began to be explored (Parkes 1945; Curtin 1965). Now, over half a century after the end of the Second World War, intensive research has provided detailed historical case studies and more general theoretical approaches to the study of anti-Semitism and anti-black racism. There is also a small but growing field of studies devoted to the hostility faced by 'white' minorities such as the Irish, Italians, and Germans, and, most recently, 'asylum seekers' (Curtis 1984; Panayi 1991; Sponza 2000;

Kushner 2003*a*). It remains the case, however, that there is little connection made or dialogue between those working in these increasingly sophisticated fields of study. Indeed, there is active resistance from some who insist on the maintenance of distinct boundaries between them. Harry Goulbourne has argued, for example, that 'there are such things as race relations... [I]n Britain these are best understood against a background of empire and decline and within a context of migration [since 1945] and the development of what is generally regarded as a British multi-cultural society'. Earlier movements of people such as those of Jews and the Irish before the Second World War were fundamentally different to the 'catalytic role black and brown people played in the process of Britain redefining her identity and place as a post-imperial nation-state'. He adds that:

whilst relations between different European groups of white people gave rise to patterns of discrimination, the emergence of the notion of racial differentiation and the subsequent race relations or relations between races arose out of the dramatic contact and integration of Africans and Asians in the world that Europe, and this instance Britain, built.

Goulbourne does not deny the hostility and oppression faced by white minorities that were 'often vicious'. But he rejects utterly what he perceives as the 'well-intentioned' but mistaken attempt to 'collapse' exclusion on the basis of colour/race with exclusion 'on the basis of nationality, culture or religion'. Such 'collapsing' may, according to Goulbourne, have political appeal as a form of unified resistance to racism, but, at an analytical level, it involves unacceptable 'compromise' (Goulbourne 1998: ix–x). In contrast, this contribution will argue that making such connections is of analytical necessity, involving the rejection of the 'race relations' approach and, instead, embracing an inclusive racialization problematic.

Robert Miles, Stephen Small, David Theo Goldberg, and others have provided a critique of the academic, political, and everyday usage of the term race relations, emphasizing how it 'reifies, and thereby legitimates' the idea of 'race'. Rather than being value free, ' "race" and "race relations" are ideological notions which are used to both construct and negotiate social relations' (Miles 1989: 73). In relation to his research on the black experience in Britain and the United States, Small warns of the dangers of employing the race relations approach—its tendency to focus on the black population as a, and often *the*, cause of racialized antagonism. Instead, he argues, 'the problem is not "race" but "racisms," not relations between "races" but relations which have been racialised, not the physical

attributes of Blacks or their presumed inferiority, but the motivations of non-Blacks and the obstacles they impose' (Small 1994: 30).
Similarly, but with a more inclusive and historically informed perspective, Goldberg (1990: xiii) has supported the 'presumption of a
single monolithic racism...being displaced by a mapping of the multifarious historical formulations of racisms. The shift here is from a
synchronic description of surface expressions reflecting "race relations" to critical anatomies of diachronic transformations between
successive racist standpoints assumed and discarded since the sixteenth century'.

Small distinguishes between the '"racialization" problematic', a
theoretical framework of analysis, and the 'process of "racialization"', that is 'a process of attribution which has been unfolding historically, and continues to unfold' (Small 1994: 33). This chapter will
concentrate on the process of racialization and its case studies will be
largely based on responses in Britain to Jewish refugees in the first half
of the twentieth century. Its subject matter and geographical focus
require some explanation in the context of this volume as a whole.

First, although more contemporary material is included, the historic angle is critical. Howard Winant was one of the first scholars
to employ the concept of racialization (Omi and Winant 1986;
Winant 1994). In his *Racial Conditions* (1994: 59), Winant highlights that 'From a *racial formation* perspective, race is understood
as a fluid, unstable and "decentered" complex of social meanings
constantly being transformed by political conflict.' Later in this
study (Winant 1994: 119), Winant asks whether the enslavement,
mass violence, cultural deracination, and general horror of Western
imperialism could have 'been attempted, let alone accomplished, if
[its] intended victims had been other Europeans?' Answering his own
question, Winant adds that 'Only the Jews, the "other within",
could be placed on the receiving end of such barbarity, and when
they were, the Jews were appropriately racialized as well.' Winant's
inclusion of the Jews is important if problematic—the Jews have
been viewed and treated as both insiders and outsiders in relation to
the idea of 'Europe', as will be explored shortly. Here, however, the
major concern is limiting the European 'other within' to the Jews. As
Winant (1994: 98) himself acknowledges, 'More than ever, the
world is preoccupied with race...Much of Europe has become thoroughly racialized—if it was not already—by its obsession with the
immigrants of former colonial subjects, the presence of former
gastarbeiter, asylum seekers, Romani, and so forth.' The relevant
phrase in the context of this essay is 'if it was not already': there are

many minority groups, large and small, who have been racialized in European history, often with violent results—Jews, Muslims, Gypsies, and those of African origin being the most prominent. Of equal significance has been the racialization of presumed types of Europeans with a hierarchy frequently established with those from the north and west being perceived as superior to those from the south and east. Much scholarship, including that of Winant, is justifiably focused on the acute and growing contemporary crises created by ongoing racialized praxis. Nevertheless, only an inclusive and historically aware approach can do full justice to understanding the complexity and dynamics of racialization processes in general.

Second, this chapter explores the relationship between Britain and what has been termed the 'myth of Europe' (Asad 2000: 13). Part of but apart from 'Europe', the British case provides a fascinating insight into the making and remaking of Europeanness. In particular, the mythologized idea of 'Englishness', as against the potentially more inclusive Britishness, has been constructed not just in opposition to the 'Celtic fringes' and minorities within, but also the continent and its inhabitants. More generally, the 'idea of Europe' itself has a long and disputed history, and scholars differ at what point individuals began to think themselves as 'European' (Hay 1968; Nelson 1992; Hale 1993; Pim den Boer 1993; Pagden 2002). In this literature, however, there is an absence of consideration of the role played by the 'othering' process in constructing both the borders and the identity of 'we Europeans'. More recently, those working within post-colonial studies have rightly stressed the central role played by the colonized in understanding who 'we' are, or are not. In an important case study, Talal Asad (2000: 11) has argued that:

Muslims are present in Europe and yet absent from it. The problem of understanding Islam in Europe is primarily...a matter of understanding how 'Europe' is conceptualised by Europeans. Europe (and the nation states of which it is constituted) is ideologically constructed in such a way that Muslim immigrants cannot be satisfactorily represented in it...they are included within and excluded from Europe at one and the same time.

Again, however, it is often the case within this new scholarship that the focus is unnecessarily and limitingly narrow—a two-volume study of *Europe and Its Others* (Barker 1985), for example, fails to mention Jews or Gypsies once. Moreover, the racialization of East Europeans has played its role in European geopolitics: myths of the uncivilized Slavs continues to impact on the ways the boundaries of Europe, and European integration, are both imagined and defined.

Third, the concentration on the Jewish case study is revealing through the ambiguities that will be exposed. The racialization processes in relation to the Jews have been in constant flux, pronounced often at times of crisis and less so in periods of greater stability. Moreover, it has been rare for *all* Jews to be racialized, or, more accurately, for all Jews to be racialized negatively. It has been common, for example, to accept as 'one of us' what were perceived as Westernized Jews as against the essentially 'oriental' Jews from the East. This bifurcated image of 'the Jew' has gone alongside 'positive' racialization in which alleged innate characteristics—superior intelligence, international power, and financial acumen—have been deemed as potentially to the wider good. However unrealistic, individually and collectively at particular points Jews have attempted to use such positive racialization to their own advantage.[2] Whilst limited in chronology, focus, and geography, Jewish immigration to Britain will still provide an excellent case study into the nature of the process and praxis of racialization.

It is significant that the 'most consistent advocate' of the 'racialization problematic' has been the historical sociologist, Robert Miles (Small 1994: 33). In both his empirical and theoretical work Miles has covered responses in Britain to a range of migrant workers—especially the Irish and post-1945 European refugees (Miles 1982; Kay and Miles 1992). Although Jews have featured less in his work, Miles has acknowledged in his later writings that responses to them as migrant workers in Britain have been racialized, especially the East European Jewish refugees at the turn of the twentieth century (Miles 1993: 133, 138–9, 143–8). Moreover, within Europe, he recognizes that 'the Other has been created not only externally to the nation state but also within, most notably in the case of the Jews' (Miles 1989: 39). Miles does not consider, other than in passing, responses to Jewish refugees from the 1930s to the early 1950s within the same framework which would have strengthened his model of the racialization of migrant labour in twentieth century Britain (Miles 1993: 139; Kushner 1995). Nevertheless, his general approach, while operating within a pronounced Marxist framework, is, in relation to the migratory groups he considers, inclusive. Indeed, Miles' historical analysis 'demonstrates that racialization and the expression of racism are not confined solely to conjectures within Western European nation states shaped by the consequences of colonial migrations' nor should they be 'interpreted as continuous and unchanging' (Miles 1993: 148–9). More generally, however, to emphasize an earlier point, it is disappointing that few working outside Jewish studies have engaged with the recent sophisticated work on the construction of the Jew which would strengthen the theoretical underpinnings of the concept of racialization (Cohen 2002).[3]

In his study of English literature and society from 1875 to 1945, Bryan Cheyette demonstrates how 'race-thinking about Jews was...a key ingredient in the emerging cultural identity of modern Britain'. Cheyette locates what he calls 'semitic racial representations' at the 'centre of literary production and more widespread social and political discourses'. With relevance to this essay, he adds that, 'Instead of a colonial or genocidal history of racism and antisemitism, [his study] is at pains to show the way in which racialized constructions of Jews and other "races" were at the heart of domestic liberalism'(Cheyette 1993: xi). Cheyette is anxious to avoid overuse of the term 'anti-Semitism' because it frequently evokes illusions to Nazi Germany, and therefore cuts off debate and sober analysis—only a few writers in Britain such as Ezra Pound or Wyndham Lewis fit easily into a fascistic form of anti-Semitism. In contrast, he utilizes the term 'semitic discourse' as it enables consideration of ambivalence and an understanding of the 'indeterminate, fluid reading of "the Jew" in literary texts' (p. 8). Returning to the work of Stephen Small, a similarity of approach if not subject matter is apparent to that of Cheyette:

If the [contemporary] USA is racialized, is it also racist?
Not necessarily. It's better to think of racism as one aspect of racialization.... While recognizing that society is racialized, I do not think that it is useful to approach ideologies by asking whether they are racist or not. Some appear to be clearly and explicitly racist. Others, which make no explicit mention of race, can still be motivated by racisms of various kinds. But explicit racist hostility, especially that based on the belief in an ideology of the natural inequality of races, is not always the primary motivation. (Small 2002: 268, 271)

Instead, Small suggests that it is more useful 'to acknowledge the diverse array of ideologies that speak to issues of race, ethnicity, national, or religious identity, and to examine them for their racialized intentions, content, and consequences' (Small 2002: 268, 271). It is with such an analytical framework that I will now turn to in the case studies of this contribution. It does not deal with the 'classic' example of racist anti-Semitism, the Holocaust, which too often is the only reference point in relation to wider discussions of the treatment of Jews in the history of Western racism; but with the everyday processes of racialization in a liberal democracy by which 'white' refugees were and continue to be constructed and responded to in Britain.

British society, culture, and politics have been situated in classic ambivalence to the rest of Europe: 'thick fog over channel—continent isolated' as the perhaps apocryphal but oft-quoted pre-1914 headline put it (Bartlett 1957: 950).[4] Arrogance, snobbery, and a belief in innate superiority have gone alongside fear, suspicion, and rivalry to undermine but never destroy the sense that Britain has been part of the family of nations that make up Europe, as well as part of its racial map. The twentieth century, and especially the impact of the two World Wars, have intensified such ambiguous thinking and have been central to the making and remaking of national identity in Britain. The ambivalence over Britain's relationship with the continent has enabled the question of closer economic cooperation, and particularly the acceptance or otherwise of the single currency, to become a highly controversial issue in British politics, dividing both major political parties and the population as a whole (Joyce 2000).

As already glossed, the construction and reconstruction of 'Englishness' at key moments has often been in relation to the continental 'other' or at least parts of it. The historian, Linda Colley, for example, has argued that national identity was defined in the long eighteenth century largely by Francophobia: 'Imagining the French as their vile opposites, as Hyde to their Jekyll, became a way for Britons . . . to contrive for themselves a converse and flattering identity' (Colley 1994: 368). Increasingly from the late nineteenth century, that role has been occupied by the Germans, demonized in the two world conflicts and still regarded as the real danger lurking behind the front of a politically and economically united European community. Yet the mythical power of the wicked Hun/evil Nazi and the relative respectability of Germanophobia in contemporary Britain should not disguise the earlier affinity felt towards Germany and German culture before the twentieth century (Kushner 2003*b*: 14–16).

The Royal marriage between Victoria and her German husband, Albert, cemented a bond in the second half of the nineteenth century that many regarded as much racial as cultural. Language, political institutions, and common law were regarded as Anglo-Saxon in origin. It has been suggested that 'Victorian historians, particularly those of Whiggish persuasion, gave a degree of scholarly legitimacy to the notion that English history was a triumph of Saxon values, a victory of superior racial character'. James Urry, a historian of anthropology, argues that for mid-Victorian England, what he calls 'Teutomania', had 'important political implications both abroad and at home. By tracing their origins to Germany, Englishmen denied their links with the French, who were considered Celtic in origin, overlaid with Latin culture' (Urry 1984: 83–4). Only in the last quarter of the nineteenth century after reunification was Germany seen as a potential enemy, a rival in the economic and imperial fields and a military threat including increasingly paranoid fears of invasion (Panayi 1991).

Historians of science are increasingly recognizing the complexity and variations in Victorian racial thinking. There was little consensus about origins, evolution, typologies, and racial hierarchies. The idea, for example, of an Indo-European Aryan race suggested that Celts and Germans 'shared both a common racial and linguistic inheritance' and to some extent queried the idea of Anglo-Saxon supremacy (Urry 1984: 84). The existence of the Aryan myth, however, did not stop the growth of powerful anti-Irish racism in mid- and later-Victorian Britain and the belief of many that the Irish migrants coming into the mainland in their hundreds of thousands were bringing with them disease, crime, and squalor (Curtis 1984). It is important to accept the existence of scientific and other racisms in the nineteenth century, although in the case of the Irish, the belief in Celtic inferiority was undoubtedly the dominant discourse. What almost all the race thinkers could agree on, however, was the real existence of races and that these needed to be measured and categorized in scientific studies focusing particularly on skull shape, and hair and eye colouring. Whilst much was to change, especially in the 1930s in response to the rise of the Nazis, even those bitterly opposed to the politicization of racism refused to abandon their use of racial typologies (Huxley and Haddon 1935).[5] But what was the impact of race science on immigration policies in the past century and a quarter when Britain became a major place of settlement?

From 1871 to 1911, the population in Britain born outside the empire increased from 157,000 to 428,000 according to the census, the latter figure representing over 1 per cent of the total. Most of these aliens were born in Europe with Russia replacing Germany by the 1890s as the most common place of origin (Holmes 1988: 20–6). By 1905, Britain had its first permanent legislation, the Aliens Act, to keep out those who it regarded as being undesirable. It is undoubtedly the case that most of the attention of those either defending free entry or demanding restriction of immigration focused on East Europeans, the vast majority of whom were Jewish (Garrard 1971; Gainer 1972; Feldman 1994, Goldberg 1993a: 55). It has been estimated that roughly half a million Jews from the 1870s to 1914 settled in Britain for at least two years, although perhaps only a third stayed permanently (Gartner 1960). Most settled in what would now be called inner city areas, especially the East End of London, the centre of social investigation and also the site of fears about the 'state of the nation' (Feldman 1994). East European Jews were clearly the largest immigrant group coming into Britain. How far, however, were they perceived as European, or as Jews, or simply as aliens?

Europeans, according to most anthropologists from the 1870s through to the inter-war period, could be divided into three racial typologies with associated physical and often mental characteristics: Teutonic, Alpine, and Mediterranean. Race scientists had some difficulty placing the Jews into this schema, although this was not the case with Robert Knox, the Scottish anatomist in his influential *The Races of Men* (1850) which inspired James Hunt's Anthropological Society of London, founded in 1863 (Stocking 1971: 376–8). Knox argued for the supremacy of Anglo-Saxons over all other races. In contrast, a Jew was always a Jew, according to Knox, incapable of true civilization and unconvertible through culture or religion: 'Nature alters not.' Knox was influential on polygenists in Britain who argued that the black races had separate origins, were naturally inferior, and indeed closer to animals than humans. The Jew, in spite of Disraeli's claims to the contrary, was not a Caucasian, argued Knox. Indeed, Knox referred to the 'African character of the Jew, his muzzle-shaped mouth and face removing him from certain other races' (Knox 1850: 198–9, 208).

Later race thinkers in Victorian Britain were less dogmatic than Knox and by 1871 the creation of the Anthropological Institute reflected a defeat for the polygenists (Lorimer 1988). Nevertheless, anthropologists and others still largely accepted, as did the growing number of Jewish anthropologists, that there was a Jewish race that could be measured and categorized. Francis Galton, the founder of eugenics, and his protégé, Karl Pearson, did so through a variety of means, including photographs (Gilman 1996: chapter 2). Pearson's study of the intelligence and health of the Jewish immigrants in the East End was categorical: they were 'inferior physically and mentally to the native population'. His conclusion was that 'The welfare of our own country is bound up with the maintenance and improvement of its stock, and our researches do not indicate that this will follow the unrestricted admission of either Jewish or any other type of immigrant' (Stone 2002: 105).

Eugenics arguments were certainly utilized by the leading and prominent anti-alien, Arnold White, at the forefront of the national efficiency movement. Unlike the Huguenots, argued White, it would be impossible to assimilate the East European Jews who would eventually take over Britain. White was more explicit in his racism than most anti-alien campaigners: Jews were Asiatics and the present immigration 'of debased and impoverished Jews from the slums of the Russian Ghetto' was particularly 'undesirable'. White pointed to the growth of anti-Semitism across Europe and concluded if action was not taken to stop alien immigration that in Britain 'the patience of Anglo-Saxons' was beginning to give way (White 1899: xi, 122, 279).

White's explicit Anglo-Saxon racism was relatively unusual, even though he was a mainstream political figure in late Victorian and Edwardian Britain (Searle 1971: 54). More typical of the anti-alienists was W. H. Wilkins of Clare College, Cambridge. Wilkins in his *The Alien Invasion* (1892) warned that Britain alone in Europe had no laws to control immigration. Wilkins was not against foreign immigration per se, but only those who would make an 'injurious effect'. Britain was having to deal 'with the invasion of some thirty or forty thousand every year of the class which under ordinary circumstances would go to fill the poor-houses and penitentiaries of Eastern Europe'. With emigration of the fittest and immigration of the weakest, 'we are drawing out good wine and pouring in bad'. Wilkins, however, wanted to 'make it clear' that he was not 'animated by...sentiments of racial or religious animosity'. He used the term 'Jew...merely to distinguish between other races and nationalities'. While it was true that 'a large proportion of [the] undesirable visitors [were] Jewish by race and religion' that had 'nothing to do with the objection to them' (Wilkins 1892: 4–6, 15, 35). Was this the case?

Like all anti-alien activists, Wilkins praised the genuine refugees of the past who had developed new industries and melded into the population. It could not, however, 'be seriously contended that the Flemings and the Huguenots have their parallel in the destitute and degraded immigrants from east of Europe, or the vagrant and vicious aliens from the South' (p. 10). Wilkins, in singling out particularly East European Jews and Italians in *The Alien Invasion*, was not merely referring to the two groups of immigrants into Britain on account of their size (the latter were far less numerous) but because he objected to their activities and indeed their nature as a whole. His concerns were as much animated by class considerations as they were by race. For White, following Knox, the Jews could never be Europeans or Anglo-Saxons because they were Asiatics. Wilkins and most of those pressing for alien control had created a racialized and internally hierarchical concept of Europe itself, and like the United States wanted to legislate against the free entry of what they saw as inferior types from the south and particularly east of the continent.

The Jewishness as well as the poverty of the East European Jews made them particularly undesirable from a racial perspective as they were linked to crime, revolution, and disease. Although they are not mentioned specifically within its clauses, it is clear that the 1905 Aliens Act was designed to keep as many poor Jews out of Britain as possible (Kushner and Knox 1999: 27–310). Some anti-restrictionists argued that alien Jews were in fact 'European white men' who were 'not of a stock inferior to our own', and one 'when it mixes with our own in course of years, goes rather to improve rather than to deteriorate the British race' (Dilke 1904: 991, 995).[6] Such pro-alien views were not only unsuccessful but also highlighted the racialized nature of the debate. There were few in Britain who were moving in the direction of the German Jewish American-based anthropologist, Franz Boas. Boas largely rejected the scientific existence of race and instead argued for the ability of immigrants and their children to adjust rapidly, both physically and mentally, to new conditions in their adopted countries (Stocking 1982). It remains that Wilkins, White, Evans Gordon, and many other leading anti-alienists had a particular animus against Jewish East European immigrants and their campaign, in this respect, was in the short term partly successful and in the long term, almost totally so.

The 1905 Act was a relatively mild measure, limited in fact to those travelling steerage—the process of racialization can never be taken in isolation and has to be combined with other factors, in this case class. It was replaced in 1914 and 1919 by far more draconian legislation which in essence ended almost all immigration into Britain and gave the government the power to detain and deport aliens it saw as racially undesirable. It is ironic that during the First World War and immediately after the legislation was used particularly against Germans in Britain, effectively destroying a community of 70,000—anti-German racism built on the earlier, positive racializing of the Anglo-Saxon which had originally enabled a bonding with all things Germanic (Kushner and Knox 1999: chapters 2 and 3).

In the inter-war period there were eugenicists, anthropologists, and others whose 'scientific' work provided a justification for the anti-alien policies of the British government which were designed in particular to keep out East European Jews and to remove the black communities in the ports that had developed particularly during the First World War (Evans 1985; Rich 1986: chapter 7). Elazar Barkan in his study of race thinking in inter-war Britain and America, entitled *The Retreat of Scientific Racism*, argues that when Karl Pearson published his extensive prewar research on East European Jews in London

LIVERPOOL JOHN MOORES UNIVERSITY
LEARNING SERVICES

in 1925, by that date 'there was no problem of alien immigration into Great Britain' (Barkan 1992: 155). In fact, it was at that point that the Conservative government was intensifying its efforts to keep out the hundreds of thousands of Jews escaping pogroms, revolution, civil war, and famine in Eastern Europe. A group of one thousand Ukrainian Jews were stranded in Britain after the United States, using racially explicit quotas to keep out East and Southern Europeans, turned them back from Ellis Island. Home Secretary Joynson-Hicks refused to allow them to stay, stating, 'that under no circumstances will I permit these unfortunate people to be absorbed into our population. It is quite impossible. They are a class of people who come from the east of Europe that we do not want, and America does not want them either' (Hicks 1925: 313–4). Intellectuals, such as Madison Grant, had been influential through their espousal of Nordic racism, in the passing of the American immigration quotas of 1921 and 1924 (Higham 1978: 316–24; King 2000).[7] In Britain, race scientists were less directly influential. Even so the racisms of the prewar period and the intense nationalism stimulated by the First World War enabled the success of anti-alienism to the extent that more aliens were deported than allowed entry throughout the 1920s (Cesarani 1987).

For the most part, however, those involved in the scientific study of race in Britain and America grew increasingly estranged from the political use of racism. Moreover, they began to question not the concept race itself but crude categorizations that did not allow for change and complexity out of population mixing. H. J. Fleure, one of the leading figures in the geographical, archaeological, and anthropological studies of race in inter-war Britain, reflected the forces of change and continuity. In his *The Peoples of Europe* (1922: 11) he argued that there was such racial diversity within Europe 'to make the idea of "European Man" a mere abstraction; we need to think rather of "European Men"'. Fleure's racialized understanding of Europe was based on diversity and not hierarchy. In the 1930s, Fleure condemned the Nazis' use of race and racism. His answer was to turn the scientific study of race against them—few Germans he believed were of the Nordic race type. Fleure was genuinely appalled at the persecution of the Jews in Germany and commented how they had contributed positively to both British and Jewish life. Again, race science was used to defend the Jews: 'It may be said that certain physical characters . . . are widespread among the Jewish elements of our populations, but they also show approximations, notably in some features of head form, to the people round about them' (Fleure 1936: 176–7).

In 1935, the scientific reaction in Britain to Nazi racialism came out in its most famous form—Julian Huxley and A. C. Haddon's *We Europeans*. Arguing for European commonality—it started with photographs of sixteen men, asking the reader to guess their specific nationality—it normalized the Jew within a Europe that was de-essentialized, emphasizing diversity throughout. And yet racist anti-Semitism was still debunked using racialized categorization and measurement. The Jews, it argued, should in racial theory be long-headed as they were Semitic in origin but were in fact as a racial type largely broad-headed like Einstein (Huxley and Haddon 1935: 96–7). The aftermath of the Second World War dealt a major blow to race science but even then it did not disappear. Indeed, its persistence at a scientific, popular, and political level has been exposed in the 'Bell Curve' debate in the United States during the 1990s and beyond (Kohn 1995).

The continuous use of race by scientific anti-racists undoubtedly added to the sense of confusion and prejudice in government and popular circles in Britain. That Jews in Eastern Europe were locally assimilated, and therefore fitted into an Eastern European racial type, according to race thinkers such as Fleure, did not actually help those trying to get into Britain in the inter-war period. As one leading Home Office official put it during the 1920s in relation to naturalization policy:

different races display very different qualities and capabilities for identifying themselves with this country ... [T]he Latin, Teuton and Scandinavian races, starting some of them, with a certain kinship with British races, are ... easily assimilated. On the other hand, Slavs, Jews and other races from Central and Eastern parts of Europe stand in a quite different position. They do not want to be assimilated ... and do not identify themselves with this country. (Cesarani 1987: 17)

Indeed, a decade later government officials reverted back to a form of Anglo-Saxon racism, much happier to accept German Jews, especially of the right class and education, as against those who came from further east. Captain Jeffes of the Foreign Office Passport Control section went across Europe in 1939 finding out who was being given visas to come to Britain as domestic servants, the most numerous form of entry for Jewish refugees. He was 'appalled to see the bad type of refugee presenting ... permits ... who were so filthily dirty both in their person and their clothing that they were utterly unfit to go inside a decent British home'.[8] As another British official stated, 'the better [racial] type of refugees ... were ruled out at the start'.[9]

Such prejudice against the *ostjuden* was to continue after 1945—an indication of how long racialized responses to the Jews persisted.

From 1945 to 1951, Britain recruited foreign workers massively to make up gaps in the workforce and help rebuild the country (Kay and Miles 1992). The Royal Commission on Population (1949: 124, 130) was explicit about what was required for the 'national interest': large-scale immigration could 'only be welcomed without reserve if the immigrants were of good human stock and were not prevented by their religion or race from intermarrying with the host population and becoming merged in it'. Not surprisingly, black workers from the New Commonwealth were rejected as the solution—migrants had to come from the continent of Europe (Paul 1997). Hundreds of thousands of Poles, Ukrainians, Latvians, Lithuanians, as well as Italians were recruited for the land, the new health service, the building industry, and transport. The object, as a Foreign Office memorandum put it in 1947, was to 'recruit as early as possible the maximum number of Displaced Persons who can help immediately to meet Britain's shortage of manpower'. It was not, however, 'to get as many Displaced Persons as possible'.[10]

Mirroring and to an extent reflecting the impact of race science and the processes of racialization in Britain over the past century on immigration policy, the memorandum showed the complexity and outright contradictions in such thinking. The selection of displaced persons, it emphasized, must be highly discriminatory to make sure that the right people were chosen. Animosity at home 'clearly prevent the recruitment of Jews' and the Volksdeutche. Nevertheless, such discrimination for the sake of justice must not be on the grounds of 'race, nationality, or residence'.[11] The Jews of the post-war displaced persons camps, largely East European survivors of the ghettos and death camps, represented roughly one quarter of their total but only 1 per cent of those chosen to come to Britain (Cesarani 1992; Kushner 1994: 227–37). Racialized myths of Europe ensured that Britain recruited almost exclusively from the continent in its vital period of post-war reconstruction. Other myths of Europe, however, similarly coming out of the legacy of race thinking, meant that it did so in a racially discriminatory way, refusing to accept Jews and others as part of its future identity; they were non-assimilable. Yet further highlighting the importance of the racialization process and its fundamental ambiguities and contradictions, the myth of British decency and superiority to the rest of Europe was actually reinforced by the Second World War and horror at the Nazis' implementation of race science in the exposed concentration camps.

Indeed, it is crucial to add that such discriminatory racialized policies by Britain continue today against the other major racial victims
of the Nazis—the Roma—and more generally against asylum-seekers,
many of whom come from Eastern Europe.

In the space available it would not be possible to do justice to all
the trends and developments in post-1945 debates and policy
towards immigration in Britain. Nevertheless, many of the features
of the racialization of immigration since the late nineteenth century,
which have been shown to have been in operation throughout the
first half of the twentieth century, continued beyond. Although much
of the public debate and state policy has focused on New
Commonwealth migration, racialization of white immigration continued. In the late 1940s and early 1950s, those from Italy and
Eastern Europe were regarded as poorer alternatives to more
Westernized immigrants such as those from the Baltic states.
Moreover, the Irish continued to be viewed as problematic even if,
for reasons of realpolitik, they were exempt from immigration control legislation in the 1960s (Paul 1997). Since the late 1980s, however, the continued racialization of white newcomers has been most
blatantly manifested in responses to asylum-seekers.

Asylum-seekers come to Britain from all parts of the globe. The
continued crises in former Yugoslavia throughout the 1990s, as well
as the persecution of the Roma in many Eastern and Central
European states, has ensured that many have come from Europe
itself. The 'whiteness' of these asylum-seekers has been used by their
opponents to deny that racism motivates their hostility. A closer
examination of the arguments used by those opposed to asylum-
seekers demolishes such excuses and in fact adds another example to
those across the twentieth century and now beyond of a racialized
discourse operating alongside a refutation of racist intent. The campaign against asylum-seekers in Britain since the late 1990s has been
unprecedented in its intensity. The vast majority of the British press,
especially the tabloids, have been opposed to asylum-seekers and the
frequency and power of its invective has no parallel. Governments,
both Conservative and Labour, and their state apparatus, have
waged war on the entry of asylum-seekers and the public, a vocifer-
ous and campaigning minority aside, have been hostile, leading to
frightening levels of violence, including murder (Kushner 2003*a*).

An editorial in the *Sun* (10 August 2003) reveals the complex
racialization process at work. the *Sun* is by far the largest circulation newspaper in Britain, and its playfulness notwithstanding, its
influence is not negligible. It was certainly in serious mode in the

editorial which was entitled 'Way of life is at stake.' Moving seam-
lessly from referring to those coming in from asylum-seekers to
'illegal immigrants', it accused the newcomers of undermining the
country's sense of identity. Such a charge, it emphasized, was not
motivated by racism. Instead, it came out of a genuine 'fear that
those who abuse our hospitality are stealing not just our money but
our character and our culture' (Kushner 2003a). The use of the term
culture rather than biological objections should not disguise the
racialization process at work here and in other government, state,
media, and popular attacks on asylum-seekers. The assumption
is that culture is an inherent obstacle to integration—the asylum-
seekers, diverse though their origins are, have been homogenized
and essentialized and thereby deemed to be un-British/un-English.
With such reasoning, their entry, like the earlier asylum-seekers,
Jews from Eastern and then Central Europe, can lead only to 'polluting the body politic' (Goldberg 1993a, b). Yet, as ever, the racialization process is complex and rarely all-embracing. Just as there
were 'desirable' and assimilable, 'whiter' Jews in the past, so the
'bogus' or 'abusive' asylum-seekers have been differentiated from
the 'genuine' refugees who deserve 'our' sympathy. Moreover, their
predecessors have been deemed to have enriched Britain in the past.
The fact that those now dubbed genuine refugees were at the time
perceived as racially undesirable aliens shows how the memory
process has further complicated the intricate and multilayered
patterns and practices of racialization (Kushner 2003a).

To conclude: in its own peculiar way, Britain's racialized myths of
Europe, which have often been used to show its essential separateness,
actually reveal its full integration into a very real if deeply disturbing
European reality. The process of racialization is complex and dynamic,
requiring an inclusive and historic framework if it is to be understood
and then meaningfully countered. Racialization cuts across such constructed binaries as white/black, colonizer/colonized, or even, as this
chapter has striven to illustrate, Europe/the rest of the world.

NOTES

1. Barkan perhaps overstates some of the changes that took place before 1939.
2. This was true to some extent with Zionists such as Chaim Weizmann in the
   First World War who exploited fears of Jewish power in British government
   circles to further his own cause.
3. Cohen provides an example which shows the complexity of race discourse and
   the need to incorporate the Jewish example.

4. Bartlett states that 'there are several versions of a supposed London newspaper headline' of which this is the best known.
5. See, for example, the lingering use of racial typologies in the anti-racist popular book *We Europeans* ascribed to Julian Huxley and A. C. Haddon but owing much also to Charles Singer.
6. Dilke contrasted the East European Jews to the 'yellow races' being allowed into the Transvaal.
7. King provides a rare attempt at comparing Britain and the United States but unfortunately, by failing to examine British policies towards aliens in the 1920s, greater similarities are underplayed in his analysis.
8. Public Record Office (PRO) HO 213/107 E409, Jeffes to Cooper, 5 June 1939.
9. Parkin, 8 May 1939 in PRO FO 371/24100 W7740.
10. PRO FO 945/500 W586, 'Recruitment of DPs for Great Britain', 24 March 1947.
11. PRO FO 945/500 W586, 'Recruitment of DPs for Great Britain', 24 March 1947.

REFERENCES

Asad, T. (2000) 'Muslims and European Identity: Can Europe Represent Islam?', in E. Hallam and B. Street (eds.), *Cultural Encounters: Representing 'Otherness.'* London: Routledge.

Barkan, E. (1992) *The Retreat of Scientific Racism: Changing Concepts of Race in Britain and the United States Between the World Wars.* Cambridge: Cambridge University Press.

Barker, F. (ed.) (1985) *Europe and its Others,* 2 vols. Colchester: University of Essex.

Bartlett, J. (1957) *Familiar Quotations,* 13th edn. London: Macmillan.

den Boer, P. et al. (1993) *The History of the Idea of Europe.* Milton Keynes: Open University.

Cesarani, D. (1987) 'Anti-Alienism in England after the First World War'. *Immigrants and Minorities* 6 (1): 5–29.

——(1992) *Justice Delayed: How Britain Became a Refuge for Nazi War Criminals.* London: Heinemann.

Cheyette, B. (1993) *Constructions of 'the Jew' in British Literature and Society: Racial Representations, 1875–1945.* Cambridge: Cambridge University Press.

Cohen, D. (2002) 'Who was Who? Race and Jews in Turn-of-the-Century Britain'. *Journal of British Studies,* 41: 460–83.

Colley, L. (1994) *Britons: Forging the Nation 1707–1837.* London: Yale University Press.

Curtin, P. (1965) *The Image of Africa: British Ideas and Action, 1780–1850.* London: Macmillan.

Curtis, L. (1984) *Nothing but the Same Old Story: The Roots of Anti-Irish Racism.* London: Information on Ireland.

Dilke, C. (29 March 1904) *Hansard* (HC) 132.

Evans, N. (1985) 'Regulating the Reserve Army: Arabs, Blacks and the Local State in Cardiff, 1919–45'. *Immigrants and Minorities,* 4 (2): 68–106.

Feldman, D. (1994) *Englishmen and Jews: Social Relations and Political Culture 1840–1914.* London: Yale University Press.

Fleure, H. (1922) *The Peoples of Europe.* London: Oxford University Press.

LIVERPOOL JOHN MOORES UNIVERSITY
Aldham Roberts L.R.C.
TEL. 0151 231 3701/3634

Fleure, H. (1936) 'Nordic Race and Culture and German Nationality'. *German Life and Letters,* 1 (1): 171–81.

Gainer, B. (1972) *The Alien Invasion: The Origins of the Aliens Act 1905.* London: Heinemann.

Garrard, J. (1971) *The English and Immigration 1880–1910.* London: Oxford University Press.

Gartner, L. (1960) 'Notes on the Statistics of Jewish Immigration to England, 1870–1914'. *Jewish Social Studies,* 22 (2): 97–102.

Gilman, S. (1996) *Smart Jews: The Construction of the Image of Jewish Superior Intelligence.* Lincoln: University of Nebraska Press.

Goldberg, D. T. (1990) 'Introduction', in Idem (ed.), *Anatomy of Racism.* Minneapolis: University of Minnesota Press.

——(1993a) *Racist Culture.* Oxford: Blackwell.

——(1993b) '"Polluting the Body Politic": Racist Discourse and Urban Location', in M. Cross and M. Keith (eds.), *Racism, the City and the State.* London: Routledge

Goulbourne, H. (1998) *Race Relations in Britain since 1945.* Basingstoke: Macmillan

Hale, J. (1993) *The Civilization of Europe in the Renaissance.* London: Longman.

Hay, D. (1968) *Europe: The Emergence of an Idea.* Edinburgh: Edinburgh University Press.

Higham, J. (1978) *Strangers in the Land: Patterns of American Nativism 1860–1925.* New York: Atheneum.

Holmes, C. (1988) *John Bull's Island: Immigration and British Society, 1871–1971.* Basingstoke: Macmillan.

Huxley, J. and Haddon, A. (1935) *We Europeans.* London: Jonathan Cape.

Joyce, C. (ed.) (2000) *Questions of Identity: Exploring the Character of Europe.* London: I B Tauris.

Joynson-Hicks, W. (11 February 1925) *Hansard* (HC) 180.

Kay, D. and Miles, R. (1992) *Refugees or Migrant Workers? The Recruitment of Displaced Persons for Industry 1946–1951,* London: Routledge.

King, D. (2000) 'Liberal and Illiberal Immigration Policy: A Comparison of Early British (1905) and US (1924) Legislation'. *Totalitarian Movements and Political Religions,* 1(1): 78–96.

Knox, R. (1850) *The Races of Men.* London: Henry Renshaw.

Kohn, M. (1995) *The Race Gallery: The Return of Racial Science.* London: Jonathan Cape.

Kushner, T. (1994) *The Holocaust and the Liberal Imagination: A Social and Cultural History* Oxford: Blackwell.

——(1995) 'Their Brothers' (and Sisters') Keeper? Refugees from Nazism and British Labour', in M. van der Linden and J. Lucassen (eds.), *Racism and the Labour Market.* Bern: Peter Lang.

——(2003a) 'Meaning Nothing But Good: Ethics, History and Asylum-Seeker Phobia in Britain'. *Patterns of Prejudice,* 37 (3): 257–76.

——(2003b) 'The Holocaust and the Museum World in Britain: A Study of Ethnography', in S. Vice (ed.), *Representing the Holocaust.* London: Frank Cass

——and Knox, K. (1999) *Refugees in an Age of Genocide.* London: Frank Cass.

Lorimer, D. (1988) 'Theoretical Racism in Late-Victorian Anthropology, 1870–1900'. *Victorian Studies,* 31 (3): 405–30.

Miles, R. (1982) *Racism and Migrant Labour.* London: Routledge and Kegan Paul

——(1989) *Racism.* London: Routledge.

——(1993) *Racism after 'Race Relations'.* London: Routledge.

Nelson, B. et al. (eds.) (1992) *The Idea of Europe.* Oxford: Berg.

Omi, M. and Winant, H. (1986) *Racial Formation in the United States: From the 1960s to the 1980s.* London: Routledge.

Pagden, A. (2002) *The Idea of Europe: From Antiquity to the European Union.* Cambridge: Cambridge University Press.

Panayi, P. (1991) *The Enemy in our Midst: Germans in Britain During the First World War.* Oxford: Berg.

Parkes, J. (1939) *The Jewish Problem in the Modern World.* London: Thornton Butterworth.

——(1945) *Antisemitism.* Harmondsworth: Penguin.

Paul, K. (1997) *Whitewashing Britain: Race and Citizenship in the Postwar Era.* Ithaca: Cornell University Press.

Rich, P. (1986) *Race and Empire in British Politics.* Cambridge: Cambridge University Press.

Royal Commission on Population (1949) *Report.* London: HMSO.

Searle, G. (1971) *The Quest for National Efficiency: A Study in British Politics and Political Thought 1899–1914.* Oxford: Oxford University Press.

Small, S. (1994) *The Black Experience in the United States and England in the 1980s.* London: Routledge.

——(2002) 'Racisms and Racialized Hostility', in D. T. Goldberg and J. Solomos (eds.), *A Companion to Racial and Ethnic Studies.* Malden: Blackwell.

Sponza, L. (2000) *Divided Loyalties: Italians in Britain During the Second World War.* Bern: Peter Lang.

Stocking, G. (1971) 'What's in a Name? The Origins of the Royal Anthropological Institute (1837–71)'. *Man,* 6: 369–90.

——(1982) *Race, Culture and Evolution: Essays in the History of Anthropology.* Chicago: University of Chicago Press.

Stone, D. (2002) *Breeding Supermen: Nietzsche, Race and Eugenics in Edwardian and Interwar Britain.* Liverpool: Liverpool University Press.

Urry, J. (1984) 'Englishmen, Celts and Iberians: The Ethnographic Survey of the United Kingdom, 1892–1899', in G. Stocking (ed.), *Functionalism Historicized: Essays on British Social Anthropology.* Madison, Wisconsin: University of Wisconsin Press.

White, A. (1899) *The Modern Jew.* London: Heinemann.

Wilkins, W. (1892) *The Alien Invasion.* London: Methuen.

Winant, H. (1994) *Racial Conditions: Politics, Theory, Comparisons.* Minneapolis: University of Minnesota Press.

CHAPTER 11

Gendered Preferences in Racialized Spaces: Cloning the Physician

Philomena Essed

One of the guessing games we used to play at my former Dutch high school went something like this: A father and son are in a car accident. The son, who needs to be operated upon immediately, is taken to the hospital by an ambulance. When the stretcher is pushed into the emergency room the only surgeon available takes one look at the patient and objects: 'I can't operate on him, he is my son'.
Question: How is this possible?

We would go at length, trying to explain how the father in the accident was not the real father, or the son not the real son, or something weird with the surgeon.... Then came the 'ha-ha-got-you' moment for the story teller: 'The surgeon was his mother!'

Gender bias hit on the head, end of story back then. But is it? The surgeon could have been a man, but gay couples were not yet in the picture. Not recognized then either were the racial dimensions involved. No doubt I was not the only one who imaged the surgeon to be a *white* man. And once we found out the surgeon was a woman, she was surely not imagined black African either. Neither did we question the cultural presuppositions of emotional detachment and neutrality—apparently the Dutch medical code would have the patient bleed rather than being operated upon by a close family member.

These different interpretations of the high school brainteaser are meant as playful reference to the theme of this essay: cloning the physician. The story came to mind thinking about 'racialization', the title of this volume. The request to contribute had put me in a predicament. Why limit myself to racialization when many share with me the view that 'race' only gets meaning in terms of a particular language or national history and in terms of gender, ethnicity, class, physical ability, and other relevant factors (Young 1990; Collins 1998; Gilman 1999). The troublesome implications of race as an overriding characteristic for claiming or rejecting human beings have been well documented. Artificial fixings of peoples in closed races and ethnicities have been and are at the heart of racism, ethnicism, and recurrent genocides (Oommen 1997; Goldberg and Solomos 2002). But even well-intentioned exceptions, notably strategic essentialism in the name of nationalist, anti-imperialist, or anti-racism struggles, turn straightjackets of projected identities and 'ethnic' fundamentalisms, often operating over the backs of women (Yuval-Davis 1997; Cockburn 1998). Admittedly, critical scholars have increasingly tried to avoid essentialisms, insisting on such notions as multiracial, hybridity, intersectionality, and multiple identifications (Crenshaw 1991; Root 1996; Werbner and Modood 1997; Essed 2001; Markus 2002). While cognizant of 'multiple' factors indeed—race, ethnicity, gender, age, ability, and so on—this alternative has its limitations too. The enumeration of A to Z factors has a way of serving as a token sign of inclusiveness, a ritual procession of differences in otherwise foremost 'racial' or gender approaches. Thus, I stated in a recent publication that the idea of 'diversity' in Dutch work organizations is little more than a fancy label, an alternative word to refer to only ethnic difference (Essed 2002). Moreover, new labels do not solve the problem that centralizing difference (and the pursuit of equity and inclusion) lets off the hook the normative practices. And business continues as usual.

There are ample publications about mechanisms of exclusion, but our critiques of racial, ethnic, gender, class, national, and other structural forms of exclusion have hardly even scratched the surface of the normative image compared to which 'Others' are perceived as different or deviant. In this chapter, I aim to shift the gaze from exclusion (of those perceived of a lesser kind or status) on the basis of perceived *difference* (e.g. race, ethnicity, gender, nationality) towards preference for *sameness*, in particular in view of maintaining (imagined) homogeneity in high status positions. With preference for sameness I mean constructed or claimed homogeneity while identifying individuals as like-minded, like-looking, like family, like 'us', like clones of the appreciated 'types'. I do not mean to put off readers with the notion of clones, let alone use it approvingly. In the course of this chapter it will be seen that 'cloning', in a cultural sense, is a well-established practice for securing privilege. Among top managers the wish to clone super-managers, like themselves, does not even seem to raise any eyebrows. One anecdotal example can be found in the words of Mr Henny de Ruiter, president-commissioner of Ahold (1) and a powerful corporate hotshot in the Netherlands. In an interview for a business magazine, in late September 2003, de Ruiter proclaims his admiration for two other hotshots, much like him heavy with commissioners' posts, saying: 'They should be cloned, but regretfully that is not possible' (Dinther 2003: 33). Within weeks of this interview one of the 'should be cloned' candidates would become de Ruiter's successor as Ahold president-commissioner. Interesting detail: journalists quoted sources qualifying de Ruiter as a 'yes-man'—'he never says no' (Dinther 2003: 30, 32) and his successor Karel Vuursteen as a man who 'just does not know how to say no' (Boogaarts 2003).

Candidates for high status professions or positions are selected through networking, and according to their closeness to a normative (preferred) image, often somehow mirroring the Self of the selector(s) (Tilly 1998). Here is another example, a different bastion of exclusive membership, the Vatican: Fall 2003, Pope John-Paul II advanced the procedure for appointing new cardinals—a few dozen in total, all men, different colours, racial, ethnic, and national backgrounds. But like the pope they are all known to be conservative. His own end nearing, the pope tries to make sure that his preference for conservatism outlives him at the highest level of the Catholic Church (next below the pope).

Preference for more of the same type points at *cultural cloning*. This seems an apt concept to refer to gatekeeping at top positions where (combinations of) racial, gender, ethnic, age, and other systemic discriminations *against* particular groups are also indicative of normative preferences *for* combinations of (perceived) masculinity, whiteness, European-ness, able-bodiedness, and related markers (Essed 2002). Cultural cloning is a process of control, of preservation, of (constructed) sameness *in view of maintaining privilege and status differences* (Essed and Goldberg 2002). Cultural cloning is different from the familiar concept of reproduction. 'Reproduction or trans-generational continuity includes preservation, repetition and sameness *as well as* transmutations, a necessary process in the extension of life forms' (Essed and Goldberg 2003). I intend to problematize the homogeneities of cultural cloning and the gatekeeping practices it entails. In light of this, professional profiles are interesting because they express norms, values, and images of competence, and the way in which these are anchored in racial, gender, national, ethnic structures, and in local and situational processes.

In order to offer more than a theoretical exercise, I apply the concept of cultural cloning to one specific high status position: the profession of physician. The choice for this profile is foremost pragmatic, assuming that most readers have at least some everyday experience with medical practices or with the health sector in general. Most of us know from our daily lives about the limited time slots available to see the doctor, the objectification of our bodies, the rigid boundaries between different specializations catering to different parts of the body, or the absolute authority physicians exert over nurses (Rosenstein et al. 2002). Choices being made in these contexts are not race neutral. But to focus only on racial manifestations does not go deep enough. Racism and other forms of exclusion are integrated into the everyday routines of medical practice, expressions of which are also determined by the nature of the medical field (Essed 1991). The other way round, routine practices in organizations follow the familiar categories and routes of power and inequality, thus privileging the ingredients that make up higher social status (Tilly 1998). A brief digression on the culture of medical organizations might be useful at this point.

'The Physician' in a (Post)Modern Work Environment

The skewed focus, in race critical research, on the injustices of exclusion holds the danger of overlooking other significant questions about the *nature* of the spaces discriminated groups do not have equal access to. What about the promise of happiness in our societies of wealth and limitless opportunity? Robert Lane insists, in his well-documented study about the loss of happiness in market democracies, that despite the fact that many citizens of advanced market democracies are satisfied with their material conditions, they feel increasingly unhappy (Lane 2001). Jock Young signals discontent about relative deprivation. He challenges the myth of merit: meritocracy can never be achieved when a high proportion of reward is undeserved, because inherited (Young 1999). Richard Sennett has studied the corrosion of character, which he perceives as one of the personal consequences of the workplace in the new capitalism (Sennett 1998). To return to the medical sector, preceding questions about how privilege is sustained through cultural cloning, another question can be whether Western physicians deserve privilege, financial comfort, and the high status they presume and enjoy. Who gains from non-holistic perceptions of health and illness? Are people healthier and happier when medicine reduces them to body parts, to be fixed under time pressure, time only seen as a scarce resource? Does one need to prolong lives no matter what, because it seems technically possible? These and other fundamental issues, though not able to be dealt with here, are part of the larger context fuelling systemic injustices.

The above questions pertain to the nature of society and in particular the place of medicine. The medical field is shaped by paradigmatic underpinnings of Western science, including the commercialization of health and bodies, the medicalization and, increasingly, the biomedicalization of our lives (Clark et al. 2003). In a constantly changing world of health care and in a world where 'new products are the lifeblood of the marketplace' the drive to create and to maintain superior competitive advantage is perceived as imperative (Spevak 2002: 32). Competencies deemed relevant to develop superior medical skills are racially and culturally charged, including among other things intelligence, rationality, emotional detachment, high ambition, high competitive drive, and a workaholic mentality prioritizing work above family. This package of requirements is likely to be attributed more generously to those perceived closer to the value systems and cultural contexts from which the elevation of these competencies emerges: (post)modern societies, whiteness, European-ness, masculinity, middle class cultural habitat, Western science habitat. In light of this, a critique of particular modes of cultural cloning (for instance through everyday racism) must be read against the background of the *total* framework of historical and societal forces supporting the cultural cloning of normative profiles of physicians, and of other top positions for that matter. Conversely, it must be seen that the quest for (racial, ethnic, gender) workplace diversity would call for a disruption of the myth of maintaining (claimed or projected) sameness. This probably explains why diversity requirements are easily read as having to deal with 'something extra', because not the same and not like the familiar business as usual (Essed 2002).

While physicians (and other high status professionals) are expected to be highly competitive, to prioritize work above family, to objectify patients, to work against the clock, to repress emotion, and to have the ability to place oneself in the shoes of others, these very working codes and conditions are conducive to generating insensitivity, condescension, impatience to listen, irritation, and disregard to the feelings of others. The demands of the physician's work presume that the working environment, colleagues and nurses, cooperate. It is *expected* that they be tolerant of disruptive behaviour. In US surveys it has been found that disruptive behaviour by physicians is rampant, while fuelling the shortage of nurses. They leave the institution for fear of retaliation, because they believe nothing ever changes, for lack of administrative support, or because of physician's lack of awareness or unwillingness to change (Pfifferling 1999; Rosenstein et al. 2002). Disruptive behaviour includes a range of everyday humiliations: physical abuse, condescension, insults, disrespect, yelling, berating patients, and abusive anger—the kind of behaviour that fluently channels into modes of everyday racism, sexism, patronizing of economically or educationally disadvantaged people, and dismissive attitudes towards critique. The survey does not make any explicit racial or gender qualifications, but indirectly there are a few indicators. It turns out that when humiliating behaviour is categorized by specialty, general surgery ranks number one, followed by cardiology, cardiovascular surgery, and neurology, areas strongly shaped by Western principles of hard sciences, dominated by masculine values.

How does this relate to cultural cloning? Arguably, profiles are not static, but many physicians are reluctant to change their behaviour, even when confronted with critical data, says one research report. Instead, 'they rationalize why the data either doesn't apply to them or is just wrong' (Marco 2002: 30). Defensiveness also points to anxieties, a sense of unease among physicians about the rapidly changing technology and the new demands of the Information Revolution. There is anger about the (postmodern) ways of managed care which has changed the relationship with patients and financial arrangements (Bottles 2000). It has been found that one of the most pressing concerns of physicians today is time pressure and that an increasing number are unhappy with their jobs (Williams and Skinner 2003). Other sources agree that in many medical organizations the culture of pacesetting and commanding leadership styles has created a crisis of leadership (Goleman, Boyatzis, et al. 2002).

Medical organizations, like other (bureaucratic) organizations in market economies, operate in a competitive market. Management in view of competitive advantage implies, besides other things, the homogenizing of practices, rules, procedures, tasks, and profiles, and in that sense, cloning as replication in the name of efficiency. Once a particular mode, product, or model has been tested to work for the defined purposes, it can be patented in order to be multiplied and applied until replaced by an improved version—think of medication, medical instruments, healing techniques, and so on, or closer to home, the computers and software we all work with. In the age of globalization, medical institutes and their physicians operate in a field with mega-high stakes, in complex conglomerations of corporate interests. Western countries protect their hold on the medical industry, among other things, with enormous financial investments in (bio)technology and pharmaceuticals, and with patents preventing the large majority of the world, mostly people of colour, from accessing (producing) cheap products and medicine (Scheper-Hughes 2000). Various feminist scholars in the area of science, technology, and the environment have called the pursuit of ultimate control over creation in all its forms, the relentless exploitation of earth's resources, quintessential symptoms of the triumph of Western masculine values underlying the process of modernization (Shiva 1989; Kirk 1995). The same value systems and the practices it entails are also constitutive of a *culture* of cloning, increasingly a global phenomenon.

Cultural Cloning and the Culture of Cloning

Globalization means in neutral terms increased interconnectedness across the world. But politically, it has come to imply that the Western (masculine) power model of technology, limitless possibilities, and the promise of wealth for those who grab the opportunity gets to be cloned across the world. Let me give an example by way of introducing the notion of cloning in a cultural sense analytically. In his book *Diploma of Whiteness: Race and Social Policy in Brazil, 1917–1945*, author Jerry Dávila recounts an anecdote about the Minister of Education and Health who presided in the late 1930s (Dávila 2003). He had called upon a group of anthropologists and national intellectuals to advise him about the physiognomy of the body of the 'future Brazilian man': 'Not the vulgar type, but the best example of the race' (p. 21). His concern about the Brazilian race had been aroused by the artist whom he had commissioned to make the statue of the future Brazilian man. The statue, meant to be placed at the entrance of the ministry of Education and Health building, did not match the sensibility of this new and modern design. The artist had come up with a representation that 'looked racially degenerate rather than virile and Aryan' (p. 21) as the minister had imagined Brazilians would evolve. The minister's dismay was a function of his belief that the modernization of Brazilian society implied that Brazilians would come to look more like clones of the hegemonic model of perfection: white, blond haired, blue eyed. Yet, the future Brazilian man could not be read only in terms of race. This idealized body represented a racialized perception of progress—Europeanization and 'genetically' uplifting (whitening)—as much as it represented a gendered perception of modernization—the triumph of masculinity. At the same time this perfectly healthy body was to project progress in terms of physical and mental capacity—as ultimate control over the disabling imperfections of nature—and as eternally 'young'—progress as the defeat of the disabling signs of ageing. Indeed, the epitome of progress was a male body beaming with Aryan masculinity.

Because body images gain meaning in a cultural context, it seems fair to suggest that the desire for Brazilian clones of this perfectly white European male body meant also for Brazilian education and health to emulate, or if I may say so, to become a clone of, the culture this body represents. The notion of cloning the culture is useful in this context because it involves emulating the modernization package the Aryan male body is perceived to represent, including modes of economic and technological development, racial ideologies, bodily aesthetics, and other ideological values, norms, images, and practices.

The paradigm of progress, Western models of human development copied and globally spread as benchmarkers of 'civilization', signifies a larger phenomenon we have called *cloning cultures* (Essed and Goldberg 2002). 'By Cloning Culture(s) we mean the social processes by which the replication of sameness—its repetition, continuation, and extension—takes place. These social processes include the embedded norms and values as well as the social ordering and structures that enable the possibilities and actualities of such replication. Modes of replication are manifest in production, in consumption, and in representational practices and images, including aesthetics' (Essed and Goldberg 2003).

Cloning culture is manifest in the systemic order of modern society, one where human and material relations are arranged according to uniformly organized institutes (school, universities, hospitals) and sections (disciplines, administration, catering). Human categories are often organized as unequal functional pairs (employers–employees, teachers–students, parents–children) and unequal biosocial pairs along lines of gender, race, ethnicity, age, abilities (man–woman, black–white, etc). At the very basis of these concepts are processes of emulation (school buildings look alike) and categories of real or attributed sameness (nation, men, women, professors, surgeons, and nurses). Cloning culture is rooted in and continually shaped by the reductionism of modern science. The modernization of healing in

Europe, including its rejection and exploitations of Otherness, has been central to that process.

The Medical Profession as Epitome of Cloning Culture

Racial ideologies—Others as inherently inferior or as only histori-cally backward, but culturally improvable under the right circum-stances—have been constitutive principles of the modern state including modern science (Goldberg 1993, 2001). In the same vein gender ideologies—cognitive intelligence above emotional intelligence (Goleman 1995); subjugation of women, destiny, nature, by men, technology, culture (Shiva 1989)—have been constitutive of modern science, including medical science.

In the making of the modern medical profession the 'men' of Amsterdam's oldest medieval city gate called *De Waag*—which means weigh house—have played an important role. *De Waag* is a small castle with four or five towers built in the 1300s or 1400s. A few years ago, I had the opportunity to visit this centrally located castle, today a buzzing cultural centre for old and new media. On my tour through *De Waag* I got shown into a beautiful room, octagonal shaped with painted portraits against the wall—masculine, pale-faced lookalikes—almost identical to the ones you come across in distinguished halls of the various Dutch university buildings. The tour guide told the story of how in the sixteenth century *De Waag* had housed the surgeons' guild, an upcoming profession at the cut-ting edge of knowledge production. The development of this new, reductionist, knowledge assumed separability and manipulability of distinctive parts—knowledge of parts of a system to be taken as knowledge of the whole. Reductionism served as the cradle for 'experts' and 'specialists' to become the only legitimate knowledge seekers—male seekers. By the sixteenth century the witch-hunts of Europe had successfully resulted in the total exclusion of women from the practice of healing (Shiva 1989).

The guild had organized their interests quite effectively, a joint ven-ture between science, justice, and the church. Surgeons needed bodies to cut and to dissect in order to improve their knowledge about the anatomy of the body. Justice provided fresh corpses. It seemed to have worked like this: in order to encourage respect for the law the bodies of executed criminals were hung in full view from the towers of *De Waag*. Later, the bodies were taken inside to the upper floor to what was called the Theatrum Anatomicum—the octagonal room occupied by the guild of surgeons. The surgeons did not only experiment on the corpses of criminals, but also on others buried in unholy ground. The church authorities, represented exclusively by white men, turned a blind eye to the business of snatching bodies from the graveyards. The surgeons objectified bodies, but in their turn they got objectified by the artistic hand rescuing the scene for exposure to future generations. In the same octagonal room, Rembrandt made his sketches in 1628 for the famous (in today's capitalist market, value 'priceless') painting 'Anatomy Lesson of Professor Tulp'.[1]

I tried to imagine the early surgeons in their struggle to become a profession (rather than a medical sect), cutting at the bodies of criminals objectified and subjected to the insatiable knowledge hunger of what would become medical science, all of which in the name of 'progress of Western civilization' driven, among other things, by the zeal to control nature through knowledge and technology. But other, contemporary images came to mind . . . of the organ industry.

I imagined a hospital room where a fresh organ gets to be implanted in a body eager to embrace life longer than it could have on its own merit. I imagined contemporary organ donors quickly being relieved of a vital organ, bodies still warm, or even still alive. But organ donors have a race, age, gender, nationality, economic position, indicative of the injustices within and between societies where some have to sell body parts in order for them and their families to survive. Thousands of people in Eastern Europe, (illegal) immigrants in northwest Europe, children in Third World countries are being deprived of parts of their body, for little or nothing. They might get killed. The integrity of their body violated for the sheer purpose of snatching away that precious organ in order to prolong the life of an economically, nationally, racially, or gender-wise more privileged human being.

Nancy Scheper-Hughes studied the organ trade in South Africa, the country where a race, gender, and economically privileged individual received the first heart transplant. The surgeon made world headlines but, on the other side, the plight of organ donors was kept from world's view:

During the apartheid years, transplant surgeons were not obligated to solicit family consent before harvesting organs (and tissues) from cadaver donors. 'Up until 1984 the conditions for transplantation were easier,' said Dr. B, a heart transplant surgeon at Groote Schuur Hospital. 'We didn't worry too much in those days. We just took the hearts we needed. But it was never a racial issue. Christiaan Barnard was very firm about this. He was one of those people who just ignored the government. Even when our hospital wards were still segregated by law, there was no race apartheid in transplant surgery.' But what he meant was that there was no hesitation in transplanting black and colored (mixed-race) 'donors' hearts—taken without consent or knowledge of family members—into the ailing bodies of their mostly white male patients. [...]. Up through the early 1990s about 85% of all heart transplant recipients at Groote Schuur Hospital were white males. (Scheper-Hughes 2000: 25)

The scarcity of transplantable organs, 'created by the technicians of transplant surgery, represents an artificial need, one that can never be satisfied, for underlying it is the unprecedented possibility of extending life indefinitely with the organs of others' (Scheper-Hughes 2000: 14).

Western science has been successful in sowing and reaping physicians with the right disposition, the willingness to accept and internalize as 'necessary in the name of progress' even the most cruel and dehumanizing demands of cloning culture. Medical science has a long history of harbouring racist, sexist, socially elitist assumptions, for instance involving human, often painful, experimentation in which imperialist, Eurocentric, and patriarchal goals have been inflicted on Others—Jews, the poor, blacks women, people of colour, and so on, with no regard to ethics (Mwaria 2001). The power that comes with Western medical authority is precious, highly rewarded financially, and in terms of social status the preservation of which requires that membership to this group remains limited and highly guarded. With a few examples, I illustrate how mundane gender, racial, and other taken-for-granted cultural imaginaries and everyday practices define this high status position by privileging those perceived as representing whiteness and masculinity, and by seeking homogeneity. Homogenizing means that a limited number of cultural and physical attributes are selected to serve as primary markers defining who belongs and who does not, who can qualify as physician and who cannot (really). Thus, otherwise complex human beings are reduced to traits representing the normative image of their profession, thereby suggesting that no other than these normative traits fit best the requirements for the profession. Examples are selected from the Dutch context, but the issue at hand does not necessarily apply to the Netherlands only.

Homogenizing Through Cultural Cloning

It has been found that 'men are selected for managerial positions because they are perceived, especially by male selectors, to be more reliable, committed and predictable, free from conflicting loyalties between home and work' (Collison and Hearn 1996). Likewise, the ideal construct of the competent medical specialist is deeply imbued with masculine values. Maya Keizer, a Dutch expert in the area of gender and health care, pictures the medical specialist as follows:

He (sic) is totally available for his job but not necessarily as accessible to patients. He is very conscious of his authority over nurses, junior doctors and trainees. He is rational and detached, and takes pride in heroic individual successes. He sees patients as objects rather than as human beings. (Keizer 2000)

The cultural process of 'cloning the physician' is facilitated in at least the following two ways: (*a*) through the dominance of masculine, European norms and values in medical cultures; and (*b*) by relating interpretations of medical competence to these norms and values. There is also an embodied dimension to cultural cloning: the white male body speaks to perceivers' sense of whiteness, and (Dutch) masculinity. Therefore, (middle class) white men will be attributed more generously than others traits qualifying them as medically competent. Others (non-whites, non-males) may have to prove more vigorously that they master the qualifying criteria in spite of their different bodies.

The highest *cloning quality* can be found among surgeons—over 96 per cent of which are (white) men. The tenacity of cultural cloning in this profession becomes even clearer when considering that the percentage of white males decreased only 4 per cent over a period of four or five centuries! In the sixteenth century all surgeons were white men. Today, even the more 'feminine' directions are still male dominated: of paediatricians, generally perceived as the specialization with the lowest status among physicians, (only) 60 per cent are white men. Gynaecologists and family doctors rate over 70 per cent (Keizer 2000).

The medical specialist is a protected profession; salaries are kept high, in private practices three times as high as in university hospitals. Opportunity hoarding operates through the creation of permanent supply shortages: there are caps on the number of medical students allowed to register per year and there are high barriers against allowing into Dutch medical practice refugees who have been physicians in their home country (Couwenbergh 2001).

In what follows I briefly highlight three modes of sustaining sameness:

Over-representation of Masculine Mentors

Cultural cloning among medical specialists does not start at the hospital entrance. When physicians, as parents, socialize their sons (or sometimes their daughters) to follow in their footsteps, cultural cloning is prestructured in the home. Many male surgeons in the Netherlands are sons of surgeons. This is not the case for the few women surgeons, most if not all of whom had to create their own paths. Cloning is also shaped by the medical sciences. Ninety-eight per cent of the full professors in medical faculties are (white) men, thus maintaining a cultural climate conducive to reinforcing existing Western, masculine values and practices.

Everyday Racism as a Mode for (White) Students to Identify with Whiteness (or the Dominant Culture)

Cultural cloning operates through everyday (gendered) racism: recurring incidents of being ignored, put down, rejected, often events that seem trivial as such but in accumulation gradually undermine self-confidence, trigger constant alertness, while causing stress, depression, or high blood pressure. For the purpose of this volume, I pay closer attention to this instrument of cultural cloning. I have selected a few experiences of Rosa N., a black woman, about the period when she was a medical student. More of her story has been published elsewhere (Essed 1991).

She recalls a class situation where the professor, a surgeon, freely expresses contempt about immigrants, racist comments meant to elicit laughter. He speaks to whiteness (in this case white Dutchness), thus advantaging those who identify as such:

We were in a surgery class. It was taught by a plastic surgeon [. . .] who told us about an industrial accident in a food processing plant, where a Turk working on a cutting machine had sliced open his hand. He even started the story with: the stupid Turk [. . .] Stupid, his hand is not a can! He said: [. . .] 'I didn't really have much confidence, but still, I wanted to save the man's hand, because, you know what it costs the Dutch government if that man loses his hand! [. . .] He gets unemployment benefits. [. . .]' So, the surgeon had to save the man's hand.

He showed us another series of slides about how he'd operated on the hand. It looked really weird [. . .] Eventually the hand started to die anyway. It looked really terrible. [. . .] The surgeon left the hand alone until it was completely black, like a hand of coal. [. . .] The hand was amputated, after all.

And then he showed the next picture. Someone's heel gone, 'that's another stupid foreigner in a factory', he says. He talks about there being so many accidents [. . .], but only with foreigners. [. . .]. But he (doesn't add) that it's foreigners who do this kind of work and that they are the highest risk group for having an accident [. . .].

While the professor speaks to Dutch whiteness when he ridicules immigrants, students respond in recognition of white bonding. They laugh along. Nobody objects to the racist comments:

The students thought it was real funny. They don't really give it much thought, because it arouses a kind of hilarity when it's told that way [...] Then everyone laughs about it. But I find such humor out of place, actually.

Whiteness as mode for bonding is further strengthened when the consensus, tolerance of racism, puts critics of racism on the spot. Moreover, those who refuse to tolerate racism are often pathologized for being oversensitive. Rosa N. is the only one in class who raises objections in public (a few white students support her later, but in private).

I waited until the man was finished. The lights went on, I told him he shouldn't make remarks like that again because they are offensive, and I chose that attitude because I thought: I must not become uncontrolled, agitated or aggressive.
Now at my work (her internship), they find me oversensitive [...], probably because I just can't let certain things pass. And I can absolutely not do that. I do not want to and I will not. So I always respond (against racism), because I just can't keep quiet.

Everyday racist discourse as a matter of joking is one mechanism to reconfirm the norm of whiteness or white Dutchness—in this case white middle class Dutchness—because calling the immigrants stupid also reinforces their lower status as factory workers. By the same token the professor could have resorted to sexist innuendos. Male managers—another masculine world—frequently use racist and sexist jokes to break the ice when they present and as a way of emphasizing their professionalism, competence, rational self-images, total confidence, detachment, and control (Cockburn 1991). Similar styles occur in classrooms heavily imbued with masculine whiteness, such as large MBA classes, where teachers who intimidate and cajole students often receive highly positive feedback. Is it relevant to mention that the resulting atmosphere of 'we' and 'us-hood'—emphasizing shared sameness—makes it often difficult for individual white or male students to disconnect from (a mixture of) racialized and gendered pressures to embrace attributed sameness for fear of repercussions? Indeed, the few students who agreed with Rosa N. expressed their support only off the record.

The story of Rosa N. a woman of Surinamese background, was published in 1991. Ten years later, in 2001, a journalistic inquiry among medical students of Iranian background—a refugee group with a substantial percentage of highly educated members including physicians in retraining—indicates that tactics of humiliation, including shouting and the use of abusive words, still serve to put ethnic students in their place (Slutzky 2001). One medical (male) student of Iranian background comments that some professors are intolerant of the fact that he speaks Dutch with an accent. Rather than asking him to repeat his question, he has had professors shout back: 'I do not understand a damn word of what you are saying.' The student comments that after a couple of put-downs you just stop asking any more questions. Another Iranian medical student, a woman, comments that some professors address non-Dutch with a hostile tone in their voice. There is also a comment about one of the professors who examines students' lab results. On his round past the test tables he visits the table of the Iranian woman, the only woman of colour, invariably last. The fact that she has to wait longer than anybody else symbolizes the perceived distance between the image her body is seen to represent and the normative image of the physician (in training).

Preference for Masculine and White (Dutch) Cultural Values in Rewarding Performance

Medical culture is not very hospitable to expressions of emotion, and least when it concerns the physicians themselves. Those who distance themselves from their own emotional lives, often white men, learn to be suspicious of their spontaneity (Seidler 1997). As a result there will be rejection if not pathologizing of compassion, instead of recognizing empathy as a humane expression of medical competence. Rosa N. gives an example when she talks about interactions with colleagues in the hospital:

Recently there was a patient who had responded unexpectedly well to treatment, after we had almost given up on her. [. . .] I wanted to show that to one of the superiors. So I said: 'come along, you gotta see this!'. That's my enthusiasm [. . .] When I noticed his whispering with the others I felt he's talking about me because [. . .] they feel I am too emotionally involved, they don't like that. You have to be detached [. . .] when making a report. That is the general trend in Holland. You may not display any emotion.

Cultural cloning, choosing automatically for sameness, for the familiar paths in the name of competence, effectiveness, and efficiency while preserving privilege, works even better when there is little time to reflect, when pressures to perform are high, and where there is a premium to quantitative output (number of patients, of operations, and so on).

Internalizing or Challenging Cultural Cloning?

Today Rosa N. would not have had more women professors, but she would have had more female company among the students—30 per cent of all students of surgery are women, 70 per cent are men. All students, men and women, majorities and ethnic minorities, are expected to internalize and accept values based in masculine and Western experiences if they want to be respected and rewarded as (future) physicians. In a recent study on women in health professions, two Dutch researchers, women, both surgeons, found that the few percentages of women among surgeons just want to be surgeons, not women or men. This radical reductionism—a one-dimensional sense of identity—fits the picture of fragmented rather than holistic approaches to patients as well. Interviewed about their study the authors firmly subscribe to masculine values, commenting that surgery is too demanding a profession to combine with family life or childcare. The surgeon has to be available 24 × 7, which is even difficult for men-husband-father surgeons—let alone women-wife-mother surgeons. They agree that a good surgeon feels emotionally detached from his work. They reject the (feminine) value of empathy with patients as human beings (Keulemans 2002).

In Eastern European countries women dominate numerically, but their advantage in numbers is offset by lower status and payment compared to the relatively small numbers of male physicians. In that respect privilege continues to be cloned along masculine lines. There are substantially more women physicians in various Western European countries and North America, but masculine values continue to dominate the cultures of medicine (Riska 2001). In all fairness, it should be mentioned that the inclusion of more women has not remained unnoticed altogether. It has been found that Dutch women physicians give less medication, thereby also providing more effective treatment. They are less inclined to engage in heroic surgery (Keizer 2000), or in unnecessary surgery. They devote more time to the social dimensions of health problems. With many women doctors opting for part-time jobs, often shared with a colleague, this might have a positive impact in particular on younger (women) doctors who want to balance family and work. These and other indications of the impact of female gender optimistically suggest that more diversity might chip away at systems of cultural cloning along (white) male gender lines.

In the meantime most doctors continue their practice as usual while some, often women, take over neglected, mostly psychological dimensions. Men more often than women lack emotional intelligence and social competence, or do not consider emotional care to be relevant. It has been found that women family doctors assume a larger share of psychosocial work. Gender-socialized as caregivers they are more open to holistic medication, illnesses placed in a larger context of family and other social relations (Keizer 2000). Patients, in particular highly educated women, feel more comfortable with women. Many women have been able to develop better communication skills than men. At the same time cultural cloning continues to work against alternative practices. The number of women medical specialists and family doctors is increasing, but medical cultures have remained largely masculine. Going against the wheels of cultural cloning comes with a price. Clearly not all physicians (want to) fit the characteristic of 'detached' and 'objectifying' as readily as the normative profile requires them to. But the time slots available to 'see' patients are not conducive to holistic and emphatic approaches to health care. A vastly spreading problem among family doctors is burnout—this is an area of medicine practice from which men are now retreating (down to 77 per cent) and women are entering.

Conclusions

I started out this chapter by stating that the exclusive focus on race, racial, and racism creates tensions with the view that one-dimensional approaches cannot sufficiently account for the complexity of racial injustices. Moreover, I have tried to transcend the paradigm of racialization in order to understand the very problem as constitutive of modernity and as an instrument of cultural cloning. I wanted to take notice of the fact that elements of domination are interconnected, reciprocate, and mutually constitutive, interwoven into more general principles of modernization. I have made a distinction between *cultural cloning*—preference for more of the same in order to secure spaces of privilege—and *cloning culture*: the culture reigned by the pursuit of control of all forms of creation (biological, nature, bodies, life itself) in view of making prototypes to be commodified for the purpose of profit. I suggested that durable inequality is deeply embedded in the nature of cloning culture: values underlying modern science (reductionism), the organization of our societies (dissecting, separating, and categorizing), the commodification of time, the marketing and corporatization of health (standardization and the cost–benefit approach), and the dehumanizing practices that go along with that (erosion of human care).

As a social scientist trained to identify and think in terms of (generalized) social categories, I have struggled throughout the text to avoid falling victim to the homogenizing think-trap myself. I may not have been as successful as I would have liked, but I did not want to fall either into the opposite trap where my own critique of mythical homogenizations would prevent me from identifying values and practices as indicators of masculinity, choices as preference for whiteness, and positions as reserved only or primarily for certain bodies and not others. The point of this chapter was not to equalize men with masculinity and white with Western. With the concept of cultural cloning and the context of cloning culture I have problematized the relation between dominant value systems and the skewed embodiments of high power positions. This critique is not new, but what is distinctive about the suggestions I have made in this chapter is to insist that racism cannot be countered without questioning and reassessing the larger package of norms, values, and practices cloning cultures stand for, while transforming (some of) their fundamental characteristics.

In questioning some of the underlying values of our culture I seek to encourage reflective elaboration on the meaning and implications of cultural cloning. What is it that we are reproducing with the cultural cloning of high status positions along lines of perceived homogeneities? I have tentatively and analytically applied the framework of cloning cultures to the cultural cloning of the profile of 'the physician'. The analysis highlighted how cloning operates through everyday racism, the privileging of masculine whiteness (Dutchness), but also as expressed in other problems emerging from and within cloning culture. Preference for sameness means investing in the continuation of the best and the worst characteristics of current high status positions including the best and the worst of the supportive social environments in which these positions are embedded. There is no question that modern medical science has been beneficial to large groups of people. But there is also another side. If dominant modes of exercising medical power and authority include tolerance for patronizing humour, derogatory remarks, fierce competition rather than cooperation, the erosion of a caring disposition, the commodification of lives and bodies, and hence the dehumanization of human kind, could it be that the dominance of whiteness and of masculine values hampers humane and wise decision-making over societal problems and the future of human kind?

Last but not least, our universities are part and parcel of shaping and cloning the physician prototype. Increasingly, education has to meet the demands of the commodification of time in the pursuit of ever higher levels of productivity. The corporate model is about managing standardized packages. We can question who this model serves. The assessment, accountability, corporate-derived, and increasingly market-driven culture of higher education has privileged quantity (number of students, of publications, of grants received) and pushed reflectivity and quality (time for students, time for authentic research) away from the centre to the margins of higher education. The current emphasis on knowledge production—the more publications the better, even when many have less and less time to read—needs to give way to other aspects, particularly the pursuit of wisdom (in using knowledge and information). The old quest for wisdom is more relevant than ever, given the (mass) destructive capacity of (technological) knowledge and the lack of progress in finding solutions to durable injustices, despite the mountains of publications that have been produced.

Acknowledgement

I am very grateful to Eegje Schoo for sharing with me many original and profound views on the nature of Dutch culture and society. In the course of my thinking and writing about 'cloning culture' she mentioned the idea of 'cultural cloning' in one of our conversations. In this chapter, I have taken the opportunity to theorize and give more flesh to the idea, while conceptualizing its relation to the larger context of cloning culture.

NOTES

1. Dutch originated mega-holding specializing in food and food-related services and operating in many countries across the world. In the year 2003, Ahold has been negatively in the news for investigations about budget fraud and excessive CEO salary. As a consequence president-commissioner de Ruiter had to resign.
2. www.vermilion-sands.com/amsterdam/gotiek/waag.html—consultated 26 November 2002.

REFERENCES

Boogaarts, R. (2003) 'Karel Vuursteen moet Ahold in de gaten houden'. *FEM Business*, 39 (27 September): 8.

Bottles, K. (2000) 'Why are Physicians so Angry?' *Physician Executive*, 26(5): 44–48.

Clark, A. E. and Mamo, L. et al. (2003) 'Biomedicalization: Technoscientific Transformations of Health, Illness, and U.S. Biomedicine'. *American Sociological Review*, 68 (April): 161–94.

Cockburn, C. (1991) *In the Way of Women: Men's Resistance to Sex Equality in Organizations*. London: Macmillan.

——(1998) *The Space Between Us: Negotiating Gender and National Identities in Conflict*. London and New York: Zed Books.

Collins, P. H. (1998) *Fighting Words: Black Women and the Search for Justice*. Minneapolis: University of Minnesota Press.

Collison, D. L. and Hearn, J. (1996) 'Breaking the Silence: On Men, Masculinities and Managements', in D. L. Collison and J. Hearn (eds.), *Men as Managers, Managers as Men: Critical Perspectives on Men, Masculinities and Managements*. London: Sage.

Couwenbergh, M. (2001) 'Buitenlandse arts behandeld als vreemd wezen (Foreign physician treated as an alien)'. *Contrast*, 18 January.

Crenshaw, K. (1991) 'Mapping the Margins: Intersectionality, Identity Politics, and Violence Against Women of Color'. *Stanford Law Review*, 43 (6): 1241–99.

Dávila, J. (2003) *Diploma of Whiteness: Race and Social Policy in Brazil, 1917–1945*. Durham, NC: Duke University Press.

Dinther, M. V. (2003) 'De val van een jaknikker'. *FEM Business*, 38 (20 September): 30–3.

Essed, P. (1991) *Understanding Everyday Racism: An Interdisciplinary Theory*. London: Sage.

——(2001) 'Multi-Identifications and Transformations: Reaching Beyond Racial and Ethnic Reductionisms'. *Social Identities*, 7 (4): 493–509.

——(2002) 'Cloning Cultural Homogeneity while Talking Diversity: Old Wine in New Bottles in Dutch Work Organizations?' *Transforming Anthropology*, 11(1): 2–12.

——and Goldberg, D. T. (2002) 'Cloning Cultures: The Social Injustices of Sameness'. *Ethnic and Racial Studies*, 25 (6): 1066–82.

—— (2003) 'Cloning Cultures'. Paper Presented at WISER, Witwatersrand University, Johannesburg, South Africa, July 29.

Gilman, S. L. (1999) *Making the Body Beautiful: A Cultural History of Aesthetic Surgery*. Princeton: Princeton University Press.

Goldberg, D. T. (1993) *Racist Culture: Philosophy and the Politics of Meaning*. Oxford: Blackwell.

——(2001) *The Racial State*. Malden, MA and Oxford: Blackwell.

——and Solomos, J. (eds.) (2002) *A Companion to Racial and Ethnic Studies*. Oxford: Blackwell.

Goleman, D. (1995) *Emotional Intelligence*. New York: Bantam Books.

——Boyatzis, R. et al. (2002) *Primal Leadership: Realizing the Power of Emotional Intelligence*. Boston: Harvard Business School Press.

Keizer, M. (2000) *Acht stellingen over gender en professionaliteit (Eight theses about gender and professionality)* Gender en professionals in de gezondheidszorg (healthcare) Den Haag: Raad voor de Volksgezondheid & Zorg (RVZ).

Keulemans, M. (2002) 'Bent ú dokter Mulder!' (Are you doctor Mulder?) Interview with Ella de Jong and Mimi Mulder. *Folia*, 55: 8–9.

Kirk, G. (1995) 'Women Resist Ecological Destruction', in G. Ashworth (ed.), *A Diplomacy of the Oppressed: New Directions in International Feminism*. London: Zed Books, pp. 69–89.

Lane, R. (2001) *The Loss of Happiness in Market Democracies*. New Haven and London: Yale University Press.

Marco, A. P. (2002) 'Why Doctors are Afraid of Numbers'. *Physician Executive* (May–June), 28 (3): 30–3.

Markus, M. (2002) 'Cultural Pluralism and the Subversion of the "Taken for Granted" World', in P. Essed and D. T. Goldberg (eds.), *Race Critical Theories: Text and Context*. Oxford and Cambridge, MA: Blackwell, pp. 393–408.

Mwaria, C. (2001) 'Biomedical Ethics, Gender and Ethnicity: Implications for Black Feminist Anthropology', in I. McClaurin (ed.), *Black Feminist Anthropology Theory, Politics, Praxis, and Poetics*. New Brunswick, NJ and London: Rutgers University Press, pp. 187–210.

Oommen, T. K. (1997) *Citizenship, Nationality and Ethnicity*. London: Polity Press

Pfifferling, J-H. (1999) 'The Disruptive Physician'. *Physician Executive*, 25 (2): 56–61.

Riska, E. (2001) *Medical Careers and Feminist Agendas: American, Scandinavian and Russian Women Physicians*. Hawthorne, NY: Aldine de Gruyter.

Root, M. (ed.) (1996) *The Multiracial Experience: Racial Borders as the New Frontiers*. Thousand Oaks, CA and London: Sage.

Rosenstein, A. H., Russell, H., et al. (2002) 'Disruptive Physician Behavior Contributes to Nursing Shortage'. *Physician Executive* (November–December), 28 (6): 8–11.

Scheper-Hughes, N. (2000) 'The Global Traffic in Human Organs'. *Current Anthropology*, 41 (2): 191–224. www.journals.uchicago.edu/CA/journal/issues/v41n2/002001/002001.html.

Seidler, V. J. (1997) *Man Enough: Embodying Masculinities*. London and New Delhi: Sage.

Sennett, R. (1998) *The Corrosion of Character*. New York and London: W.W. Norton.

Shiva, V. (1989) *Staying Alive: Women, Ecology and Development*. London: Zed Books.

Slutzky, M. (2001) 'Sommige docenten hebben de pest aan buitenlanders' (Some teachers hate foreigners). *Contrast*, (18 januari): 5.

Spevak, C. (2002) 'The Competitive Advantage: Strategic Thinking for Physician Leaders'. *Physician Executive* (January–February 2003), 29 (1): 20–34.

Tilly, C. (1998) *Durable Inequality*. Berkeley: University of California Press.

Werbner, P. and Modood, T. (eds.) (1997) *Debating Cultural Hybridity: Multi-cultural Identities and the Politics of Anti-Racism*. London: Zed Books.

Williams, E. S. and Skinner, A. C. (2003) 'Outcomes of Physician Job Satisfaction: A Narrative Review, Implications and Directions for Future Research'. *Health Care Management Review*, 28 (2): 119–40.

Young, I. M. (1990) *Justice and the Politics of Difference*. Princeton: Princeton University Press.

——(1999) *The Exclusive Society: Social Exclusion, Crime and Difference in Late Modernity*. London: Sage.

Yuval-Davis, N. (1997) *Gender and Nation*. London: Sage.

CHAPTER 12

Racialization and the Public Spaces of the Multicultural City

Michael Keith

The language through which contemporary cultural diversity in the multicultural city is described has become increasingly problematic. In part this problem of description is nothing particularly new. The validity of the paradigm of 'race relations' sociology (Miles 1982, 1987; Rex and Mason 1986; Banton 1987), the status of the analytical concept of 'race' (with or without inverted commas), and the orientalizing roots and routes of academic regimes of scrutiny through which ethnicity becomes visible, have all taken vocabulary as ethically contentious and analytically moot. More recently, Paul Gilroy (2000) has called powerfully to move beyond race-thinking towards the abolition of what he describes as 'raciology'.

This chapter attempts to consider how these challenges might make us think differently about how we come to think and discuss the multicultural cities of the twenty-first century. The chapter is rooted in a number of research projects in contemporary London at the Centre for Urban and Community Research at Goldsmiths College.[1] It speaks directly at the level of the political contestation of the multicultural city but in a manner that is rooted in the banal empiricism of social research that makes the insertion of the times and spaces of the urban into the abstractions of cultural or political theory an imperative. The register of voice is attempting to argue the salience of the traces of historicity and spatiality in making sense of the multicultural city but also to problems that I believe are universal to cities of the twenty-first century across the globe. In order to do so, the chapter suggests that the notion of mutability of racial subjects that is at the heart of most concepts of racialization must be set within its context. The concepts of historicity and spatiality are consequently essential to a contextualization of the theoretical language of racialization. This is nowhere more clearly demonstrated than in the contemporary metropolis.

Conventionally, the focus on processes of racialization appeals to a set of analytical perspectives that emphasize the contingent construction and deployment of ideologies of racial difference in politics, in the labour process, and in patterns of collective consumption (Miles 1989; Malik 1996; Solomos and Back 1996; Back and Solomos 2000). It is certainly the case that languages of race tend to imply a more coercive sense of the processes through which collective subjects are generated. In contrast, in both its anthropological histories and its more contemporary deployment in identity politics, cognate notions of ethnicity have tended to stress processes of sentiment, affiliation, and identification that circumscribe processes of cultural reproduction.

However, a couplet that echoes a binary comparison of the voluntarism of ethnicities (new and old) with the determinism of collective subject-making in race rhetorics may be equally problematic. The modern self as much as the ethnic group is generated through framings of power and subjectivity that describe limits of individual autonomy and freedom (Rose 1999). The body of the individual as much as the collective bears traces of history constructing identity and refracting identification through regimes of performativity and scopic regimes of visibility (Butler 1999; Moore et al. 2003). Such thinking qualifies the degree to which racial or ethnic identities can be measured within a straightforwardly deterministic calculus.

Yet the recognition across a range of scholarship that a descriptive framing may be suitable in one place and time and not at another does tend to shift emphasis on to the contexts in which languages of cultural difference become significant. In particular, the privileging of contact between different cultures and values in debates around notions of hybridity and creolization has tended to raise the stakes when considering the sorts of cultures that are being 'mixed' and the sorts of novelty that emerges in the worlds of twenty-first century capitalism. The city plays an increasingly significant role in conceptualizing these dynamics. In this sense the multiculturalism of the cities of the twenty-first century is both demographically inevitable and politically challenging. Demographies of difference are concentrated in city space as the societies of the 'north' fail to reproduce their populations and economic change drives the motor of migration. Normative models for the organization of the self, the family, the community, and the neighbourhood stretch beyond the boundaries of the nation-state through diasporic world links and transnational forms of identification. And as the transformation of societies across the globe progresses apace, the world witnesses both an accelerated pattern of urbanization and a concentration of patterns of cultural difference in the increasingly dominant form of the cosmopolitan metropolis.

Mainstream political theory has cast these debates of citizenship, belonging, and identity largely within the theoretical terrain of the construction of the public realm. In such a context migrant minorities are variously incorporated, licensed, excluded, or assimilated within the conventional polis (Kymlicka 1995; Parekh 2000). However, the problem of thinking through the interplay of contemporary urbanism and processes of racialization is that the conventionally narrated notion of the 'receiving society' defining 'racial groups' through forces of racialization in the crucible of the metropolis is subverted by the simultaneous transformations of both racial identities in flux and the globalizing metropolis itself.

Political theory has debated at length the possibilities for the public sphere to become a site for deliberative democracy to negotiate the political settlement of the city (Arendt 1958; Habermas 1991; Benhabib 1992, 1996; Calhoun 1992). As Richard Sennett has described, it has been less adept at a coming to terms with a notion of the public realm that stresses the visual order of the metropolis and the plural urban worlds stressed in Simmelian theorization of city life (Sennett 2000). The very complexity of the spaces of the city challenge the degree to which the metropolis can be rationalized or subjected to a singular moral order or governmental rule (Boyer 1983). In this context, the existence of processes of 'race-making' or racialization within the city pose some important challenges both to the value of the term itself and to its deployment in the cosmopolitan stews of hope and despair that make up most of the twenty-first century metropolises.

Social Policy, Racialization, and the Multicultural City

It is in this sense that this chapter attempts to address the problems of living together in conditions of multicultural urbanism. If the multiculturalism of the cities of the twenty-first century is both demographically inevitable and politically challenging then we must address simultaneously problems that are both ethical and analytical.

Ethically, we need to consider what it means to live in cities that are constituted by communities that may be the products of both different histories and histories of differences that bear the imprint of colonialism, slavery, and domination. *Analytically*, we need to recognize also that such communities may be constituted through globalized networks of sentiment and allegiance. Just as the economic drivers of contemporary capitalist globalization challenge the sovereignty of the nation-state, the flows of labour as well as capital create transnational networks of culture and people.

Across the world the city provides a privileged arena in which such challenges are realized. So this contribution to this volume on racialization is also written from a position which believes that an engagement with the structures of government is inevitable. There is a tendency in some literatures (from both the left and the right of the political spectrum) to romanticize the world beyond the boundaries of the state and to promote the virtues of civil society and community mobilization. Keith (1995*a*, *b*, 2004) has suggested that it is important to understand that such civil society forms are framed within regimes of governmental power and that such romance might limit rather than progress our movement towards cosmopolis.[2] Alternatively, the disciplinary rise of cultural studies in the academy has tended to focus attention on the cultural dynamics of the production of the multicultural, at times distracting attention from the institutional forms of governance within which multiculture is set.

In the allure of the contemporary global city cosmopolitanism, diversity, and difference shimmer for a moment. Racism, nationalism, ethnic cleansing, and xenophobia return as urban nightmares. Indeed, the challenge of discussions that link urbanism to race, multiculture, and forms and norms of intolerance is that both the subject (the city) and the object (multiculture) of debate keep on disappearing before our eyes only to resurface in different forms.

The city appears so solid until we look for its boundaries. The streets appear to offer certainty until we find the beach beneath the cobblestones, the secret narratives of the hidden spaces of private lives, and alternative public spheres of association and dissent. When history is the voice of the powerful, geography is the prerogative of both the explorer and the mapmaker. We do not always wish to take such voices and such cartographies for granted. The chronology of a Sydney or a London appears to offer the reassurance of a historical ordering of things. This happened and then that. Until you realize that as Peter Ackroyd (2001) has described with the capital of the United Kingdom and Peter Carey (2001) with Sydney, the city has a biography that suffers always from the unreliable and imperfect flaws of the narrator. In contrast, the historiography of the city tells us how chronology has been used to make sense of the city and that *histories* are normally written by the winners, the voices of the dispossessed relegated to the marginalia.

Similarly, though rarely acknowledged, the demography of most of the major metropolises of the twenty-first century is in large part a product of migration. These migrations can come from the same country (as with the migrant growth of the first industrial metropolises) or they may bring folk from across the globe to a New York or Hong Kong. The categoric certainties of this demography may appear to offer an alternative register of a kind. The transnational movements are locked into patterns of urban residence and city labour markets, creating the classic patterning of jobs, homes, and power marked by the mosaic of multiculturalism. The city variously accommodates, assimilates, or stigmatizes these racialized patterns through its form. The multicultural city mosaic (of Shanghai or Karachi or Bombay as much as London or Chicago or Sydney) is classically subjected to the institutional logics of the melting pot and the reproduction of segregation and the ghetto. But both the exigencies of exogamy and the more prosaic realities of cultural flows that subvert ethnic boundary markers disrupt such narratives. The hybrid forms of multiculture and the increasingly hyphenated forms of demographic mixing challenge a rubric that makes the city visible as a competing arena of ethnic cultures precisely because these cultures do not stand still to be photographed, analysed, and measured.

So we search for a vocabulary that captures the changing cartography of the multicultural city. We are aware that the very act of description potentially ossifies and so such a vocabulary needs to be careful about its categoric forms. And we are aware that we write in the shadow of all the other people that have written about cities and have written about multiculturalism and the processes of race-making that even created its own subdiscipline of studies of *race relations*. So much in the shadows that the deep meanings that attach themselves to the shape of the city and the lexicon of urbanism form part of our cultural present. An urban sensibility structures the very act of writing about the city.

In this sense in social policy terms we need to understand how multiculture is made problematic in urban policy and the occasions and the reasons when it is not. This is not a revised form of the race relations situations of an earlier Weberian formation. It is instead to focus attention on *the manufacture* of both the problems of social

policy and the speaking positions of those who become its subjects
and seek to address them. Both are historically and geographically
contingent. In this sense a juxtaposition of multiculturalism and integration as logical opposites is analytically flawed because the latter
depends on an articulation of the former.[3]

At some places and times 'the problem' within policy discourse ties
ethnicity to demography (as in debates that describe escalating numbers of asylum-seekers or putative flows of migrant labour in the
newly expanded European Union). At other times and places the
problem within policy may invoke cultures that cover geographically
discrete demographics (as in the normative challenges of Islamic faith
or the loaded calculation of black single parenthood). At other times
again as Solomos' work has repeatedly described policy discourse
around issues as diverse as employment practice or policing may
generate racial difference through regimes of racialization (Solomos
1988, 1993).

Even in the official statistics that probably underenumerated
migrant flows, London accommodated an increase in its population
by almost a million between 1991 and 2001. This passed almost
without comment in the decade in which it happened but has
become a major topic of concern in the early twenty-first century.
How much was this due to the high proportions of Canadian,
Americans, Australians, and South Africans (re)settling in the city
and who bore the markers of a certain kind of whiteness? But how
much also was this caused by the sense in which many of the migrations of Lithuanians, Muscovites, and refugees from international
traumas in the Baltic and the horn of Africa were rendered invisible
by the spaces of the city?

What is undisputable is that we are confronted by a situation in
which the certainties of academic disciplines that take (often implicitly) the nation-state as the principal building bloc of 'sociologies' or
histories or politics or cultural anthropologies are challenged by the
messiness of the contemporary city. The social organization of city
resources may sit *babushka doll* like within neat hierarchies of central, regional, and local state power but flows of culture, capital, and
population subvert such taxonomies. And what is argued here is that
the very vocabularies that are used to capture these new realities confront some very old problems within the loose array of writing and
thought that we might call *urbanism*.

Specifically, we need a new heuristic compass with which to navigate the contemporary city. Historically, we might place cities
research on a spectrum that crosses the west–east of conventional

and critical literatures. Conventional urban studies approaches tend to reify the social and economic order of the city (and strive to maximize its functionality and optimize its working form). Critical analysis in contrast seeks to undermine this naturalized ordering of buildings and people (and expose their patterned artifice as inscriptions of injustice and reified inequalities of power and capital).

The phenomenon of patterns of residential settlement and cognate debates around gentrification exemplify this contrast between the conventional and the critical. Critical struggles to reduce the processes of gentrification to the Ricardian rent curve vie with a boosterist urbanism that narrates the city as a site of consumption and measures successful growth precisely in terms of enhanced capital valorization of residential preferences in the new districts of Jerusalem, Los Angeles, or Paris. But such a spectrum is necessarily two-dimensional in nature. It cannot adapt to the transnational challenge of globalization and the ethical challenge of multiculture.

To do so demands insertion into both urban studies academic debates and public concern, with the future of the multiculture of globalizing cities a second spectrum. It is fundamentally a product of moral philosophy and it challenges both economistic and cultural readings of the urban. It runs north–south between communitarian and liberal traces of moral philosophy but it is realized in the cities of multiculture in ferocious debates that our west–east spectrum cannot locate.[4]

The spectrum creates a tension between the strange and the familiar and relates particularly to how we come to know the city and how we valorize either its *knowability* or its *anonymity*. The city has long been a site in which newness comes into the world. It has historically been the crucible of economic, political, and cultural change precisely because old values and old orderings are disrupted by the tumult of city life. This produces the quintessentially urban horrors of populist fanaticism as well as the metropolitan potential for enlightenment critique. The city is consequently paradoxically or ambivalently located between these tensions, the sites of the city that display the most intense forms of intolerance are commonly also those that demonstrate the potential for the most intimate forms of cultural dialogue. To be analytically plausible or ethically useful an understanding that privileges the notion of racialization consequently must be able to account for such agonism and paradox.

We need to recognize that the polar north and related points east, west, and south provide a compass *for* but not a road map *towards* the good city. They identify a constitutive tension in the ordering of city life that sits agonistically within its frame. The additional (north–south) dimension speaks to some of the fundamental tensions in moral philosophy but it also resonates within cartographies of contemporary multiculturalism. Significantly, the choreography of the debates within contemporary moral philosophy and those in multiculture are homologous with long-standing arguments around how we consider the ethical markings of the spaces of the city. Unless we understand how the city draws together, displaces, and explodes these tensions we will continue to misrepresent the challenges multiculturalism poses to an understanding of contemporary urbanism. Most significantly of all, such tensions speak directly both to the social policy questions that figure how we might *organize* the multicultural city and also to the academic questions that address how we might *know* it.

At one extreme the city has commonly welcomed the *strange* and the *unknowable*. The migrant, the refugee, the indigenous culture, and the newly arrived potentially see the city differently. Seeing the niche market or the scope to innovate as well as challenging the received wisdom and ascendant hierarchies of power, the arrival of new people and migrant groups in the city potentially renews its lifeblood. The discursively ephemeral may suddenly become symbolically central. The hidden histories of colonialism and empire, slavery and suppression of native peoples may resurface from their cells in the subconscious of the city. But they do not do so straightforwardly.

In contrast, the communitarian sense of the *familiar* unit of the ethically *knowable* and the moral legitimacy of the neighbourhood speaks directly to debates that confuse the west–east typologies of what might conventionally be described as reactionary (coded as politically *right*) and progressive (coded as politically *left*) urbanisms. The sets of values that privilege the speaking positions of minoritarian voices may rapidly have to defend the ground on which their claims are being made. The right to police arrivals in such a (real or metaphoric) neighbourhood challenges such speaking authority. This speaks directly to urban policy concerns in terms of property rights, gender relations, schooling, visible sexualities, the control of subsidized rental residence (through state or social landlord provision), and the rights of cultural recognition in the marketplace of employment law and practice. The liberal indifference to the markers of identity likewise speaks directly to the rights to avoid discrimination, racial harassment, the symbolic and real violence of cultural intolerance. Crudely, our compass is complicated by this new spectrum. We can see both a right-wing and a left-wing communitarianism in the multicultural cities of the twenty-first century. The right of neighbourhoods to be turned into Business Improvement Districts and police themselves and the right of local communities to take self-governing actions against the homeless, the anti-social, and the badly behaved appeal to the traditional constituencies of the right. The sense of community grassroots organization against property capital, protests against road extensions, building on green land, and school closures speaks to the traditional agendas of the left. *Both* are communitarian in *both* their moral stance and their invoked urbanisms. They share ethical roots but differ significantly in their city visions and political routes.

But equally the right to be freed from state restrictions against wearing particular clothes or to exercise personal religious preference and the right to limit the state's power to arbitrary violence and to police the spaces of the city tends to be celebrated likewise on the left. Yet alternative strictures that limit state interference in the markets that structure the spatialized city realizations of Ricardian rent curves, the imperatives of global capitalism, or government interference in market relations speak to a liberalism that few on the left would identify as their own. Straightforwardly, this cautions us to be more careful with our vocabulary. There is a liberalism of the left and of the right. Neoconservatism is not necessarily best identified as neoliberal and cannot be subsumed in catch-all notions such as the revanchist city when we are identifying the enemies of progressive urbanism.

The extra dimension of this moral compass becomes more not less complicated by the realities of city multiculturalism across the twenty-first century globe. Recognitions of the rights of indigenous and native peoples and migrant minorities sit squarely within the fourfold tensions of critical urbanism, functional city building, communitarian valorization and stigma, and the problem of liberalism. It does not always sit easily. The case in favour of migration for the benefits of the economy of the city play against reactionary debates on the threats of migration to constructions of solidarity. They speak also to more complex debates about which cultural rights of migrant minorities should be recognized and which suppressed by the governance structures of the well-run city.

These are traced through the way economic and social change are realized and managed in the city. But equally significantly, the extra dimension of the north–south of our compass is complicated yet further by the dimensionalities of urban space and city temporalities.

Can the rights of recognition of Islamic schools in twenty-first century London, Paris, or Brisbane be spoken about in the same register that gave church schools state recognition of Jesuit education in
England or in the deep-rooted enlightenment anti-clerical voice of
nineteenth century France? Are the sites that are cherished as migratory zones of transition—metaphorical Ellis Islands of multiculture—to be naturalized for these processes of change or analysed for
their contingency. The East End of London is sometimes spoken of
in these terms. In the vernacular for some it has always (always is
such a plastic adverb) been the site where migrant minorities arrive
in London and then move on again. There is a sense of it as a space
of *the changing same*. Reassuring narratives of assimilatory tolerance follow each other in centuries old succession and frame our
understanding of the space itself and its setting within the city. But
how does such fleeting transition sit with the aggressive gentrification of the same city spaces in the late twentieth century. Alternative
narratives would render the spaces of today's East End visible as the
logical frontier of capital appropriation, even as scholars such as
Neil Smith have taught us to be careful about the deployment of the
metaphor of the frontier itself (Smith 1991, 1996).

The Mutability of Cosmopolitan Racial Subjects

Demographic fractions of a city population do not constitute communities. Communities are built, imagined, performed, and fought
for; frequently in struggles for justice and resources *against* the state.
Commonly, such identities rest also on resistance to other forms of
dominance in the city ranging from the spatialization of capital to the
populist will of the people. In this context, a striking feature in contemporary literature about multicultural cities is a tendency either to
privilege culture (at the expense of institutional context) or to
privilege demography (at the expense of the significance of meaning).

To the extent that an analysis of racialization implies a stress on
notions of becoming rather than being, this separation of culture
from institutional form and demography from cultural production
may be empirically predictable but is invariably analytically problematic. Empirical academic studies potentially reify minority presence through ascribed ethnicities that are monitored, counted, and
measured in terms of demographic penetration of political systems,
employment profiles, and attempts to promote equal opportunities.
Such measurement may be pragmatically progressive and politically

defensible but inevitably it highlights the 'border problems' of definitions of demographic fixity that reveal the absurdity of racial languages enshrined in policies of affirmative action and census monitoring (Goldberg 2002). Likewise, study of cultural production that privileges creativity that emerges from dialogue between traditions in the arts or in everyday life implicitly argues against the taxonomies of either ethnicized or racialized pigeonholes. But such arguments may undermine the case for institutional recognition of forms of cultural racism in the institutions that govern precisely these activities.

The contingencies that are explicit in such dilemmas lead logically to a focus on the sites in which the markers of race and ethnicity become significant in defining life chances, and other social and ethical outcomes. In this sense, it is essential to link the historical transition of racialized categories to the places in which their descriptive power is relevant at one moment and changes over time.

In a related sense the interplay between the spaces of the city and identity politics has the capacity to generate arenas of cultural identification and ethical contest. Alexander Negt and Oscar Kluge argued that it was possible to describe such self-autonomous arenas of debate and deliberation as a proletarian public sphere (Negt and Kluge 1993), a concept that Paul Gilroy has developed productively to consider the routing of black diasporic cultures through the *alternative public spheres* of the city (Gilroy 1993*a*, *b*). Drawing on Gilroy, in this sense it is possible to conceptualize how community struggles have produced 'alternative public spheres', commonly in the cultural realm: in youth culture, in musical culture, in voluntary and religious associations. These arenas are political, though they are not always seen as such (Back and Keith 1999; Back et al. 2003). They do not fit straightforwardly within the conventional languages of political science. They are most readily seen as Goffmanesque framings of social and moral life. Erving Goffman's metaphor of the stage and the dramaturgical analysis of ethnographies of such worlds is an essential tool in rendering comprehensible the complexities of city life (Goffman 1974). It is in the dance hall that gender politics is most clearly performed, in the church and the Mosque where faith-based transnational identities are deliberated, and on the football pitch where forms and norms of masculinity may be contested.

Crucially, the demographic make-up of the alternative public sphere may be marked by specific fractions of ethnicity but the key characteristic of the multicultural city is that it is in such spaces that new identities are generated and new solidarities are formed. In this sense, the spaces themselves become constitutive features of the manner in which racial identity is defined. Both the (successful or unsuccessful) reproduction of social values or norms and the emergence of new ways of seeing and thinking through patterns of creolization and hybridity are quite literally site-dependent.

Migration to cities of the capitalist north brings together cultures from across the globe. An analytical focus on the patterns of creolization and hybridization in the work of authors such as Appadurai, Back, Bhabha, Gilroy, and many other scholars in cultural studies has produced both important debates about the performative nature of intercultural dialogue and also significant concerns about the terms and limits of such processes. Simultaneously, studies in political science and sociology have considered the degrees to which individual migrant minorities (and sometimes migrant majorities) have succeeded within the institutional networks of city politics, education, welfare, class formation, or different economic sectors (Modood 1997; Runnymede Trust 2000). In the former literature 'the cosmopolitan' assumes a sign of cultural transformation through mixing; in the latter it stands as a valorized sign of reified diversity. Yet there are problems with both a decontextualized account of the powers of creolization and with histories of migrant minorities that plot their relative successes and failures by privileging the temporalities of generational change and advance. Such problems can be addressed through a consideration of the spatialization of both performativity and institutional form.

The Historicity and Spatiality of the Racialized City

Context and description become important drivers of academic analysis of racialization in a register of voice that foregrounds the salience of the traces of historicity and spatiality in making sense of the multicultural city. It is essential to place the mutability of racial subjects within the times and spaces of the city on which such identities are staged. To exemplify through the British context it is relevant to consider the identification category of blackness as both politically and analytically a significant sign of cultural difference at some times but not at others. Barnor Hesse has explored the manner in which the temporalities of the post-1945 *Windrush* generation potentially narrates a misleading uniformity of the Caribbean experience in the United Kingdom (Hesse 1993). Generalization of the Fordist labour demand of those years and the settlement of the British black experience is meaningful at times but can inadvertently downplay the significance of other settlements and histories that reach back further, not least in the port cities of Liverpool, Bristol, and London. The typology of Barbados, Jamaica, Guyana, Nevis, and other small islands is likewise contingently significant. The term 'Asian' in a British context used to capture demographic fractions from across the (sometimes twice) migrant diasporas of the Indian subcontinent is similarly both contested and at times meaningful. The badge of Islam similarly again both unites and divides.

In the United States, the Hispanicization of cities at some times appears analytically meaningful, at others masks a cartography of 'new' and 'old' migrations that bear the imprint of different economic moments of the late twentieth century and very different political trajectories of homeland and settlement (cf. Davis 2000) between demographies that cross Mexican, Central American, Puerto Rican, and the Spanish-speaking Caribbean diasporas. The contested vocabularies through which this process is described foreground slightly different invocations of ethnic identity that stretch across the nuances of Hispanic, Latino, and Chicano appellations.

It is precisely the mutability of racial subjects that makes the urban arena simultaneously both exciting and dangerous; the scene of Les Back's metropolitan paradox on which both the most extreme moments of racial terror and intense forms of intercultural dialogue are staged (Back 1996: chapters 5 and 6). The increasingly diverse nature of contemporary cities has to be understood as taking place through this process of staging and place-making of the neighbourhoods of the city. The city is constituted both as a cartography of sites through which communities identify themselves in the migrant metropolis and as spaces that are appropriated in the performance of community-making. Both these forms of spatialization literally *take place* within specific regimes of national, transnational, and local governance and power that mark their constitution.

To take just one example in the area of Deptford in south London, the genesis of a sense of a black community can only be understood in terms of struggles that were simultaneously local and global. In the 1970s, Communist Party Black South African exiles from apartheid South Africa worked alongside West African migrants and African Caribbean churches in the campaign against SUS[5] the police criminalization of young black men under the Victorian common law of suspicion (Keith 1993). The area witnessed a number of racial attacks and fire bombings, some associated with National Front activity. In 1980, in a case many suspected involved horrific arson, thirteen died at a party in the New Cross fire in this part of London. The wave of resentment spread out across the city in subsequent months and in 1981 a national march from the inner suburbs to the central areas of the West End of London made the black spaces of the inner suburbs visible in the political heart of London. These individual struggles and campaigns structured the emergence of a sense of community that was specifically staged in Deptford but also appealed to a metropolitan sense of blackness that confronted British racism.

The ethical resolutions of multiculture are challenged and reconfigured both spatially and institutionally. Consequently, the public spaces of the city and the institutional structures of democratic power are racialized both demographically and culturally. Across the United Kingdom a sense of struggle is historically linked to a debate about the nature of 'representation' whereby the penetration of the political apparatus of the state and representative politics is contested alongside the representation of black and migrant minority subjectivities in the expressive cultures of music, literature, clothing, and sport.

Equally pointedly, in a mainstream European and American context the fragility of categories of whiteness becomes visible under closer empirical scrutiny. There is not a point in the history of London when cultural differences have not played a significant role in shaping the life of the city. Masked by a historical gaze that normally erases such conflicts, it is possible to narrate London's biography through the lens of ethnic difference. The struggles between Vikings and Danes resulted in a prefigured residential apartheid in the city, rural migrations from the Celtic fringe were embossed in place names, and communal strife and the religious moments of dissent and riot through centuries were invariably culturally inflected. Peter Ackroyd has even argued that for much of the eleventh to the thirteenth centuries the capital represented the heart of Saxon merchant resistance (as city-state) to Norman aristocratic dominance of the fledgling nation-state (Ackroyd 2001).

To the present day in the city there is a beating of the bounds of Catholic Wapping that are marched on the Feast of the Virgin Mary, distinguishing the area from the Jewish territory north of the Highway. Throughout the early decades of the twentieth century violent conflict characterized relations between these two turfs but in the early twenty-first century they appear echoes of an anachronism. As Stedman-Jones (1989) has described, the white 'Eastender' was culturally defined in a manner that conflated such racial differences.

It is against such histories that it is important to consider the particular development of the recent past. The acceleration of migrant flows and the global reach of migrant labour in the twenty-first century markets makes the current city different in degrees of multicultural complexity rather than different in kind from its historical counterpart. But what has changed is the manner in which transnational links of globalized culture challenge the assumed or explicit normative models of assimilation. Assimilation rests on the appeal of the homogenizing force of the nation-state. The twenty-first century city may or may not outlive the nation-state but its multicultural nature disrupts the national political settlement analytically and challenges the straightforward sense of a national culture ethically. And against the setting of mainstream (national) cultures and conventional (national and local) political participation, migrant communities have historically created for themselves discursive sites through which newly localized versions of culture and politics develop.

In such settings cultural production is marked by both homeplace and site of settlement. In comforting narratives of Whiggish assimilationism the Italian community in the United States create pizza that is subsequently re-exported back to mainland Italy. Bangladeshi 'lascars' or seamen invent the curry in London that eventually becomes the national dish of the United Kingdom, displacing the quintessentially English fish and chips that historically owe their lineage to the combination of French *pommes frites* and Jewish traditions of frying fish that characterized the East End of the city in preceding decades.

More powerfully, in the interstices of state and civil society the city facilitates the genesis of alternative public spheres. In the manner of Negt and Kluge's description of the proletarian public sphere, migrant minorities struggle to build their known sites of association and discussion. These may provide the arenas in debating societies and working class associations for the circulation of transnational and diasporic constructions like Jewish international socialism that followed the work of Rudolph Rocker through twentieth century Whitechapel (Gidley 2002) or the exilic politics that runs from Marx and Lenin to the colonial struggles of migrant Africa and Asia in early twentieth century London. And just as London's colonial past was characterized by sites of diasporic dissent and exchange of ideas, its post-colonial present provides us with both the high profile work of the Finsbury Park mosque and the low profile work of women's politics in the Bengali-run Jagonari Women's Centre in Whitechapel. Each in turn becomes a deliberative arena for the mediation of the forces that impose racialized identity and the discursive construction of new forms of collective identification. They are spaces through which the history of the present is contested in the language of contemporary urbanism.

For the purposes of this chapter, two features remain important about such changes. *First,* the city itself becomes a *theatre* of many different—and sometimes irreconcilable—sets of cultural values, ideologies of the economic and the political, dynamics of social change. The dramaturgical metaphor links directly with the centrality of a Goffmanesque understanding of the mutability of racial subjects already considered. The nature of such cultural incommensurability provides a central organizing principle of much post-colonial and post-structural social theory. In particular, it informs the notion of a cosmopolitanism of hybridity and creolization promoted in the work of Homi Bhabha (1997; Bhabha et al. 2000). Similarly, Salman Rushdie has described the capacity to foster and subsume such incommensurable realities as the defining feature of the city and the central thematic of his own work (Rushdie 1992).

Second, the staging of such debates within the theatre of the city changes the cultures that distinguish migrant minorities in the first place. Diasporic communities are changed by the very processes of cultural reproduction and cultural dialogue in which they are implicated. In France the everyday lives of the *banlieu* so strikingly demonstrated in Kassiewitz's film *La Haine* restructure the nature of Moroccan, West African, and 'indigenous' French urban culture. In Birmingham, Manchester, and London in the United Kingdom the communities of the former Commonwealth reclaim the nature of what it means to be black, Jamaican, or West Indian; Sylheti, Bengali, or South Asian as 'new ethnicities' emerge that are articulated through *the spatialization of culture* within the city. But simultaneously what is risibly described at times as the 'host' culture changes likewise. Similarly, the Hispanic takeover of the American metropolis makes sense within the categorizing imperative of the narration of the 'Magical Urbanism' of Mike Davis but this very categorization, contingently both false and valid, obscures both the demographic discontinuities between Mexico and El Salvador and the city habitus of specific communities of new migrations (Davis 2000).

Performativity and Racialization

In this sense we return to the tension that exists between the reassuring voice of the communitarian and the idealism of liberal individualism. In a volume that considers processes of racialization such tensions are best understood through a consideration of the process of manufacture that is central to the term.

How race becomes visible might structure our thinking about the nature of processes of racialization. Many authors that have written about the public sphere—Richard Sennett (1977, 2000), Hannah Arendt (1958), Iris Marion Young (1990)—have stressed the right of the citizens of the city to create and define the polis through deliberative debate and creative performance in the present. But the city invariably testifies to the presence of the past within its contemporary form. The manner in which these traces of other times and different spaces become relevant depends on the constitution of arenas of debate and resource allocation in the city. Configurations of life chances relate directly to the historical imprint of city settlement and employment. Educational chances are determined in part by the quality of local schools, life expectancy in part is dictated by the quality of housing stock into which you are born. The middle class use their cartographies of the social to promote disproportionate access to the welfare state; the ethnic enclave is potentially both a testament to institutionally racist exclusion and a source of social capital and networking. And the multicultural imprint of the city is itself a legacy of the processes of (frequently collective) consumption through which segregation occurred in residence and the division of labour was racialized. Concentration promotes a voting bloc that may generate access to political power; dispersal may signify assimilatory success but renders invisible presence itself. So in both its spatialities and its historicities the appeal to move beyond race, to end raciology, is continually rebutted as much by legacy as by intent.

Through a liberal lens, the rights of self-organization and relative autonomy valorize state subsidized religious education but may balk at the degree to which a communitarian moral calculus is inscribed in the teaching of Catholic, Jewish, or Islamic schools. Through a communitarian lens the settlement and marketing of one part of East London as Banglatown in the 1990s is potentially an act of strategic essentialism. It can be seen as a self-defence mechanism for a community of interest to contest the displacing forces of gentrification that make the area too expensive to live in. Yet it may also ossify a particular notion of community values within it. In work with colleagues, young Bengali women aged 13–14 expressed to Back, Cohen, and Keith their preference for the 'racist space' of the Isle of Dogs to the surveillance of Banglatown, its open spaces relatively free of the patrician gaze and community regulation (Back and Keith 1999).

Through a communitarian lens, the self-organization of migrant communities against the injustices of racist intolerance depends on an appeal to a sense of sentiment that defines certain kinds of racialized solidarity. Yet in appealing against police malpractice, state-sponsored discrimination in housing allocation, or disproportionate exclusion from schools, the fundamental basis of appeal can become that of liberal individualism. The right for markers of individual difference not to matter is in part an appeal to a progressive liberalism that valorizes the equal treatment of all. Yet to the extent that such campaigns for the rights of the city appeal to forms of state regulation of the city itself, they must appeal to a notion of governmental practice in a liberal register. The ambiguity of this position recurs in the politics of the multicultural metropolis and the racialization of city spaces.

As the twenty-first century city becomes more complex, the pluralization of processes of racialization sits uneasily within the city. An appeal for 'no borders' marks certain claims for the free movement of labour and endorses the creation of new migrant minorities in cities of affluence. This appeal to freedom of movement is at times shared by the liberal left and also the neoliberal right. But to the extent that cities appeal to a sense of common sentiment, a shared identity that prefigures political deliberation over the allocation of welfare services and employment chances, such a register may speak against certain collective interests. A communitarian sense of geographical scale (such as the neighbourhood) or ethnic solidarity (and identity) may feel less sanguine about such rapidly changing urban forms. It is this context that the reassuring certainties of the couplet black and Asian to describe the multicultural world of twentieth century British cities is challenged by new migrations of the 1990s boom years, particularly in London.

It is why the debates on migration rapidly become more complex in the cities of twenty-first century Europe and North America. When we understand the agonistic politics of the liberal and the communitarian that define the multicultural condition some seemingly perverse debates are clarified a little. In the United Kingdom in 2004 the easier categorizations of race are subverted by debates around new migrants arriving from Eastern Europe. Scholars on the left—including Marxist economist Bob Rowthorn—have questioned whether such migrant flows threaten processes of welfare reform by undermining the legitimacy of the welfare state (Rowthorn 2003). But the appeal from the British left to a common sense of social solidarity is premised on an appeal not only to an anachronistic notion of nation building but also a curiously Kantian sense of communal loyalty. This particular clock cannot be turned back. A return to what Ali Rattansi (2004) has identified as a new assimilationism is both analytically and ethically flawed.

Ostensibly abstract debates have a populist resonance that replays many of the histories of the 1960s. An understanding of the racialization of the public spaces of the city is instructive to frame both their popular appeal and their analytical value. The public spaces of the contemporary city are characterized by forms of rationality and sentiment that transcend national boundaries. The spaces of cultural difference in the metropolis in this sense do not configure within the nation-state but cut across it. Transnational sentiment and cosmopolitan challenge create the city as a site where the rational interest of the urban (e.g. the demand for migrant labour in contemporary London) does not necessarily correspond with the articulated sentiment of the nation (e.g. in the auction of populist hostility to new migrants and asylum-seekers).

Conclusion

This chapter has suggested that the notion of racialization is help-ful in understanding the multicultural metropolis but only contin-gently so. There is a danger that the term itself implies a much greater sense of certainty than reality delivers. If we take from Simmel the centrality of the flux of the city in challenging the edit-ing processes of rationality, we begin to understand the importance of context in structuring processes of identity manufacture and the manner in which racisms construct racial boundaries. Inflected through the spaces of the city, both the creativity of processes of hybridization and creolization and the enduring scars of raciology and pernicious intolerance can be seen as simultaneously realized rather than juxtaposed.

NOTES

1. See www.goldsmiths.ac.uk/cucr.
2. The point being made here is that (after Foucault) we need to consider how regimes of governmentality map the transactional boundary state and civil soci-ety in ways that facilitate the emergence of some forms of social movements, domination, and resistance but do not allow others.
3. On 3 April 2004, Trevor Phillips, the head of the Commission for Racial Equality, argued that multiculturalism and integration were mutually exclusive

because 'Multiculturalism suggests a separateness' that integration does not (*The Times*, 3 April 2004, p. 9). His statement reified the demography of multiculture while simultaneously diminishing its ethical challenge.

4. In this sense, Richard Rorty has argued that the tensions between the communitarian and the liberal structure debates in contemporary moral philosophy and run through the identity, loyalty, and difference. See Rorty, R. (1998) 'Justice as a Larger Loyalty', in P. Cheah and B. Robbins (eds.), *Cosmopolitics: Thinking and Feeling Beyond the Nation*. Minneapolis and London: University of Minnesota Press.

5. The offence of SUS (short for 'suspicion') was based on a Victorian bye-law that allowed two men of good faith to arrest and charge an individual who was about to commit a crime. In the 1970s SUS was seen to be used almost entirely in London and in a massively disproportionate way against young black men, particularly in specific parts of the city. SUS was repealed following Lord Scarman's inquiry into the Brixton disorders of 1981.

REFERENCES

Ackroyd, P. (2001) *London: A Biography*. London: Vintage.

Arendt, H. (1958) *The Human Condition*. Chicago: University of Chicago Press.

Back, L. (1996) *New Ethnicities and Urban Culture*. London: UCL Press.

——Keith, M. (1999) ' "Rights and Wrongs": Youth, Community and Narratives of Racial Violence', in P. Cohen (ed.), *New Ethnicities, Old racisms*. London: Zed Books.

Back, L. and Solomos, J. (eds.) (2000) *Theories of Race and Racism: A Reader*. London and New York: Routledge.

——Khan, A., Shukra, K., and Solomos, J. (2001) 'Democratic Governance and Ethnic Minority Political Participation'. ESRC Conference, University of Manchester, 22 March.

——(2003) 'Democratic Governance and Ethnic Minority Political Participation in Contemporary Britain'. ESRC Final Report.

Banton, M. (1987) *Racial Theories*. Cambridge: Cambridge University Press.

Boyer, C. (1983) *Dreaming the Rational City*. Cambridge, MA: MIT Press.

Benhabib, S. (1992) 'Models of Public Space: Hannah Arendt, the Liberal Tradition, and Jürgen Habermas', in C. Calhoun (ed.), *Habermas and the Public Sphere*. Cambridge, MA: MIT Press.

——(1996) *Democracy and Difference: Changing Boundaries of the Political*. Princeton: Princeton University Press.

Bhabha, H. (1997) *Minority Culture and Creative Anxiet*. From British Council (2003) Reinventing Britain web site.

——Pollock, S., Breckenridge, C., and Chakrabarty, D. (2000) 'Cosmopolitanisms'. *Public Culture*, 12 (3): 577–91.

Butler, J. (1999) *Gender Trouble: Feminism and the Subversion of Identity*. London: Routledge.

Carey, P. (2001) *30 Days in Sydney: A Wildly Distorted Account*. London: Bloomsbury.

Calhoun, C. (ed.) (1992) *Habermas and the Public Sphere*. Cambridge, MA: MIT Press.

Davis, M. (2000) *Magical Urbanism: Latinos Reinvent the US Big City*. London: Verso.

Gidley, B. P. (2002) *Citizenship and Belonging: East London Jewish Radicals 1903–1918*. Ph.D. thesis, University of London.

Gilroy, P. (1993*a*) *The Black Atlantic: Modernity and Double Consciousness*. London: Verso.

——(1993*b*) *Small Acts: Thoughts on the Politics of Black Cultures*. London: Serpent's Tail.

——(2000) *Between Camps: Nations, Culture and the Allure of Race*. London: Allen Lane.

Goffman, E. (1974) *Frame Analysis: An Essay on the Organization of Experience*. Boston: Northeastern University Press.

Goldberg, D. (2002) *The Racial State*. Oxford: Blackwell.

Habermas, J. (1991) *The Structural Transformation of the Public Sphere: An Inquiry into a Category of Bourgeois Society* (Thomas Burger, trans.). Cambridge, MA: MIT Press.

Hesse, B. (1993) 'Black to Front and Black Again: Racialization Through Contested Times and Spaces', in M. Keith and S. Pile (eds.), *Place and the Politics of Identity*. London: Routledge.

Keith, M. (1993) *Race, Riots and Policing: Lore and Disorder in a Multi-Racist Society*. London: UCL Press.

——(1995*a*) 'Ethnic Entrepreneurs and Street Rebels; Looking Inside the Inner City', in S. Pile and N. Thrift (eds.), *Mapping the Subject*. London: Routledge.

——(1995*b*) 'Conclusion', in S. Pile and M. Keith (eds.), *Geographies of Resistance*. London: Routledge.

——(2004) *After the Cosmopolitan*. London: Routledge.

Kymlicka (1995) *Multicultural Citizenship: A Liberal Theory of Minority Rights*. Oxford: Clarendon Press.

Malik, K. (1996) *The Meaning of Race*. London: Routledge.

Miles, R. (1982) *Racism and Migrant Labour*. London: Routledge and Kegan Paul.

——(1987) 'Recent Marxist Theories of Nationalism and the Issue of Racism'. *British Journal of Sociology*, XXXVIII, 1: 24–43.

——(1989) *Racism*. London: Routledge.

Modood, T. (1997) *Ethnic Minorities in Britain: Diversity and Disadvantage*. London: Policy Studies Institute.

Moore, D., Kosek, J., and Pandian, A. (eds.) (2003) *Race, Nature and the Politics of Difference*. Durham, NC and London: Duke University Press.

Negt, O. and Kluge, A. (1993) *Public Sphere and Experience*. Minneapolis: University of Minnesota Press.

Parekh, B. (2000) *Rethinking Multiculturalism: Cultural Diversity and Political Theory*. Cambridge: Cambridge University Press.

Rattansi, A. (2003) 'Who's British? Prospect and the New Assimilationism', in Runnymede Trust (ed.), *Cohesion, Community and Citizenship*. London: Runnymede Trust.

——(2004) 'A False Dilemma? *Guardian*, 26 February.

Rex, J. and Mason, D. (eds.) (1986) *Theories of Race and Ethnic Relations*. Cambridge: Cambridge University Press.

Rorty, R. (1998) 'Justice as a Larger Loyalty', in P. Cheah and B. Robbins (eds.), *Cosmopolitics: Thinking and Feeling Beyond the Nation*. Minneapolis and London: University of Minnesota Press.

Rose, N. (1999) *Powers of Freedom: Reframing Political Thought*. Cambridge: Cambridge University Press.

Rowthorn, B. (2003) 'A Question of Responsibility'. Open Democracy www.opendemocracy.net/debates/article-10-96-1554.jsp#16.

Runnymede Trust (2000) *The Future of Multiethnic Britain*. London: Runnymede Trust.

Rushdie, S. (1992) *Imaginary Homelands: Essays and Criticism 1981–1991*. London: Penguin.

Sennett, R. (1977) *The Fall of Public Man*. New York: Alfred A. Knopf.

——(2000) 'Reflections on the Public Realm', in G. Bridge and S. Watson (eds.), *The City Reader*. Oxford: Blackwell.

Smith, N. (1991) 'Mapping the Gentrification Frontier', in M. Keith and A. Rogers (eds.), *Hollow Promises? Reality and Rhetoric in the Inner City*. London: Mansell.

——(1996) *The New Urban Frontier*. London and New York: Routledge.

Solomos, J. (1988) *Black Youth, Racism and the State: The Politics of Ideology and Policy*. Cambridge: Cambridge University Press.

——(1993) *Race and Racism in Britain*. Basingstoke: Macmillan Press.

——and Back, L. (1996) *Racism and Society*. Basingstoke: Macmillan.

Stedman-Jones, G. (1989) 'The Cockney and the Nation 1780–1988', in D. Feldman and G. Stedman-Jones (eds.), *Metropolis London: Histories and Representations since 1800*. London: Routledge.

Young, I. M. (1990) *Justice and the Politics of Difference*. Princeton: Princeton University Press.

CHAPTER 13

The Uses of Racialization: The Time-spaces and Subject-objects of the Raced Body

ALI RATTANSI

It is my view that whatever its limitations, the concept of racialization is indispensable and marks an advance in the study of what is generally called 'race and ethnic relations'. It cannot replace other concepts. But it functions to *open up* avenues of inquiry and understanding that the blunt attribution of 'racism' has a tendency to close down. However, many of the difficulties faced by the notion of racialization are analogous to and intimately connected to the dilemmas thrown up by usages of 'race' and racism in the social sciences. As in this volume as a whole, any discussion of racialization thus inevitably overlaps with definitions of race and analyses of racism, and my contribution is no exception. And similarly, its value only becomes apparent in substantive research.

The question then is what the idea of racialization enables as a productive resource in debates over race and racism. What are the uses of racialization? The answer takes us on a journey over a wide theoretical terrain and into empirical analyses involving serious conflicts of interpretation.

On Vocabularies

Racialization, as a potentially useful concept in the vocabulary of the field generally labelled race and ethnic relations, occupies a position somewhere between race and racism. This relation may be seen as a spectrum, with racialization standing in a variable location along the way. Or it may be conceptually visualized as one corner of a triangle with mutual interconnections between the three constituent elements.

Whatever the trope or form of modelling or conceptualization, the concept of racialization encounters a serious problem. It is parasitic, for its meaning(s), on prior definitions of race and racism. But race, it can be argued, is an 'empty category' (Rustin 1991: 57), or more appropriately, in Laclau's theorization, a category which functions as a 'floating signifier' (1990) which can be made to include a range of signified features depending on the way it is articulated with different elements in varying discourses. Moreover, racism as Miles has complained with some justification is liable to seemingly endless inflation (1989; Miles and Brown 2003). All of which leads to the conclusion that like most social science concepts, racism is an 'essentially contested' notion. Consensus on its meaning is unlikely.

The result is a chronic instability and potential vacuity at the very heart of the concept of racialization. It is nevertheless a seductive, indeed irresistible addition to the theoretical vocabulary of sociology in particular. Its attraction lies in its emphasis on process (Barot and Bird 2001). Race simply describes and racism suggests singularity and closure, in contradistinction to the dynamic implied by racialization. Of course, one reasonable attempt at preventing closure is the now generally accepted usage of racisms to signal plurality as well as changeability. But this laudable strategy compounds the problem for racialization, for we are now confronted by myriad racialization*s*.

The fact that the modern concept of race has always included biological and cultural elements and that cultural elements have increasingly come to the fore in the wake of developments in modern genetics—indeed this is partly why race is a floating signifier—has meant that distinctions between race, 'ethnicity', and 'nation', always blurred, have become murkier still. Public discourses, private utterances, and practices such as immigration and asylum policy and other institutional processes contain elements of all three in a confusing mix.

Derridean inspired deconstructions of the binaries race/ethnicity and race/nation are thus easy to accomplish. But supposedly obvious distinctions between 'old' and 'new' racisms thereby also become destabilized (Rattansi 1994: 53–6). Wittgensteinian resources may also be called upon to highlight the 'family resemblance' between these terms to make substantially the same deconstructive move

(Rattansi 1994: 53; for those surprised by the conjoining of Derrida and Wittgenstein in this context, see Staten 1984, especially pp. 82–3).

Add to this the necessary decentring and de-essentialization of racist, ethnic, and other identities and the de-essentializing of social and institutional processes (Rattansi 1994: 29–33) and the prospects for anything but a formal role for the concept of racialization begin to look distinctly unpropitious. However, it does enable an opening for discourses and practices to be seen as complex and shifting configurations of the biological and the cultural, with a variable intertwining of race, ethnicity, nation, ethnicity, gender, class, and sexuality, and this as we shall see is an intellectually fertile resource (see also Rattansi 2002).

Nevertheless, the relatively mobile signifier that is race and the plurality of racisms gnaw away at the architectural stability of the concept of racialization and its associated theorizations. Goldberg's frustration with the problematic nature of the concept and his reported demands to his students for rigour in usage are entirely understandable and laudable (Goldberg 2002: 1 and Goldberg, this volume). His delineation of six key contemporary racisms—and it is not difficult to list more—serves to demonstrate the complexity of the problems involved and the inability of racialization to help in differentiating what is and what is not to count as racism, nor how many are really important, nor what forces shape and reshape them, nor the strategies that might effect deracialization. Or at least, not without a great deal more theoretical and empirical labour.

Which is just as well. The danger of a too 'thick' concept of racialization would be its presumption regarding processes on the ground, so to speak, which only substantive excavation can reveal.

The argument presented so far should dispel doubts that readers may have entertained about whether many of the chapters in this collection are *really* about racialization. The point about being about racialization is about analysing a panoply of related issues and processes. The value of the concept lies precisely in pointing not just at race and racism, but beyond them in their manifold imbrications. But what role does this leave for the concept in substantive analysis?

States of Racialization

A reading of Michael Banton's contribution to this volume should immediately dispel any uncertainty that arises about the substantive content of racialization. If claims about the racialization involved in specific processes at particular historical periods can actually be refuted then it may be suggested that the concept of racialization cannot be as 'thin' or 'empty' as all that.

In any case, given that Banton, Miles, and others have wanted to restrict the racialization label to discourses and/or processes that explicitly invoke biologically based categorization, it cannot be argued that racialization denotes nothing or even relatively little. It is a *relatively* empty signifier. But to what extent the inclusion of bio-logical classification as a defining element of discourses and practices helps to resolve disputes about actual events, outcomes, and effects is not easy to specify. A more detailed engagement with the empirical concerns raised by Banton's argument is obviously required to illu-minate further the way debates about racialization can (and to what degree they cannot) be a productive way forward in understanding processes, and claims and counterclaims involving race and racism.

Banton's allusion to Hansen's critique of the 'racialization school' and its interpretation of the formation of British immigration policy in the period after the Second World War provides rich material for unpacking the kinds of difficulties that arise when the concept of racialization is deployed.

Drawing upon his own earlier investigation (Banton 1985: 29–48) and Hansen's recent account (Hansen 2000), Banton's conclusion echoes that of Hansen: 'the claims of the "racialization school" are palpable nonsense' (Banton, chapter 2, this volume, note 5). Banton's and Hansen's dissatisfaction is directed at research and interpretation by Carter et al. (1993), Carter et al. (1996), Solomos (1989, 1993), and Paul (1997). Whether this group of authors can be said to con-stitute a racialization school is not a point that need detain us, although I note in passing that the exact degree of unity between these different authors does not appear to have been established by its critics with any rigour.

The disagreements as set out by the critics of the racialization school relate in particular to the background and passing of the 1962 Commonwealth Immigrants Act. This changed the rights of free entry into the United Kingdom for citizens of the United Kingdom and Commonwealth as enshrined in the British Nationality Act of 1948. A number of interrelated questions appear to be at issue in this debate. To what extent was *state* opposition to immigration as initiated by the 1962 Act driven by *popular* racist hostility to black and Asian immigration? How far could popular racism itself be said to have been influenced by debates among politicians or debates initiated by politicians? What was the effect on public attitudes of immigration legislation that arguably always framed the immigrant as the problem rather than regarding racism in Britain as the main issue? Were politicians and other policy-makers such as civil servants motivated by racism to any degree in their desire to restrict black and Asian immigration? (This inflow was sometimes referred to as 'coloured' and at other times labelled 'immigration from the New Commonwealth'; as we shall see, particular forms of categorization of this immigration in this period are of great significance in illuminating the questions involved in the debate surrounding the claims of the racialization school and its critics). These questions go to the heart of the debate as to the role of the state as a racist agent and as one, or *the* key influence in racializing policies and popular attitudes to race and immigration.

There are other issues at stake too. Was the state monolithically racist or were there significant divisions among politicians and civil servants and between these two groups? Were there conflicts of view between different departments of state, for example, the Colonial and Commonwealth Office, the Foreign Office, the Ministry of Labour, and the Ministry of Health, and what was the significance of any such conflicts for understanding the role of the state in the racialization of the immigration issue in post-war British politics and culture?

At first sight it may appear that these historical questions can only have a tangential bearing on the conceptual and theoretical clarification I am trying to establish. However, it is my argument that it is only by engaging with this debate in a little detail that the difficulties inherent in the deployment of the concept of racialization become evident as well as susceptible to remedy and repair.

It is to Hansen that we must turn for an extended critique of the so-called racialization school and for an alternative interpretation. Hansen represents the racialization school's analysis as a form of determinism in which the British state had decided, in the 1950s, before public opinion had turned against mass immigration, that black and Asian immigration would harm the British 'racial character'; that state policies were a crucial influence which racialized immigration as an issue, partly by framing the immigrants as 'the problem' rather than racism or housing shortages; the state thus helped establish a public framework which defined the British nation as essentially white and thus by implication represented coloured as more or less inassimilable.

In criticism, Hansen advances the following arguments. First, that the racialization school's quotations from primary sources in the state archives are selective and refer to marginal figures. Second, that there were strong, principled, and influential instances of opposition to racist immigration controls within the state, but which are ignored within the racialization school's account. And finally, that the interpretation offered by the racialization school ignores factors such as 'the role of public hostility, housing shortages and other local pressures, a lingering attachment to empire in the Conservative party, Commonwealth ideals in the Labour Party and common-wealth states' opposition to migration restrictions' (Hansen 2000: 13). The state's role in racializing the immigration issue is thus grossly exaggerated. The claims of the racialization school in this regard are 'palpable nonsense', says Hansen, a judgement which as we have seen is repeated by Banton in this volume.

It is important to Hansen's argument that racism was supposedly much more a feature of 'society' rather than the state, with politicians being 'liberal' while it was the public that was 'illiberal'. For Hansen, the thesis of racialization by the state becomes 'incoherent' when this is acknowledged. The 'construction of a racist national identity' by the state was simply not necessary. In effect his argument is that it was already in place, as evidenced by massive public hostility to black and Asian immigration (Hansen 2000: 15).

However, examined more closely, Hansen's own analysis is shot through with caveats and equivocations which seriously weaken the force of his critique of the racialization school. This is not to suggest that the racialization thesis can be accepted as it stands. Elsewhere, I have presented a critique and reformulation framed in different terms (Rattansi 2002) and will draw upon it here. Before doing so, I will examine the problematic character of Hansen's analysis in order to highlight the difficulties that arise in debates over *what* is to count as racialization and in understanding *how* and *why* it takes the forms it does.

For example, the strength of Hansen's objections is considerably diluted by his own admission that 'anti-racist' opposition to restrictions on black and Asian immigration was restricted to just one member of the Conservative Cabinet, Lennox-Boyd (pp. 63, 72). Moreover, this turns out on closer inspection to be not a principled anti-racist stand so much as a pragmatic move, being based on Lennox-Boyd's perception that discriminatory immigration controls would be 'fiercely resented' in West Indian, African, and Pacific dependencies. 'I must *therefore* record that I could not agree to legislation confined to Colonial immigrants [rather than the whole Commonwealth, including the white Dominions]' (cited in Hansen 2000: 77, emphasis added).

Note too that even the Colonial Office, the main department of state opposed to the imposition of racially based immigration controls, only supported West Indian immigration. It favoured restrictions on migrants from India and Pakistan on the grounds that while 'West Indians were viewed as industrious, reliable and talented, Indians and Pakistanis were seen to be lazy, feckless and difficult to place in employment' (Hansen 2000: 85).

Interestingly, the accusation of palpable nonsense against the racialization school now reduces to the limp assertion that although these 'comments against Asians possess all the nuance of barroom prejudice, they demonstrate that black immigration, far from inciting fear and loathing across parties and the bureaucracy, had strong support within at least one major office of state' (Hansen 2000: 85).

Moreover, although Hansen claims that illiberalism (there is here a coyness about using 'racism' which as we shall see is significant, as a form of discursive *deracialization*) was a property of society and not the state, he cites evidence to support the view that senior government ministers held off imposing controls on black and Asian immigration because there was not enough indication of hostility among the white British population (Hansen 2000: 67–8). On their own admission ministers thought that neither the white population nor 'liberal opinion'—thus aligning with illiberal opinion—was ready for restrictive measures (Hansen 2000: 68, 72).

It is also significant that Hansen admits that public opinion against coloured immigration hardened considerably in the run up to the 1962 Immigration Act, thus giving support to the racialization school's thesis that the state's actions played a part in racializing British popular attitudes to blacks and Asians (Hansen 2000: 14).

What different interpretations of the racialization process define as racism is obviously of some importance. Hansen's conceptual confusion in this context simply adds to his difficulties when he attempts to argue that there is only scanty evidence of racism among politicians, for he provides two definitions of racism, on the same page. Compare the following:

there were instances [amongst politicians and civil servants] of what can be characterized as racism (when this is understood as a desire to exclude black immigrants because they are black). (Hansen 2000: 15)

Racism, understood as an assumption of ethnic inferiority, has since the war been marginal to and politically insignificant among politicians and bureaucrats. Throughout the postwar period, both were significantly more liberal than the public to which politicians owed their office (Hansen 2000: 15).

In a curious reversal of the usual analytical conventions which have distinguished between discourses and policies which support discrimination on grounds of cultural difference (the so-called 'new racism') and racial inferiority ('old racism'), Hansen simply adds confusion to the racialization debate by invoking racial (white/black) difference and cultural (ethnic) inferiorization as the forms of racism that are at issue. One might ask, in any case, what those who wanted to keep blacks out because they were black, objected to about blackness? Just their blackness? Or did blackness signify inferiority? And what about the comments about Asians and their characteristics which clearly implied their inferiority?

Indeed, Hansen has to concede the existence and influence of assumptions of what he calls 'imperialist assumptions of European superiority' (Hansen 2000: 63) to the policy-making process, as well as the effect of the notion that the 'coloured community is certainly no part of the concept of England or Britain to which people of British stock throughout the Commonwealth are attached' (cited in Hansen 2000: 67).

There are several other weaknesses in Hansen's argument which I shall set aside for present purposes. The point though is that comparing the accounts offered by Hansen and the racialization school suggests the conclusion that neither is able to provide definitive evidence to clinch the argument. Moreover, there is a vagueness on both sides as to what degree of evidence is required about the extent of racism—assuming a common definition could be agreed—among politicians, civil servants, and the white British population to support one case or the other. Hansen, for example, underplays evidence such as the frantic attempts by the earlier, Labour government of Attlee in the 1940s to prevent potential West Indian immigrants from setting sail on the famous SS *Windrush* from Jamaica and the fact that the active opposition to the recruitment of coloured workers from the West Indies and the Indian subcontinent only subsided, briefly, when the alternative supply of white workers displaced from Eastern Europe had dried up (Dean 1987; Carter et al. 1993: 57–60). On the other hand, it is arguable that the racialization school is indeed only able to provide relatively patchy evidence of racism among influential politicians and civil servants and neither side has reliable evidence on the precise character of white British public opinion on immigration for the *whole* of the post-Second World War period.

It should already be clear, then, that a crucial debate about the racialization of the British polity is bedevilled by imprecise claims, the absence of detailed empirical evidence, and lack of clarity on how crucial terms such as racism are to be deployed. At the very least, the conclusion one might draw from a reading of the debate between the racialization school and its critics is that the value of the concept of racialization itself is hostage to clarity in defining key terms, especially racism, and greater specificity in relation to claims about attitudes and practices across a wide range of institutions and sectors of the population. This would then be consistent with the argument presented at the beginning of this chapter regarding the interdependence of the concept of racialization with other concepts and the need for rigorous empirical research if the promise of the notion is to be realized.

However, an altogether more important analytical issue is revealed by a consideration of the conflicting interpretations presented by the racialization school and Hansen. This concerns the multilayered character of the racialization process and the need to theorize this multidimensionality in an appropriate framework. The problem of settling accounts around how and to what degree racialization occurred during this historical period is hampered by the remarkably narrow analytical framing of the debate and the specificity of the vocabulary used, especially by Hansen.

What Reeves (1983) has referred to as 'discoursive deracialization' (and for which I shall use the term discursive deracialization) is a notable feature of Hansen's interpretation *and* of the language of many of the relevant political actors in this disputed narrative.

For example, the anxieties of the British establishment about 'coloured immigration' are described by Hansen in the following terms:

There was, to be sure, a deep unease among senior bureaucrats and Cabinet ministers about non-white immigration and few people were enthusiastic about it. (Hansen 2000: 63)

The nature of the 'deep unease' and the 'hypocrisy' also referred to in this context are simply left unexplored. The degree to which both might reflect forms of racism is an issue that is simply evaded. Instead, assumptions about their generally benign character are implied throughout Hansen's interpretation.

Most damaging of all to Hansen's alternative to the racialization school is his consistent, discursively deracialized, and in effect unwitting argument that the entire political culture within which the policy debates about immigration into Britain occurred *were already profoundly racialized*. That is, it is Hansen's contention that the 1948 Nationality Act, which allowed unrestricted entry into Britain for all UK and Commonwealth citizens, was formulated in these terms only in order to keep robust links with the 'Old' (white) Commonwealth. Hansen is quite clear that free entry had been enshrined in the 1948 legislation on the assumption that only those from the *white* Commonwealth would want to come to the United Kingdom.

Indeed, Hansen's historical account of the period from the end of the Second World War onwards rests on the assumption that politicians, civil servants, and indeed more or less the whole (white) British nation throughout this era were united in their opposition to any idea of creating a multiracial or multicultural country. To put it differently: what Hansen's account suggests is that state did not have to take a lead and play a strong active role in racializing British national identity and policy-making because racialization, indeed racism, was a deeply embedded, taken for granted part of the national culture and institutionalized in the 1948 Nationality Act.

Consider the following selection from a large number of similar judgements by Hansen on postwar British immigration policy:

At no point did British politicians or civil servants consider restricting Old Commonwealth [white] citizens to enter the United Kingdom freely and to enjoy the full rights of citizenship. By contrast, they were only superficially and residually committed to the entry rights of New Commonwealth [black and Asian] citizens... Boxed in by their ideological [sic] commitment to Old Commonwealth citizens' right to come to Britain, Conservatives opted for no controls. (Hansen 2000: 18)

The commitment expressed by politicians in 1948 to the traditional laissez faire policy [of immigration] was a commitment to these [white] individuals' right to enter the United Kingdom. It is unremarkable [sic] that, as the right of free entry was exercised in ever-larger numbers of non-white immigrants, civil servants expressed less enthusiasm for it. (Hansen 2000: 66)

[I]mmigration as a political issue was created by substantial migration from the ['coloured'] New Commonwealth. Had post-war migration been solely from the [white] Old Dominions' citizens, there would have been no interest in restricting it. (Hansen 2000: 76–7)

Note Hansen's consistent attempt to play down and indeed discursively deracialize the obvious racially discriminatory sentiments that drove the British state's immigration policy. The commitment to *white* immigration is rephrased as an 'ideological' commitment to links with the Old Commonwealth of Australia, New Zealand, and

Canada. The nature of the ideological underpinnings, blatantly racialized as evidenced by Hansen's own descriptions, is left unexamined or unexplained. It is regarded as 'unremarkable' that civil servants' attitude to immigration changed when more non-white immigrants began to enter the country.

In fact what is remarkable is that Hansen fails to grasp how strongly a different and more powerful racialization thesis emerges from his judgements on post-war British immigration policy. Indeed the conclusions to be drawn from the analysis and evidence presented by both sides is startling. The racialization school appears to have seriously *underestimated* the degree to which governments and departments of state worked within racialized and indeed broadly racist assumptions about the British nation and the undesirability of black and Asian immigration. Hansen's critique, on the other hand, only succeeds, to the extent that it does, by revealing that the debate about racialization needs to focus not merely on actual, stated racist and racialized assumptions, but on the taken for granted, enveloping framework within which policy options were set out and debated. And this framework was one which relied on a premise difficult to describe as other than racist, that only immigration from the white 'Old Commonwealth' countries was acceptable, while that from the coloured New Commonwealth was obviously ('naturally') undesirable and to be stopped as soon as practically possible, given a variety of constraints not least of which was the desire to find a way of allowing white Commonwealth immigration to continue if at all possible.

Hansen's own account bears ample testimony to this form of racialization, indeed underpins his critique of the racialization school. In the light of this, Solomos' claim (challenged by Banton in this volume) and that of the racialization school as a whole that post-war debates about immigration were, at bottom, about race seems to remain generally intact.

Precisely how racist the debates were would depend on definitions of racism, but the colour consciousness driving the British state's policy agenda would appear to fall generally within all definitions, including Banton's, given the explicit reference to biological markers in defining the relevant populations.

Multidimensionality, 'Non-decisions', and 'Common Sense'

A key purpose of my detailed examination of the purported critique of the racialization school should now be clear. It was to reveal, through consideration of a dense case study, that racialization has to be understood as multidimensional. Both explicit statements and underlying taken for granted assumptions have to be analysed. The broad consensus that characterized the policy preferences of successive British governments and civil servants did not have to be explicitly stated in all discussions precisely because it was a form of common sense that infused all aspects of thinking about immigration policy. Reeves's notion of discursive deracialization captures an important element of the way, paradoxically, that racialization processes work. It should also be clear that the long-standing debate in political science about the different faces of power and the ways in which forms of 'non-decision-making' and various structures and cultures of routine agenda setting operate are acutely relevant to understanding the politics of racialization (Lukes 1972; Carnoy 1984; Dunleavy and O'Leary 1987).

The framing assumptions of the British state, it should be clear, concern *whiteness*, and its associated 'chains of equivalence'—to use Laclau's form of discourse analysis—regarding 'European', 'Western', 'civilized', 'Christian', and so forth. These have historically been deeply woven into the fabric and texture of political culture, the formation of the state, and the popular imagination. And a consideration of the debates shows, if more evidence was required, that the turn to 'whiteness' in the study of race and ethnic relations has been long overdue (Dyer 1997; Frankenberg 1997; Hill 1997; Jacobson 1998; Ware and Back 2002).

A number of questions remain. While I have suggested that it is difficult to see the policy assumptions and practices of the British state as anything other than broadly racist, ingenious redefinitions—in effect, other forms of discursive deracialization—may always make it possible to represent these as something less odious and thus attempt to sustain the thesis that somehow the British political elite remained liberal and non-racist and held out for as long as possible against the pressures of an illiberal, racist, white national population.

Moreover, other difficulties may also arise. Debates may become unproductive if analyses remain imprisoned within a rigid racist/non-racist grid when interpreting the intentions and actions of particular actors involved in policy and other processes. Ambivalence and contradiction, as I and others have argued, should be regarded as 'normal' features of identities (Rattansi 1994: 28–34, 63–74).[1] It is likely that key political actors and bureaucrats in the British state had varying degrees of attachment to notions of fairness and non-racial practice. The fact that Britain had been involved in fighting a war against an explicitly racist state, Nazi Germany, might have had a constraining influence on the way the British state could now conduct its external relations with its non-white colonies. There were other factors, such as the influence that openly racist immigration policy might have had on the leaders of nationalist movements in the colonies, especially given the context of the cold war and the left-leanings of many of the independence movements, and the fact that the governments of the white Dominions of Australia and New Zealand were trying hard to deflect attention away from their blatantly white-only immigration policies but which might have been questioned if a broader debate had been sparked by open racial discrimination in Britain's own proposals.

Also, given the generic complexity of the idea of race, politicians and civil servants as well as ordinary citizens are likely to have operated with a *mélange* of notions of race, nation, ethnicity, and cultural difference. This is where the concept of racialization reveals its strengths. It keeps open, and subject to empirical investigation, the degree to which racism per se animated the intentions and practices of actors and institutions, and also keeps the analysis alert to the variety of different ways in which the issue of race might appear in combination with questions of class, gender, sexuality, and nation. The idea of racialization can function to prevent the sort of closure and polarization that is provoked by having to create a simple racist/non-racist labelling of identities, subjectivities, intentions, practices, and outcomes (cf. Hansen 2000: 248–9). It is interesting to note in this context that Carter's recent 'critical realist' reinterpretation of the post-war immigration debates, although drawing on a sophisticated theoretical infrastructure, adds surprisingly little to the understanding he and his colleagues from the racialization school had already provided (Carter 2000). In part, this appears to stem from its failure to break out of relatively rigid racist/non-racist binaries, as well as by its neglect of issues of deracialized discourses, the framing effect of common sense cultures of whiteness, and an appreciation of the insights of those who have emphasized the role of non-decision-making and agenda setting (Carter 2000: 108–38).

The framework adopted here would indicate that it would not be unusual to find confusion, ambivalence, contradiction, and differing degrees of commitment to overt racism in debates in Cabinet, committees in departments of state, and political party meetings of MPs and activists. Examining a relatively long historical period of racialization is thus likely to reveal conflicts, hesitancies, and periods of uncertainty in policy. Although it is clear that the overwhelming sentiment was one which took it for granted that coloured immigration was undesirable and to be avoided as far as practically possible, this is by no means the whole story nor can it be the end point of the analysis.

For example, I have emphasized elsewhere that the British state's immigration policies in this period also have to be understood in the light of highly *sexualized* racist anxieties—completely ignored by Hansen and only incidental to the account of the racialization school—which mobilized a variety of stereotyped conceptions of the sexuality of black men and of working class white women. There were severe anxieties, too, about the development of dangerous spaces in cities such as Liverpool where it was thought that a 'new Harlem' was springing into existence, combining drugs, prostitution, and general criminality, thus condensing into one image a range of fears around race, sexuality, class, and potentially uncontrollable urban locales (Dean 1993; Rattansi 2002: 56).

Racializing States: Foucault and Beyond

If forms, states, and processes of racialization are likely to be complex and internally contradictory this is no less true of racializing state apparatuses and the governments that come to occupy the executive branch. Decades of debates on the functioning of the state in Western liberal democracies have established beyond doubt that it is a mistake to treat the state as monolithic. Different ministries and departments of state are charged with carrying out specific governmental tasks and in the process develop relatively autonomous interests, are subject to relatively separate sets of pressures, and have to compete with other branches of state for financial resources. Unsurprisingly, all these features were present in the immigration debates considered above. Moreover, Hansen is right to draw attention to the way in which, once the 1948 Nationality Act was in place, it created constraints or 'path dependence' regarding future policy options (Hansen 2000: 30–1).

However, if understood in the context of the *longue durée* it is also important to recognize how conceptions of race, and especially whiteness, as remarked earlier, have in the modern period been central to the formation of Western states and even to the ideologies of liberalism that have underpinned the formation of the liberal democratic parliamentary polity. Two contributions by Goldberg

(1993, 2002) have been seminal in this regard (see also Parekh 1995). It is now clear that debates about colonialism, decolonization, immigration, various aspects of domestic governmentality, foreign policy, and so forth have occurred within an overarching racialized unity and racial hierarchy which have privileged whiteness and its discursive links with varieties of Western, European, and masculine imaginaries.

The work of Michel Foucault has provided important analytical and theoretical resources in a newer understanding which treats race not as an optional 'add-on' to the workings of Western states, but as inscribed within their formation, cultures, and working practices from their origins in early modernity. A number of authors have deployed his insights into 'bio-politics', 'disciplinary' technologies, 'regimes of truth', processes of 'normalisation', and 'governmentality' as part of a conceptualization of racial, or racialized, or white governmentality (Stoler 1995, 1997; Hesse 1997; Goldberg 2002; Rattansi 2002; Brah, Chapter 3, this volume; Nayak 2003, Chapter 7, this volume).

Compressing a potentially book-length discussion, the productiveness of Foucault's work may be seen in his understanding of the state's practices in the management of 'populations' within territories, combining biology—management of the purity of the stock, health, sexuality, and spatial distribution of the population—and culture, in creating disciplined bodies and identities with a strong racialized, especially white character. The most sustained development of these ideas can be found in Goldberg's recent *Racial States* (2002) and all students of racialization are in his debt for the rigour with which key Foucauldian themes have finally been brought into the mainstream of the analysis of both racialization and the state.

As I have shown earlier, once the inscription of whiteness within Western states, and in this particular case the British state, is recognized, the relative absence of overt racist and racializing enunciations and their record in documents in state archives becomes wholly understandable. In routine state practices this is not, *pace* Reeves, the operation of discursive deracialization so much as the working of a racialized common culture or common sense. One may borrow Giddens's notion of 'practical consciousness' to conceptualize the forms in which this common sense is involved in individual practices. In Foucauldian, general post-structuralist, and other forms of discourse analysis, what is not said and what does not have to be said can be as significant, sometimes more so, than what is explicitly said. Reeves and other students of racialization, though, are right about the way in which the terminology of race may be sanitized and coded in ways that attempt to make it immune to charges of racism. Solomos and Back's analysis of the discursive strategies used by local politicians in Birmingham (1995: 114–123) is instructive in this regard, and the work of discourse analysts researching within different traditions, such as Wetherell and Potter and van Dijk have also made a significant contribution (van Dijk 1987, 1993; Wetherell and Potter 1993; van den Berg 2003) although it is important to note that Solomos and Back, in common with van Dijk, tend to underplay ambivalence and overemphasize conscious rhetorical strategy (van den Berg 2003: 123).

Foucault's expanded notion of networks of power-knowledge, in which the activities of the central state apparatus are only one, though very important, nodal point also draws attention to wider parameters of the state's management of populations in a racializing manner. Successive British governments, including those of the 1950s, charged various local and regional apparatuses and organizations with collecting a range of information about ethnoracially classified sections of the population (Dean 1987, 1993; Carter et al. 1993).

Historically, censuses have been important in colonial and domestic rule, and investigations by administrators, anthropologists, travellers, journalists, and a variety of voyeurs have fed the state with information on 'native' and lower-class domestic populations (Mitchell 1988; Bayly 1996; Cohn 1996). The surveillance, knowledge-gathering, and normalizing capacities of contemporary state apparatuses have given extraordinary scope for the development of Foucault's original insights into governmentality. Governmentality studies have mushroomed (see Dean 1999 for a general discussion).

However, there are dangers in an overreliance on Foucauldian optics. Despite gestures to the contrary, Foucault's work and general strategy of inquiry remained underdeveloped with regard to the complex networks of resistance to configurations of top-down projects of national and local governmentality. His theorzation and analyses of subjectivities, reflexivity, and identity formation remained rudimentary. Despite his emphasis on the microphysics of power his actual insights into the operation of 'micro' interactions, processes, and negotiations of power lacked the richness of his understanding of broader processes. Moreover, his attachment to a 'thin' concept of the subject, reflected partly in his hostility to psychoanalysis, is a serious handicap in recognizing the emotional attachments and conflicts involved in any analysis of racialized power.

Thick descriptions and the empathetic portrayal of the lived experience of racialized interactions require an open-ended, eclectic approach to theoretical resources, including recourse to the still relevant insights of Gramsci, although the usefulness of the concept of hegemony for the understanding of racialization cannot be explored further in this chapter.

For the present, note one other lacuna in Foucauldian approaches which require urgent repair. While Stoler's recovery of Foucault's reflections on the bio-politics of race and state racism, and Goldberg's Foucauldian exploration of the parameters of racial states, have been invaluable in highlighting the state–race articulations which have formed Western states, what is underplayed is the significance of *nation* (Stoler 1995: 93; Goldberg 2002: 118–22). Race and nation have been equally important in the formation of Western states and, by colonial domination and resistance, and imperial extension, in the formation of practically all states.

While it has been important to bring race back into state theory and analysis, the massive significance of nationalism in the formation and continued significance of what, even in a globalized and increasingly post- and supranational world, is a system of nation-states should not be underestimated. The mobilizing power of the idea of the nation has been crucial to the formation of newer ethnonational-cultural racisms and the new wars of the late twentieth and early twenty-first century and, in different contexts, to the newer racializations such as Hindu nationalism in India.

Indeed, it is my argument that the appropriate framework for understanding racialization is the 'race–nation–ethnicity complex', in its articulation with sexuality, gender, and class (Rattansi 2002; Rattansi 2005).

Reproductions and Articulations

The reproduction of race and nation occurs, then, through the workings of the state and myriad social interactions in a wide range of social fields, sites, and institutional contexts. But how exactly are these complex processes to be theorized? Some of the difficult issues have been explored above. Other seemingly intractable questions remain.

In a now famous formulation, Michael Omi and Howard Winant conceptualized race as an 'unstable and "decentred" complex of social meanings constantly being transformed by political struggle' (1986: 68). Building on this form of analysis and bringing to bear a fuller range of post-structuralist and 'postmodernist' resources of decentring and de-essentialization, I have attempted a more elaborate theoretical framework for the understanding of racism, processes of racialization, and the formation of identities (1994, 1995, 2000, 2002). This is part of a broader post-Marxist sensibility in sociology, cultural studies, feminism, and political theory which attempts to retain Marxian and Weberian insights into the significance of pressures generated by markets and the need for capital accumulation, and the key role of the unequal distribution of economic, political, and cultural resources, but without succumbing to the untenable reductionism of the idea of the economy or class or the relations of production as the ultimate determinants in the last or indeed the first instance (Laclau and Mouffe 1985; Giddens 1990, 1994; Laclau 1990; Anthias and Yuval-Davis 1992; Bauman 1992; Brah 1996; Anthias 2002).

Patriarchal forms, sexualized relations, classed, gendered, and sexualized racisms, nationalisms, ethnic attachments, differing structural characteristics of national states, all play contextually variable roles in influencing the character of social life (Brah 1996). To refer simply to 'capitalist society' or 'global capitalism' as the grand container within which relations of gender or racialization take place cannot now be regarded as an adequate form of analysis. On the other hand, whether the very concept of structure has now to give way to notions of 'networks', 'mobilities', and 'complexity' (Castells 1997; Urry 2000, 2003) is also becoming a matter for debate although not one that can be pursued here.

Whatever form of theorization is adopted, it has to find ways of analysing both reproductions and transformations, articulations, rearticulations, and disarticulations. A focus on a specific, contentious racialization process, *institutional racism*, provides a convenient illustration of the issues involved.

Power, Structure, and Agency

It is neither possible nor necessary to provide a comprehensive discussion of the debates over the usage of institutional racism. I shall simply concentrate on a number of salient issues.

Whether this is explicitly acknowledged or not, the concept of institutional racism functions primarily as a mode of understanding the reproduction of racism via racialization processes over time and in specific sites. And it draws attention, wittingly or not, to the power relations involved. Much of the confusion over its deployment especially, but not only, in public debates, derives from a failure to make clear that it does not provide a general analysis of the origins of racism as well as its reproduction. Hence the constant conflation and confusion, accusation and counteraccusation regarding the relation between individual intentions, individual attitudes, and prejudices, more collective cultures of social interaction such as the 'canteen culture' of police forces, and routine institutional practices which may or may not have any racial motive in their development and continued operation and may have variable outcomes.

In so far as the focus of analysis should be on the complex interplay of these elements, as well as their articulation with divisions of gender and class, it should be clear that what is being analysed is not so much institutional racism *tout court*, but the workings of processes of racialization within institutions, with variable outcomes for racialized populations both within institutions such as schools, hospitals, police forces, and so forth, and those who are in some sense 'outside' the institution, such as parents, or black youth who become the objects of police practices.

There are several advantages to a change in conceptualization from institutional racism to institutional racialization. First, as I have analysed elsewhere (Rattansi 1994: 62–3) it cannot be assumed that there is uniformity of racist culture and practice throughout any particular institution such as a school or police force. Second, it allows an exploration of the ways in which racism may articulate with other forms of identification and differentiation, for example, gender. Here the examples of the way in which particular conceptions and cultures of violent masculinity were important in the racially motivated murder of an Asian schoolboy in Manchester, as well as the differing responses of black girls and boys to racialized schooling processes, serve as ample reminders of the need to understand racism always in its articulations and therefore as a complex process involving varying degrees of racialization (Macdonald et al. 1989; Rattansi 1992: 20, 28; Sewell 1997; Nayak 2003; NSO 2004). Third, it also allows for an understanding of the intersection between race and sexuality, especially as evident in the anxieties of white males, and a focus on the potent male black body. The examples here are legion; the popular media treatment of the great black British sprinter Linford Christie and his 'lunchbox'—read supposedly very large-sized genitals—is typical of an all too common form of anxious 'othering' which also serves to place black British males outside the nation (see Rattansi 2000: 126). Fourth, more broadly, it highlights the generally complex interplay between identities, discourses, and the specificities of temporal and spatial context (Rattansi 1994: 32–3, 63–7; Nayak 2003).

Now, it is certainly the case that in public discourses the vocabulary of institutional racialization cannot have the same mobilizing—
nor polarizing—force that the accusation of institutional racism can
have. And legally a clear notion of racial discrimination is also
required. But these demands cannot be allowed to oversimplify
social scientific analyses. The blunt attribution of institutional
racism can occlude articulations with other social divisions, create
the impression of monolithic racism in practices and identities, and
fails to point up the complex relation between identities, intentions,
and outcomes.

It may, by connotation and implication, also oversimplify the
workings of power, rules, and knowledge within institutional configurations and organizational practices, unless specified in greater
detail and nuance. For example, decisions by local government officers regarding the allocation of public housing to families is part of
a process of bio-politics in the Foucauldian sense. Judgements about
the suitability of families wanting housing or waiting to be rehoused
contain elements of norms that are classed, raced, and gendered.
'Gatekeepers', white or non-white, are usually middle class and
deploy criteria of acceptability such as cleanliness, style of decor,
behaviour of children, size of family, the deportment of the mother,
which can work against white working class, black, and Asian families. The involvement of social workers and other professionals may
bring into play specialized social scientific knowledges regarding the
behaviour of families towards children and their attitudes to schooling which may feed into outcomes that affect the fate of families.[2]

For all these reasons and more, the use of racialization rather than
racism opens up the investigation to articulations and complexity,
rather than being nudged to closure by a focus on a singular disad-
vantaging operational feature. Another example of what may seem
like straightforwardly racist practice, the selling panic created by
estate agents in particular neighbourhoods as 'coloured' families buy
houses (Harrison and Phillips 2002), is thoroughly classed as well,
operating in middle class and owner-occupying sections of working
class areas. 'White flight' is a more complex racialized phenomenon
than might appear at first sight, even more so in the light of more
recent events in parts of London where middle class Asians are
reported to be moving out in the wake of the housing of refugees and
asylum-seekers close by.

For the social sciences the concept of institutional racism also
poses other analytical and theoretical difficulties. These relate to the
overlapping issues of structure and agency, and micro and macro

levels. For instance, what exactly are to count as 'institutions' and where are the boundaries around them to be drawn? What is 'inside' and what is 'outside' institutions and how are the relations between them, especially of cause and effect, to be analysed? What are the relevant distinctions between institutions, organizations, and social collectivities of other kinds?

Some of the difficulties of analysis as well as recommended changes in practices in non-racist directions can be illustrated by taking the problem of understanding variations in school achievement between children from different ethnic groups. Is the school or the local and national education system the relevant institution? What about the relation between the class and ethnic composition of the neighbourhood?

The concept of articulations is particularly important here. Positivist quantitative analyses usually attempt to disaggregate questions of class, ethnicity, and gender as separate factors whose causal efficacy can then be assessed by statistical methods. But this is to misunderstand how class and gender, for example, are already racialized and ethnicized. The formation, lived experiences, and treatment by teachers and other agents of white middle class or working class girls over their whole childhood and school life are known to be different to those of black and Asian girls of different class origins. The 'class' cannot be 'taken out' of the ethnicity and the gender and assessed separately except in a superficial manner, and any recommendations based on this type of analysis may be misleading. The cultures of local education systems and individual schools may also be relevantly different.

The problems of weighting different factors and drawing boundaries to differentiate the inside and outside of institutions is also relevant to analyses of prisons and the criminal justice system, workplaces and labour markets, and so forth. Again, while for policy purposes and for some research, relatively pragmatic decisions might be made about differentiating organizations such as schools or prisons from their environments, serious long-term research into educational processes or those involving the criminal justice system cannot rest content with the concept of institutional racism. But the problems go much wider than the field of race and ethnic relations, for it concerns much broader issues in sociology, especially, about the relevant fields and sites of causal and analytical focus, and the effectivity and responsibility of particular agents and agencies.

Two final illustrations will suffice to indicate the range of problems involved. Take, first, the issue of the under-representation of ethnic minorities in mass media organizations such as newspapers and television. The idea of institutional racism may highlight the taken for granted ways in which recruitment of white journalists, editors, producers, and other workers takes place. But the assumption cannot be made that the way in which the media portray or represent ethnic minorities in these mass media is simply a function of white personnel or that the employment of more members of the minorities will necessarily change the forms that representations will take. A cultural and aesthetic perspective broader than that offered by 'institutional racism' is required. Otherwise, as happened in the United Kingdom, the attempt to remedy the portrayal of ethnic minorities simply reverses negative into 'positive images'—read stereotypes—which stifle attempts to open up practices of representation to the genuine differences of sexuality, ethnicity, and cultural politics in the ethnic minorities (Bailey 1987; Hall 1992; Rattansi 1992: 33–5).

The attempt to obtain an exact parity between the proportions of members of ethnic minorities in the population and in employing organizations also provides an illustration of the ways in which the relatively narrow focus provided by notions of institutional racism may work in ways which set targets that are to some or other degree inappropriate. For example, to take the case of local employers, exactly what is to count as 'local'? In London targets are known to vary between reflecting the population of the city as a whole, and local boroughs such as Westminster or Islington. The question is not only one of what is and what is not local, but whether it is desirable and possible for particular occupational structures to reflect ethnic composition in any precise manner, especially without taking into account the influences of class and gender.

While the concept of racialization may sensitize policy-makers and especially researchers more to the complexities of analysing and remedying what conventionally comes under the rubric of institutional racism, there are of course limits on what it can do. The onus is then upon the deployment of other, more sophisticated conceptualizations of social structures and processes in general.

For example, is an understanding of racism in the United Kingdom or any other nation-state a matter of somehow 'adding up' all the racializations to be found in various micro sites? The problem with this sort of additive model is that it becomes vulnerable to the simplistic view that the micro and the macro somehow 'reflect' each other—as in the claim that racism in the police merely reflects or mirrors that in the wider society and is a matter of a number of the numbers of 'rotten apples' always being present in both. Instead, racialization, if seen as part of internally disarticulated processes, needs to be researched in a manner sensitive to its disjunctive qualities and therefore also aware of the specificities of particular institutional sites and their practices. Moreover, one might ask about the degree to which it is possible to talk about national patterns of variation and to what degree differentiations have to be made in more varied and complex ways, especially in a rapidly globalizing and post-national age where the forms of racism may have myriad interconnections with events and agencies that only in the recent past would have been regarded as geographically too distant to be immediately relevant. The case of so-called 'Islamophobia', as we shall see, is an obvious example of this type of problem of temporality and spatiality in the analysis of institutions, locales, and social spaces.

Identities, Discourses, and Ideologies

In my earlier commentary on the debate over the racialization thesis in post-war British politics, I have argued that one major problem bedevilling a productive understanding of processes of racialization is the assumption that racist identities can be labelled strictly as 'racist' or 'non-racist'. A binarism and reductionism of this kind fails to capture the complexities, ambivalencies, and contradictory character of how racism works as part of individual's identificatory trajectories over time and in their specific contexts. The conceptual underpinning of this more complex understanding in psychoanalytic, post-structuralist, and newer social psychological theorizing is something I have explored in greater detail elsewhere (Rattansi 1992, 1994, 1995). I have also pointed up the need to incorporate notions of self-reflexivity in the understanding of agency in order to avoid the pitfalls of a tendency towards determinism in some forms of post-structuralism (Rattansi 1999).[3] I will therefore not rehearse these points here, except to underline the necessity of incorporating these types of insight into rethinking racism and racialization.

What I wish to do here is to reflect on how the concept of ideology can be conjoined to these more complex conceptualizations of identificatory processes. In recent years the concept of ideology has found less favour in analyses of racism and racialization, mostly because of its tendency to reduce discourses to untenable notions of class and other 'interests' that are as it were pre-given, with racism being regarded as merely a cloak or rationalization of these interests.

These reductionisms often dovetail with conceptions of agents or subjects as unitary, irrational, and 'prejudiced', or suffering from 'false consciousness', despite being incorporated into relatively sophisticated analyses such as that by Phizacklea and Miles (1980; for a critical discussion see Rattansi 1992: 31–3).

But critiques of rationalist forms of anti-racism, drawing upon the move away from concepts such as ideology and prejudice, can be taken too far. It is important to stress that subjects can be mistaken or partially mistaken about the social processes of which they are a part, for a variety of reasons, not least because of the reliance on selective and misleading media reporting and framing of events. And views can be changed when faced by different facts and access to alternative frameworks. A telling recent example is the British National Party (BNP) councillor in Burnley, elected on a party platform that local Asians had had disproportionate access to public funding, a point repeatedly made in the local media as well, who resigned from the BNP after realizing, having held office for a short time, that she had been misled and had misunderstood the real situation as regards funding.[4] Questions arise here about understanding differential commitments to racism and racializing frames of reference. A simple labelling of this particular councillor as racist could easily lead to a pathologization and determinism that is an inherent danger in conceptions of the subject insensitive to the decentring of identities and the complex interplay of identifications, public discourses, and the relative rationality and self-reflexivity of agents.

The concept of ideology is also important in highlighting a tendency, noted by Marx very early in his writings, in *The German Ideology* (1846), for social relations to become naturalized, that is, to be seen as inevitable, immutable, and part of 'human nature', a discursive form particularly evident in representations of race and racialized difference. Barthes's concept of 'myth' underscores what he also regarded as a similar tendency in processes of signification (1973). There are issues here about how public and personal narratives as well as collective memories are shaped which are well beyond the scope of this chapter.

The question of pathologization is one that is relevant not merely to the categorization of individuals but discourses and social collectivities as well. This is evident in the now popular concept of Islamophobia. The component elements of the configuration were systematized recently in a publication by the Runnymede Trust in Britain (Runnymede Trust 1997). In a critical response, Halliday (1999) has pointed out that the notion is not always helpful, especially in its tendency to homogenize a wide range of phenomena involving relations between 'Islam' and the 'West' over a period of several centuries. Miles and Brown (2003: 163–8), in turn, have attempted to clarify some of the ways in which anti-Islamic discourses and racialization intersect to create exclusionary practices against Muslim populations, especially in Western Europe and North America. They quite rightly insist on a rigorous differentiation between specifically racialized discourses and practices and those involving religion. In practice, as Miles and Brown are well aware, the two often coalesce. This was evident recently in Britain in the wake the BBC's suspension of a morning talk show after its host, the former Labour MP Robert Kilroy-Silk, published a newspaper article entitled 'We owe Arabs nothing' which, in its combination of the homogenization of Islamic histories and cultures and their conflation with Arabs as a geoethnoracial category— not to mention its arrogant ignorance of the cultures and regions—might be regarded as a typical piece of Islamophobia (Kilroy-Silk 2004).

My concern here is to highlight a hitherto neglected aspect of the concept: its tendency to pathologize. The use of the vocabulary of 'phobia' has a tendency to treat the phenomenon as an illness and as a form of irrationality. Witness the way the British left of centre weekly, the *New Statesman*, advertised an article entitled Islamophobia by William Dalrymple (2004): 'It's not just Robert Kilroy-Silk who rants against Arab culture and Muslim faith. Prejudice against Islam has become a disease, and attacks on mosques are now routine.' Recent attempts to highlight rising anti-Semitism are often couched in similar terms. Former Labour Cabinet Minister, Stephen Byers, chair of the UK Parliamentary Committee Against Antisemitism, argued recently that 'Anti-semitism is not rational. It is...a virus and it mutates. It will not be defeated unless it is treated as an act of senseless hatred that has no logic, no reason and no justification' (2004). It is tempting to retort, on the contrary, that anti-Semitism will never be defeated if it is treated as a 'senseless', disease-causing biological organism.

The strictures that apply against the pathologization of individuals' attitudes and identifications are equally relevant to the tendency to treat complex discursive and institutional configurations as forms of illness and therefore 'irrational' and open to 'treatment' in medically analogous forms (Rattansi 1992: 25–9). This type of analysis essentializes and dehistoricizes, ignoring contradictions, ambivalences, and complex imbrications with other discourses and social divisions, and the manner in which the discourses work effectively as frameworks for explanation and 'making sense' of events and lived experiences. Again, as with the concepts of prejudice and false consciousness, the intellectual and political labour of reflection, discursive invention, and reinvention is squeezed out by this sort of reductionism and oversimplification while also not allowing multidimensional and sophisticated counterstrategies.

The relevance of racialization in this context lies in its opening up the investigation to the *degrees* to which, and the forms whereby, biological and cultural immutabilities and inferiorizations are present in different versions and particular instances of anti-Islamic, anti-Muslim, and anti-Semitic statements and practices.

However, whatever the merits of deploying the concept of racialization in social scientific analyses, its use in public discourses in other contexts is subject to limitations. It cannot replace racism nor anti-racism. Anti-racialization, for instance, cannot have the same mobilizing force nor political charge despite incorporating a necessary complexity. A sort of strategic essentialism, as advocated by Spivak in other contexts, becomes relevant, although supplementing the analysis with the notion of racialization, and therefore with the guiding idea of articulations, keeps the crucial need for alliances as well as simultaneous strategies against various intertwined inequalities and divisions constantly in view. Racialization tells us that racism is never simply racism, but always exists in complex imbrication with nation, ethnicity, class, gender, and sexuality, and therefore a dismantling of racism also requires, simultaneously as well as in the long run, a strategy to reduce relevant class inequalities, forms of masculinity, nationalisms, and other social features whereby racisms are reproduced in particular sites.[5] The need to guard against pathologizations is not built into the fabric of the concept, but has to be insisted upon as a necessary corollary.

To be Continued: The Cultural Dilemmas of Embodiment

Levi-Strauss noted a long time ago that the fact that humans are both biological and cultural beings means that they have constantly to resolve a puzzle about the relation between biology and culture. Race, in my view, is one of the key ways in which an attempt has been made in modernity to illuminate how embodiment and signification, biology and culture are intrinsic to being. This is not to underplay the role of race in the justification of slavery and imperial and colonial dominations, but to add another dimension to our understanding of the phenomenon of racialization. The tendency to treat bodies metonymically, as indicating answers to larger puzzles about cultural difference, is not surprising, and there is a likelihood that some or other version of biological explanation, even if functioning as part of a broader framework, will continue to be seductive. The new genetics, as many have noted, is giving a new lease of life to concepts of race (Kohn 1995; Brah, this volume). Moreover, the continuing loose, widespread, and institutionalized usage of race in the United Kingdom, as in 'Race Relations' legislation and in official bodies such as the Commission for Racial Equality, gives currency and circulation to the notion. Elsewhere, ideologies centred around Afrocentrism have used the concept of race in resistant but nevertheless unfortunate mode.

And a common sense deployment of race continues to survive in the unlikeliest of contexts. Progressive, sophisticated intellectuals succumb to the temptation to racialize in an unreflective manner that bodes ill for attempts to purge the ordinary cultures of everyday lives of the tendency to racialize. One of Britain's most highly regarded intellectuals and editor of *Critical Quarterly*, Colin McCabe, in an obituary of another prominent intellectual, Paul Hirst, makes a revealing comment:

I only realised that Paul was Jewish about a year ago when he referred to himself, to my then surprise, as Jewish. He was such a quintessentially English character that it was a bit surprising that he was not of Anglo-Saxon stock. But it is difficult to imagine an Anglo-Saxon with quite so much of the Jewish mother about them—so that fitted. He was always extraordinarily solicitous—were you fed, were you wrapped up warm, would you be careful crossing the road. (MacCabe 2003)

The combination of biological reductionism, cultural essentialism, and judgement of individual personality could have come straight from a nineteenth century narrative. In a sense it did. This is the continuing legacy of race as it is reinscribed in contemporary common sense, somehow bypassing in this instance even the relative sophistication of the new cultural racisms.

It is hardly surprising that in the heat of intense geopolitical conflict, and fuelled by ill-conceived theories of the global 'clash of civilizations', such notions continue as well. Erhud Barak's claim (*Guardian*, 27 May 2002), while recalling the Camp David negotiations with the Palestinians, that 'Arabs don't suffer from the problem of telling lies that exists in Judaeo-Christian culture' neatly encapsulates the combination of race, geography, and culture intrinsic to most racializations.

The problem will be with us for just a while yet, then, to put it in the mildest possible manner. More than ever, therefore, we need the concept of racialization; challenges to the phenomena it names; sophisticated theoretical frameworks to analyse its operation; and rigorous empirical research to unpack its complex articulations with other forms of cultural essentialization, biological reductionism, and configurations of power, knowledge, and inequality.

NOTES

1. Small (2002: 271–2) has recently reiterated the need to move away from simple racist/non-racist couplets in the analysis of racialization. However, he does not provide a reconceptualization of identities, subjectivities, and general social processes in terms of decentring and deessentialization that in my view is required to create a secure theoretical basis for undermining commonly used racist/non-racist differentiations. In other respects though, there are many overlaps in my argument and his (see also Brah, Chapter 3, this volume).
2. For some of the ways in which more conventional social research on housing and schooling may be reconceptualized using Foucauldian insights; see Rattansi (1994: 61–2).
3. On the basis of a selective reading of my work, Carter (2000), in his 'critical realist' contribution to recent debates, criticizes me for ignoring issues of agency and reflexivity (2000: 24).
4. The illustration comes of course from media reporting as well. See 'BNP loses another Burnley councillor' (*Guardian*, 27 February 2004).
5. Some of the relevant issues are discussed in Anthias and Lloyd (2002).

REFERENCES

Anthias, F. (2002) 'Gender, Ethnicity and Social Stratification: Rethinking Inequalities', in S. Fenton and H. Bradley (eds.), *Ethnicity and Economy: 'Race and Class' Revisited*. Basingstoke: Palgrave Macmillan.
——and Yuval-Davis, N. (1992) *Racialized Boundaries*. London: Routledge.
——and Lloyd, C. (eds.) (2002) *Rethinking Anti-racisms: From Theory to Practice*. London: Routledge.
Bailey, D. A. (1987) 'Re-thinking Black Representations'. *Ten-8*, 31.
Banton, M. (1985) *Creating Racial Harmony*. Cambridge: Cambridge University Press.
Barot, R. and Bird, J. (2001) 'Racialisation: The Genealogy and Critique of a Concept'. *Ethnic and Racial Studies*, 24 (4): 601–18.
Barthes, R. (1973) *Mythologies*. London: Paladin.
Bauman, Z. (1992) *Intimations of Postmodernity*. London: Routledge.
Bayly, C. (1996) *Empire and Information*. Cambridge: Cambridge University Press.

Brah, A. (1996) *Cartographies of Diaspora*. London: Routledge.

Byers, S. (2004) 'Antisemitism is a virus and it mutates'. *Guardian*, 15 March.

Carnoy, M. (1984) *The State and Political Theory*. Princeton: Princeton University Press.

Carter, B. (2000) *Realism and Race: Concepts of Race in Sociological Research*. London: Routledge.

——Harris, C., and Joshi, S. (1993) 'The 1951–55 Conservative Government and the Racialization of Black Immigration', in W. James and C. Harris (eds.), *Inside Babylon: The Caribbean Diaspora in Britain*. London: Verso.

——Green, M., and Halpern, R. (1996) 'Immigration Policy and the Racialization of Migrant Labour: The Construction of National Identities in the USA and Britain'. *Ethnic and Racial Studies*, 19 (1): 135–57.

Castells, M. (1997) *The Network Society*. Oxford: Blackwell.

Cohn, B. (1996) *Colonialism and its Forms of Knowledge*. Princeton: Princeton University Press.

Dalrymple, W. (2004) 'Islamophobia'. *New Statesman*. London, 19 January.

Dean, D. (1987) 'Coping with Colonial Immigration, the Cold War and Colonial Policy: the Labour Government and Black Communities in Great Britain 145–51'. *Immigrants and Minorities*, 6 (3): 305–34.

——(1993) 'The Conservative Government and the 1962 Commonwealth Immigration Act: The Inside Story'. *Race and Class*, 35 (2): 57-74.

Dean, M. (1999) *Governmentality*. London: Sage.

Dunleavy, P. and O'Leary, B. (1987) *Power and the State*. London: Macmillan.

Dyer, R. (1997) *White*. London: Routledge.

Frankenberg, D. (ed.) (1997) *Displacing Whiteness*. Durham, NC: Duke University Press.

Giddens, A. (1990) *The Consequences of Modernity*. Cambridge: Polity Press.

——(1994) *Beyond Left and Right*. Cambridge: Polity Press.

Hall, S. (1992) 'New Ethnicities', in J. Donald and A. Rattansi (eds.), *'Race', Culture and Difference*. London: Sage.

Hesse, B. (1997) 'White Governmentality: Urbanism, Nationalism, Racism', in S. Westwood and J. Williams (eds.), *Imagining Cities*. London: Routledge.

Goldberg, D. (1993) *Racist Culture*. Oxford: Blackwell.

——(2002) *The Racial State*. Oxford: Blackwell.

Halliday, F. (1999) ' "Islamophobia" Reconsidered'. *Ethnic and Racial Studies*, 22(5): 892–902.

Hansen, R. (2000) *Citizenship and Immigration in Post-war Britain*. Oxford: Oxford University Press.

Harrison, M. and Phillips, D. (2002) *Housing and Black Ethnic Minority Communities*. London: Office of the Deputy Prime Minister.

Hill, M. (ed.) (1997) *Whiteness: A Critical Reader*. New York: New York University Press.

Jacobson, M. F. (1998) *Whiteness of a Different Colour*. Cambridge, MA: Harvard University Press.

Kilroy-Silk, R. (2004) 'We Owe Arabs Nothing'. *Daily Express*. London, 4 January.

Kohn, M. (1995) *The Race Gallery*. London: Jonathan Cape.

Laclau, E. (1990) *New Reflections on the Revolutions of Our Time*. London: Verso.

——and Mouffe, C. (1985) *Hegemony and Socialist Strategy*. London: Verso.

Lukes, S. (1972) *Power: A Radical View*. London: Macmillan.

MacCabe, C. (2003) 'The Legacy of Paul Hirst'. (www.opendemocracy.net/themes/article.jsp?id=10&articled=1308#27).

Macdonald, I., Bhavnani, R., Khan, L., and John, G. (1989) *Murder in the Playground*. London: Longsight Press.

Miles, R. (1989) *Racism*. London: Routledge.

——and Brown, M. (2003) *Racism*, 2nd edn. London: Routledge.

Mitchell, T. (1988) *Colonising Egypt*. Berkeley: University of California Press.

Nayak, A. (2003) *Race, Place and Globalisation: Youth Cultures in a Changing World*. Oxford: Berg.

NSO (National Statistics Online) (2004) National Statistical Office, UK, www.statistics.gov.uk

Omi, M. and Winant, H. (1986) *Racial Formation in the United States*. London: Routledge.

Parekh, B. (1995) 'Liberalism and Colonialism: A Critique of Locke and Mill', in J. Pieterse and B. Parekh (eds.). *The Decolonisation of the Imagination*. London: Zed Press.

Paul, K. (1997) *Whitewashing Britain: Race and Citizenship in the Postwar Era*. Ithaca: Cornell University Press.

Phizacklea, A. and Miles, R. (1980) *Labour and Racism*. London: Routledge.

Rattansi, A. (1992) 'Changing the Subject? Racism, Culture and Education', in J. Donald and A. Rattansi (eds.), *'Race', Culture and Difference*. London: Sage.

——(1994) 'Western Racisms, Ethnicities and Identities in a "Postmodern" Frame', in A. Rattansi and S. Westwood (eds.), *Racism, Modernity and Identity*. Cambridge: Polity Press.

——(1995) 'Just Framing: Racism and Ethnicity in a "Postmodern" Framework', in L. Nicholson and S. Seidman (eds.), *Social Postmodernism: Beyond Identity Politics*. New York and Cambridge: Cambridge University Press.

Rattansi, A. (1999) 'Racism, Postmodernism and Reflexive Multiculturalism', in S. May (ed.), *Critical Multiculturalism*. London: Falmer Press.

——(2000) 'On Being and Not Being Brown/Black British: Racism, Class, Sexuality and Ethnicity in Post-Imperial Britain'. *Interventions*. 2 (1): 118–34.

——(2002) 'Racism, Sexuality and Political Economy: Marxism/Foucault/ Mostmodernism', in S. Fenton and H. Bradley (eds.), *Ethnicity and Economy: 'Race and Class' Revisited*. Basingstoke: Palgrave Macmillan.

——(2005) *Racism: Contemporary Perspectives*. London: Sage.

Reeves, F. (1983) *British Racial Discourse*. Cambridge: Cambridge University Press

Runnymede Trust (1997) *Islamophobia: A Consultative Document*. London: Runnymede Trust.

Rustin, M. (1991) *The Good Society and the Inner World: Psychoanalysis, Politics and Culture*. London: Verso.

Sewell, T. (1997) *Black Masculinities and Schooling: How Black Boys Survive Modern Schooling*. Stoke on Trent: Trentham Books.

Small, S. (2002) 'Racisms and Racial Hostility at the Start of the New Millenium' in D. T. Goldberg and J. Solomos (eds.), *A Companion to Racial and Ethnic Studies*. Oxford: Blackwell.

Solomos, J. (1989) *Race and Racism in Contemporary Britain*. Basingstoke: Macmillan.

——(1993) *Race and Racism in Britain*, 2nd edn. Basingstoke: Macmillan.

——and Back, L. (1995) *Race, Politics and Social Change*. London: Routledge.

Staten, H. (1984) *Wittgenstein and Derrida*. London: University of Nebraska Press

Stoler, A. L. (1995) *Race and the Education of Desire: Foucault's History of Sexuality and the Colonial Order of Things*. Durham, NC: Duke University Press.

——(1997) 'Racial Histories and their Regimes of Truth', in D. Davies (ed.), *Political Power and Social Theory*. Westport, CT: JAI Press.

Urry, J. (2000) *Sociology Beyond Societies: Mobilities for the Twenty-First Century.* London: Routledge.

——(2003) *Global Complexity.* Cambridge: Polity Press.

van den Berg, H. (2003) 'Contradictions in Interview Discourse', in van den Berg, H., Wetherell, M., and Houtkoop-Steenstra, H. (eds.), *Analyzing Race Talk.* Cambridge: Cambridge University Press.

Ware, V. and Back, L. (2002) *Out of Whiteness.* Chicago: University of Chicago Press.

Wetherell, M. and Potter, J. (1993) *Mapping the Language of Racism.* Hemel Hempstead: Harvester Wheatsheaf.

INDEX